THE JOURNEY OF A JEW
FROM BAGHDAD

J. DANIEL KHAZZOOM

Mairin Khazzoom
Ellen Graham

ACNOWLEDGEMNTS

I owe a debt of gratitude to two special individuals – Mairin Khazzoom for her unstinting help in every stage of writing my memoir during the last six years and to Ellen Graham for her labor of love in editing the first two parts of my memoir and sections of its third part.

I thank Joan Ominsky and Dr. Steve Ominsky for their incisive comments on the entire manuscript and thank Pat King for guiding my effort at the early stages of my writing. I thank also the many who read and commented on various sections of the manuscript or helped with sources, references and photographs.

J. Daniel Khazzoom.

PREFACE

Several times in my life, I have leaped off a precipice into the unknown.

In 1951, at the age of 18, I left my family and the country of my birth, Iraq, to settle in the new state of Israel. Along with more than 850,000 other Jews from Arab lands, I was escaping persecution and seeking sanctuary in the Jewish homeland. With the rise of Arab nationalism during the nineteen thirties and forties, the everyday hatred directed toward Iraq's Jews by our Muslim neighbors snowballed into fearsome terror. Still, we did not decide to upend our lives lightly. Most of us who joined this migration left behind homes, loved ones, businesses and bank accounts in order to live in peace and security among fellow Jews.

One of my aims in writing my story is to document a way of life that vanished with this exodus: the rich Babylonian Jewish culture that had flourished since ancient times in Iraq. I hope, too, that my story will help put the current bloodshed in Iraq in a larger historical context. Though not on a scale comparable to that in present day Iraq, much of the torture, assassination, bombing, kidnapping, hand cutting and beheading that dominate today's headlines (and that mistakenly many tend to attribute to the presence of our troops in Iraq) much of that is what we lived through and endured, except that at the time there were no TV cameras and no reporters to report to the world on what happening to us. Iraq was and remains a violent society. Saddam Hussein was not an aberration. He is a product of that culture of violence, I witnessed this inherent violence of Iraqi society over and over as a child. However much I tried to erase it from memory, terror is imprinted on my soul. What remains—what I have been unable to shed—is a harrowing instinct to be prepared to flee at any moment.

For decades after I left Iraq, I faced a quandary every morning when dressing. I would pause to consider whether I should put on both my socks before slipping into my shoes— or, instead, first put on one sock and shoe before putting on the other sock and shoe. The source of this irrational obsession? Trying to decide whether, if I were forced to flee just then, it would be better to be wearing at least one shoe than in my stocking feet. And only in the past few years have I stopped hiding money under the rug in my study-- ready cash should I suddenly need to run.

I was young and had little to lose by way of material assets when I left Iraq. But my departure marked the first of many tearful partings and separations that would be my family's fate amid the incessant turbulence in the Middle East. For seven years after leaving Baghdad, I had no word from my parents who I'd left behind. To communicate would have put their lives at risk. Eventually, they and my siblings followed me to Israel. But it was 22 years before I was reunited with my oldest sister, Jamila, who remained in Baghdad with her husband until 1972.

Life in Israel was a huge comedown for the refugees that streamed in from Arab lands, swamping the new nation's ability to provide jobs, housing, and even food. More painfully, we encountered discrimination by the East Europeans, who branded Jews from the Middle East "Arabs," and derided our language and customs as primitive. So in 1958, I once more ventured into the unknown. I again took leave of my family-- to get my doctorate, marry, start a family and build a career as an economist in the United States and Canada.

The price of freedom has been almost unbearably high. The dispersal from our homeland, the expropriation of our possessions, the years of anxious separation and the demoralizing economic strains of life in Israel would ultimately tear at our once-close family bonds. The passage of time has helped repair the breach, but it came too late for some of my relatives, who died penniless and alone in Israel.

I am an American now, living a comfortable life as a retired academic in sun-splashed California. But even in this free and open society the dark frights of the past have ambushed me at unexpected moments:

On Sunday, January 27, 1969, I was engulfed by a strange feeling that I had never experienced before. I had an inexplicable but overwhelming sense that something terrible was about to happen, that the few of us left in Baghdad were about to be taken away from us. Try as I might, I was unable to shake that feeling. My immediate family was safe with me and the news reports contained nothing unusual. Unable to sleep, I even called my father in Israel. He reassured me that nothing untoward had happened there. Yet our conversation did nothing to dispel my mounting sense of dread. What was causing this premonition of impending doom?

The very next day, I received my answer. Baghdad's radio informed a horrified world that a military tribunal had convicted nine Jews of espionage for Israel and had ordered them summarily executed. The prisoners were publicly hanged in Liberation Square in Central Baghdad before jeering mobs. Just before their hangings, the gallows were inspected by Saddam Hussein, then Iraq's vice president, who toured the square in an open car.

That day was declared a day of national celebration in Iraq. Dancers were summoned to perform under the gallows. People were provided free rides in trams and buses, so that they could come and celebrate under the corpses. Loudspeakers announced that at 4 p.m. the bodies would be brought down so that the mob could deal with them in the streets.

The news of the hangings shattered me. To this day, I shiver at the thought that the wave of terror might have led the battered remnant of Baghdad's Jewish community to disavow its sons. Who went to claim the bodies of the nine "spies" after the mob had finished dragging them through the streets, without fear of being arrested as a spy sympathizer? Were there ten courageous souls left in Baghdad to recite in public our ancestral Kaddish in memory of the victims of Iraqi atrocity?

During the Gulf War, news reports of Iraq's brutality in Kuwait again reopened old wounds, resurrecting frightening memories of Baghdad's Jewish community crumbling under Iraqi atrocities.

During the third week of August 1990 a correspondent for the Washington Post who had managed to escape from

Kuwait was interviewed on "The McNeil-Lehrer Report." She told of the terror she had experienced while living under the Iraqi occupation.

"Once they see you," she said of the Iraqis, "they get ideas about what to do with you. To stay alive, you stay indoors, you never go out, and hope they will not come after you. But the nights brought the greatest fear."

So it was with my family, as we huddled inside our Baghdad home in 1941, listening as a rampaging mob moved closer to our neighborhood, bursting into homes and massacring Jews.

"This woman is telling our story," I told my wife.

I was visiting Israel in September 2000, during the outbreak of the Palestinian intifada against Israel. When I watched televised images of the mobs throwing stones and surging forward with hate in their eyes, it once again summoned up our dark days in Baghdad. I was so disturbed that I could not sleep. I cut short my trip to Israel and flew back to the States, grateful to escape the abhorrent scenes of raw hatred. In Baghdad, when I was growing up, there was nowhere to go. We were trapped.

During that flight, I reflected on one of the reasons I have chosen to live in this country. While American society can't claim to be free of anti-Semitism or other forms of bigotry, what distinguishes our system is that such attitudes are neither sanctioned by our laws, nor shared by the vast majority of the public. I had occasion to witness this first-hand: When synagogues in Sacramento, California were targeted by arsonists in 2000, both Christian and Jewish citizens rallied around to support the Jewish congregations that were victimized. The true moral measure of a society, then, is demonstrated not just when the targets of bigotry rise up to fight it, but when those in the community who are *not* victimized feel compelled to condemn acts of hate. In Iraq, there was no one willing to fight side by side with us.

When the U.S. invasion of Iraq began in 2003, people asked me how I felt about it. I could only say that I hoped Iraq would move toward becoming a more humane society, and in the process serve as a catalyst for the transformation of

6

the Arab world.   But as I write this, such an outcome seems elusive.

Sometimes people ask me if I would not want one day to visit Baghdad, my birthplace. My answer is—and always will be--an emphatic "Absolutely Not." What I remember fondly about our life in Baghdad is the warm loving life within the Jewish community of Baghdad. That was the only community that showed care and love. Now that the community is no more, I do not care for the rest. Baghdad is nothing more than a hollow shell for me, and I will never set foot on that G-d forsaken land ever again.

--

Sacramento, California, 2013

PART ONE - IRAQ

BY THE RIVERS OF BABYLON

AN ANCIENT COMMUNITY

I was born a Jew in Baghdad, in the Muslim country of Iraq. My roots there go back centuries: Legend has it that our first Khazzoom ancestor was born in Baghdad six hundred and fifty years ago.

Daniel - April 7, 1934   Daniel -two years later - June 11, 1936

Even though Iraq was a land of plenty, I was painfully aware from an early age that it wasn't my promised land. And because of my experiences growing up there, I have never identified myself as Iraqi, but rather as a Jew from Baghdad. The community that nurtured me was a cloistered, self-contained enclave within the often-hostile city at large. Although Baghdad's Jews were not confined to a walled ghetto, we lived in what might be described as a cultural or spiritual ghetto, within a repressive state. We had minimal contact with the Arabs around us and were subject to separate restrictive laws. There were quotas limiting the number of Jews who could serve in Parliament, for example, and for most of my youth we were not permitted to leave the country.

15

Sometimes, in my younger years, the exit regulations could be bent with a bribe, but there was no recourse for the whim of clerks who, willy-nilly, denied permission to travel abroad. It was a country ruled by men, not law.

In Baghdad, my world consisted of family, synagogue and school, tightly bound by ancient tradition and the seasonal progression of religious holidays. The outward security that this close-knit world provided, however, was illusory. For outside the safety of my family's embrace lurked ever-present threats: We didn't set foot in exclusively Muslim neighborhoods. In Baghdad in those times, Jewish children were frequent victims of harassment or theft on the street--or worse, kidnappings or beatings. Even as a small child, I internalized the anxiety that came from knowing we could never let down our guard, and that at any moment it might be necessary to flee for our lives. These fears proved all too prescient, when the pervasive, almost routine, sense of alienation and dread culminated in full-scale terror: the 1941 *farhood*, or massacre of Baghdad's Jews that my family and I narrowly escaped.

In school, we were taught how some of the world's earliest and greatest civilizations took root in the lands that make up modern Iraq, which acquired its present name when the Arab Caliph Omar conquered it from the Persians in 634 CE. I never developed a feel for the true size of the country until I traveled with my parents from Baghdad to Basra in Southern Iraq when I was twelve. The trip took twenty-four hours by train. Much later I learned that Iraq is more than three times as large as New York State and twenty times as large as Israel.

Pinning down facts about the country of my birth was always a dubious proposition, because the government controlled the flow of information and it was a highly unreliable source. In the early forties, the official estimate of Iraq's population was 4.5 million. Two years later, the estimate had jumped to 14.5 million—with no explanation or investigation of the obvious discrepancy. The information vacuum and our starvation for news would worsen in the following years, intensifying our sense of peril.

Iraq produced most of the food it needed, but had very minimal industrial capacity and most industrial products were imported. Oil was first discovered in Karkouk, in northeastern Iraq, in 1927. Early estimates put the country's oil endowment in excess of one hundred billion barrels. By the mid-1930s, the Iraq Petroleum Company (IPC) had acquired sole rights to develop the oil fields in Northern Iraq in return for paying royalties to the Iraqi government, and IPC opened a pipeline from Mosul to Tripoli in Lebanon and to Haifa in what is now Israel, and the export of oil began in earnest. Soon Iraq became one of the world's leading producers and exporters of oil, with oil revenues contributing roughly fifty per cent of the gross domestic product. Little of this sudden wealth trickled down to the population, however. In the corrupt regime of Iraq, which wallowed in bribes and kickbacks, a good chunk of the oil revenue went to line the pockets of public officials, cabinet members, the royal family and their cronies, instead of being channeled to meet social needs and enhance the welfare of Iraq's citizens.

Though oil was cheap in Iraq, the very poor couldn't afford it and used cow dung and wood as fuel. They seldom used lamps, rising and going to bed with the sun except on nights when the moon was full.

The city of Baghdad was founded in 762 CE by the Muslim Abbasid Caliph al-Mansour. Prior to that, Baghdad was a suburb of Ctesiphon, the capital of the Sassanid dynasty (226 CE – 636 CE). My father told me that Baghdad is a Persian word meaning "beautiful orchard," that a small Jewish community was known to have lived there some five centuries before the Abbasid dynasty chose it as its capital, and that over time the community grew to become the center of learning for world Jewry.

Growing up, the history of Iraq and Baghdad didn't concern or interest me particularly. Rather, I identified with the history and achievements of the Babylonian Jewish community, the oldest Jewish community in existence, whose history goes back two thousand six hundred years and predated the arrival of Arabs in these lands by many centuries.

My ancestors were exiled from Palestine, our Promised Land, to Babylonia after the destruction of the First Temple in Jerusalem in 586 BCE. They settled along a canal in a region called Kebar near Babylon, about fifty miles southwest of present-day Baghdad. And it was there that they composed the ode that Jews recite the world over to this day: "By the rivers of Babylon, there we sat and wept, as we remembered Zion." In Iraq when I was growing up, it was customary to read this ode only once a year, on *Tish'a Be Ab*, the day when we remember the destruction of Jerusalem and the Temple's torching. And we read it from the depths of our souls. The ground under our feet was where it had all happened. There was the Tigris—one of the rivers of Babylon—before our very eyes, less than a hundred yards away from the synagogue in which I grew up. For us, Babylonian Jews, the calamity was a living thing - not something that had happened in the distant past. We were where we were because our ancestors were exiled here. We were the exiled.

Those early settlers went on to establish other new towns in Babylonia not long after they arrived. One, called Tel-Aviv, became the communal and spiritual center of the elders of the Jewish community. "And I came to the exile community that dwelt in Tel Aviv by the Kebar Canal, and I remained where they dwelt. And for seven days I sat there stunned among them." (Ezekiel 3:15). Tel Aviv is significant not only because of the prominent people who resided there, but also because of the message that underlay its name: We are down today, but we are not giving up. A brighter future lies ahead. Tel Aviv is made up of two Hebrew words: Tel, which means a mound of ruins -- and that is probably how my ancestors saw things when they were led to Babylon, having lost their homeland, their spiritual center, their families, their homes, and their dignity. The second word is Aviv, meaning the spring season, symbolizing revival and rejuvenation. So the name means "it is all ruins now, but it will blossom again; spring is ahead, and we will rebound." Fittingly, on May 21, 1910, the modern city of Tel Aviv in

Israel was officially named after the city established by Jewish exiles in Babylonia.

The history of this community, with its theme of hope and invincibility, is the history of the Jewish people. Babylon is where most Jewish practices and traditions originated -- public prayer, the prayer book, the synagogue, and the magnum opus of them all – the Babylonian Talmud.

But what characterized the Babylonian Jewish community more than anything else were its institutions of learning. The Babylonian Academies of Nehardea, Sura and Pumbeditha were the Ivy League institutions of the Jewish world. It was in those Academies that the Babylonian Talmud was written. The academies' leaders were bold and civic-minded; they were erudite and original thinkers.

The traveler Pethahiah of Regensburg, Germany, who visited Babylon in the late twelfth century, reported on the erudition of Babylonian Jewry: "There is not an ignoramus throughout the lands of Babylon... who does not know all the twenty-four Books in their punctuation and accuracy ... The Hazzan does not read in the Torah, but the one who is called to the Torah reads it himself ... Babylonia is an entirely different world."

The Jews of Babylon were Sephardim, a term used to include those descending from the Iberian Peninsula, North Africa, and Asia, whose laws, customs, liturgy and language differ from those of the Ashkenazi Jews, who originated in central and Eastern Europe. The vernacular language of my community was Judeo-Arabic, rather than the Yiddish, or Judeo-German, spoken by Ashkenazim. Sephardim tend to be more inclusive and more lenient in their practices than Ashkenazim, and so we have not been fragmented into groups like the Orthodox, Conservative, Reform, and Reconstructionist branches of Ashkenazi Judaism. We Sephardic Jews all pray in the same synagogue, regardless of our level of observance or degree of belief—or non-belief.

A kaleidoscope of colors, a cacophony of sounds, and a myriad of impressions run through my mind when I think of my childhood in the ancient city of Baghdad. Sometimes

19

the pictures form clear images; at times everything is blurred. Even the years seem jumbled together; I know definitely when some things happened; other things I can't place on a definite time line.

In the late nineteen forties, Baghdad's population was reported as 450,000, with most residents clustered into neighborhoods segregated by religion. About 65% of the population were Muslim, 25%—100,000 to 110,000—were Jewish, and about 10% we re Christian. My family, along with most of the population, lived on what was known as the Rassafa side of the Tigris River, where government buildings, commercial offices, schools and hospitals were concentrated. An inviting boardwalk studded with large houses and mansions, cafes and coffee shops ran along the Rassafa riverbank. But in the shadow of these grand residences was another world entirely: dusty, unpaved alleys crowded with squalid shacks where large families lived without electricity or running water among their cows and sheep. Karkh, the other side of the Tigris, was wild, green and sparsely populated mainly by poor Arabs living in tin shanties or huts made of cowhide, dung and mud.

When I was in my teens two modern bridges were erected spanning the Tigris. The two bridges ramped up steeply from the Rassafa side and then ramped down just as steeply toward the Karkh side. I remember the climb, because when I rode my bicycle to play tennis on the Karkh side I was breathless by the time I reached the top. My experience with the floating bridges that these modern bridges replaced was very different.

At the best of times a floating bridge never felt solid under my feet, but under the weight of a moving car it rocked alarmingly. Up and down it went, taking my stomach with it. Staying on the bank was safer. From there I could watch the undulating bridge or the rowboats that ferried people from one side of the river to the other. Sometimes several rowboats were tied together and tugged across the river by a motorboat, serving as a makeshift ferry to the other side of the Tigris.

Baghdad had two wide boulevards. Ghazi Street cut

through the lower-class part of town, and we mostly avoided it. Rasheed Street ran along the Tigris, and was crowded with hotels, stores, movie houses and restaurants. In my neighborhood, a thick hedge of pink and white oleanders grew along the median. Flowing brooks, fed with water from the Tigris nearby and shaded by stands of towering eucalyptus, separated the wide sidewalks from the traffic. On summer nights, when we slept on the rooftop of our home to get relief from the blistering heat—daytime temperatures often surpassed 110 degrees F. --we were lulled to sleep by the soothing croaking of the frogs that made their homes in the brooks.

Only once in my memory did the thermometer drop to freezing level in Baghdad. I was walking home from school on Rasheed Street when I noticed a big crowd gathered in a circle, excitedly pointing to something on the ground. When I got closer I could see a thin crust of ice on a puddle of water. I was astonished. It was the only time in my life before coming to the U.S. that I saw frozen water on the ground. That afternoon, the Ministry of Education closed all public and private schools in Baghdad until further notice.

Though automobiles were still a relative rarity, Baghdad's streets roiled with activity during the workday. Hackney carriages, buses, and taxis jostled each other in the bustling thoroughfare, where in lieu of traffic lights, policemen attempted to bring some order to the whirling chaos. Snarls and bottlenecks were commonplace, especially when a carriage horse would stumble and fall. Drivers whipped their horses mercilessly or honked their horns in annoyance, causing other horses to rear up in panic. Tempers flared, and sometimes drivers came to blows— fisticuffs being the all-too-typical way to settle disputes in those days.

We probably had as many paved streets as we did in Baghdad largely because tar, a byproduct of oil refining, was so readily available. My father and I loved the smell of tar and the smell of gasoline, and we often walked on a newly tarred road to enjoy its fragrance. Sometimes we even walked to a gas station to sniff the air.

Trade and finance in Iraq were mostly in Jewish and Christian hands, divided about equally. Some Jewish families owned banks, and many employees at major banks were Jewish—experience that stood them in good stead when they immigrated to Israel. There were also numerous small bankers in the Jewish community, known as *sarraf.* Some of them would sit outside banks or other business establishments downtown, rolling money in their hands. Others had large offices and staffs. Not much paperwork was involved; financial transactions were based largely on trust. One of my classmates related how his father, a *sarraf,* conducted business: Someone would drop a roll of banknotes on his desk worth, say, 100 dinars. (Up until 1948, 1 dinar = $5) His father wouldn't bother to count the money then and there. Nor would the depositor wait to get a receipt.

In the textile and produce markets, peddlers and shoppers haggled at top volume over the price of everything from a single orange to fine jewelry and bolts of silk. Untold hours were wasted negotiating every transaction in a stylized dance of parry-and-thrust between merchant and customer: The shopkeeper's mock indignation when a price was deemed too high or a scale's accuracy was questioned; then exasperation, signified by a turban heatedly flung to the ground; finally the shrug of grudging acquiescence as a lower price was agreed upon. Men—Arabs barefoot in long robes and Jews in mostly Western dress-- congregated in the markets, coffee shops and cafes playing dominoes or backgammon before crowds of onlookers. Women were rarely seen on the street.

While Islam forbade the consumption of alcohol, this stricture was honored mainly in the breach. Spirits were available—sub rosa--at coffee shops, where patrons could quietly indulge while still maintaining an abstemious image at home. It was rumored that some of the wealthier Arabs drank perfume, which presumably didn't violate the letter of the law, but did play havoc with their digestive systems. There was one dry cleaning establishment said to be a secret drinking establishment. Perhaps it was a result of their inhalation of fumes from chemicals, but I observed several people emerge from that establishment in a drunken state.

Amid the hubbub of an emerging modern city, rural ways persisted as they had from ancient times. Tall date palms abounded in our neighborhood. Iraq was then the world's largest producer and exporter of dates—the government claimed some seventy varieties grew there. Dates were cheap, so the poor depended on them for sustenance, often eating nothing more than a date sandwich and tea as their main meal. To harvest dates, workers with hooks strapped to their bare feet and sickles tucked in their belts would scramble up the palms' spiny trunks to harvest the delicious fruit. As the trees bent precariously under their weight, I would watch transfixed, sure they would fall, but they never did.

On Saturdays Baghdad virtually came to a halt for the Sabbath. Arab-owned coffee shops and movie theaters remained open, but most markets and commercial centers were shut down. There was an aura of serenity in the air as the din of traffic fell silent. My father and I were in the habit of strolling the neighborhood on Saturday afternoons. Often, we would simply stand and listen to the pleasant cool water flowing in the brooks and the rustle of the leaves of the fragrant eucalyptus stirring in the wind. I liked to watch fishermen cast their nets from boats close to the riverbank. They worked in pairs: One would walk barefoot along the rocky shore, pulling the boat against the current while the other managed the nets from the boat.

Diseases ravaged the city, and we had to be conscious of dirt and contamination. My parents took every precaution to shield us from those diseases. Every year we were inoculated against typhoid. But there was no inoculation against malaria, and I suffered from recurring malaria four years in a row. I remember being terrified, shaking uncontrollably as I lay in bed, unable to stop my teeth from chattering, while my mother stood by, looking helpless. She put more covers on me, shoved hot water bottles into my bed, and sometimes she just threw herself over me to try and arrest the shaking or stop the intermittent hallucinations. I was treated with quinine, a powerful medication, which damaged my middle ear, causing me even until now to suffer from vertigo.

When I was ten I suffered from a severe case of jaundice, another common disease in Iraq. I was so ill that I did not want to eat or drink. It took me weeks to recover.

Nor were my siblings spared, suffering illnesses ranging from smallpox to chronic digestive disorders.

When I was a boy, my grandmother used to sing "*Baghdad Sit Leblad*," or "Baghdad the lady of the cities of the world." Was this an instance of the victim identifying with the oppressor? Or was it perhaps a tribute to the only Baghdad my grandmother knew, the Jewish Baghdad of my memories.

A LOVE STORY

My father, Abraham Kh'doury, and my mother, Looloo Raby, were maternal first cousins. Abraham was born in 1890, the second child of a family of three boys. Looloo, born in 1901, was the second child of a prosperous family of five girls and four boys. Her father was a wealthy banker and businessman, and the family lived in an imposing home in downtown Baghdad.

My paternal grandmother, Farha, had hoped for a girl when my father was born. She was advised that a surefire recipe for fulfilling this wish the next time was to have her newborn son wear earrings. So she had her infant Abraham's ears pierced. The earrings were too heavy for his tender earlobes, but Grandmother Farha didn't waver. She must have been disappointed when she gave birth, a year later, to another boy. In the meantime, the earrings had succeeded in slicing each of her baby's earlobes in two, a scar he would carry for the remainder of his life.

Abraham was left fatherless at age three, when Grandfather Abboudi died in a cholera epidemic that swept through Baghdad. My grandmother and her three young sons then became the responsibility of my father's paternal grandfather, Jacob, a grocer who barely eked out a living.

There was no social safety net in Iraq. Though Babylonian Jews did care for the poor, the epidemic had left so many needy widows and widowers that they taxed the resources of the community beyond its limits. Ultimately Farha and her sons moved in with her brother Joseph, who worked as a sarraf, or independent banker. With him, they were relatively better off economically than with Grandfather Jacob, but it was still a life of poverty.

My parents, March 29, 1924
Mama, pregnant with S'haq, is
wearing a diamond necklace she treasured, a present my father had bought for her.

Early widowhood brought with it enormous hardship. My grandmother had no chance of remarrying. Rarely did anyone in Iraq want to marry a widow, certainly not one with three children. She couldn't earn a living - generally, women didn't work outside their homes. Undoubtedly she felt she was a burden to her brother and his family. Every morsel that one of her children ate at Joseph's table was one no longer available for her brother, his wife, or their children. There must have been times when she got the message they were no longer welcome, yet she had nowhere else to go. How does one spend a lifetime under such conditions? The conflicts such dependency undoubtedly caused in the entire family may partly explain my father's sometimes-capricious nature, which led to our frequent clashes as I was growing up.

My father spoke fondly of his Uncle Joseph and the debt he owed him. But he never shared details about his daily life while growing up in his uncle's home. And, although he maintained contact with cousins from his other maternal aunts and uncles, I don't remember him staying in touch with any of Joseph's children. Was there a sense of guilt toward Joseph's family that he couldn't confront? Or was it simply that Joseph's children felt they had had enough of my father and his brothers?

Within his immediate family, Abraham was the most prominent and the best –educated, but he did not always value education. When he was eleven, he told his mother he was going to drop out of school.

"Wonderful," she said. "I feel lonely at home by myself. You'll keep me company. It will be good for both of us. You'll see."

But my father quickly realized he was heading for a dead end. Education was his only way out of poverty. He asked his principal's forgiveness for his foolishness, and the school agreed to take him back. He never cut school after that.

Indeed, after graduation he studied law in Istanbul, Turkey, the center of learning in the Middle East at the time, and went on to become one of the prominent lawyers of his time. One evening, when we were all assembled in our "glass" room, with its glass doors and enormous kerosene chandelier, he read from his memoirs about his long-ago trip to Istanbul. He told a harrowing story of how the horse-drawn carriage that took him and other travelers to Turkey lost its way in a blinding snowstorm. Before the storm subsided, my father said he nearly froze to death on the way to Istanbul's prestigious law school.

Ottoman certification of membership in the legal profession
On top, the logo of the Ottoman Empire; at the lower left,
picture of my father wearing the Ottoman fez

My mother was the last daughter in her family not to receive a modern education. Her younger sisters attended the same French school that my sisters and I attended. Looloo attended *stayee*, literally meaning "my master," a small private school where she was taught to read the prayers and *sh'bahoth*--the religious paeans—in Hebrew. She also learned to read and write Judeo-Arabic, the language of the Jews of Iraq. My mother never learned to read or write Arabic, and that was typical for most people of her generation. She didn't attend *stayee* long, and she had few opportunities to practice what she had learned. By the time I was growing up, she could no longer remember how to read Hebrew, but she still remembered a lot of the *sh'bahoth* and some of the prayers by heart.

My father, eleven years older than his cousin Looloo, became attached to her when she was a baby and married her when she turned seventeen. Baba loved to tell us children about Looloo, the toddler he knew and cherished.

Hebrew scripts of Judeo-Arabic (Notice that it is written under the line)

"She was a sandwich thief," he would say winking at us. "I would drop by Aunt Aziza's house on the way to school to play with her and do you know what she used to do?"

"No, Baba. Tell us, tell us," we would say, our faces shining with excitement.

"She would grab my schoolbag and rummage through it, tossing every item on the floor until she found my radish sandwich."

"Is that so?" my mother would ask, hiding a smile.

"What would she do with the sandwich, Baba?" we would ask, grinning at our mother. We knew what was coming next.

"She would drop my bag, crawl to the corner of the room with the prize in her hand and eat every last bit of my sandwich."

" And what did you do, Baba? Why didn't you try to get your sandwich back before Mama had eaten it?"

"I couldn't do that. How could I deprive your mother of anything she wanted?"

We were silent then, watching the loving glances our parents exchanged, secure in their love for each other and for us.

But being children we couldn't let the matter rest.

"So what did you have to eat, Baba?"

" I starved the rest of the day," he'd say, rubbing his stomach.

Mama chuckled as we children ganged up and reproached her for leaving Baba to starve.

"Enough, children," Baba would tell us. "Your mother has made up for her thieving ways."

Then he would point to the radishes Mama made sure to have on our Sabbath table every Friday night.

My father and mother continued to meet frequently when they were children, during regular family visits. When Abraham returned from law school in Istanbul, he declared his love for Looloo and asked her parents for permission to marry her. My maternal grandfather, Silman, put his foot down. His daughter's suitor was fatherless, came from a poor family, and his grandfather was only a grocer – clearly an undistinguished pedigree. Even though some saw my father as a rising star, Grandpa Silman was not impressed. My maternal grandmother, Aziza, favored the marriage, but women didn't have a voice in such decisions. My mother wanted to marry my father, but she, too, had to keep quiet. Nothing could be done without Grandpa Silman's consent. He wanted to find a more suitable husband for his daughter through the traditional channel – an arranged marriage.

Such unions were facilitated by Jewish matchmakers, mostly women, known as *dellalat*. The *dellalat* provided the parents of eligible men with a list of eligible women, describing their family backgrounds and social status. They provided similar information about the bachelors to the women's parents, and helped negotiate the size of the dowry that the prospective groom expected as part of the matrimonial settlement.

Every detail of family background, history and social status was scrutinized and weighed. When both sides were satisfied that a match was conceivable, a rendezvous was set up, ostensibly to give the eligible man, woman, and their families an opportunity to meet and get acquainted. In fact, however, the meeting was intended to give the young man and his parents the opportunity to look over the woman and decide if she was attractive enough. Rarely did the prospective bride have an equal say, or any say at all, in the choice of a mate.

When the bachelor and his family decided there was a basis for a deal, negotiating the size of the dowry began in earnest. Haggling over price, so ingrained in Middle Eastern culture, naturally came into play when settling on a dowry. (Muslim customs were no less offensive, except that the bridegroom was expected to pay the bride's family for rights to marry their daughter.)

My father detested this custom and wanted no part of it. He loved my mother and rejected the notion that her parents should pay him to marry her. But his feelings were immaterial; both he and my mother were helpless in the face of Grandpa Silman's opposition.

Abraham hoped for a breakthrough. Then opportunity—in the form of a potential disaster-- knocked on his door.

It happened that a few months after my father's return from Istanbul, the Tigris reached dangerously high levels and threatened to flood Baghdad. The Tigris ran through the middle of the city, and the bank was perilously low on the populated Rassafa side of the river. In times of flood, people sought refuge on the Karkh side of the Tigris, where the bank was higher.

When Abraham realized that there was a danger of flooding, he went straight to my mother's home and told her he wanted her to take the boat with him across the Tigris to the Karkh side, where they would stay until the flood subsided. She agreed to join him.

Her decision was scandalous by the standards of the day. Going out with a man at night without a chaperone was considered disreputable; going away with a man for several days was unforgivable. If what she did became known, no man would ever want to marry her. But that didn't deter either of my parents.

When they returned, the news of what had happened spread like wildfire. Grandpa Silman realized he was outmaneuvered; he had no choice but to give in. My parents were married shortly thereafter. Mama was just 17, and Baba was 28.

Their love was the talk of the town, even during the time I was growing up. In Iraq it was considered bad taste to show affection in public. My father flouted this custom, too, putting his arm around Mama's shoulders in public. Their behavior drew stares and set tongues to wagging.

THE FAMILY ARMY

My parents had ten children – six daughters and four sons. In the western world a family of this size is uncommon; in Iraq it was not. Women in Iraq married young, and many gave birth to seven or eight children before reaching thirty. Mama had nine children by the time she was thirty-one. In 1896, the rabbis in Iraq issued a ban on marriage when the bride was less than sixteen. Though violations still occurred -- Aunt Guerjiyi, my mother's older sister, was married in 1913 when she was fourteen -- the ban held pretty well.

My sisters' names are a mix of Arabic, Hebrew, French and Spanish, and they are variants of beautiful, pretty, pleasant, glorious, sunny. My brothers and I had Hebrew names only.

My father was the only breadwinner in the family. He literally had an army to feed, clothe and educate. Yet my parents spared no effort, and we lived in physical comfort. I marvel at how they managed.

My mother's hazel eyes radiated love and compassion. Unlike my father, with whom I often clashed in a classic father-son power struggle, Mama didn't believe in physical punishment. Only once do I remember her spanking me, and she was seized with remorse afterward. While I knew my mother loved me without reserve, sometimes I wondered if my father loved me at all. Then he would show me kindness, and I would feel secure in his love—though never totally secure.

The Khazzoom Family, 1934
Front row l to r: Latifa, Helwa, Jacob Meir; second row l to r: Reyna, Muzli, Baba with two-year old Daniel, Mama, Jamila. My brother, S'haq, isn't in the picture; my brother, Abboudi, died before I was born; my sister, Valentine Nouriya, wasn't born yet

He was a bundle of contradictions. He fought fiercely against corporal punishment in Jewish schools, but didn't hesitate to beat me. He went out of his way to avoid embarrassing people. But at times he humiliated my brother, some of my sisters, and me. He boasted about my accomplishments to his friends, clients and leaders of the community, but seemed to relish the times when events knocked me down and brought me to my knees. Living in an Arab milieu, he had assimilated some of that culture's rigid patriarchal views about family. Growing up, I was baffled by his behavior, and, when I was younger, I was often afraid of him and the power he wielded over my life.

On a number of occasions my father put on Arab attire.
Nine-year old Jacob, Abraham, and four-year old Daniel.

The happiest times I remember from my childhood in Baghdad are those when the family was gathered together. On winter nights we sat around the *sopa,* or kerosene heater, roasting chestnuts, boiling water for tea, or just watching the flames through the heater's many-colored apertures. When we turned out the lights, the colorful flames illuminated the room, casting dancing shadows on the walls and on the Persian rugs that covered our couches. I nestled into my chair feeling secure and warm, despite the chill wind that whistled though the cracks in ill-fitting windows and doors. It seemed then as if danger was far away and could never touch us.

Sometimes, in the dark winter evenings, we would hear the turnip vendors, or *abu'l shalgham,* in the street. For children in Baghdad, these peddlers were as eagerly anticipated as Good Humor trucks. We would rush outside and, just as quickly, run shivering back into the house to savor our piping hot, newly purchased turnips in front of the kerosene heater. Cooked with dates, the turnips' sweetness seemed to melt on our tongues.

My parents' second child, Abboudi, died at age two, eleven years before I was born. In Iraq, as in the rest of the developing world, male infant mortality was high. In spite of the superior hygienic conditions within the Jewish community, male infant mortality was high there too, and Abboudi fell victim to it. My mother often spoke lovingly of him, although she never explained the exact cause of his death. I think she never recovered from the devastation of his loss. My brother S'haq, my parents' fifth child, died at seventeen.

I was the next to youngest in the family, and before my birth my parents made a pilgrimage to the tomb of the Prophet Daniel in northern Iraq, as was customary among Babylonian Jews during *sh'buoth*, the holiday of pilgrimage that commemorates God's gift of the Torah to the Jewish people on Mt. Sinai. They pledged that if my mother gave birth to a boy they would name him Daniel. I was born a few days later. But because I was named at a time of worsening persecution of the Jews, my parents thought it would be safer to make Daniel my second name and give me Yousif—the Arabic counterpart of Joseph—as a first name. Within the safe confines of our home, however, Mama would sometimes tenderly call me "Dannu." Years later, in Israel, I toyed with the idea of dropping Joseph, or Yousif, as reminders of the oppressive times when we had to hide our Jewish identity. Eventually I recognized that tyranny would always be an integral part of my history. So I decided to keep only the initial J., as a symbol of my life under Iraqi repression.

My oldest sister, Jamila, was a sort of second mother, teacher, confidant and friend to me. Our mother gave birth to Jamila when she was eighteen, and their relationship was more like that of sisters than of mother and daughter. In Iraq, the eldest daughter was expected to help with housekeeping and caring for the family, and so, by a fluke of birth order,

Jamila was robbed of much of her childhood. Although we had domestic help, she was the first one up in the morning to wash the courtyard and kitchen floors, make tea in the samovar, boil the unpasteurized milk, and prepare breakfast.

Jamila had a nurse's healing touch. Once, when I was nine years old I became ill and had a high fever. Our family doctor, Ammu Guerji, came for a house call - Ammu, or uncle, being an honorary title, since Guerji was actually my mother's cousin. Ammu Guerji looked after all of my family's medical needs, and never took a penny in return.

Ammu Guerji was not sure what could be behind my high fever, and he looked worried. I was scared, and Jamila noticed. If she was afraid of contracting my mysterious illness, no one ever knew. She put her arms around me and lay beside me through the night. I was worried she would catch my disease and die. But deep down, I felt reassured in her arms. I closed my eyes and fell asleep and was back on my feet a week later. We never knew what caused my illness. But I never forgot Jamila's devotion.

In Iraq, families with many children tended to be lax in educating their girls, sending the boys to good schools and the girls to substandard institutions. Not so with my parents. They sent my sisters and me to the l'Ecole de l'Alliance Israelite, the elite French school, and the most expensive of all private schools in Iraq. It was my brother Jacob, not my sisters, who was sent to a lesser school. Jacob couldn't take the demanding curriculum of l'Alliance.

As a child, Jamila became fluent in French at l'Alliance. But because of her duties at home, she had to drop out of school in her mid-teens. When I began attending l'Alliance, she walked me through my punishing French homework assignments. Jamila was my all-knowing idol; it seemed there was no French word she had not mastered. As I progressed, I encountered more and more uncommon words, and as usual I asked Jamila for their meaning. When she didn't know, she just said so matter-of-factly. Together we looked up the word in the dictionary. That was the first lesson I learned from her - there was nothing wrong, nothing embarrassing about admitting I didn't know. No one, not even Jamila, could possibly know all there was to know.

Jamila was my father's favorite. She was the only one of his children who ever accompanied him to the King's Palace. In his official capacity as a member of the Governing Council of Central Iraq, Baba was occasionally invited to the Palace to join in celebrations. Usually, only male guests were invited. The Palace made an exception one time, when they invited a famous Egyptian singer to perform at a gala celebration of the King's birthday. For that one time, invitees were allowed to bring their wives along. Baba got Palace approval to have Jamila accompany him, along with my mother. It was probably my father's way of letting Jamila know he loved her and appreciated how she put herself out for the rest of us.

Mama and Jamila had long dresses sewn specially for the occasion. They were a dazzling combination of crimson and pink silk. Baba was horrified at how sheer the dresses were, until Mama assured him they were to be worn over very modest under dresses.

My sister Muzli was tall and slender, with straight black hair and an elegant sense of style. She loathed housework, but loved the outdoors, and she found her niche in running the family errands. She would leave mid-morning for the market downtown, where she bought snaps and buttons that Mama needed, took our shoes to the shoemaker, stopped at the watchmaker for a watchband or a repair, and scoured stores for the linens we needed.

Like several of my older sisters, Muzli dropped out of school during intermediate school. I don't remember them getting any argument from our parents about this decision; it was the societal norm. On days when Muzli didn't go to the market, she would loll on the balcony in the sun reading novels. At night she listened to Radio Cairo until it signed off. During those broadcasts, she knit feverishly and with amazing skill, producing all of our sweaters and scarves as well as Baba's socks.

Reyna, the fourth child in our family, was the one who often orchestrated our evenings around the *sopa,* our kerosene heater, making sure we had roasted chestnuts and cups of tea. She was eight years older than I. Mama told me that Reyna had been the most beautiful of all her children, but at an early age, her face had been ravaged by smallpox. Thereafter, she was taunted by her classmates about the scars on her face. Neighbors and friends shunned her. The cumulative effect of the unfriendly world surrounding her took its toll. She distanced herself from almost everyone, and she rejected others before they had a chance to reject her.

Reyna was a great go-getter. No one in our family was a match for her. I suspect that if she had been a man with the same talent, she would have been "forgiven" for her smallpox scars. But in the Babylonian Jewish community there was a double standard. It was acceptable for a man to have scars or to wear eyeglasses - no doors were closed to him. But a Jewish girl who wore eyeglasses was unlikely ever to get married because of this "blemish." To marry her off, her parents would have to literally buy a husband for her. Accordingly, nearsighted girls avoided wearing eyeglasses at all cost. They would stumble and fall, if that was what it took to hide their "blemish." Reyna couldn't hide hers - it was there for all to see, and she was brutally penalized for that.

When Jamila got married, Helwa, my parents' seventh child, became Mama's right hand. She got up early in the morning, prepared our breakfast and our lunches, washed the dishes and swept the floor, and then got herself ready to go to school. The night before, she had polished our shoes. She would line them up by the wall. "Here they are: the shoes of the army," she would laugh. Helwa has always been a clown and inveterate mimic, who brightened our family gatherings with witty impersonations.

Latifa was my parents' mischievous eighth child, and my closest companion growing up. Latifa's original name was Doris. When she was a baby, she became very ill and my parents feared she was on the verge of dying. In desperation, they changed her name to Latifa. Their belief was that the heavenly decree of death is issued against a person as he is, with his name being an integral part of his person. By changing the person's name, the heavenly decree would no longer apply to him, and his life would be spared. Latifa didn't die.

In a family as large as ours, we children paired off and tended to be closest to the siblings nearest us in age. Valentine was my father's "old age child," the baby of the family on whom he doted. She was so much younger than the rest of us—six years younger than me—that she didn't have a special playmate in the family. But she was such a sunny, good-natured child—with exotic blond curls—that my sisters liked to take her to school to show her off. My sister, Jamila was present at Valentine's birth, where she witnessed just how deeply devalued girl children were among the Jews of Iraq. Boys were a parent's social security in old age, whereas girls grew up to marry and require dowries. Jamila told me she was aghast when she heard the midwife mutter an expletive at the sight of the infant girl, and declared that she wished she could put her hands around Valentine's neck and choke her to death.

Because there were so many of us, my parents didn't have enough time to fully accommodate the emotional needs of each child. Some of us who had special difficulties, particularly my sister Reyna, suffered from the lack of adequate attention. I know my father was aware of this, and I believe it tormented him. He was knowledgeable about psychology, and often reiterated with obvious regret his inability to give more time to us. Fortunately, Mama's even, gentle nature helped compensate. I owe my resilience and much of my self-confidence to her unconditional love and unrelenting message that I was special.

S'HAQ: OUR HIDDEN BROTHER

My brother S'haq was seven years older than I. He never teased me as my brother Jacob did or hugged me as my sister Jamila did. I remember him sometimes reaching out a hand to me as he muttered something unintelligible. S'haq couldn't speak. He was retarded.

When I think about him now, it is the pain in his eyes

that calls to me. I wonder what sense S'haq made of his life, or if he could even think about himself in those terms. Did I imagine puzzlement on his face when he saw me playing backgammon with our father? He clearly was happy when the family sang and, with a big grin on his twisted features, he clapped his hands along with the rest of us. S'haq was part of our family, but he never appeared in our family pictures and I have no pictures of him. He exists only in my mind and in my heart.

My mother had conflicted feelings about S'haq. In addition to being retarded he was also an epileptic, a terrifying disease in those early years. Nobody knew how to treat it, and epileptics were shunned. The Babylonian Jewish community was known for its humanitarian leadership. For example, it established the School for the Blind, a school where students learned trades and received such a rich music education that many of them won leading positions in Baghdad's orchestra. But alongside enlightened attitudes stood the inconsistent and backward view that retardation and epilepsy were punishments from God visited on a family for some sin the parents had committed. S'haq, who had done no wrong, was a blot on our escutcheon and had to be hidden. When company came, S'haq was hustled away out of sight.

Families were large, and it was hard for the community to keep track of every single member, but news of S'haq's existence leaked out beyond our immediate circle. I was sitting in the salon one day when two hard-faced women we barely knew came to call. They sipped their tea, their lips speaking words of no account, their eyes watchful, and their ears alert. Finally, her patience at an end, one of them blurted out:

"We heard you have a crazy person living here."

My mother shook her head.

"There is so such person here."

I wonder how she felt as she denied her son's existence.

Mama and Jamila were responsible for S'haq's daily care. As he grew larger the task became more difficult. He was incontinent, and keeping him clean was a monumental task. My mother looked as if she were bent under the weight of the world when she cleaned him. "Will this never end? I don't know how much longer I can deal with it," she would say, choking back tears.

Baba, equally despondent, devoted much time and energy to finding a cure for S'haq's condition. He dragged him from doctor to doctor, spending so much time at it that he postponed looking for a husband for Jamila until she was almost past marriageable age.

When S'haq was eleven, my father took him to a hospital in Jerusalem. The doctors there promised to see what they could do to cure his condition. Baba left him in the hospital and went to take care of his own business in Palestine. On his way to catch the bus back to Baghdad, my father stopped at the hospital to visit S'haq carrying several kilos of large sweet grapes he had bought in Jerusalem. S'haq fell on the grapes, devouring the whole bag. It was obvious that S'haq was either refusing to eat or being starved. Baba immediately dressed him and took him back to Baghdad.

While S'haq lived at home for the next six years, my father didn't lessen his efforts to find a doctor who would cure him. We never talked about S'haq outside the family; it was as though he didn't exist. But because Abboudi had died in infancy, S'haq was the oldest son, and my parents were known among close friends as Abu S'haq (S'haq's father) and Um S'haq (S'haq's mother).

When S'haq turned seventeen, my father took him to a Jewish hospital in Beirut. This time he returned home without my brother. The house felt different without him. I missed him sitting at the table with us while either Mama or Jamila fed him. I missed the strange sounds he sometimes made and the odd way he walked as he made his way around the house. I wondered how he felt being in a strange place, so far away from home and everyone he knew.

Three days after Baba arrived home from Beirut, a telegram was delivered from the hospital. All it said was "We're sorry." I learned about the telegram much later. No one told us about it at the time. I saw the stricken look on

Baba's face that day and wondered what had happened. Mama's face crumpled as she turned away. Mama and several relatives who came in later that afternoon sat on the floor, a sign of mourning in Jewish tradition. Yet when we asked what had happened, the answer was, "Nothing."

I was confused. My parents seemed to be in mourning, but they never explained why. Gradually I came to realize that S'haq had died—he probably starved himself to death--but I was still afraid to ask my parents about my brother's death. Now I realize that a lot of confusion surrounded his death.

S'haq was seventeen years old when he died, but because he had not learned to speak, he was not seen as having reached the age of *bar miswah*. He had never taken his place as an adult within the Jewish community and, as such, the family was technically not supposed to sit Shib'a, the traditional seven days of mourning, for him. Nor were my parents required to follow ordinary mourning rituals. Baba, however, chose to mourn S'haq's death fully. He wore a black tie for a year following his death—to work and to the synagogue, where he went every morning to say Kaddish for S'haq. My parents mourned S'haq's loss; they mourned the man he had never become. They had never talked about him in life; how could they begin to talk about him in death? These days of mourning were a difficult time for them. But they were no less difficult for us children, who didn't know how to behave. A pall hung over the house, and we couldn't see beyond the fog of grief and sadness swirling around us.

One thing, however, was clear to me.

My father saw how S'haq's need for constant care was wearing down my mother, and felt it was up to him to relieve my mother of that responsibility. And so he had taken S'haq to Beirut. It broke my heart when, during this period of mourning, my mother, speaking from the depths of her grief and guilt, said of my father: "He rushed him to Beirut knowing that they would kill him." I believe Baba heard my mother's outburst, but he just turned away in silence. That is what I remember most from this period: Baba's silence. It seemed to me that my father's lips were closed forever.

S'haq is often in my thoughts. Before our first child was born, my wife and I decided to call the baby S'haq if it were a boy. My mother was upset. "It is an unlucky name in our family," she said. I suspect she was relieved when our first child was a girl, whom we named Aziza for my mother's mother. But even though my mother thought S'haq was an unlucky name, she refused to be known as Um Jacob (Jacob's mother) after my brother Jacob, who was her oldest son after S'haq's death. For years thereafter, Mama chose to be known as Um S'haq.

My siblings and I never speak of S'haq now. I believe that I am the last to hold him in my memory. When I donate prayer books to my synagogue I usually dedicate them to a loved one. Several carried this inscription:

In Memory of My Brother S'HAQ
DIED AT AGE 17
In A Hospital in BEIRUT AWAY FROM HOME AND FAMILY.
PROFESSOR J.DANIEL KHAZZOOM.

FAMILY ENVIRONMENT

I was born in a sprawling house in the older downtown section of Baghdad. Its design was typical of the old-style Jewish homes of that city. It was rectangular, built of brick with wooden columns and steel beams, and featured an open interior courtyard. The courtyard provided security; it was dangerous for Jewish children to play outside on the street. The second and higher-level floors were built around the perimeter of the building, and they had wide walkways that overhung the courtyard. Railings enclosed the walkways and stairs led up from the courtyard to the roofs, where we could stand by the balustrade and look down at the busy street below.

Viewed from the street, large houses could appear

deceptively small behind their high walls. Once my father took me with him to the Baghdad home of a judge he knew and I was astonished to enter a vast interior wood where ostriches, peacocks, and all manner of other exotic birds were kept among tall trees.

Courtyard, second floor and balustrade of a Baghdadian Jewish home
identical in design to the home I was born in.
From G. S. Golany, *Vernacular House Design* (Or Yehuda, Israel: Babylonian Jewry
Heritage Center, 1994).

The open architecture and hot dry climate invited all manner of unwelcome creatures inside. Like all houses in Baghdad, ours was infested with fat lizards, scorpions and, sometimes, snakes. Once, when Jamila was gathering wood to cook our Sabbath meal, she was bitten by a scorpion hiding in the woodpile. Another time, when I was very small, we found two huge spotted snakes in the house. The man we called to catch them refused the job when it became clear the snakes were mating. "Why do you want to separate them?" he said. "They are just having fun." I lived in dread of those snakes, for I had heard a version of the Adam and Eve story asserting that if a snake bit you on the heel it meant certain death. Ever after, I kept my feet tightly wrapped in a blanket when I slept, even in hot weather.

When I was eight, my family moved to the more modern section of Baghdad. I remember Latifa saw the new house before I did. I also remember how excited she was by the prospect of moving.

"You will be so happy when you see the new house," she told me. "We ate sugar when we bought this house."

Babylonian Jews commonly used Latifa's expression of optimism whenever they embarked on a new enterprise. Every new deal was going to be a sweet one. For two days we shoveled sugar into our mouths at every opportunity, savoring the sweetness of moving to a new home.

Exterior view of the houses in the neighborhood in which I grew up - Reyna, with our nephew, Rony, on the Tigris' boardwalk near our home, 1949

The night before the move, my parents were up until all hours. They had received cash for the house they had sold, and they needed to count it. What made the task more onerous was that the money—the then-spectacular sum of around $25,000-- was all in one-dinar notes. The buyers transported the cash in a trunk to our new house—an unguarded treasure that could have vanished had robbers chosen that night to break in. The entire family—uncles, aunts, and grandmother—gathered at our home for a boisterous conference about how to safely carry these riches to the bank. After much argument, my uncles divided the money up in small bundles and took it separately to make deposits.

Before surrendering the old, empty house to the buyer, my father and I went for a last visit. Baba walked into every room, stood silently, slowly moving his eyes over every corner, as if impressing it all to memory. He was quiet, and I didn't want to disturb him. But I realized what must have been going through his mind when we got to what used to be my bedroom. Here was where my bed had stood, and here was where my brother's bed had been. Here was the window through which the sun shone in the morning to cheer us all up, and there was the high ceiling on which the rain drummed during winter nights. It was cozy and secure in that warm room. There was a part of me that would never leave that house; was that how my father felt too?

Because cars and trucks were scarce, and of almost no use in the narrow streets of old Baghdad, laborers had to carry our furniture on foot to the new house. My grandmother had given my parents an enormous wooden chest about 8 feet by 3 feet in size. A Kurdish porter carried it on his back the entire mile or so to the new house. He was a small man, and was struggling for air by the time he arrived. I still can see the sweat dripping from the tip of his nose as he tried to untie the strap around his head to rest the chest on the ground. I just stood and gaped at him. Why did I not even bother to offer him a glass of water? I was the product of a culture that thought of the Kurds as less than human. Yet they were hardworking people – certainly unlike most other Iraqi Arabs, who tended to avoid strenuous physical exertion.

Our new home was actually two houses connected by a corridor. The back house was where the cooking and the laundry were done, but the front house was always immaculate. Rich Persian rugs covered the floors and the chairs in the salon. Though smaller than the old house, the new house was only yards away from the banks of the Tigris. From the front balcony, you could sit and watch the glittering river that played such an important role in our lives. At night the moon seemed to swim in the sky and in the water below. My mother would get up at dawn and watch the sun rise over the river. Sometimes when I sat with her, I wondered if she was thinking about how my father took her across the river during the flood before they were married.

In the spring, the Tigris rose to its full height, sometimes almost overflowing its banks. Looking at the swollen river flowing majestically under the trees, I was awed by its power, by the depth of its mystery. As the river rose, water filled our basement. I liked to think of it as a lake under our house. I used to drag one of our huge laundry tubs to the basement and launch my makeshift boat on our private lake. Using a broom handle to row, I tried to steer my vessel from one side of the basement to the other, and was frustrated when my tub only went in circles.

I told my grandmother about my exploits, and she laughed. "The water came into our basement when I was a little girl," she said. "My father used to buy several turtles and put them in the water in the basement. He claimed it purified the water."

Although I loved to watch the mighty Tigris as it rose to its full height during the spring, I dreaded the perils associated with the rising river.

When the river threatened to break its banks, it was a dangerous time for men to be on the streets. At times like these, both old and young were pressed into service to stem the rising waters by diverting the flow into reservoirs. A great majority of these men were either Jewish or exceedingly poor. The military picked them off the streets and, under pain of death, compelled them to help with flood control. Sometimes the reservoir walls broke, and had to be repaired. The work was forced slave labor, never paid.

The floods also drew out hustlers, like the Muslim man who would offer to carry people across the street so they wouldn't get their feet wet. Midway across, he'd threaten to dump his passenger in the water unless he paid him more than what they had agreed on.

A MAN AHEAD OF HIS TIME

I both respected and feared my father. His suffering as an orphan growing up in abject poverty undoubtedly accounted for his contradictory nature: On the one hand, a pious man of wisdom with a keen social conscience; on the other a father who swung from tenderness to cruelty with his own children.

I remember the nights he came home in the evening tired from a long day of work, and marvel at how he overcame his weariness to sit and play the *ood*, or lute, for us. We sang and clapped, happy to enjoy a musical evening with our father.

We used to play *tawlee,* or backgammon, with him, and he loved to be caught cheating. He took cards from the deck surreptitiously, or would upset the game board and rearrange it to his advantage. He cheated so brazenly that he invited discovery by us children, all the while affecting an innocent look. We clamored for payment of a penalty and he would oblige. But he never ceased playing his cheating game, even when he was advanced in years.

The good times, sadly, were tempered by my father's capricious, authoritarian nature, which kept me continually off balance.

Sometimes I felt close to him, like the times I'd put oil in his dwindling hair and played with it, making his hair stick close to his head or stand up in spikes. Then we would laugh together, and I was glad he was my father.

My own hair was thick and curly and I was proud of it. Sometimes my father watched me as I combed my hair in front of the mirror. I knew he was displeased with my vanity, but I never realized the depths of his disapproval.

One day I was at his office when he asked his messenger, Saleem, to take me to the barber. I took no particular notice of the whispered consultation he had with Saleem, but went to the barbershop trustingly. There, it was

Saleem's turn to whisper in the barber's ear. It wasn't until the barber had taken off all my hair, leaving me nearly bald, that I realized what my father had engineered. When I went home, Mama was upset to see what had happened.

"Why did you do that to your hair?"

I didn't know what to say - that I was the victim of a cruel conspiracy my father had orchestrated? I went to the bedroom to look in the mirror. I ran my hand over my shorn head and wept. I felt violated.

Two weeks later when school started, my hair had not grown back, and my schoolmates mocked and teased me. I tried to ignore the taunts, but deep inside I felt bitter and angry. My hostility was directed not at my schoolmates, but at my father, who probably had wanted to take me down a peg by asserting his patriarchal authority.

L to R: Helwa, Valentine, Latifa; Daniel in back
Passport picture taken several weeks after my hair had been shorn

My father and I locked horns frequently and many times it ended in a beating for me. We were both strong-willed and had firm opinions. Neither of us was willing to yield, but my father was stronger than me. I refused to give in despite the beatings, and he punished me by not speaking to me for a week or so. I remember the Friday nights at *kiddush* time when I was being given the silent treatment. We ordinarily kissed our parents' hands on the eve of the

48

Sabbath as a sign of respect. But on those nights, my father would push me away silently and refuse to let me kiss his hands. It took persuasion and intercession on my mother's part before I would be allowed to approach him. Did my father realize how terrifying and hurtful his silence and rejection were? I can only conclude that having no father of his own, he did not realize the terrorizing effects of his wrath on his children.

We struggled constantly over matters as trivial as my sneakers. Our school devoted only one hour a week to gym, at which time we were required to wear sneakers. I looked forward to that hour of physical exercise, but my father forbade me to participate, believing it distracted me from my studies. Still, on gym days, I always put on my sneakers and tried to leave the house without being seen. Occasionally I managed to get away with it. But my father knew me too well. Most of the time, he would wait inside the dining room door until I walked into the vestibule and reached to open the front door. Then he would appear, his face looking like thunder on a stormy day.

"Why are you wearing sneakers? Go back and put on your shoes. You are not allowed to participate in athletics."

I had no choice but to obey, but I didn't obey willingly. We fought repeatedly over my defiance of his ban. "I command you," he roared once. My face then was the one that was as black as thunder.

One particularly disturbing altercation occurred after a bus in which Reyna and Jacob were riding was rear-ended by a car driven at high speed by a member of a powerful family of Muslim multi-millionaires, the Orphalies. When the police arrived, Jacob truthfully described what had happened. Later, my immediate family and some uncles were sitting in the parlor when Jacob returned, looking proud of himself having done the right thing. As he stood explaining what had transpired, my father jumped from his seat, walked toward him and spat in his face. I can still see the terror in Jacob's eyes as he reacted to what was indeed an act of terror. Jacob had acted honestly and legally, just as my father would have. Perhaps my father was worried that our family would be the target of revenge. Perhaps he needed to show his power in front of those present. In any case, it was a nauseating thing to watch.

Yet sometimes he surprised me. I was seven years old and in the second grade when my father made me a promise: "If you rank first or second in your class, I will buy you a watch."

I wanted that watch, and was terribly disappointed when I ranked eighth in my class. I looked at my report card and hated that eight written in bold script. Before I knew it, my finger went into my mouth and then I was erasing the eight and replacing it with a two written in second-grade script. My father looked at the report card and then looked at me. He could see what I had done, but he could also see how much I wanted that watch.

"I can see I have to buy you a watch, Daniel," he said. And he did!

As I grew older, my father included me in activities and expeditions that made me feel grown up. The language he wrote best was Turkish, but he had to write documents in Arabic, and those he asked me go over to correct his Arabic or write the documents from scratch for him. Then he would brag to his friends and colleagues.

"See this document? My son Daniel wrote it for me. Doesn't he write with a fine hand?"

Another time he took me with him to view a piece of land he had bought. It was in an area inhabited by Bedouins. The Bedouins lived in tents, and I had never seen a tent before. When my father was talking to the man who had sold him the land, I edged closer to one of the tents and peeked inside. All of a sudden four or five enormous dogs appeared out of nowhere and attacked me. I was flat on the ground screaming in terror when my father rescued me. I was never so happy to feel his arms around me. He was my protector, just as he was every night when he barricaded our door against intruders. At times such as those I felt safe with my father.

Baba was a self-made man guided by enlightened

ideas and principles, a man ahead of his time. In his public life, I remember his sensitivity to the plight of the poor, the less fortunate, and the rejects of society and his fights on their behalf. I remember his commitment to Jewish ideals, his service to the community, and his belief in equal education for boys and girls. It was from him, and later from my sisters, that I got my first lessons about women's dignity and women's rights.

My father was a man of strong principles. He never bought goods made in Japan during World War II. He bought goods made in England.

"The British are our friends, and I support them," he would say.

Nine members of the Civil Council (with son of one of the Council members)
My father seated in front row, second from the left.

Sometimes people scoffed at him.

"What difference can one man buying British goods make?" they would ask.

"I stick to my principles," he would reply.

In 1926 my father was elected to the Babylonian Jewish community's civil council, *mijlis eljismani*, a body of unpaid community leaders that managed the civil affairs of the community. He was appointed the head of its education committee, which oversaw the Jewish school system.

L'Ecole de l'Alliance Israelite was part of an

international network of primary and secondary schools established in Paris, and in Baghdad there was one Alliance for boys and another for girls. The Jewish community regularly sent messengers to France to recruit the finest teachers for the boys' Alliance. As an inducement to a prospective teacher, the candidate's wife might be offered a teaching post at the girls' Alliance. Some of the wives turned out to be excellent teachers. Others didn't.

My father felt l'Alliance's girls were being short-changed. He proposed that the two schools merge, thus giving girls and boys the same quality of education. This caused an uproar in the Jewish community. Several accused my father of undermining Judaism by advocating coeducation. When he insisted on the plan, my parents' home was cordoned off for nearly two months and there were threats on his life. But he didn't give in. My father was an observant Jew and had no intention of undermining Judaism. He simply saw injustice and wanted it corrected.

A compromise was proposed: Teachers at the boys' Alliance would devote half their time to teaching in the girls' Alliance. Since my father's interest was in ensuring an equally good education for all students, he agreed to the compromise. Unfortunately, when he left his position in 1928, the compromise fell into disuse, and practices reverted to the earlier system.

My father also fought against corporal punishment in the Jewish schools. On one occasion a teacher beat a student, and the student's mother reported the incident. The teacher was unrepentant. The education committee wrote to the principal recommending that the teacher be dismissed, but the principal, who agreed with the teacher, balked. Since the committee had no jurisdiction over the teacher so long as the principal was in place, the committee dismissed the principal and appointed the committee's chairman—my father--acting principal. In that capacity, he fired the offending teacher.

Once again, Baba had succeeded in stirring up the Jewish community. To many, the education committee's "harshness" was incomprehensible. But eventually most became reconciled to it. Corporal punishment never completely stopped. Incidents went unreported. But when a teacher was caught beating a pupil, it was understood by all that he or she risked dismissal.

I visited with my father in the homes of appellate and supreme court justices and was with him in the company of men of wealth and power. It was from him that I learned early on not to be cowed by titles or awed by wealth or social status, but to judge people by their character and humanity. It was by observing him defy bullies and speak out on unpopular issues that I developed the courage to stand up for my own beliefs.

Some of these traits had begun to rub off on me by the time I was 14, when I tangled with a renowned medical specialist. I developed swollen glands, and my father made an appointment for me with a Muslim doctor. This was unusual. We never went to see Muslim doctors because many were said to have received their doctorates fraudulently, and we weren't sure of their competence. But this one was reputed to be the best in his field. My father couldn't accompany me to the doctor on the day of the appointment and sent my brother, Jacob, with me.

"Explain your symptoms," the doctor said, addressing me in the Muslim dialect and peering down the length of his nose at me.

When Jews conversed with Muslims in Iraq it was understood that both would use the Muslim dialect. Muslims never stooped to use the Jewish dialect. For me, this practice screamed Muslim superiority, and I refused to learn the Muslim dialect. "The Muslim will speak to me in my own language," I vowed.

I then recited my symptoms in Judeo-Arabic.

"The glands on the back of my neck are swollen and they hurt when I touch them or turn my head," I explained.

The doctor shook his head, signaling he didn't understand. I detailed my symptoms again and again, but the doctor just kept shaking his head.

Judeo-Arabic contains Hebrew and Aramaic words and expressions that, to a non-Jew, are incomprehensible. Still, there was enough Arabic in our dialect that a Muslim can understand the gist of what is being said. But my doctor wouldn't admit to understanding a word. He continued to shake his head. Perhaps he felt it was an effrontery that I spoke to him in the language of the despised Jews, and was determined not to admit to understanding anything I said. But I was just as determined. He would admit to understanding my language or we would leave without his treating me, and that is exactly what happened.

That night, on the roof of our home, where we slept on summer nights, Jacob gave vent to his anger, just as we were about to go to sleep.

"What got into you? Don't you know that you should have spoken to the doctor in the Muslim dialect? Baba had waited for this appointment for two months, and you blew it. You've wasted the visit. He is going to be so mad at you."

Jacob had me worried about Baba's reaction. The next morning when I saw my father he didn't seem angry. I even detected a glimmer of admiration in his eyes as he patted my head.

"You'll have to recover without the help of that doctor, son."

And indeed I did. The bumps in the back of my neck were gone of their own accord within a few weeks.

The charity commandment, or *sedaka*, was instilled in us children early, mainly through Baba's example. Once, a tailor who rented his store from my father took ill and was bedridden for weeks. He was young and had a large family. When the tailor came back to work, he stopped at our home to see my father. He was pale, had lost a lot of weight, and looked frail. He sat on the couch with a worried look on his face. In his hand, he held a quarter dinar bill, the equivalent of about $1.25. In a broken voice, he told my father he had intended to pay his accumulated rent, which I believe was close to ten dinars, but had only a quarter dinar toward what he owed. My father nearly broke down when he saw the tailor extend his hand to offer the small sum.

" I don't want any money," he said. "You don't owe me any money. Take the quarter dinar to your family and feed your children."

Having surmounted the poverty of his youth, my father tried to inspire others who were struggling to get by.

One time he met a friend walking with his wife on Rasheed Street. He was an electrical engineer who had studied in Berlin and returned with his German wife to practice in Baghdad. The couple appeared dejected. The wife was pregnant; they felt they didn't have the means to support a child, and had decided on an abortion. They were on their way to the hospital, when they met my father and confided their plight to him. He told them,

"Don't you know that when God sends a child, He sends his sustenance with him? You have nothing to worry about. Go home and welcome your baby when it is born."

The two looked at each other, looked at my father, then turned around and went back home. They had a baby boy. In time, the engineer's business picked up. He and his wife had more children. Once a year, on the birthday of their first-born son, the engineer and his wife took their son to visit my father, and they thanked him for changing the course of their life on that fateful day.

Occasionally, my father did pro bono legal work, including risky cases involving Jews suing Muslims on criminal charges. These were no-win situations. Either the Jew lost in court, or if he won, the Jew or his lawyer—or both—were subjected to violence; some were murdered. Jewish plaintiffs and lawyers weren't the only victims of such recriminations, but they were most frequently targeted. Not surprisingly, Jews seldom took Muslims to court on criminal charges.

One criminal case may have led to an attempt on my father's life. When he was waiting for a bus one day, a man with a knife attacked him. Baba wrestled his assailant to the ground and stood on top of him until the police came. When he arrived home he was bleeding and furious.

We never learned the motive for the attack. The police didn't charge the assailant and released him without an explanation. We suspected the crime was an act of vengeance connected to Baba's legal representation of a victim in a criminal suit against a Muslim.

My father in court attire

Although I wish my father and I had never butted heads, I suppose, given our temperaments and the generational gap, it was inevitable. But all that pales by comparison to what I now remember of my father. I remember him with much love. I remember my father more for his warmth and caring as a parent and for his commitment to enlightened ideas and principles as a human being - than I remember him for his foibles and inconsistencies.

MAMA'S GENTLE STRENGTH

The foundation of my mother's relationship with my father was laid when she risked scandal to cross the Tigris with him during the flood before they were married. I believe that set the tone of mutual trust and caring the two of them shared throughout their life.

Considering the time and place, their marriage was

one of co-equals. There was no community property in Iraq, and it was common that a man who bought a house for his family would have the house recorded in his name. Yet in the case of our family homes, ownership was in both of my parents' names.

My father was responsible for our finances, but my mother was his trusted advisor on major decisions. During the early years of World War II, Baba invested a large sum of money in 100-kilo bags of sugar and rice. Three years into the war, sugar and rice became scarce, rationing was imposed and the price of these two commodities went up. I was present one evening when a friend of the family, a seasoned businessman, came to visit my parents. During the discussion, he urged my father to take advantage of the high commodity prices and sell his holdings of sugar and rice. Instead of responding to his friend, my father turned to my mother to listen to what she had to say. This was almost unheard of in Iraq, where men made the decisions, big or small, without consulting with their wives.

Many times I heard women in Iraq demur when it came to making a major decision—about their own or their family's lives. "I am only a woman," they would say. My mother, however, didn't shrink from asserting herself. There was a clear division of responsibilities, but outside of my father's legal work, I don't think Mama hesitated to exert her influence. When she wanted something she made her wishes known and as often as not my father would go along.

Mama was a wonderful homemaker. Baba never second-guessed her, never complained that she was buying too much, even though I know there were times when he couldn't keep up with all the expenses. Mama tailored her menus to Baba's likes and dislikes. The only times I remember him complaining about her cooking was when the chicken soup had too much tomato for his liking.

During the summer when school was out, we used to wait impatiently for the moment my mother poured the steamy, pearly rice out of the big pot in the late morning hours, uncovering the thick layer of crispy browned rice at the bottom of the pot. It was *h'kaka* time. Everyone took turns helping scrape out the *h'kaka* with an enormous spatula. Each of us children got a piece on a plate. Some of us poured soup over it to soften it; some ate it as is. There was utter silence. One could hear only the crackling sound as we cracked the crunchy *h'kaka* between our teeth.

There were nine of us to care for when I was growing up. And S'haq's illness added an extra burden. Still she made time to be with us, to tell us stories about her childhood, her family, and the old Baghdad of her youth. She taught us the songs that she had learned from my grandparents, and we sat and sang together.

She was sensitive about her lack of a modern education, and it distressed her when her Alliance-trained younger sisters came over to help us children with our French homework. Mama often told me how much she regretted not being able to help us herself. "I feel as if I am a useless piece of wood," she would tell me.

Mama devoted a lot of her attention to me, her favorite child. She felt I was special, and she conveyed the message in words and deeds. I loved being singled out, but sometimes it made me uncomfortable.

During the school year our lunch was usually cooked rice and chicken soup, with vegetables and desserts. I never liked chicken soup and would skip it. One day, Mama decided to cook a different chicken dish, just enough for me. For my siblings, she served the usual soup. Mama had an anxious expression when I came to the table. It torments me to this day when I think of the anxiety I must have caused her by being so finicky. Her face lit up when she saw me enjoying the new dish. Before long, Latifa complained that she didn't want to eat chicken soup either, but wanted what I was having. Mama told her there was enough only for me. Now I couldn't enjoy my meal knowing my sister wanted some. So I took half of what I had on my plate and put it on Latifa's plate. Mama beamed with admiration.

My mother never missed an opportunity to praise the positive she saw in me – a good deed, a gentle statement, an organized desk, or neat handwriting. I don't remember her ever criticizing me. When she pointed to a shortcoming, it was always with caring and love.

Mama was a lot more understanding of the needs of growing young men and women than my father was, and she shielded us from my father's wrath whenever we did things that Baba disapproved of. Muzli and Reyna often slipped out to the movies on Sabbath afternoons. That was a violation of the Sabbath and it would have infuriated Baba, but he never knew about it--Mama covered for them. Jacob blew out the kerosene-stove fire one Sabbath day. Muzli and Reyna were aghast; having anything to do with fire on the Sabbath is prohibited by Jewish tradition. But my father never got wind of Jacob's transgression. Mama kept everyone quiet.

Only once do I remember her giving me a spanking. It was in the "*Omer*" period, between Passover and *sh'buoth*, when the weather changed unexpectedly from too hot to too cold, and from sunny to rainy. We called that period *Omer el mijnoon,* the crazy *Omer.* During *Omer,* it was difficult to decide where we should sleep. Sometimes it was too hot to sleep in the bedroom, but many times when we took our beds to the rooftops we were rained out at midnight.

I must have been eleven on that particular *Omer* night. I wanted to have my bed moved up to the rooftop. Mama felt it was too early to do so. It was hot, and I couldn't sleep. I kept going to her room to complain. After waking her up for the third or fourth time, Mama took me back to my bed, and gave me one swat, saying, "You sleep now!" I was taken aback. I never expected her to spank me, and I believe Mama was taken aback, too. She immediately put her arm around me and sat next to me in bed. I fell asleep. The next morning when she saw me she gave me a big hug and asked me if I had slept well. I grumbled. But we made up.

In 1944, when I was twelve, my mother suffered crippling stomach pains and was bedridden for weeks. Our doctor, Ammu Guerji, diagnosed gallstones and told my father that she needed surgery. Baba wanted her to be hospitalized in Meir Elias Hospital, an institution maintained by the Jewish community. That it was costly was not a consideration, as far as he was concerned. He also wanted the finest in surgeons. Ammu Guerji had a colleague in London who specialized in gallbladder, and Baba flew him to Iraq to operate on Mama.   By the time she had left the hospital, the cost had nearly exhausted my parents' assets.

Baba, Reyna, uncles, aunts and cousins accompanied her to the hospital. Although my brother and five of my sisters stayed at home, the house felt empty. It felt dark, even though it was daylight. I was out of my wits. Could Mama die? She told me that morning that she had seen her father in a dream the night before. He was dressed in white and held a twig of green myrtle in his hand, which he gave to my mother. Then he disappeared. Mama said she felt reassured.   In the traditional interpretation of dreams, white meant peace, green symbolized life and, in the Babylonian tradition, green myrtle symbolized Elijah's blessing. Mama decided that Grandpa Silman was telling her that she would be safe and wouldn't die. But that was only a dream. What if she did die? What would I do?

A week later, Uncle Moshe took me to visit Mama in the hospital. I had never been to a hospital before. Meir Elias was a sprawling facility, surrounded by lush gardens that seemed to stretch for miles. As we walked the corridors, I was fascinated that the floors were made of some material—perhaps cork—that muffled the sound of our footsteps. Mama's large single room overlooked a beautiful field.

I walked toward Mama's bed. Her eyes were closed, and she had a big rubber tube implanted in her stomach that dripped a yellow fluid into a big jar attached to her bed. I learned later that the fluid was bile. Looking pale, Mama opened her eyes slowly. I wanted to run and hug her, but I was afraid I might hurt her or pull the tube out of her stomach. I stood still by her bedside and looked at her. She moved her left arm slowly and put her hand on my shoulder. It felt so good to feel her touch that I cried.

I visited her again two weeks later. She was sitting up, the pink had returned to her cheeks, and she had a smile on her face. A thin tube had replaced the big one.

This time I spent more time with Mama. She told me that when the anesthesiologist came to place the mask on her face, she asked him to wait. She lifted her right hand, covered her eyes, and recited the "*Sh'ma Yisrael*," the central prayer Jews are taught to try to make the last thing they utter before they die: "Hear O Israel, the Lord is one...." Then she turned to the anesthesiologist and motioned to him that now she was ready.

Unlike the quiet that prevailed during my first visit, this time the hallways near Mama's room were bustling with barefoot people dressed in Arab robes and turbans. Men armed with rifles stood guard at the entrance to the room next door. It seemed that the head of a tribe from Southern Iraq was hospitalized in the room next door. He had hauled the tribe's treasure with him, all cash, stacked in one big suitcase, which he kept under his hospital bed. The armed men were there to protect the suitcase.

The hospital prohibited firearms on its premises. But the sheikh didn't care, and no one could take him on without risking bloodshed. Later we learned from Meir Elias' administrator that, at the end of his treatment, the sheikh and his armed entourage left the hospital without paying the bill.

To my delight, Mama recovered, and all my fears proved unwarranted. She came home to be, as always, the heart and soul of our family, the center of it all. The household again hummed efficiently, thanks to her considerable administrative skill and boundless energy.

Mama oversaw the women who came every two weeks to wash our clothes. They were professional washerwomen who moved from house to house, their wrinkled fingers lifting the clothes in and out of the water, moving them from the washing tub to the rinsing tub, hanging them outside on the roof in the summer and inside in a special room hung with yards and yards of clothesline in the winter. A kerosene heater hastened the drying of the clothes in that room. Sometimes I peeked into that room. The sour smell of clothes drying inside was different from the fresh clean smell of clothes drying in the sun.

When the clothes were dry, my mother examined each piece for signs of wear and tear. It was then that the sewing machine came out, and I would be called upon to assist her. I was in charge of turning the wheel of the sewing machine, and I can still hear the click-clack of the machine and Mama's voice saying: "Turn the wheel now. Stop it. Stop now, Dannu."

Our society was not a throwaway society. We mended everything - clothes, shoes, and household items. A cousin of my mother's had his shoes repaired so often, adding sole after sole, that he unintentionally ended up adding a couple of inches to his height. When I first came to live in the United States, I had difficulty throwing away worn-out underwear.

We bought kerosene from a peddler who walked the streets dragging a cart that held a large tank of the fuel. Mama often sent me out with a can to purchase the kerosene, and I watched the kerosene flow from the spigot in the tank into my can. We knew there never would be a shortage of that fuel. We used gasoline to clean clothes that couldn't be washed in soap and water. This cleaning was done in the courtyard.

I almost started a conflagration with kerosene when I was about ten years old. Mama left me to watch a fire she had started in a hibachi pot in the courtyard. She had doused the charcoal with kerosene, but the fire began to dwindle after she put me in charge. I decided to improve on matters by pouring additional fuel on the fire. The resulting blaze scared me half to death. Luckily, Mama was keeping an eye on me from the kitchen window. She rushed to pull me back from the wall of flames and held me in her arms. Silently we stood together watching the flames until they receded and the charcoal began to turn red.

It was Mama who supervised the annual production of date syrup, or *silan.* For this major undertaking, a specialized team of professionals came to the house carrying their big pots and heavy equipment with them. The dates were boiled in water until they were reduced to syrup. The syrup was strained and boiled again until it had thickened to the proper consistency. They extracted syrup from a variety of dates—one favorite of mine tasted like sweet persimmons, another like honey. We mixed the sweet *silan* with sesame paste as a dessert, spread it on bread, and poured it over omelets and pancakes. Most importantly, it was mixed with crushed walnuts to make haroset, what we called *hillaik*, for our *shettakha (seder)* table during the Passover.

There was so much to do to prepare for Passover, and Mama was at the hub of it all. The weather then could be changeable, but spring was in the air and we were relieved to finally come out of hibernation. A week or so before the holiday, we began to move beds to the roof in preparation for sleeping on the rooftop. All the dark, heavy drapes came down, and in their place we hung beautifully embroidered white curtains that wafted in the breeze. We replaced the Persian rugs on our sofas and benches with white embroidered covers. We didn't own a vacuum cleaner, so Mama always hired four or five Kurds to roll up the rugs and lug them up to the roof to shake out the dust. The job was hard even for a team of this size, for the rugs were extremely heavy. But in their usual fashion, the Kurds worked without a break until all the rugs were clean, mothballed and put into storage for summer. Mama spent the whole day under the searing sun on the rooftop, ready to lend a helping hand to the workers and making sure they had enough water to drink. When they were finished, the shiny white floor tile was exposed to view and our house was ready for summer.
Roses came to full bloom around Passover time. And it was the season to make rosewater, or *miwaghd*, for use in cooking. The week before the *miwaghd* was distilled, sacks of rose petals stood in the corner of our storeroom from which the smell of roses drifted out to permeate the house. When the team arrived with their distilling equipment, it was a momentous occasion. I watched the steam rise from the boiling water steeped with rose petals. The steam was condensed and the distilled rosewater was bottled for future use. The bottles stood on the shelf long after the perfume had faded from the house, but just looking at them summoned up the scent of roses. It seemed to me that the smell of rosewater was at the core of our lives, spilling its

fragrance everywhere.

Mama always bought us new clothes for Passover. It was especially important that our new shoes squeak to demonstrate beyond doubt they were brand new. One of our neighbors had six boys, and they regularly passed by our house on their way to the synagogue. The father walked ahead and the children marched in a column behind him - nothing unusual, except during Passover they sounded like a marching regiment: One big pair of squeaky shoes followed by six other pairs, each with its own peculiar squeak.

On their holidays, Arabs bought squeaky new shoes, too. But more often than not, Arab men walked barefoot carrying their shoes, called *yamanee*, in their hands. They were proud of their *yamanee* and didn't want them to get dirty. Clean feet were not, apparently, a priority.

A week before the Passover, we baked our *massah*, thin round crackers of unleavened bread, twelve to fourteen inches in diameter. My mother, my siblings and I rolled the dough. Wearing a thick head cover and with hands and arms covered, my sister Jamila stood in front of a large wood-burning clay oven and stuck our thin-rolled dough directly on the hot walls of the oven. She pulled those that had already cooked and lay them on a large table to cool. We had to be careful not to bring food to our work area, for fear of getting the unleavened dough in contact with leavened food. On the eve of the Passover itself, we baked a dozen thick, soft *massah* for use on the *shettakha* plate.

Passover was a time for mutual visits and renewed friendship, and Mama oversaw the preparations for the occasion. Friends dropped in to wish us a happy Passover. My father, mother, and my siblings and I came out to greet them and join them in the living room. They sipped Turkish coffee we served in demitasse and munched on masafan (star-shaped marzipan), louzeena, Hajji Bada (round shaped marzipan), and other goodies Mama had prepared for the occasion. We sat and chatted together. No one stayed long. There were too many families to visit. Sometimes it was a madhouse trying to keep the fresh Turkish coffee coming with every new wave of visitors or, as sometimes happened, with a bunching up of visitors.

We, too, went to pay visits to friends. Sometimes we ran breathlessly from one place to another trying to make the whole list. Most of the time we returned home exhausted. I still loved those visits. I enjoyed the sense of renewed friendship they elicited, and I loved to cross paths with the throngs of visitors, constantly coming, constantly going.

Baba's greeting card
We left the card behind when the family we went to visit was out-
Card depicts a handshake with the biblical blessing "Happy Holiday" and a personal blessing commonly used by the Sephardim "May You Be Credited with Many Happy Years".

My own family's greeting card 5730 (1970), patterned after my father's

Those mutual visits were something special. They were unique to the holiday, and they did a lot to reinforce our festive feel of the day.

Some practices at the *shettakha* table are unique to

Babylonian Jewry. We follow the *Kabala,* or rituals Jewish mysticism, and break the massah into a large piece in the shape of the Hebrew letter *wow* and a smaller one in the shape of the Hebrew letter *daleth.*

The cutting of the *massah* was one of the highlights of the evening. We sat up straight, eyes fixed on our father's fingers, as he painstakingly cut the unleavened bread into the proper shapes. When he succeeded we all let out a triumphant cry, as he lifted each piece up high.

"Is this a *wow?*" he'd ask.

"Yea," we would all clap.

"Is this a *daleth?*"

"Yea," we would all scream.

Baba wrapped the *wow* piece in a large white linen cloth, tied the linen across his back and shoulder, and recited in Hebrew: "This is how our ancestors came out of Egypt - they hurriedly bundled what they possessed and carried it on their shoulders." Then he would run around the table to reenact the Israelites' hurried exodus, as we all shouted, "Go! Go! Quick! Quick!" He then untied the bundle, turning it over first to Jacob and then to me to follow suit. Being the youngest son, I got the honor of keeping the linen tied to my back until it was time to distribute pieces of the *massah* to everyone at the table. On the last day of Passover my father and I ritually took leftover *massah* to the fish in the Tigris. I laughed to see their gaping mouths appear like magic out of the water, waiting to be fed their *massah.*

We took turns chanting the *haggadah,* or Passover story, in order of age—first Jamila, the eldest, then Muzli, all the way to Valentine, the youngest. When Valentine had finished reading her portion, we started over. Some portions of the *haggadah* were lively and had beautiful tunes. But everyone hated the portion about the "wicked" child who disdains his traditions and ancestors. That portion followed another that portrayed the "wise" child who honors his heritage.

Since Jamila was the oldest, she always got to read about the wise child. Muzli, the second child, always got saddled with the portion about the despicable wicked child.

She protested bitterly but no one else would trade with her. She was the second child, this was the second portion, and that was it! So it went every year until Jamila got married and left the house to celebrate with her husband. Then Muzli became the first in the family. She got to read about the wonderful wise child!

She was not so fortunate many years later, when my siblings and I had gathered for Passover and shared the reading of the *haggadah* not by birth order, but by our random seating order around the table. When it was Muzli's turn to read, what section did she draw? We collapsed with laughter when it turned out to be her old nemesis, the wicked child.

HEARTBREAK AND MARRIAGE

As the next to youngest child, I was often perplexed by the family dramas unfolding around me, particularly when it came to my older sisters and matters of the heart.

In the summer of 1939, Baba arranged for Mama, Muzli, Reyna and Jacob to spend the summer in Beirut. He felt that a change of scene might help cure my three siblings of a chronic stomach ailment that was afflicting them. Beirut was known for its beauty, its gorgeous mountains, and its majestic view of the Mediterranean. Uncle Moshe, who accompanied my mother and my siblings on the trip, wrote to us fairly regularly about the great time everyone was having in Beirut.

When they all returned home at the end of August, I peppered my sisters and brother with questions.

"What is it like in Beirut?" I asked. Reyna and Jacob merely shrugged, but the light in Muzli's eyes could have lit up the world. She danced around the house, clapping her hands to the music emanating from the radio.

"It was wonderful, wonderful! Beirut is wonderful!"

Later I went to my mother.

"Why is Muzli so happy?"

My mother looked up. All she would say was that

Muzli lived in a dream world and wouldn't be happy for much longer.

"We have to follow the traditions. Muzli has to understand that. What would happen to Jamila if Muzli were to get married before Jamila?"

It was very puzzling, but, as usual, it was Latifa who explained it all to me. She was only ten months older than I, but her eyes and ears missed nothing. We were together in the courtyard pumping the spinning top my mother had brought me from Beirut.

Muzli, right, and Reyna, left, by a waterfall in Beirut, 1939

Latifa tapped my shoulder.

"You know why Muzli is so happy?"

"No," I replied, "Do you want another turn with the top?" I was feigning disinterest, for I knew Latifa would have to be coaxed to tell if she realized how badly I wanted to know.

"Never mind the top," she said impatiently. "When Mama, Muzli, Reyna, and Jacob were in Beirut they used to go to a café to spend the evenings. There, a man from Jerusalem used to join them to play cards. But he really was not interested in cards--he was interested only in Muzli. He wanted to marry her. And Muzli liked him, too."

"Muzli is getting married? Will she be going to

Beirut? I would like to go to Beirut, too."

"No, silly. Jamila is older than Muzli and she isn't married yet. Mama wouldn't allow her to get married before Jamila."

Latifa went back to spinning the top. I went back to my mother.

"Is it true that someone wanted to get married to Muzli in Beirut?"

"Yes," Mama explained. "But I told him that he couldn't marry Muzli because Muzli is younger than Jamila. If we let Muzli get married first, people will think there is something wrong with Jamila, and nobody will want to marry her."

"And what happened?"

"He kept coming back," Mama continued. "And I told him the same thing every time he asked to marry Muzli."

My mother looked proud of herself for sticking to tradition.

"And what happened to the man?"

"I don't know. He probably went back to Jerusalem."

Muzli's smile faded as the days went by. She talked wistfully of her time in Beirut, but she never talked about the man.

Twelve years later, Muzli married Naim. Years after that, when we were sitting together in a park near Muzli's home, she told me sadly about a dream she had the night of her wedding. The man she had met in Beirut appeared in a dark alley holding a kerosene lamp. There was no one else in the alley – just the two of them. He walked slowly toward Muzli. He had a sad look on his face. He stopped in front of her. He raised his lamp and took a long look at her face; said nothing. Then he turned off the lantern and vanished in the dark.

Our community's rigid insistence that daughters be married off in order of age—oldest first—was but one of the harsh marriage customs that cast a pall over my family for years, as pressure mounted to find husbands for my sisters. Unmarried women were not highly regarded by Babylonian Jews. Marriage bestowed respectability and desirability on a woman. The families of future husbands often took advantage of the situation and demanded huge dowries from the bride's family—humiliating for the women and often reducing their families to penury.

Marrying off a daughter imposed strictures on the bachelors, too. Bachelors were expected to postpone marrying until all of their sisters were married off. Otherwise, rumors would spread that the single sister was unmarriageable, that she had a "blemish." Bachelors also were expected to pay their sisters' dowries when the father was deceased or didn't have adequate funds. My maternal uncle, Sion, never married. By the time his youngest sister, my Aunt Nazeema, was married off, Sion was in his fifties and considered himself too old. He died not long afterward. I mourned his life, and what his surrender to those antiquated traditions had done to him. He was a compassionate man and would have made a loving husband and a nurturing father.

My parents had married for love and by mutual agreement. There was no dowry and no talk of money. They had always impressed on us children that it was demeaning to make marriage conditional on money. But then I watched as they suffered through the despised dowry and bargaining route, in order to get Jamila married off. I resented what it did to them and to Jamila. I resented it no less when it was time to find a mate for Reyna.

Uncle Moshe oversaw the search for Reyna's husband after they had immigrated to Israel, because my parents had stayed behind in Baghdad. The months went by, but whenever a match seemed near at hand, the deal fell through - either because of Reyna's smallpox scars, or the prospective bridegroom's demands for horrific dowries, which were probably not unrelated to the smallpox. Reyna was hurt. She wept and stopped eating.

And then the inevitable happened. Helwa and Latifa, who were younger than Reyna, met men they wanted to marry. I supported them in their plans to marry before Reyna. Reyna was hurt by this, believing that if her younger sisters married ahead of her it would dim her own chances of marriage. Because I so despised these outlandish rules, I was dismissive when Reyna broached the subject with me, and I very much regret that now. I wish I had been more understanding of her plight.

Helwa and Latifa went ahead and married before their older sister. Then Reyna met a man she liked, the first one she had ever opened up to. Like Reyna, he had been afflicted with smallpox as a child. Reyna fell in love, and they talked about getting married. But his parents forbade the match unless our family came up with an exorbitant dowry. They stopped seeing each other and Reyna was heartbroken. I believe he cared for her, but lacked the backbone to stand up to his parents. He wrote Reyna a letter after their breakup, and addressed the envelope to "Reyna Khazzoom the Precious."

Not long after the breakup, we learned that he was scheduled to marry a woman his parents had found for him. But the story had a tragic ending. On the day of his wedding, he got out of his taxicab to cross the street. A car ran a red light and struck him. He died that night. Reyna sat in mourning. She withdrew more into herself.

I believe that was the only man she ever loved.

Two years later, Reyna married Saleh, a soft-spoken mailman. It was arranged marriage. Reyna and Saleh had a son, Gideon. For a while she seemed happy—her in-laws adored her, and made no secret of the fact they were honored to have their son marry into our family. But Reyna's relationship with Saleh quickly deteriorated. They remained married, but led the life of two divorced people under the same roof. Reyna wouldn't consider divorce, for fear she would never remarry.

Heartbreak aside, the dowry system - and the enormous financial stakes involved - sewed discord and treachery within families, including ours. Jamila's marriage to Ezra Hay was arranged in the late nineteen forties, and my father promised that she would have a dowry of five thousand dinars, the equivalent of $25,000. However, the money that Jamila spent on her trousseau and furnishings for her new home could be deducted from the total. Because of this,

Jamila had to keep a strict accounting of every penny she spent.

No sooner was Jamila's marriage arranged than my father gave her money to go shopping. It was then that my manipulative aunt, Khala Toya, stepped in. She volunteered to help Jamila select a trousseau.

"And now a dress for me," Khala Toya would say to Jamila as they browsed in a store. "Your father can well afford it."

My father had always disliked Khala Toya, considering her a troublemaker, which indeed she was. But I don't think even he knew the extent of her perfidy. Jamila was unable to refuse her, even when Khala Toya bought wedding clothes for her sons with my father's money. Jamila was afraid to confess to my father: How could she tell him that Khala Toya had appropriated the money, without creating deep divisions within the family and casting a dark shadow over the coming wedding?

Later, I overheard my father and Jamila going over her trousseau account.

"Jamila, what has happened to you?" he scolded. "What has happened to the money? I gave you one hundred dinars yesterday, and you can only account for seventy. I want you to have the best that money can buy, but this is money for which I must account to Ezra's family. If you can't account for the missing money, I will have to make it up when I hand over your dowry. Did you lose it? Are the bills incorrect? Were you cheated by some wily merchant?"

I could hear the despair in Jamila's voice, as she twisted her skirt between her fingers and looked at the ground.

"I will do better, Baba. I am really sorry."

"Do try, Jamila."

But every time Jamila went shopping it was the same story, and I grew to hate Khala Toya when I heard Jamila stammer her excuses to my father.

In Iraq, children lived with their parents at least until they got married. When daughters married they often remained in close proximity to their parents. In the old section of Baghdad, some parents bought newlyweds a house across the street from their own, and built an enclosed bridge to connect the two residences. One family who lived in a huge house across the street from us had four of their married sons with their wives and children living with them in the same house.

When Jamila got married, the nuptial agreement stipulated that my parents rent a house for her in our neighborhood where her husband Ezra, his parents, his five brothers and his sister would come to reside with the newlyweds. My parents paid a huge sum of money for the rent. Jamila's in-laws paid nothing. They occupied six rooms and the whole first floor in the house. My sister and Ezra occupied only small two.

HARD BARGAINING

In our Baghdad neighborhood, we were surrounded by family. All my aunts, uncles, cousins and grandmothers lived within a radius of a few blocks. And for the most part, the extended family pulled together. In our world, women never shopped for fruits and vegetables; the men folk did that. But in our family, it was Uncle Moshe, and not my busy father, who did our shopping.

Every evening Uncle Moshe would make a list of what my mother needed him to buy at the market the next day. He usually hired an Arab porter to help him carry his purchases. Often, he'd buy a dozen or so watermelons for us. They were placed in a large cloth, knotted into a bundle, and one end of the cloth was tied around a porter's head so that he could carry them. My uncle walked by the porter's side to ensure the watermelons reached their destination safely. There was the assumption that one or more of them might be sold en route to passers-by on the street.

My uncle was a commodities broker. The Baghdad market was a loose, unruly system, very different from the sophisticated commodity market in the U.S. He had a list of merchant clients who wanted to buy or sell certain commodities and he generally knew where to find the potential seller or buyer. He served as the intermediary to arrive at a mutually acceptable price. Usually this involved shuttling back and forth many times between all the parties involved, using every trick in the book to cajole, pressure, plead and haggle to seal the deal.

He never went to work before eleven on any given day; his mornings were spent marketing for us. I remember times when he said he had a hot deal and would have to go to work early (still meaning no earlier than nine a.m.). On those rare occasions, he didn't do the daily purchases for us.

His partner often called us in the mornings, looking for Uncle Moshe, saying he needed to finalize a deal and wanted Moshe's extra push. But Uncle Moshe was busy doing our shopping. The partnership didn't last. Apparently Uncle Moshe still made enough to live comfortably with his wife, Khala (Aunt) Guerjiyi, my mother's older sister. They didn't have children and lived alone in a huge house. Uncle Moshe was our second father, as we were his surrogate children.

The only shopping for food my mother did was from street peddlers. If, for example, she ran out of tomatoes, she would hail one of the peddlers. Then the fun—the inevitable ritual of haggling --would begin. My mother would point to the tomatoes she wanted, and the peddler would place them on one side of his scale, with a large stone on the other side.

"Just two kilos," he would tell my mother, holding out his hand for the payment.

My mother would shake her head.

"No! No! I want you to use proper weights."

It was the peddler's turn to shake his head, as he stared at my mother, amazed and outraged by her request.

"By *Allah* I swear, this stone weighs exactly two kilos."

"I'm sure it does, but I still want you to use proper weights," my mother would insist.

In the end, my mother won, the peddler producing his weights but still raising his eyes to heaven, his arms thrown wide to emphasize his outrage at his honesty being questioned, and by a woman at that.

We never bought *laban* (yogurt) on the street, since my mother always made ours. But the Arab women who sold it fascinated us. The *laban* was packed into huge tubs about two feet in diameter, and the *laban* sellers carried these containers on their heads. Even my father was mesmerized by the ability of these women to walk and run with the tubs on their heads and, as often as not, a baby strapped on their backs. I remember one day Baba shaking his head in disbelief as he counted twelve tubs on one woman's head.

As a sanitation measure, our unpasturized milk was always boiled as soon as we brought it into the house. Once when I was four years old, I spotted a jug of newly boiled milk covered with muslin on the kitchen table. The steam was escaping through the muslin, and I wanted to investigate. I pulled on the tablecloth to help me climb on the table. Before I knew it, I was covered in boiling milk, and the jug lay in pieces on the floor. My skin was blistered and everyone in the house was near hysterics.

We bought our milk from Arabs who lived in settlements about eight blocks from our house. Usually one of my sisters and I walked there carrying our own bottles with us, bottles into which the cows were milked directly via a funnel. Sometimes the cow wouldn't let the milk down, and a calf was put to the cow's teat to induce her to give milk. As soon as the milk began to flow, the calf was pushed away from its mother. Even though we were waiting for our milk, my sympathies were all with the hungry, lowing calf.

Many of the Arabs who owned the cows had several wives. I remember one man in particular who had two wives. The first was extremely plain, and she was the one who milked the cows. His second wife was young and beautiful. I still remember her name – Shamsiya. I could see how much the man valued Shamsiya. Everyone in the settlement knew she was her husband's favorite. I felt sorry for the sullen, silent first wife, who had to do all the work. Then one day I realized neither woman had an easy life.

My sister Latifa was with me, and we were watching

the first wife milk a cow. Suddenly a woman's screams rang out in the quiet evening air. I was frozen, as I watched the Arab repeatedly kick and beat up his young wife, who was on the ground trying to protect herself with her hands. I thought the first wife might interfere. But she looked terrified, and continued milking. I was horrified.

"What happened?" I asked Latifa.

"The young woman had just walked out of the hut, where she had left her young son asleep. The baby woke up and began to cry, just as the husband appeared on the scene. The husband is beating up the mother for not taking better care of his son."

I was incensed by the man's cruelty.

Latifa shook her head.

"There's nothing we can do about it."

I clenched my hands into tight fists even though I knew Latifa was right. "Just be happy Mama doesn't have to put up with a husband who beats her," I thought to myself.

That night, as my mother tucked me into bed, I said: "Aren't you glad you're not married to an Arab?" My mother smiled.

"You say the strangest things, Dannu. I couldn't be married to an Arab. I'm Jewish, and Jews don't marry Arabs. Go to sleep now."

We distrusted the Arabs and seldom did business with them. One day when I was five, we heard a big commotion outside one of the tailor's shops on the first floor of our house. I went up to the third floor to watch what was happening. A big crowd had gathered outside the shop. In the thick of it stood a brawny Muslim holding a suit in his hands, screaming at the tailor, whom he had apparently dragged into the street. The tailor looked frail and his eyes spoke of terror. The Muslim slapped him and seized him by the throat and shook him hard. The tailor's eyes began to bulge in his head and I screamed for my mother.

"Mama, he's killing him. He's killing him."

My mother joined me at the window and put her arm around me.

"It's how they cheat," she said softly.

We learned later that the Muslim had ordered a suit from the tailor a few weeks before a religious holiday. He had chosen the cloth from some the tailor had in stock and had agreed to pay for both the material and labor when the suit was ready. When the suit was finished and the time came to pay, the Muslim claimed the suit was not to his liking.

"Doesn't the man know the tailor would have fixed the suit to the Muslim's liking?" I asked.

"Of course he does," my mother replied, "but it's not what the Muslim wants. He wants a suit without having to pay for it."

We both watched as the Muslim shook the tailor one more time, spat in his face and threw him forcefully to the ground. I flinched at the sound of the tailor's body hitting the ground. Then I saw the Muslim put the folded suit under his arm and walk away.

This was but one of many instances of Muslims exploiting Baghdad's Jewish community. When I was older, I once bought a new Passover suit from a Muslim shopkeeper who didn't have a fitting room in his store. He assured me that I could return the suit for a refund if it didn't fit. When it turned out to be too small and I took it back, he refused to give me my money back.

The tensions between Muslim and Jew were a constant of my boyhood. I especially hated Ramadan, a sacred month of fasting in the Muslim world, for that was the time of the frightful drumming.

Daily, in the wee hours of the morning, men would walk the streets beating drums so that people would wake up to eat and recite their prayers before dawn. Everyone was supposed to be awake at that hour, whether or not he was a Muslim. The relentless, frightening rhythms were the same as those played for Muslim funeral processions. While the drummers were walking the streets and filling the airwaves with their beat, the *muezzin*, or cleric, would ascend to the top of the mosque's minaret and call the faithful to prayer. In the din, I would lie awake, staring into the darkness, anxiously awaiting the pale morning light.

The Muslim calendar is lunar, so Ramadan can fall during any season of the year. The worst time was when it fell in the summer and our beds were on the roof. No one got much sleep then. The calls and drumbeats began even earlier than in the winter. The fact that Jews and Christians constituted over a third of the population of Baghdad and didn't pray in mosques was of no import.

That reasoning applied to other Ramadan constraints as well. When I was about thirteen, a Jew was arrested for smoking in the street during Ramadan. He was brought before a judge the following day. When told of the so-called crime, the judge raised his eyebrows in horror.

"How dare you? Don't you know that smoking in public during the month of Ramadan is forbidden?"

The judge went on to preside over the case, as the smell of the cigarette on which he was puffing filled the courtroom. The month of Ramadan had not ended at the time.

SABBATH IN BAGHDAD

The Sabbath and the annual cycle of Jewish holidays imparted a calm amid danger and drew us closer together in the safety of home and synagogue. Whether during joyous feasts or solemn liturgy, I could picture Jews all over the world being blessed as we were, and felt a connection with every Jew who had gone before us. Even though the practices of Babylonian Jewry differed radically from Ashkenazi Jews, the events we celebrated were the same. It was a long, unbroken chain that linked us one to another.

On Fridays, the coming of the Sabbath was in the air—in the throngs crowding Jewish bakeries early on Friday morning, in the bustling Jewish barbershops, in the brisk business at candy stores, in the early closings of the textile market and other Jewish shops. Smiling people radiated happiness. The day of rest was around the corner.

On Friday evenings we celebrated the *kiddush*, a ceremony of welcoming the Sabbath, which began with the lighting of the *kerrayee* at sundown. The *kerrayee*, a glass bowl filled with sesame oil and water, hung from the ceiling on three silver chains. A silver Star of David, into which fitted seven homemade palm wicks, nestled on the bottom of the bowl. In the winter, when the sun set early, and we wanted the flame to last several hours into the evening, my mother used more oil than water. In the summer she used more water than oil.

Kerrayee – Babylonian Menorah for Sabbath and holidays.
A replica of my parents' Kerrayee, made in Ghana

Mama set up the *mady*, as the festive table was known, laying out the customary Babylonian flat bread: four round pieces, each about fifteen inches in diameter laid in pairs back to back so that it seemed there were in reality only two pieces. This method, which was done to simulate the type of bread configuration used in the Temple, is unique to Babylonian

Baker taking baked Babylonian flat bread out of the clay oven.

Babylonian synagogue in Ramat Gan, Israel, patterned after the Babylonian synagogues in Iraq.
The Tebah, lectern, is where the services are conducted. The seats, (covered with Persian rugs) on the Tebah are for the elders of the community. Covered with curtains upfront, the *hekhal*, Ark of Law, is where the Torah scrolls are kept.

Jews. Mama placed the full saltcellar beside the bread, covering the bread with an embroidered cloth. Then she filled the *kiddush* cup with grape juice and set it on the table next to a big bunch of lush green myrtle ready for the *kiddush* ceremony.

My parents' *kiddush* cup

Standing in front of the *kerrayee* and watching it being lit was a spiritual experience that deepened as I grew older. It evokes in me a sense of peace and fellowship, transporting me beyond the everyday to a new world where tension has melted away. Once Mama had lit the *kerrayee*, my father and I, sometimes my brother and I, headed for Meir Elyahoo synagogue, one block from our home. Services were held whenever a *minyan*, a forum of ten men, had assembled. Successions of *minyaneem* were formed, as soon as ten men showed up. Each minyan met in a separate room in the sprawling Meir Elyahoo building.

There is a Jewish tradition that when the Sabbath arrives at Friday's sundown, every Jew is endowed with an additional soul for the duration of the Sabbath. The added soul, it is said, raises the Jew from the vale of woe, opens a new wonderful world for her and lifts her spirits.

Standing next to my mother, Baba held the *kiddush* cup and recited the traditional prayer to sanctify the Sabbath, just as God had sanctified the day. We all drank from the cup of grape juice, but beforehand we kissed our parents' hands, a sign of respect in the Middle East that always rekindled my connection to our parents.

My parents' *kiddush* cup was given to them by my maternal grandmother when they married. At one time, the cup's lid was crowned by six branches, on which a dove of peace perched. With the rise of Arab nationalism in the 1940's, the Iraqi authorities treated any Jew who possessed a Star of David or any other six-cornered object as a traitor. When midnight searches of Jewish homes turned up such items, the penalty for "Zionist sympathies" was a minimum seven-year jail term. So my father had a silversmith remove the six branches. That left the dove wobbling atop the lid—an apt reflection of our shaky situation in Iraq.

Every Friday morning, Mama got up while stars were still out to prepare the bountiful meal for that night. There was always *kibba*, a ball of dough made of ground rice stuffed with ground meat, vegetables and cardamom and cooked with mutton or chicken; fried *shibboot*, fish that abounded in the Tigris; and our favorite crispy potato pancakes filled with ground meat, vegetables, lots of raisins, almonds, walnuts and condiments.

We bundled up in the cold winter nights before we sat for *kiddush*, for we didn't light a fire on the Sabbath, as stipulated in the Torah. For extra warmth, fun and love, we huddled around Mama, burying our hands under her thick furry robe-de-chambre and in her armpits. Immobilized, she would laugh and protest, "What are you doing to me, children? I can't even move." Baba wore his camel-skin cloak to keep warm. I remember when I was three or four, I used to sit on his lap at dinnertime and snuggle inside his thick cloak.

For an hour or more we sang s*h'bahoth*, the Sabbath paeans. Then it was time for the *nimnamot*—treats like nuts, roasted watermelon seeds, sheets of dried apricot, and *louzeena* (a diamond-shaped confection made of quince or orange peel cooked in sugar and sprinkled with ground nuts or coconut); *h'lawa* (halva); *sha'ir elbanat* (literally meaning, girls' hair – a crispy confection made of thin strings of halva) and the ever-present *simismiyee* (sesame bar). Often Baba or Uncle Moshe would come home on Friday afternoon loaded with Sabbath treats.

Our father was a good storyteller, and *nimnamot* time was also the time for listening to his stories.   He had us wide-eyed and on the edge of our seats with his tale of escaping conscription into the Turkish army during World War I. His plan was to head for British-occupied Basra in the southern part of Iraq. He set out from Baghdad on foot, traveling through primitive tribal areas. At one point he got passage on a riverboat, where a Muslim cleric spotted him as a Jew. When they pulled into port, the cleric told local tribesmen, "There's a dog on the upper deck—get him." My father was rounded up with some other Jewish passengers and marched in a column to a clearing where they were about to be shot. The tribesmen fumbled the job—they attempted to use one bullet to shoot the entire line of prisoners--and in the confusion my father slipped away.

As he told it, it was not long before he encountered another tribal group. This time, he decided to try to outwit them. In this region, the chiefs were identifiable by distinctive turbans decorated with some thirty or forty dangling tassels. Baba knew that according to tribal law, anyone who succeeded in tying two of those tassels together put himself under the protection of the chief, who was honor bound to protect him. He sought out the tribal leader and ducked behind his broad body. As they scuffled, my father managed to tie two tassels together. The tribesmen were forced to let him go.

Once my father reached safety, he began writing a memoir of his escape. In those days, straight pins were used much like paper clips to hold sheets of paper together. My father kept his pins in a cup. Becoming thirsty, he absent-mindedly used the cup full of pins to dip out some water to

drink. He was aghast when he realized what he'd done—
especially since no pins remained in the empty cup.

"You drank the pins!" we children would scream,
amazed that after narrowly escaping a firing squad he might
have succumbed to such an ignoble end.

But of course the story had a happy ending. Baba
explained that when he had dipped the cup in the water basin
the pins had fallen out before he'd taken a drink.

In our synagogue, we held the Sabbath morning
services in two shifts early in the day - at five and at seven.
Jacob and I attended the second shift with our father, but
even that was too early for us. Jacob grumbled and
complained and many times Baba, tired of fighting, allowed
him to stay in bed. I didn't like to get up early either, but my
love of the services overcame my reluctance. Besides, I liked
to dress in my Sabbath clothes and wear the watch Baba had
given me. Until I reached the age of twelve, the only day I
could wear it was Saturday, when my father could protect me
from the thieves who preyed on Jewish children walking
alone.

On Saturday morning we read from the *sefer Torah*
the weekly Torah portion. Bar miswah boys and prospective
bridegrooms were honored with reading from the Torah.
Afterwards, the congregation went wild wishing them good
luck. Women ululated, a sign of happiness in the Middle
East, and tossed candies in front of the honorees. On such
occasions, we were treated with a visit by Phrayim abu'l
sh'bahoth, "Ephraim the Singer of Paeans," and his traveling
choir.

Phrayim's history intrigued me. Once he had gone to
Palestine for an operation while his family waited and prayed
for his safe return. His family's hopes were dashed and they
shed bitter tears when a telegram arrived saying Phrayim had
died. Garments were rent, and the community gathered in
Phrayim's house to mourn with the family sitting shib'a. In
the midst of the wailing and the praying, the door opened and
Phrayim walked in. Many of those present screamed and
some fainted, thinking he was a ghost.

Mourning turned to joy and the fateful telegram was

closely examined, but it yielded no clues identifying its sender. From then on we thought of Phrayim as one who had returned from the dead to celebrate joyous occasions with us.

An open Babylonian sefer Torah

We didn't eat or drink on the Sabbath morning until after we had returned from services and recited the morning *kiddush*. My parents had a sparkling, tall electric kettle that we used only on the Sabbath morning for brewing tea. They viewed cooking on the Sabbath as a violation of the Torah commandments against working and lighting fire on that

85

day. I don't know how they reconciled this with using an electric kettle on the Sabbath.

During my youth, Babylonian rabbis tried to convince the Jewish community that turning on electricity was the same as turning on fire. Some especially observant Jews went to extraordinary lengths to obey the Torah injunction. Some tied the electric switch to the key that winds an alarm clock and set the clock to go off late on Friday night. When the alarm rang and the key turned back, it pulled the string and turned off the lights.

Our Sabbath breakfast followed tea. *Bayth al t'beet,* eggs that Mama had set to cook on Friday had by now turned a deep brown color and tasted delicious. On a cold Sabbath day, we would roll the unpeeled eggs between the palms of our hands, put them under our arm pits or stuff them into our pants' pockets. We made sandwiches of *bayth al t'beet,* parsley, salad, Italian peppers, pickled cucumbers, spring onions, and sliced tomatoes - all rolled in Babylonian flat bread.

On sunny Saturdays, we sat on our balcony to watch the crowds of Jewish families strolling along the Tigris' banks. Jewish residents of mansions along the Tigris filled their balconies, too. Some played *tawlee* or dominos; others sipped tea or Turkish coffee or cracked roasted watermelon seeds; and some simply gazed at the river.

Many times those idyllic scenes were marred by sudden assaults by Muslims. Some of the attackers were young hoodlums; most were not so young, and many were well dressed. Jewish men and women were beaten, some women were stripped of their jewelry, and some girls, including one time my sister Latifa, were sexually assaulted. On those occasions the police were usually nowhere to be seen, and, if they did come, they frequently took up cudgels against the Jews.

Strangely enough--maybe out of denial, undying optimism, or perhaps sheer resignation on the part of Jews--those Sabbath strolls never ceased, even though they thinned out as the noose tightened around the throat of our community during the second half of the nineteen forties.

But my sister Latifa's experience by the river is one that probably still casts a shadow over her memories of those walks. I believe I am the only one with whom she shared the story.

Sometimes on Saturday nights in the summertime I went up to the rooftop before it was time to go to bed. I wanted to lie on my bed in the dark and imagine myself moving from star to star through the vast reaches of the impenetrable sky.

Fourteen-year old Latifa joined me that evening. Her soft voice didn't at first disturb my reverie.

"Are you awake, Daniel?" she asked.

"Um, um."

"Something awful happened to me today."

I wasn't giving her my full attention until she began to cry. I sat up and put my arms around her.

"What is it, Latifa?"

"By the river, by the river ---".

Her heart-wrenching cries swallowed her voice. I didn't know how to help her.

"I'll go get Mama."

At this Latifa became almost hysterical.

"No, no. I don't want her to know. I don't want anyone to know. It's awful."

"Sh, sh. It's okay. I won't tell. What happened, Latifa?"

Slowly, through hiccups and sobs, the story emerged. A bunch of young Muslim hoodlums had approached Latifa when she was walking by the river with her girlfriends. For some reason, they singled out Latifa, ran their hands over her body and grabbed her genitals, all the time laughing and daring her to resist.

"I was so scared, Daniel. I was so afraid. When a group of older people from our community came close to us, the boys ran away."

I rocked my sister in my arms until her sobs lessened and she wiped her eyes. I wanted to rush into the night, find those boys and make them pay for violating my sister. But I was as helpless as she was. I told myself I wanted to be in a place where nobody interfered with the joys of the Sabbath, where we Jews could live in peace. In Iraq, if there was peace, it was an uneasy peace.

At noontime, we usually went to the synagogue for Sabbath *minha*, midday services. I associated returning from these services with my favorite meal of the week – the *t'beet*. We lived in a predominantly Jewish neighborhood, but many of our neighbors didn't attend *minha* services. The streets were quiet at that time of the day, and, as we returned home, we could hear through the open windows the clatter of cutlery-- the sounds of our neighbors plowing through their *t'beet*. The urge to pick up speed and hurry home to our own *t'beet* was irresistible.

My mother did all the everyday cooking on a multi-burner kerosene stove. But the *t'beet* was the one meal she cooked the old-fashioned way – over a wood fire. *T'beet* is a dish made of rice, vegetables, cardamom, raisins, occasionally nuts and condiments, all stuffed in chicken skin sewn into a pouch, and cooked in a big pot filled with rice, chicken, tomato and onion. The pot was placed on a specially built *kanoon*, an elevated three-walled brick pit, just wide enough to hold the pot securely until the following afternoon. Layers of padded burlap covered the entire pit to hold in the heat.

To cook in advance for a day like the Sabbath when Jews are not allowed to adjust fire intensity required Mama to have the skill of an acrobat and the divination of an infallible seer. Everyone wanted the *t'beet* to come out piping hot, crisp brown. Mama had to balance the wood fire intensity and the amount of food she had put in the pot with her guess of how cold or how warm it was likely to be. There was no weather service in Baghdad, and of course no weather prediction is infallible. Although Mama never talked about it, I believe that *t'beet* making was a source of anxiety for her, and indeed for any woman who had to play that kind of balancing act. We let out a big scream of joy when we sat in our dining room and saw the clouds of steam rising from the crispy brown *t'beet* coming our way. I could see how happy that made Mama. But I can also remember her disappointed look when, of all things, on a cold Sabbath day the fire went out, and the *t'beet* came out lukewarm or cold. No one criticized, but Mama must have felt she had failed to deliver when the cries of joy were muted.

I wish I had been as aware then as I am now of what my mother must have felt on those occasions.

Though I took it for granted at the time, my religion was an important part of my young years and remains so still. I am sure *hakham* Moshe never realized the deep impression he left on my youthful mind.

From the time when I was eleven or so until he passed away, when I was close to sixteen, *hakham* Moshe made the trek every Saturday afternoon from downtown Baghdad, where he lived, to our neighborhood's synagogue to give his two-hour *daroosh* - commentary - on the weekly portion of the Torah. I, too, would make the trek from our home to the synagogue, just to listen to *hakham* Moshe. He was a man who spoke to my soul, to my heart, and to my mind.

Hakham Moshe wore the traditional attire common to Babylonian rabbis – a long robe that snapped in the middle from top to bottom, and a three-inch sash made of silk or wool, depending on the season, which he wore around his waist. On his head he wore the distinct turban, *amama,* worn by Babylonian rabbis, which clearly differentiated a rabbi from a Moslem cleric.

Hakham Moshe carried himself with dignity, and in spite of the simplicity of his attire he looked elegantly dressed. He was an articulate speaker, incredibly lucid. His presentation was structured and focused. He started with a topic drawn from the Sabbath Torah portion and weaved it in with the ordinary events of our lives. He was adept at making his audience see the practical relevance of Torah teaching and its applicability to every day life.

Almost without fail I attended *hakham* Moshe's *daroosh* on Saturday afternoons. The synagogue was full to overflowing during his *daroosh.* People arrived an hour before his scheduled talk to secure a seat where they would have a direct view of him when he spoke. I learned a lot from *hakham* Moshe's *daroosh*. I was amazed at how much I gained and how much I was able to retain so effortlessly.

Hakham Moshe died young. I believe he was in his middle forties when he passed away. I was devastated to learn of his death. He left young children behind; one of his children was a student in the boys' Alliance. He was younger than I. There was no social security in Iraq. *Hakham* Moshe had no savings, and the Jewish community provided no pension for its rabbinical employees. His family fell on hard times after his death. His son in our boys' Alliance received free clothing from the community after his father's death.

I missed *hakham* Moshe. Throughout the rest of my adult life, I searched for someone that could take his place in my life. I met rabbis who had some of his traits, but I have not met his match yet.

But my Sabbath learning experience with *hakham* Moshe remained with me. When my children were growing up in San Francisco, we studied together on Saturday afternoon from the *Ben Ish Hai*, a compendium of Jewish code written by the twentieth century Babylonian luminary *hakham* Yosef Hayeem, which was built around the weekly Torah portions. In many ways, *hakham* Yosef was similar to *hakham* Moshe. Unlike many of his predecessors who wrote in a tortured language that could be understood only by the learned few, *hakham* Yosef wrote in a simple down-to-earth language. I remember fondly those times when the four of us huddled together on Saturday afternoon and studied the *Ben Ish Hai*. But in my heart I thanked *hakham* Moshe for showing me the simplicity and the relevance of Jewish learning during those remarkable Sabbath afternoon *daroush*.

I felt melancholy as the Sabbath came to a close at sundown on Saturday. Sunday was a regular school day for us, and there was always the worry about homework that had to be done that night, or a Sunday exam that loomed large.

After supper I took off my Sabbath clothes and carefully hung them in place until the next week, and polished my Sabbath shoes. Then it was back to my desk and the perpetual wringer of homework and exams.

I no longer experience the unmitigated sweetness of those Friday nights in faraway Baghdad. I am more cognizant now of the inferior role assigned to women in traditional Judaism.

Whenever I visit Israel, I still make a point of attending the Babylonian synagogue nearby. I delight in being at one with the congregation standing up to chant the *Lekha Dodi*, a hymn sung by Jews all over the world as they welcome the Sabbath: "Come beloved Israel, greet thy bride, welcome the coming of Sabbath tide".

The last time I attended services in the Babylonian synagogue in Ramat Gan, Israel, was in 2004. I closed my eyes and listened as the singing filled the synagogue. Tears filled my eyes, as the soaring song reached into the depths of my soul. But I came back to reality as soon as the *Lekha Dodi* ended. I looked up and saw the women sitting in the balcony. As in other traditional synagogues, women are required to sit separately from men. The honor of being called to the Torah is reserved for men only. Why can't women lead the services, if they accept the same obligations that have traditionally been the exclusive domain of the Jewish male?

I love praying in a Babylonian synagogue, and long to go back and connect with my roots unreservedly. But it is a bittersweet experience these days. I am no longer what I was in my teens.

For many years now, I have been attending a conservative synagogue where men and women sit together and where women conduct the services and read the Torah. This pleases me no end. But the synagogue's liturgy is exclusively Ashkenazi. I long for my heritage, and I long for the way we celebrated the Sabbath. Yet when I go to a Babylonian synagogue, there is a part of me that says I am a stranger to that world. I am in a place that violates my deeply held principles.

It has been painful to deal with the reality that I am neither here nor there.

A CULTURE OF INCESSANT WORK

Education began at a tender age for Jewish boys in Baghdad. My first recollection of schooling goes back to when I was three years old, sitting next to my Hebrew tutor "*M'allim* M'nashee," or Teacher Menasha. An elderly man with a snow-white beard, he wore the traditional fez, a long white robe and a beige cloak called *abayi*. He was my brother's tutor before I was added to his list; he came to our home six days a week to teach me the Hebrew basics and to teach Jacob the Bible.

Every time I pronounced a word correctly or asked about something I didn't understand, *M'allim* M'nashee would shower me with praise. "I am proud of you, my son. You are doing so well," he would say. Naturally I waited eagerly for his arrival every day. Jacob, however, was not interested in religion. He dreaded *M'allim* M'nashee's visits.

After of my lesson, our tutor would go in search of him, calling "Jacob, Jacob, where are you?" At this point Jacob would squeal, break cover and run up the stairs to the roof. *M'allim* M'nashee, afraid of tripping, would bunch up his *abayi* behind him with both hands. He would then follow Jacob, trying to run, his head bent over as his body leaned first to one side and then to the other. Even I had trouble stifling my laughter.

If he was caught, Jacob refused to sit still. Halfway through a lesson he would get up and race around the walkway that encircled the second floor of our house. Eventually, our teacher would give up and sink, panting, into a chair.

I felt sorry for our tutor, but Jacob's antipathy to religion was such that he never stopped to think how hard all of this was on *M'allim* M'nashee. To this day, Jacob mocks my adherence to the tenets of Judaism.

As I grew older, *M'allim* M'nashee taught me prayers and the Bible. He stopped coming when his health deteriorated. His difficulty with Jacob may have hastened his retirement. My parents then retained a younger Hebrew tutor. By this time, they had given up on Jacob and hired the tutor just for me.

When I was five years old, my parents enrolled me in *Asile*, a two-year kindergarten held in the magnificent girls' school, l'Ecole de l'Alliance Israelite. In Alliance's *Asile*, boys and girls were taught in the same classrooms.

The girls' Alliance building was a Moorish-style structure, with massive pillars, arched passageways, airy classrooms, and large courtyards. The philanthropist Sir Elly Kh'doury (1867 - 1944), who lived in Hong Kong and who was a graduate of the boys' Alliance in Baghdad, donated the building in 1911 in honor of his wife.

Everything in the girls' Alliance was vast, including my *Asile* class. We were taught in French and Judeo-Arabic. Three of our four teachers were graduates of the girls' Alliance; the fourth, Mrs. Sabbagh, was French, and a strict, no-nonsense disciplinarian. My other teachers were kind, but my favorite was Mademoiselle Sim'ha. She lived in my neighborhood, and never disciplined students with a stick as Mrs. Sabbagh did.

My overall recollection of my time at *Asile* is one of loads of work in the classroom and long daily "*devoirs*," or homework. Those years were not marked by the play and fun typical of American kindergartens. There was a constant push to cram more and more learning into our heads.

Even at this young age, fear of discipline loomed large. One evening when I was six years old I was roughhousing with Jacob in our courtyard, while my older sister Muzli stood watching from the balcony. In those years I tried to stay out of Muzli's way, for she was bossy and seemed to enjoy making trouble. That evening Jacob challenged me to climb on his back. I grabbed his shirt and tried to climb, but slipped and tore his shirt. Muzli's eyes blazed.

"Wait till you get the punishment you deserve," she

Front of the girls' Alliance Israelite School, Baghdad

Formation in one of the girls' Alliance courtyards before the start of classes

scolded. "I am going to write a letter to your teacher and tell her to punish you for your rowdiness."

I had trouble sleeping that night. I worried that my teacher would make me stand in the corner, or make me recite a deprecating statement about rowdy children. She might even hit me with that long stick of hers.

The next day, Muzli handed me the letter to carry to my teacher. For some reason she left the envelope unsealed. My sister Helwa walked with me to school, but neither of us said a word. At school, I opened the letter before we went to class. It was in French, and I couldn't read it, and Helwa could decipher only a few words.

With great trepidation, I handed the letter to my teacher. I was immensely relieved when all she did was tell me gently not to do it again.

When I returned home, Muzli was waiting, and she demanded to know how my teacher had punished me. I balked and ran to my mother and told her what had happened. Mama was furious with Muzli for tormenting me, and for writing to my teacher without her permission.

After two years at *Asile*, I moved on to the boys' Alliance Israelite.

The boys' Alliance, which opened in 1864, was the first modern school in Iraq. The girls' Alliance opened three decades later. Both were part of a worldwide network of schools established by l'Alliance Israelite Universelle, which was founded by a group of French Jewish intellectuals in 1860. The schools served as links within the Jewish world to channel information about communities in duress and to provide a vehicle for mobilize help defending Jewish liberties worldwide.

The visionary behind this educational network was the Sephardic rabbi Judah Alkalai (1798-1878) of Sarajevo. Its formation grew in part out of the 1858 Mortara affair, the abduction of a six-year-old Jewish child, Edgardo Mortara, by papal gendarmes in Bologna, Italy, on the pretext that his Catholic babysitter had baptized him while his parents were gone for the evening.

The boys' Alliance that I attended played a major role in alerting the headquarters in Paris when Baghdad's Jewish community was threatened. It also served as a conduit for channeling financial help to stricken communities in Russia and elsewhere in the world. And while rabbis and observant Jews elsewhere tended to send their children to religious schools, Baghdad's leading rabbis sent their children to l'Alliance, even though it was secular.

L'Alliance gave us quality education that matched France's best schools. But we students were never told about its international humanitarian work, possibly because our teachers feared a crackdown at a time of rising Arab nationalism.

A view from the Tebah (Lectern) of the Sasson synagogue in the boys' Alliance

While impressive, the building that housed the boys' Alliance was not as large as the girls', but I still loved it—even though we froze during the winter in our drafty classrooms. The school's magnificent Sasson synagogue was named for Sir Albert David Sasson, a scion of the Baghdadian family known as the "Rothschilds of the East." Sir Albert had donated the school building in 1872 and a large portrait of him hung in our school. Gazing upon it I felt grateful to Sir

Albert for his contribution to my education.

L'Alliance was competitive, and so was I. We were required to take three midterm exams and a final every year. We were ranked according to our test scores and given *le bulletin*, a quarterly report card to take home. The class seating order was rearranged every quarter to reflect our new ranking. Those who ranked ahead got to sit ahead, those who ranked last were placed in the back rows. One of our teachers, Monsieur Sabbagh, used to make a show of it. He was wont to remind the one who ranked last, *"Mets toi tout a fait au coin, tout a fait au fond de la classe,"* meaning "You sit at the corner, all the way in the back," a humiliating situation for any student. It was harsh, and it fostered cutthroat competition. I usually ranked in the single digits, occasionally first, and in the heedless way of young people, was oblivious to the feelings of those I displaced when I moved ahead in rank.

Classes were held six days a week, Sunday through Friday, and the emphasis was on science and the French language. We also learned a smattering of English, and classical Arabic. I became good at reading and writing Arabic, even though I spoke only the Judeo-Arabic dialect.

I enjoyed learning and resented those who disrupted class. One of my teachers, though an excellent scholar, had no control over his students. Mayhem reigned in his classes, which made it impossible for those of us who wanted to learn to do so. One morning, I came to the classroom before anyone else and wrote on the blackboard: "A committee has been formed to take note of and report to the authorities the names of students who are creating disturbances in this class." Nobody figured out that the committee in question was a committee of one. I could see students looking at one another, wondering who was on the committee, but the end result was that the disturbances came to an end.

There were other class interruptions created by the school. Fees at the Alliance were pretty steep, and sometimes parents put off paying them. The school accountant, carrying with him a sheaf of papers, looking self-important as he peered at us over his glasses, would visit the classroom and call out the names of the students whose parents were in arrears. These students would be sent home until their parents came up with the money. Sometimes the students would protest, saying their parents had paid the fees, but these, too, would be sent home to bring back the receipt for the payment. As a general rule, we were never allowed to leave school during the school day, and some students were happy to get a break from their studies under any pretext. I remember Haim, one of my fellow students, always insisting he had to go and get the receipt, though his parents always paid on time, and the accountant never suggested he owed the school money.

Several of my classmates came from needy families and received scholarships. None of this was publicized to save embarrassing the poor. Poverty was a stigma, and people were even more sensitive about it than today. One day, when I was in the fifth grade, we were all surprised when a few students showed up wearing identical suits. It didn't take long to decipher the puzzle. Those were the students who had received free clothing from the Jewish community. To save on cost, all the suits were made from the same material and cut from the same simple design. The needy students' cover had been blown. But to the community's credit, it rectified the error. New one-of-a-kind suits were made for each student.

Every Friday, our classes dedicated the first few minutes to collect *sedaka,* charity, from the students. Sharing our blessings with others was a lesson instilled in us from my *Asile* days. Baba would give me a small daily allowance to spend in the school canteen. He never made it a condition, but he always reminded me to set aside part of my allowance to donate at *sedaka* time.

Around *purim* and Passover, items donated by the students were auctioned off in class, with the proceeds going to the needy. Roses were always in bloom then and we often auctioned off donated bouquets.

One day a student brought a huge bouquet of red roses from his home garden. The teacher decided to auction it last. The longer it took for the bouquet's turn to come, the more tantalized I got, for I wanted it badly. When the teacher finally held up the bouquet, I immediately bid. I had meant to open with twenty fils, the equivalent of about ten cents at the time, but found myself blurting out seventy instead. That stunned everybody, including me, but I was too embarrassed to retract. No one in the class wanted to bid higher, so I had to pay seventy fils for a bouquet that sold for less than twenty fils in the market. Worse still, I had no one to blame but myself. How was I going to pay for it from my small daily allowance?

Mama came to my rescue. "It is good to help the poor," Mama said as she handed me the seventy fils, "but be careful next time."

Our school's emphasis on charity didn't squelch a vexing cultural trait that many Jews in Iraq had absorbed from the Arab world around them: competitive gift giving, and the relentless one-upmanship it inspired. I had an extremely wealthy classmate who regularly treated me to ice cream. I, in turn, was expected to reciprocate with a bigger and better treat for him. He then would top my gesture and so it went, back and forth, quickly exhausting my relatively meager allowance. The unending race upward had nothing to do with generosity, and everything to do with shaming the party who couldn't keep up.

The world beyond Iraq's borders always beckoned to me. My first exposure to that wider world came through my hobby of collecting stamps. When the school initiated a pen pal program, I participated, mainly to acquire foreign stamps.

I remember two pen pals in particular, an American girl and a girl in Switzerland. My Swiss pen pal and I corresponded in French. I envied her descriptions of her country's freedom and her life free from fear. It was not as easy corresponding with my American friend, but Jacob--who went to an all-English school-- helped me with my letters to her.

For some reason I received more letters than any other student in class. I brought all the letters to school to share with my classmates. I was fond of my pen pals and thought of them as my particular friends. One day I received a letter from my American friend telling me she had received a letter from a boy in my class named William. I realized that William, not having any particular luck with the pen pal assigned to him, had copied the name and address of my pen pal when I brought her letter to school. In the way of young boys, I was outraged. I wrote to her immediately, telling her what a thief and despicable character William was. I felt completely justified in doing this; after all, William had encroached on my territory and tried to steal my special friend. I don't remember what happened after that; it is the memory of my reaction to William's imagined perfidy that stays with me.

My American pen pal

L'Alliance was an elite sanctuary of learning. But it couldn't entirely shield us from the dangers beyond its gates. It was a hard fact that the Muslims I knew tended to settle arguments with force, rather than discussion. They fought with one another at the drop of a hat—and it was not at all unusual to see two Muslims in a street in Baghdad literally tearing at each other, without anyone taking notice of them. Nor did Muslims need an excuse to make Jews the object of their attacks. My father always stressed what the Torah taught us: Justice, justice thou shalt pursue. But there was no justice on the streets of Baghdad, no safety. We never knew when we would be cornered, spat on, or robbed of our book bags or jewelry.

One morning I was waiting in line for the city bus on my way to school. I was in intermediate school at the time and was traveling by myself. The bus was late, and the line grew very long. In front of me in the line was a burly Arab in his mid-forties, dressed in a white gown and the traditional Arab cloak and turban. The bus finally arrived. All of a sudden, everyone in the back pushed forward. I was going over an algebra problem in my head, barely aware of what was happening, when I was hurled against the man in front of me. He whirled around angrily. His huge hand sliced through the air and hit me a resounding blow on the cheek.

I reeled from the force of the blow, and could feel my head spin. As I staggered and fought to regain my balance, I heard the voice of my maternal uncle, Khalu Sion, behind me. I had not seen him, but Uncle Sion was standing at the back of the line and had witnessed what had happened.

My uncle, a wiry man in his early forties, half the size of the man who had hit me, raised himself to his full height, as he looked my attacker straight in the face. His voice was thick with anger.

"What gives you the right to hit him? Who do you think you are? Let me see you raise your hand to him again."

The big bully stood open-mouthed, staring at Khalu Sion, not knowing what to say. He seemed stunned. Finally, he managed to reply.

"Why should it matter to you?"

" It does matter to me," Khalu Sion responded emphatically. He's my nephew."

Khalu Sion put his hand reassuringly on my shoulder, as he renewed his challenge to the bully.

"Let me see you raise your hand to him again."

The man muttered something I couldn't understand as he lowered his eyes and slunk away. Khala Sion stayed by my side until the next bus arrived. I stood with him, proud he was my uncle, hoping I would have his courage some day.

Khalu (Uncle) Sion March 11, 1984

Less than a year before this incident, I was rescued by a complete stranger.

I was walking home from school alone. Four or five Arab teenagers approached and formed a circle around me.

"Just a few minutes ago you were on Sa'adoon Street, and you came up to us and spat on us," the tallest one said to me.

I am sure my voice shook when I denied the accusation.

"I wasn't even on that street," I said. "I walked through Rasheed Street."

"That is right. It was on Rasheed Street that you spat on us."

They closed in tighter, their jeering faces leaning toward mine.

It was a beautiful balmy spring afternoon. I remember the dry street, the sun, the gentle breeze, and the sour taste of terror rising in my throat and spilling into my mouth, as the thugs tightened their circle around me, leaving no room for escape. I knew I was doomed. The thought flashed into my mind that they might have knives. I wanted to run, but the circle around me was too tight and, besides that, my feet were frozen to the pavement.

Then just as their leader raised his fist, a big Jewish man happened to pass by. Even in my terrified state, I noticed he was tall and muscular, dressed in a dark suit and wearing black-rimmed glasses. The young man must have been in his mid- twenties, but to my young eyes he looked very adult. I despaired as he walked past us, but then caught my breath as he suddenly whirled back just as the youths were closing in to strike. He met my eyes for a moment and then put one hand on his hip, as he sternly asked my attackers to move on.

My body sagged with relief, for I could feel my rescuer's strength. I knew he would brook no nonsense, and my attackers got the message, too. They stopped for a moment and scanned the street, only to see it was almost deserted. There was no prospect of a Muslim gang coming to their aid should they choose to tangle with the young man. Their faces fell as they figured they were no match for him. Casting sullen looks at both of us, they scattered.

I thanked my rescuer, and he walked slowly ahead of me, as I proceeded on my way toward the riverbank and home.

At the end of each school year, Iraq's Ministry of Education held national exams for those who had completed the primary, intermediate, and secondary grades. The ministry issued certificates to those who passed the exams.

We heard horror stories about shenanigans that went on with those exams and with the ministry's certificates. There were rumors about people who bought their certificates from the ministry. Bribery for advance disclosure of the exam questions was rampant. One of our Arab neighbors, a high school graduate of a government school, told us how the official test was made available to him for a price, and he described a well-oiled network that orchestrated the operation. To avoid flagrancy, the network revealed only a limited number of questions, just enough to carry a total of sixty per cent of the test score, so that the person who paid the bribe would just squeeze by without attracting suspicion. The advance release time of those leaks was limited to five hours before the start of the exam, to minimize the time available for disseminating the test among students who didn't pay the bribe.

I was dubious about the government tests and certificates, considering them not worth the trouble. I was focused on my French education and, from a young age, dreamed of leaving Iraq. But I wasn't sure I'd ever be allowed to do so, and realized that as long as we lived in Iraq, we couldn't ignore the government exams.

Our teachers had no concept of rest or rejuvenation through relaxation. The message I got throughout was that rest was waste; time had to be filled with work.

The girls' Alliance was no different - a similar culture of interminable work and ruthless competition. When my youngest sister, Valentine, was in the fifth grade, my sister Reyna took her under her wing and worked with her non-stop on her homework. Reyna disliked Joyce, a second cousin of ours and a classmate of Valentine's. Joyce was a blonde, blue-eyed girl who exuded self-confidence and ranked first in her class. Reyna was determined to have Valentine dislodge Joyce from top rank, and worked hard with Valentine. Valentine became dependent on Reyna, and in Valentine's mind dislodging Joyce became an obsession.

I remember how tense poor Valentine was the night before the year-end bulletin's release. It was summer time, and we were sleeping on the rooftop. Before she lay down in bed, Valentine lifted her eyes up to the sky and prayed that she would be the first in her class. I boiled with anger at how Reyna had reduced my little sister to a nervous wreck.

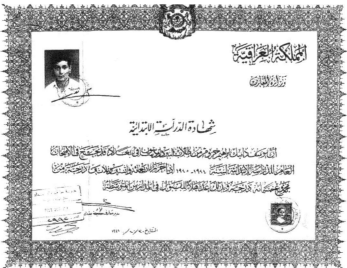

My certificate of primary school education (written in the flowery script of the Koran)

Graduates of l' Alliance's Primary, 1944-1945. Daniel third from left in second row from front.

The following day, Valentine went off to school to get the *bulletin*. Two hours into that tense morning, our doorbell rang. Reyna went to the door, but before it swung open I could hear Valentine proclaiming from the other side, "Oula! Oula!"- "First, First!" She held the *bulletin* high and her curly blonde hair fluttered in the wind. She jumped and hopped, and looked so relieved. She had been vindicated - Joyce dropped to second place. Reyna won the battle vicariously.

As much as I despised the relentless workload, in time it became part of me. During my first year in secondary school, I was exempted from the finals because of a perfect score. Nonetheless, I spent the whole week before the exam studying for the finals anyway. I struggled later in life to learn to take time off.

RESPITE AND RENEWAL

The Jewish holidays brought us periodic—and welcome-- respite.

Hanukkah was peaceful and charming in its simplicity; in a Moslem country, Christmas came and went without notice, and thus there was no seasonal glitter to emulate as there is in the U.S. I remember *hanukkah* in Baghdad as a quiet holiday that radiated serenity.

School was out on the first day of *hanukkah*. During the eight days of *hanukkah* Baba came home early to light the candles and spend the rest of the evening with us. My parents had a beautiful half-circular *hanukkiyah* made of silver, which had a mirror inserted behind the candleholders so that the lighted candles reflected in the mirror, creating a mysterious effect. Unfortunately I never got to ask my parents about the history or origin of that *hanukkiyah*. Baba had a replica made for me in Ghana, and he had the Hebrew inscription on the *hanukkiyah* done in Tel Aviv. I, in turn, had replicas of my *hanukkiyah* made for my two daughters.

Baba lit the candles every night with a beeswax candle, as is the practice among Sephardi Jews. When he finished lighting, we all joined together in singing in unison an ancient Babylonian paean "Yah Hassel Yona Me'hakka":

Lord, rescue the dove (Israel) from the fishhook (of captivity)
Her tears gushing in prayer to you
And she will rejoice in you, her King,
In the eight days of *hanukkah.*

Although it is the practice among Jews to put their lit *hanukkiyah* in their windows for all to see, in Baghdad it was dangerous to do so. We always kept our *hanukkiyah* inside for fear of vandalism by the Muslims. For the same reason we kept our Mezuzahs always on the inside, never on the outside.

Babylonian *hanukkiyah* my father commissioned for me -
a replica of the *hanukkiyah* my parents lit in Baghdad

Our *hanukkah* dinner was ordinary -- no special *hanukkah* dish. But what made the dinner special was my father's presence with us for the whole eight nights of *hanukkah*, which lent a festive atmosphere to the evening. Sometimes when we had five or more candles lit, we would turn out the light and eat our meal by candlelight. Though the *hanukkah* candles are never supposed to be used in a utilitarian way, Baba explained we could do this because an extra candle, the *shamash*, which perched high up in the *hanukkiyah*'s candleholder, was lit and it could be used to

107

give useful light. At the end of our meal we recited *birkath hamazon*, the grace-after-meal – something we did not do on other nights.

We gave gifts on *hanukkah*, but only to Yeshiba students, and we did what we could to make their life more comfortable. Perhaps that was our community's way to assert its defiance of the Antiochus Epiphanes of our times. In the second century BCE, Antiochus Epiphanes banned the study of Torah, but the Maccabees and their followers resisted and won the battle. Subsequent generations dedicated the eight days of *hanukkah* to commemorating the victory of the Maccabees over their oppressors. Perhaps by singling out for support the Yeshiba students, the carriers of the banner of Jewish learning, Babylonian Jewry was attempting to reaffirm its commitment to religious survival and the preservation of Judaism – just as the Maccabees had done centuries before when they resisted the ban of Antiochus Epiphanes.

Tu bish'bat was known among us, Babylonian Jews, as *tif'kaie elsedgagh*, the blossoming of the trees -- the day we celebrated as the Jewish New Year of the Trees. School was out on *tif'kaie elsedgagh*. Many in our community spent the day in the fields with nature and said a prayer of thanks to God for the blossoming trees they came across.

On the eve of the holiday we gathered in our living room around a long table that Mama had prepared. It was set with plates filled with every conceivable fruit of the season; there was also a medley of dried fruits. And there was one fruit that was always a must in my family– a big sweet watermelon. Even though it was not the season for watermelon, Ammu Moshe always managed to find one for us.

Baba led the evening celebration. We took turns in reciting a blessing over each fruit and thanked God for the bounty of the earth. No one wanted to eat dinner that night. We stuffed ourselves with the yummy mixture of dried fruits that filled the table.

It was cold and windy during that time of the year, but we had our protector, our *sopa* (kerosene heater) with the red and blue windows sitting majestically in our midst. Sometimes the whistling wind outside blasted hard, and it rattled our windows. Sometimes we could feel the cold wind whiz inside our room.

Reyna sat by the *sopa* roasting chestnuts and brewing` tea for the rest of us. Every now and then we headed for the sofa to warm ourselves, sip on a cup of tea or grab a roasted chestnut, all courtesy of Reyna.

Mama filled a bagful of dried fruits for each one of us. She had sewed those bags especially for the occasion. She made sure to also fill a bag for the domestic that worked in our home.

No one cared for breakfast or lunch on *tif'kaie elsedgagh* day. We munched on the dried fruits in our bags. I remember spending most of the day sitting in the sun on the balcony with my bag of dried fruits in hand. It was a wonderful, relaxed day. Nothing eventful happened during that day, except perhaps for the lines that formed at the bathrooms. There just weren't enough bathrooms in our house -- there were only two, but there were eight of us children, all having stuffed ourselves with dried fruit, all of us paying the price for our indulgence.

Our biggest feast of the year came on the traditional New Year, *rosh hashana*. A week or two beforehand, my parents bought a sheep and kept it the courtyard of our backhouse. I never had a pet, and I loved having the sheep in our house. I'd pet its soft wool and put my arms around it as it regarded me with its soft brown eyes. I used to talk to it and felt it was listening to me. My siblings and I used to feed it fresh watermelon rind, and it seemed to never tire of it. But it was always a bittersweet experience to have the sheep in our midst. I had to steel myself from becoming too attached, knowing it was destined to be the centerpiece of our *rosh hashana* table. But my reminders to myself always fell by the wayside. I always got attached to the sheep.

Then came the awful reckoning: three or four *kasher* butchers came at night, always in a hurry. They had other places to go to, other sheep to slaughter that night. It was a juggernaut. They headed straight for the back house, for the poor little sheep. I wanted to run away. I wanted to hide. But there was no hiding place far enough away. One time I ran to the rooftop. But I still heard the cry of the terror-stricken sheep when the butchers hurriedly turned it on its back and held it to the ground as they feverishly pulled the wool around its neck to clear the way for their knife. And then I heard its one loud snore as it drew its last breath.

"Why are we doing this?" I used to think for myself. "We want to he happy and celebrate *rosh hashana*. Does this give us the right to slit the throat of the poor little sheep? Is this really what is supposed to make us happy?"

I was sick to my stomach. I looked at the sky hoping to catch a glimpse of the soul of my little sheep as it traveled up high to heaven. Sometimes I cried. Sometimes I could not.

As I grew older it became increasingly difficult for me to eat the festive meal of *rosh hashana*. I was never able to get over the cruelty of slaughtering those peaceful creatures. Outwardly I joined in the happiness of eating the biggest and most elaborate meal of the year, but deep down I felt uncomfortable to think of the poor sheep on whose flesh we were now feasting. What right did we have to take its life? What right did we have to take the life of any animal? I sometimes felt an urge to walk away from the dining table on *rosh hashana* day. I did not want to be part of that cruel world. I did not want to eat meat. Those poor things were entitled to their lives. We had no right to deprive them of their lives just because we wanted to stuff our stomach.

I didn't realize it then, but the seeds of my later becoming a vegetarian were sown then during those *rosh hashana* days.

Rosh hashana falls at the beginning of Tashri – the first month of the Jewish calendar. Beginning a month before that, we observed a forty-day period of soul-searching and reflection, and we recited daily *s'lihoth* -- special prayers of forgiveness and repentance. We started *s'lihoth* an hour before dawn. It was customary for the sexton to make the rounds among the faithful and knock on their doors to wake them up in time for *s'lihoth*. We could hear him knock on the door of our neighbors; at that time of the year we slept on the roof.

There was something unique about getting up in the wee hours of the night for *s'lihoth*, looking in silence at the star-studded sky above in the midst of total darkness, reflecting on the far reaches of the beyond, and pondering what God would want us to do to be better human beings.

I attended *s'lihoth* many times during my childhood. I remember throngs of people, too, walking hurriedly toward the synagogue for *s'lihoth*. Even some of those who did not regularly attend the Sabbath services often showed up for *s'lihoth*. Since so many attended *s'lihoth*, nobody walked alone to the synagogue. That was fortunate since it was not safe to walk the streets of Baghdad in the dark. There was safety in numbers. And there was faith that God Almighty would be our protector.

We sang most of the *s'lihoth* prayers in unison, and the melodies were gorgeous. There was something inspiring about those services, and we all joined in with vigor. I felt as if we were all traveling together, hand in hand, on the road of the faithful, that we were all bonded together in our bid for forgiveness for our misdeeds. We were humbled by our frailties but uplifted by our resolve to do better.

Years later when I was living in San Francisco, I often traveled with my family from San Francisco to Los Angeles to attend *s'lihoth* at Kahal Joseph, a congregation that followed the Babylonian traditions. The services at Kahal Joseph brought back warm memories of my years of growing up. My family too came to love them. But there was also something extra that attracted my children – at the end of *s'lihoth*, the congregants were served tea with milk and cheese-and-cucumber sandwiches, a popular snack among Babylonian Jews. My children, too, loved cheese-and-cucumber sandwiches and they looked forward to the their favorite snack.

One day only tea and milk was served - no cheese-and-cucumber sandwiches. My children would have none of that, and they staged a protest demonstration.

"You mean we came all the way from San Francisco to Los Angeles only to find that there will be no cheese-and-cucumber sandwich? We won't have tea without cheese-and-cucumber sandwiches! You can't break with traditions".

The congregants thought it was hilarious. The sexton sheepishly went to the refrigerator and put cheese and cucumbers on the table, much to the delight of my children.

On the eve of *rosh hashana* our congregation held *"hattarath nedareem"* – annulment of vows – a ceremony in which ten congregants acted as a tribunal. Standing before the tribunal, the rest of the congregants confessed they had made vows to themselves, which they had failed to fulfill, and petitioned the tribunal to annul those vows. In Jewish traditions vows made to oneself are a promise to God, and they remain in force until they are either fulfilled or annulled by a tribunal. The tribunal granted the annulment requested by the congregants, with the hope that "Just as this earthly tribunal annulled them so may the Heavenly Tribunal agree and annul them ...". The tribunal had no authority to grant annulment of vows or promises made to another person or institution. That required the express consent of the other party.

The roles were then reversed. Ten judges were selected from the members of the congregation who had been absolved of their vows and they, in turn, served as a tribunal for the men who had served on the first tribunal.

During my lifetime I participated in many *hattarath nedareem*. But I could not help feeling that I was participating in a make belief show. Why could I not just say directly to God what I had to say before the "tribunal" to clear my conscience and do better next time around? Why did I need the intercession of a show tribunal, of all things?

I stopped attending.

My maternal uncle Sion told me that, in addition to *Hattarath Nedareem*, it was the practice of some people to subject themselves to *malkoth*, lashing, as a punishment for their misses. The person who submitted himself to *malkoth* exposed his back to the sexton who administered ringing lashes with a belt to the bared back. Some had the stamina to

112

withstand many lashes; some were able to take only one or two. My paternal uncle Moshe confirmed uncle Sion's story.

Many in our community made a point of taking a ritual bath, immersion in naturally flowing water, on the eve of *rosh hashana*, to reinforce their sense of purity. Many Jewish houses in Baghdad were fitted with artesian wells to serve as ritual baths for their residents. The house in which I was born had an artesian well. There were steps down to the well with rails to assist in making a steady descent to the running water deep below. During my earlier years of childhood both of my parents took their ritual bath in the well in our home.

My father went to visit the gravesites of my grandparents on the eve of *rosh hashana*, but he was always secretive about those visits. For some reason I never understood, Babylonian Jews had a thing about letting children in on any thing that had to do with death, cemeteries and dead people. If I ever learned about one of Baba's visits, it was only by inference.

The *kiddush* on the eve of *rosh hashana* was special. Several types of fruit and vegetables were brought to the table. We recited a special wish in Aramaic while eating each one. My father would lift up a piece of pomegranate and take the lead in reciting the "*yehi rasoan*" blessing – "May it be Your will, our God, that we be as full of good deeds in the coming year as there are seeds in this pomegranate." Then each one of us would take a turn, reciting the same wish over a piece of pomegranate. Following that there were some ten assortments of fruits and vegetables to go through, so it took quite a while. In the meantime, we cracked jokes and made funny comments- all in high spirits. This was the time to be jolly, which would augur well for a happy and anger-free new year.

On *rosh hashana* morning services started when it was still dark, and they were held on the roof of our synagogue, which was partly covered with canvas to protect against the hot sun. For me there was something special about those services. Was it the fading stars in the midst of the cupola above? Was it the infinite expanse, which always scared me, yet attracted me as a magnet? I do not know. But I felt intensely the presence of God in our midst. Did the rest of the congregants feel the same way, I used to wonder?

I put on my prayer shawl, sat next to Baba and opened my prayer book. But my mind was not on the services. My eyes remained fixated on the heavens until the stars had faded away and the rays of the rising sun filled the sky.

The services were very long. At the end we rushed home for *kiddush* and breakfast. We had nothing to eat or drink before we left for the services.

Members of my family used to gather before lunchtime at Ammu Moshe's home to read the book of Psalms and selections from *zohar*, the book of Splendor. The gathering, known as *hatheema*, the Sealing -- perhaps an allusion to the sealing of heavenly books on the fate of each individual – is unique to the Babylonian Jewish community. It was instituted in the mid eighteenth century by Iraq's Chief Rabbi Sadka Huseen. I did not particularly enjoy *hatheema*. Baba really hated it. He railed against it, complaining that it was too burdensome for a day of rest, but he never seemed to be able to cut himself loose from it. He always attended.

We avoided consuming sour, sharp, or salty food during *rosh hashana*. We avoided eating eggs also, because eggs symbolized grief and were eaten by mourners upon their return from the funeral. Sweet food augured a sweet year. We also avoided dark colors; white, symbolizing purity, was the color of choice. Some wouldn't drink coffee because it was black.

Sometimes I struggled during the afternoon to keep my eyes open, but tradition frowned on taking naps on *rosh hashana* day. Napping during that day was seen as a bad omen, a foreboding of bad luck during the coming year. I did not want to take a chance on bad luck. I would sing and I would stand up and I would walk around whenever my eyelids got too heavy. But many times I could not fight it, and went to sleep in our hammock in the courtyard. My parents never made an issue of it.

We blew the *shofar*, or ram's horn, in the synagogue.

The short, curly horn used by the Babylonian Jews has a deep, resonant sound different from the longer *shofars* used in Ashkenazi services. The sound of the *shofar* penetrated to the depths of my soul, seeming to transport me across a boundless world. The experience always left me shaken but strangely uplifted. The sound of the *shofar* echoes from my childhood through all the years that followed.

I never once failed to hear the *shofar* as far back as I can remember, although once I came within a hairsbreadth of not being there.

During my teaching career, I developed chronic pain in both my shoulders that made it difficult for me to raise my arm to write on the blackboard. X-rays showed the ligaments in both shoulders were badly torn, and surgery was required. The earliest the operation could be scheduled was the day before *rosh hashana*. The day before the operation, I presented myself at the hospital for preparatory tests. I was given a hospital gown and left in a room to wait, allowing me time to think.

I pondered how I'd never before missed the sacred sound of the *shofar*. "This year I'll be lying in bed under sedation or on the operating table, while Jews all over the world listen to the *shofar*," I thought. I'd be betraying something precious by missing that. "I can't do it," I decided. "I won't."

I dressed, told the attending nurse I was not going through with the operation and checked myself out of the hospital.

I was in agony during the two days of *rosh hashana*, but I did hear the sound of the *shofar* on both days of the holiday. I felt connected with my past, my ancestry, and with Jews all around the world who were celebrating as I was.

When the holiday was over I went to see my internist. An old-fashioned physician, he advised me to wrap heating pads around my shoulders when I went to bed. I followed his advice. After three weeks, the pain was gone.

When school started I could freely lift both arms and could use the blackboard without pain. Though I never rescheduled the surgery, my shoulders have not hurt since.

What happened to those torn ligaments? They said they couldn't be repaired without surgery. Who did the repair work? Was it the heating pad? Was it the s*hofar*? Whatever it was, I'm glad I listened to that little voice inside that told me I should not miss the sound of the *shofar* on that memorable *rosh hashana* day.

My favorite hymn of the *rosh hashana* services was a hymn on the sacrifice of Isaac "*eth sha'arei rasoan*", When the Gates of Mercy are opened, by the twelfth century poet Judah Ib'n Abbas of Fez, Morocco. We chanted that hymn before the blowing of the *shofar*. Every one was engaged; every one was moved by the story of the sacrifice of Isaac. I chanted my heart out. But there was also that little discomfort that increasingly troubled me from my younger days. Why were we exalting a father who was about to sacrifice his son? Was that really such a great thing, something to remember with pride? But my love for the chant swamped my growing sense of discomfort at the story, and I continued to sing. I loved the tune.

In time things became too uncomfortable for me. In one of his stanza, Ib'n Abbas' described the exchange between Sarah and Abraham, when Abraham was on his way to offer their son as a sacrifice. "Abraham said to Sarah 'your dear Isaac is growing up but has not learned the services of Heaven. I will go and teach him what God has decreed for him'. She said 'Go, my lord, but go not too far'. He answered, 'Let your heart trust in God' ". I cry every time we come to that stanza. It shakes me up. How could he have done that? He lied to her! He pulled the wool over her eyes! I was aware that the exchange between Abraham and Sarah was poetic. Still, what right did Abraham have to strip Sarah of their only child, even if he were not planning on sacrificing him?

I had similar difficulties with the daily prayers recited in the synagogue, which include the biblical passage where God tells Abraham "Take your son, your only son, whom you love, Isaac, and ...offer him ...as a burnt offering". Jews beg the Almighty in their daily prayers to consider in their favor the merit of Abraham's eagerness to carry out God's command, even though they themselves may not be worthy of God's favorable treatment. Was Abraham's alacrity to offer his son as a sacrifice because he believed that God had told him to do so, really a meritorious act? I wondered about that for years when I was growing up. What do we do to day when a father determines that he should sacrifice his son because he believed God had told him to do so? Do we exalt him in our prayers or do we put him in jail? Why should Jews exalt Abraham's alacrity to offer his son as a sacrifice?

To day, whenever I go the synagogue for daily services, I skip the part of the daily liturgy that appeals to God for his favor on the strength of Abraham's eagerness to sacrifice his son. And when *eth sha'arei rasoan* is sung in our synagogue on *rosh hashana*, I do not participate in the singing - and that one I regret the most. I feel I have torn myself away from my roots. I love the tune as much as ever. That hymn reminds me of tender days in my childhood when I sat next to my father in the synagogue and saw him watch me proudly as I sang the hymn at the top of my lungs.

I paid a price for moving forward, for changing outlook.

Yom kippoor is the most solemn day in the Jewish calendar. We stuffed ourselves with watermelon and gulped water before beginning the twenty-five-hour fast. At the synagogue, chairs were shoved into the aisles to accommodate the overflow crowd, and the threat of fire and stampede was always present. We didn't wear leather shoes or belts on this day because they were seen as a sign of pride. But we did wear sneakers. My mother told me that when she was a girl, Jews walked to the synagogue on *yom kippoor* in their stocking feet. Arabs scattered broken glass in the streets around the synagogue while the services were in progress. The streets were not well lit, and it was dark by the time the services were over. Many worshippers returned home with bleeding feet. My sneakers kept my feet safe, but the rigors of the day exhausted me, and though I knew how important it was, it was always a relief to know we wouldn't have to face *yom kippoor* for another full year.

Tish'a be'ab, the day on which the Temple was torched, Jews were exiled to Babylon, and the Jewish Commonwealth came to an end had a special meaning for Babylonian Jews.

The depth of feeling I experienced in Baghdad, as I listened to the haunting melody of the ode "By the rivers of Babylon, there we sat and wept as we remembered Zion" was greater than any I have felt since leaving Iraq. There was a palpable sense of sadness at the calamity that had befallen the Jewish people.

I remember the last year I attended *tish'a be'ab* services in Baghdad. We were approaching the point in the services where the leader was to announce the number of years since the destruction of the Jewish homeland. It was a tense moment. We stood in silence. Sorrow was reflected on every face in the congregation. The leader of the services, eyes closed, seemed to be struggling to speak. Then in a cracking voice, with moments of silence puncturing his words, he made the announcement.

"To day, we in the city of Baghdad, count one thousand eight hundred and eighty-two years since the torching of our holy Temple and the [second] destruction of our homeland". People wrung their hands. A few clapped. Was it a mistake, or were they applauding because somehow we survived two millennia of persecution? Some men wept openly; women in the balcony wiped their tears. Would our Temple ever be rebuilt? A new Jewish state had just been established. But ever since the 1930s, Iraq's capricious laws governing the Jews' ability to leave the country had become progressively more restrictive. Would the Iraqis ever allow us to join our brethren in Israel? Would the exile of Babylonian Jewry ever come to an end?

Many fasted from sundown to sundown. I, like the rest of my family, fasted from sundown until the time of the Torah reading in the morning of *tish'a be'ab*. And instead of putting on our prayer shawl and phylacteries in the synagogue, as was the general practice, my father, Jacob, and I put them on in our home - each one privately, in a separate room. We recited a short prayer, then took off the shawl and phylacteries, and headed for the synagogue. Babylonian Jews viewed wearing the prayer shawl and phylacteries in public as an adornment, which is inappropriate for *tish'a be'ab*.

Our *sefer Torah*, which during the year was adorned with brocade or white velvet, was covered with a black cloth on *tish'a be'ab*. Congregants, heads bent, marched in a slow procession behind the Torah. At the end of Torah reading, we read from the book of Jeremiah, both in Hebrew and Judeo-Arabic. As a child, I was taught that prayers should be read only in Hebrew. I guess the Babylonian rabbis feared that Judeo-Arabic might discourage people from learning Hebrew and end up displacing Hebrew in the liturgy. The reading from Jeremiah on *tish'a be'ab* was one of only two exceptions where the Babylonian rabbis had permitted the use of Judeo-Arabic in liturgy - the other being the Passover *haggadah*.

Some of the Babylonian tunes for *tish'a be'ab* were mournful; some were haunting, and we sang them in unison. The beauty of those tunes accentuated my pain at the historic event that brought us to the synagogue that day.

One blind beggar came to our synagogue every year on *tish'a be'ab*. He jingled coins in one hand while his other hand lay on the shoulder of his son, who led him up and down the aisles. Every now and then he would stop and take the lead in intoning one of those passages with the beautiful tunes. He had a ringing voice, and he sang with emotion. Everyone listened, everyone seemed to be moved. He brought tears to my eyes. What a tragedy that he was doomed never to see the sunlight, never to see the faces of his children.

At home we sat around my father and listened as he read the story of Hannah and her seven children, how they were massacred one by one for refusing to abandon Judaism – an example of the tragedies that befell the Jewish people when they lost their independence and were at the mercy of ruthless rulers. Hannah's was a moving story.

By mid-afternoon, the somber mood of the day in our home shifted to a lighter gear, as we prepared for ice cream making. It felt good to leave the somber mood behind. We filled our big ice cream maker with milk sweetened with heaps of sugar and sprinkled with crushed cardamom and rose water, and we took turns working its crank. Jacob, sitting on a stool, led the pack. He would open the ice cream maker every now and then and, with a dull knife, scrape the frozen milk from the walls of the inner container. Every time he opened the container, there were cries of impatience.

"Time to eat the ice cream. We've been waiting for too long."

"It will taste so much better, when it gets really frozen," Jacob reassured us.

Finally the moment we were waiting for arrived: Jacob declared the ice cream ready to eat. Everyone's cup was filled to the brim. It looked gorgeous - snow white chunks of ice cream. And there was a second serving when we finished the first. My parents joined in our eating frenzy.

I was thrilled when, in the mid sixties, I came across an electric ice cream maker that looked just like the manual one we had in Baghdad. I bought it, knowing it would make a wonderful present for my mother. Mama loved our cranky old ice cream maker. She would love this one, too. I would take it with us on our first trip to Israel. But it never made it to Mama's hands. Mama passed away before we made it to Israel.

I loved kite flying, and late afternoon on *tish'a be'ab* was kite-flying time. For days before *tish'a be'ab*, my siblings, cousins, and I were busy helping each other make kites – big kites, small kites, kites with two colors, kites with many colors, kites with light but long tails, kites with short but heavy tails, square kites, triangular kites ...

I remember running along the roof with the kite behind me to get it to fly. It did not always work smoothly. One time I backed up into one of the vats of tomatoes my mother had left to dry in the sun. My siblings laughed as I continued to run with my kite, covered though I was from top to bottom with tomato paste. I can still feel the joy of those times when the wind cooperated, and my kite took off. I watched it as it faded into a tiny speck in the distance and then tied its string to the railing surrounding the roof. Sometimes my kite's line became entangled with that of a neighbor's flying from an adjacent railing, and I watched in horror as the two tangled kites took a nosedive to the earth in a place where I could never reach them. But it was a delight when I got up the next day and found my little kite still flying, a shining star, way way up above, in the azure sky.

Festive *purim*, popularly known among Babylonian Jews as *m'djalla*, was my favorite holiday. It commemorates the deliverance of the Jews of Persia from destruction during the reign of Xerxes I. In Iraq we celebrated it for a full three weeks during the spring.

We children all looked forward to the special *m'djalla* gambling money our parents gave us weeks in advance. We spent every spare minute playing games of chance, such as *dosa* and *naksh el'yihood,* (literally, "the embroidery of the Jews"), or bingo. Gambling was our way of thumbing our noses at Haman, the minister of Xerxes who, in the 5th Century BCE, tossed dice to determine which month to annihilate the Jews in the Persian Empire.

The games of chance brought us together with our parents and the extended family, who all gambled with us. Life was one big party: Gathered around the card table, we shared special *m'djalla* sweets and treats, told jokes and shared stories. Later, it felt good to share some of our gambling gains with the less fortunate in our community.

I loved the times when Baba served as the dealer for the *dosa* game. He was supposed to deal his card first and then everyone else's card. He had to pay those whose hand beat his and collect from those whose hand fell short of his. But Baba reversed the order to heighten the excitement. He dealt all the other cards first, slowly and with relish. Only then did he show his card.

"I am going to win this game," he would tease. "Get your money ready! My card is going to beat you all!"

"No it won't! No it won't!" we would scream, as some waved their hands dismissively and others bounced in their seats.

121

All our cards were on the table. Now it was time to show his. Tension mounted as Baba took his own good time. He would slowly look each one of us in the eye.

"What do you think?" he would ask.

"Come on. Show us. You are too scared to open your card. Show us," some of us would blurt out.

Baba accepted the challenge. Then the room was filled with cries of joy and groans of disappointment.

Baba gave us our main allowance on the first day of the holiday. Then came our aunts and uncles, one by one, all of them adding to our *m'djalla*. The amount increased as we grew older. I got about 10 dinars (the equivalent of about $50) when I was ten.

Our *m'djalla* money had not been circulated before -- crisp, crackling currency and shiny, newly minted coins. I assumed every Jewish child received shining new money on *m'djalla* day. I was surprised when one time I showed a fourth-grade classmate some of my *m'djalla* allowance and he told me he had never seen shining money before.

"Don't you get *m'djalla* money from your parents, aunts and uncles?" I asked.

"Yes, I do. But where can you get shining coins or crisp paper money?"

When I asked my father about it, I learned that we could thank Khalu Guerji, my maternal uncle. Khalu Guerji was the Assistant Minister of Finance for Currency, the office that minted money, and so he was in a position to sell new money to my family.

A week or so before *m'djalla*, Mama, my siblings and I gathered around a large round table, with rolling pins in hand and a large bowl of dough in front of us to make *m'djalla* cookies. We made *b'abeu b'tamegh* - round cookies filled with dates and covered with sesame seeds; my favorite *simboosak b'shakar* —crisp turnovers filled with walnuts, sugar, cardamom and rosewater; and *simboosak b'jibin*, turnovers filled with Feta cheese and eggs. Wearing a thick head cover and with hands and arms covered, Jamila stood in front of our wood-burning clay oven and stuck our doughy cookies on the hot walls of the oven. Sometimes one or two of

122

my aunts joined us on those afternoons. We took a tea break periodically and sat and chatted, all looking forward to the coming *m'djalla* day.

And on *m'djalla* day, it was Muzli's specialty to make us our crispy brown Zingoola, the funnel cake that we adored. No one knew how to make those cakes as crisp as Muzli did.

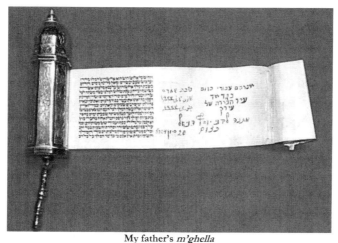

My father's *m'ghella*
Baba dedicated the *m'ghella* " to my son Joseph Daniel Khazzoom" on May 31, 1964.
The inscription shows also the date when he purchased it

Sometimes *m'djalla* services in the jam-packed synagogue verged on pandemonium. We read the *m'ghella*, the scroll of Esther, four times during the two days of *m'djalla*. Every time the reader uttered the hated Haman's name, dozens of cap guns went off simultaneously. The poor walked the aisles of the synagogue asking for help, rolling coins in their hands. No one could be turned down. This was the day to be generous.

On *m'djalla* day a Jewish band roamed our neighborhood. I particularly remember the drummer, a short fellow, whose drum was almost as big as he was. We couldn't see his face, just his feet marching along, his hands swinging drumsticks in the air and crashing them with enormous force

123

against the drum. The drumbeat rattled the surroundings, but was always out of synch with the music, adding to the general hilarity.

For a young boy, the *sukkoth* holiday was another exciting diversion. One of its highpoints was watching the workmen erect our traditional outdoor booth, or *sukkah*, where we visited with friends and family, took meals and sometimes even slept. My parents used a *sukkah* that my maternal grandparents had passed down to them. Supported by huge columns, it was so enormous it required a carpenter and three helpers to build and take down. Once, when I was seven years old, I was kibitzing while a workman perched atop a ladder trying to bolt our *sukkah* to the second floor. Suddenly, the structure began to tilt. The three men standing on the first floor let out a horrified cry, and rushed to keep it from collapsing. I stood rooted to the ground in terror, while the structure tilted in my direction.

My parents were horrified at the near miss. At the end of the holiday, when the carpenter and his crew came to take down the *sukkah*, Baba told them to take it away. From that year on, Mama used the metallic frame and four poles of a huge custom-made bed as the supports for the *sukkah.*

The *sukkah* symbolizes the ramshackle dwellings that housed the Israelites during their 40 years in the wilderness after leaving Egypt. Ours had a ceiling loosely covered with palm fronds and was elaborately decorated with bundles of fruit and snow-white embroidered curtains. Silver bowls filled with sweetmeats and Camel cigarettes stood atop a table at the entrance. My father didn't smoke, but he enjoyed sitting next to a smoker and smelling the cigarette smoke.

Atop the bench facing the entrance to the *sukkah* stood the Chair of Elyahoo, or the Chair of Elijah, with silver finials adorning its four corners. The chair, holding a set of the five books of Torah, predated my birth and perhaps the birth of my older siblings. But that relic is gone with the rest, as my parents had to leave most of their possessions behind when they left Iraq in 1958 and immigrated to Israel.

Sukkoth was a time of balmy weather and pleasant outdoor living, and we received our guests and visitors in the *sukkah.* One friend could always be counted on to show up on *sukkoth,* and that was the man we called "Ghahmeen el Akhas" – Ghahmeen the Mute. A handsome, thoughtful man in his fifties, Ghahmeen always came neatly dressed in suit and tie. I was fascinated by the thick tufts of hair sprouting from his ears, and had to stifle the urge to tug at them. Ghahmeen's vocal chords had never fully developed, but this infirmity didn't prevent him from being fully engaged in conversation.

Babylonian Chair of Elyahoo with the Pentateuch and embroidered cover.
The chair was smuggled out of Baghdad in the late nineties. I had it refurbished.

My father and Uncle Moshe seemed to be able to decipher some of what he said, but what he lacked in vocal ability he made up for in body language. If you were to see him on a silent movie screen deep in conversation, if you were to watch his attentive expression, his emphatic gestures as he tried to reinforce a point, the puffing on his pipe as he listened raptly, you would never guess he was mute.

On one visit he made it known that he had forgotten his omnipresent pipe. Uncle Moshe offered him a cigarette. Ghahmeen signaled with raised eyebrows, a shake of his head and a wave of his hand that one cigarette was not enough. He

125

motioned with a V sign that he wanted two. Uncle Moshe complied. If Ghahmeen's intention was to show off in front of us children, he succeeded. I still remember his look of contentment as he leaned back puffing on two cigarettes at once, while we watched in amazement.

Ghahmeen was a man devoid of self-pity, who appeared at peace with the hand fate had dealt him. I often wondered how he managed to take the bus, do his shopping, choose the cloth for his suits, and haggle with the tailor or shoemaker. No one knew where he worked or how he managed to pay his bills. No one knew what happened to him during the mass exodus from Iraq. He couldn't read newspapers. Did he know about the one-year window when the Jews were given the opportunity to file a petition to leave Iraq? Did he stay behind? If he did, did he know why his friends began to suddenly vanish?

Sh'buoth, the anniversary of the giving of the Torah to the Jewish people on Mt Sinai, is known among Babylonian Jews as *eed el'zyagha*, the holiday of pilgrimage. During the *sh'buoth* period, many went on a pilgrimage to the burial sites of major biblical figures, such as Ezra the Scribe, and the prophets Ezekiel and, Daniel.

There were many traditions associated with *sh'buoth*. That was the holiday on which Mama made *kahi*, the traditional Babylonian pastry fashioned out of layers of thin dough separated by melted butter and fried to crisp. We ate it sprinkled with castor sugar or dipped in *silan*. I ate it smothered with *silan*.

In the afternoon, my father, brother and I took turns chanting the *az'haroth*, a poem of admonitions by the eleventh century Spanish poet, Shlomo Ib'n Gabirol. My mother and sisters sat with us as we chanted the *az'haroth* in the traditional Babylonian melody. I still chant the *az'haroth* every year on *sh'buoth* day in that same melody I had learned during my years of growing up in Baghdad.

Tomb of Ezra the Scribe on the Tigris River in Uzer, near Basra in southern Iraq
Tomb is in building with cupola

We spent the first night of *sh'buoth*, studying sacred texts, and just before sunrise, we headed for the synagogue to start morning prayers. My Hebrew tutor explained to me that the vigil might have evolved from a tradition among the pious to demonstrate their devotion by rising early and synchronizing their morning prayers with the break of dawn. In Iraq we spoke fondly of those people and had a name for them: *wathikeem* – the pious of old.

I remember Mama telling me how the sexton of her synagogue used to knock on their door in the wee hours of the morning to wake up my grandfather to attend services at dawn. And I still remember the sexton of our synagogue. He would knock on our neighbor's door, softly call his name, and wait until he heard our neighbor's voice confirming he was up before moving on to the next house. I always felt a sense of reassurance whenever I heard his voice in those early hours of the morning. Sometimes I got up to watch him through my bedroom window. On rainy night he carried a kerosene lantern to help him avoid puddles. I felt for him, as I watched him shiver in the cold. He never seemed to be dressed warmly enough, never wore gloves, and he rubbed his hands to keep them warm as he waited to hear our neighbor's voice. I marveled at his piety. He was not paid to get up early to wake up the congregants. He did it out of the goodness of his

127

heart.

But on the night of *sh'buoth*, there was no need to waken people at dawn. We stayed up all night – all of us, young and old, men and women, pious and impious alike. We called the *sh'buoth* vigil *tikkun leil sh'buoth*. My Hebrew tutor explained to me that it was not enough to just observe the anniversary of the giving of the Torah; one needed also to experience the receiving of the Torah. And for that, one had to prepare oneself for that awesome event by spending the night studying sacred texts and focusing on the great wonder G-d brought to the world with the giving of the Torah.

My family faithfully observed *tikkun leil sh'buoth*. We spent the night reading from a compendium of Jewish sacred texts. Together with members of the extended family and friends, we attended the vigil in the home of Ammu (Uncle) Moshe, my father's older brother. We gathered at around eight p.m. (It got dark early in Baghdad). We held the vigil in the house's courtyard. During that time of the year, it was pleasant to be outdoors at night. The view of the sky and the sparkling stars above added to the spiritual feel of the occasion.

The erudite from among the participants led the discussions and commentaries. But there was always a push to make sure that everything in the compendium was read before dawn, even though many could not understand what was being read. People took turns reading aloud a section or two. The reading followed the seating order. We, children, often changed our seating place in order to get to read more portions. Aunt Guerjiyi served hot drinks – Turkish coffee, tea and a specially prepared sweet drink known as *meghli*.

At midnight, we took a break. It was time for blessings, *z'man b'rakhoth*. Aunt Guerjiyi served fruits and cakes. Everyone recited aloud the blessing over the food, and all present responded enthusiastically as one chorus: Amen. But there was more to the break than the ritual blessing and eating. There was a sense of togetherness, a sense of pride and, in a country such as Iraq where life was precarious, there was a deep sense of gratitude we were alive to celebrate the occasion one more time.

128

We lit candles in memory of loved ones. Any one, young or old, man or woman could light as many candles as he or she wished. We whispered a short prayer from the heart. The candles stood in the far corner of the courtyard. I felt a deep sense of mystery and reverence for those who were no longer with us, as I watched the glittering flames. Where were the souls of those loved ones for whom we had lit the candles? Where could they be?

People tried hard to stay awake. For many, it was a challenge to keep their eyes open. I stayed awake throughout; the vigil had a mystical meaning for me. I felt a deep sense of awe for the day of the giving of the Torah.

One year, when I was eleven years old, I went up to the roof at Uncle Moshe's home, some fifteen minutes before dawn. The roof was one level above the courtyard. I sat on one of the beds on the roof. I could hear the participants singing the traditional closing hymn: "*yom yom odeh la el*" – "Day in day out, I thank God for giving us the Torah." That song meant that the vigil had come to an end and that it was time to head for the synagogue for services. People sang with renewed vigor. There was a sense of relief, triumph, and pride. We had made it. We had followed in the footsteps of our ancestors, staying up all night engaged in Torah study.

On the roof, the cool breeze blew gently. I looked at the sky and I thought to myself, "This is the moment when G-d appeared at Sinai. This was the day when G-d gave us the Torah." I stared at the fading stars. It was a quiet, solemn moment. I felt the divine presence all around me, and I felt it in my bones. I stood motionless and let it wash over me. It was a moment of inspiration such as I had never experienced before. And for a fleeting moment, I felt as if I had melted away. I was no longer standing on this earth. I was way out there in the universe. I had merged with the cosmos.

It was awesome.

I went downstairs. I was dazed. Nothing looked real. I saw my father and put my arms around him. I needed his reassurance. Baba took my hand. He gave me a long pensive look. It seemed as if I had managed to communicate to him what I had just experienced without uttering a word.

Slowly the two of us walked together and headed for the synagogue.

TRANQUIL INTERLUDES

My childhood in Baghdad, safe in the bosom of my family, was in many ways a wonderful life. It was the threat from outside that finally destroyed it. Those days are gone and I feel their loss. In the early days, we had no intimations of the terror and upheaval that the future held, and, for the most part, we enjoyed what life brought us. Some of my fondest memories are of our summertime swims in the Tigris River.

(Left) Floater for training beginners carved out of the trunk of a palm tree (right).

When I was about ten, our father arranged for swimming lessons for Jacob and me. Our instructor swam in the river beside us with a huge inner tube around his waist. We could hold on to this tube any time we felt tired. We had an extra safeguard in our "floaters," pieces of the spiky bark of palm trees that were padded and attached to our bodies. I wore three of these floaters; Jacob—who was less enamored of the water than I-- wore four. Within three days, I had discarded one of my floaters and joined the group that swam all across the mile-wide Tigris and back. From then on, swimming became my summer passion.

Every morning during that summer, my father, Jacob and I made our way to the bridge in downtown Baghdad to meet our swimming instructors and about 50 other young Jewish boys who swam together. Often, we'd watch the young gymnast who dove from the top of one of the bridge's beams and did breathtaking acrobatics in midair before hitting the water.

Our swims took us to the opposite bank of the Tigris, a wild and green place where we were able to glimpse the strange practices of the tribal people who lived there. My father called them the "Sun Worshippers," and they immersed animals in the water before killing them for food. Women from the tribe stood in the water at the edge of the river, their black hair loose about their faces, their wet skirts flapping around their knees, their brawny arms holding a hen, a rooster or a sheep. They bent toward the water and muttered incantations, as they dunked the animals in the water. The shrill voices of the women mingled with the squawking of the hens, the crowing of the roosters, and the bleating of the sheep. All of the animals struggled to escape, the hens' wings flapping and churning up the water, the sheep's feet waving in the air, as they tried to find a footing in the riverbed. Sometimes the women ended up flat on their backs in the water, while an escaping hen or sheep flew or scurried toward the shore. There it was recaptured by other women waiting on the bank, guarding the animals next in line for immersion. The women took no notice of us as we stood in the water at a safe distance and watched wide-eyed.

During the summer, my father, Jacob and I would wake up before dawn and after our daily prayers, head for the river. I envied the boys who arrived early, for they got extra time in the water before the lessons began. One morning I decided to remedy that situation by turning the clocks in our home back so the alarm would ring early. Unfortunately I overdid it. The alarm sounded two hours earlier than usual. That puzzled my father and my brother. I kept mum. That morning we arrived at the bridge before anybody else and we had lots of time for swimming. If my father figured out what had happened to the clock, he never shared that information with me.

The freedom of the outdoors was a rare pleasure in my tightly sheltered world. As a small boy I had a tricycle that I wasn't allowed to ride in the street. We children were not allowed to venture beyond the walls of our home. As I grew older, bicycles were forbidden to me by my father— probably because there were so many collisions that left cyclists dead. I didn't listen. I had my own tutoring money, and I began riding a rented bicycle along the Tigris until I was alone in the wilderness. Cycling gave me an almost unheard of taste of freedom. One day, however, my exhilaration was interrupted when I fell off the bicycle and broke my wrist. I rode back to the rental shop in agony and went home to be comforted by my mother and roundly castigated by my father.

The matter of the bicycle was eventually resolved in my favor. My sister Jamila's husband, Ezra, worked for an agency that imported luxury bicycles from England, and he arranged for me to buy a shiny new BSA bicycle. Other members of the family sided with me against my father, and he was forced to give in. When I registered to leave Iraq and my possessions were confiscated, the only item that I missed was that beloved bicycle.

I never dreamed of owning a car. In Iraq cars were headaches. They broke down frequently and the few garages charged exorbitant sums for repairs. Ammu Guerji, our family doctor, owned several cars to ensure that he always had one in working condition. He employed a chauffeur who doubled as a mechanic. When members of my immediate family wanted to get from one place to another, we took the bus, walked, or hired a taxicab or a hackney carriage.

The horse-driven hackneys were slower and more expensive than buses, but much more fun. Often we had an eccentric driver who flouted traffic rules and the police alike. He burst into full-throated song and danced while navigating the clogged streets. When the police signaled him to stop, he gave them a raspberry and kept going through an intersection, while cars swerved to avoid colliding with us. We children giggled with delight at his outrageous—and dangerous--antics. It was exciting to be the center of attention, and to see someone make fools of the police we dreaded but couldn't ourselves defy.

BAR MISWAH

In Iraq the coming of age for girls, *bath miswah*, and for boys, *bar miswah*, marked the time when a girl turned twelve-and-a-half and a boy thirteen years and five days. At that age, they were considered adults, subject to the privileges and obligations of a Jewish adult. A religious ceremony and festivities marked *bar miswah*; nothing was done to celebrate a young woman's *bath miswah*.

My *bar miswah* ceremony, on June 24, 1945, was held in my parents' home. As part of the ceremony, it was the custom to have the elder of the family demonstrate to the *bar miswah* boy how to put on the *tefilleen*, the phylacteries. Baba invited his close friend, Iraq's *hakham bashi* (Chief Rabbi) Sasson Kh'doury, to serve as the honored elder for my ceremony.

The house was in a hubbub hours before the celebration. A chef prepared special dishes; servants swept the floors, washed the courtyard and walkways, dusted the furniture, and polished the windows. Everyone in the family was busy doing something. A sense of urgency seemed to have gripped everyone - everyone, that is, except me.

"What is the big deal?" I kept asking myself. The rabbi would show me how to put on the *tefilleen*. But I knew how to do that. I had watched my father put on the *tefilleen* many times. I would be reading from the Torah for the assembled guests. But I read Hebrew well, and I was not worried that I might stumble. Why did people around me have to get so excited? Why was it necessary to wash all the walkways upstairs, shine the glass of every window?

On a sandbar in the Tigris near our home, on my *bar miswah* day

Even now, as I look back, I am amazed at how nonchalant I was. But I realize I was the last in my family to become *bar miswah*, and my mother wanted it to be a big day. I remember her telling my father that she didn't want the day to slip by hardly noticed, as it had on Jacob's *bar miswah* day.

"I am not going to have another son. This is my last one," she told my father when he suggested we forgo a big celebration.

Early that afternoon, a friend and I sneaked out and walked the few yards from our home to the Tigris to take a swim. The sun shone brightly, the water sparkled and it felt wonderful to be away from the commotion at the house. I felt I was entitled to do what gave me most pleasure that day. It was fun to find a sandbar and lie on it in the middle of the river, surrounded by water.

The ceremony went without a hitch. Our home was filled to capacity with friends, family and neighbors. The most important guest for me was Mademoiselle Sim'ha, my favorite kindergarten teacher. Everyone seemed to have a good time. Mama radiated happiness, having gotten her wish.

On my *bar miswah* day, June 24, 1945
The *hakham bashi* Sasson Kh'doury shows me how to put on the *tefilleen*. I wore
Sesseed (prayer shawl) and Sidara (Iraq's national hat). *Hakham* Sasson wore the
Babylonian rabbinical vestment and *amama, or* head cover.

On the following Sabbath, I was called to read my
portion from the Torah scroll. I went with the same self-
confidence I'd felt on my bar miswah day. I knew that portion
by heart. But as I stood face to face in front of the Torah
scroll, my self-assurance vanished. It was the first time I had
seen the script of a Torah scroll up close. Always before, I had
practiced my portion using my printed Torah book, which
had all sentences and paragraphs marked. But the script in
the Torah scroll was one uninterrupted blur. I could have
begun intoning my portion from memory, but somehow I was
fixated on the script in front of me. Today Torah readers
practice from a *tikkoon lakor'eem,* a book that replicates the
Torah script, and they are not taken by surprise when they

On my *bar miswah* day, June 24, 1945

I sat in front of *hakham bashi* Sasson Kh'doury and read the Torah passages commanding the wearing of *tefilleen*, as my father (seated at the left end of the sofa with a Sidara on his head) and guests listened.

Guests and family members
Maternal grandma Aziza (with the white head gear) seated in the center of front row.
Standing in the back, l to r: Mama, Reyna, Saleem (cousin), Helwa and Muzli.
Latifa, seated at the extreme left; Aunt Guerjiyi, seated 4th from the left, with white dress, facing to the right.

come face to face with the script of the Torah scroll.

The service leader must have sensed my bewilderment. Perhaps other *bar miswah* boys had had a similar experience. With his head lowered close to my ear, he began intoning my Torah portion softly. That jump-started me. It took my mind off the bewildering scroll. I started reading, and it all came back.

When I finished, the service leader looked at me with a smile and intoned the traditional blessing "Hazak Obaroukh" – "May you be strong and blessed." I could never thank him enough.

In 1948 I passed the French Brevet –the equivalent of a high school graduation exam--and, with that, my Alliance days came to an end. I had yet to complete the ministry of education's Arabic program. So I transferred to Shamash School, where I prepared for the Arabic secondary school test.

Shamash, a modern school operated by the Jewish community, was established in 1928. It was housed in an enormous structure donated by three Baghdadian brothers - Benjamin, Jacob, and Joseph Shamash. Shamash prepared its students to sit for the University of London's Matriculation. Like other Alliance graduates, I had limited training in English. But when I took the Matriculation exam, I stuck to plain and simple writing. When the results were announced, and my name was among those who had passed, I felt emboldened.

There was talk in Shamash about an advanced test in English - English Proficiency. I was warned that nine out of ten Shamash veterans - those who had five years of high school English instruction - failed the test. Undeterred, I took time off from my regular study to prepare for the Proficiency.

I passed the written part of the test, but there was the oral part to contend with. The examiner gave me a text to read aloud and told me we would discuss it when I had finished reading it. Discuss it? Discussion in French or in Judeo-Arabic I could handle, but I couldn't speak two sentences in English without stumbling. Still, I had no choice. In for a penny, in for a pound, I said to myself, and began reading. It was difficult reading; there were many words I had not encountered before. Even now, when I see a word in English for the first time, my tendency is to pronounce it the French way. I did the same thing with that text. The examiner ended the session abruptly. "This is Chinese," he growled in disgust. I didn't need to tell him it was Chinese to me, too. Humbled, I went back to my regular class work.

Alliance graduates tended to stick together and didn't mix much with Shamash veterans. It was snobbishness on our part. But I thought highly of a number of my teachers. I remember my Shamash science teacher, the late Dr. Nissim Ezra Nissim, a graduate of the University of Michigan at Ann Arbor, a bright, lucid and dedicated teacher. Dr. Nissim was one of those needy students whose graduate work was fully paid for by our community.

Dr. Nissim reinforced what I'd learned first from my sister Jamila: that we couldn't know everything, that knowledge is too wide to be encompassed by any one person. When a student asked a question that he couldn't answer, Dr. Nissim readily confessed his ignorance, promising to research the question and get an answer. Another teacher might have dismissed the question or blustered his way through with a half-baked response. Not Dr. Nissim. He respected knowledge too much.

And there was Mr. Rogers, one of our English teachers. Mr. Rogers was a chubby, middle-aged Englishman, with blue eyes and thinning blonde hair. He had left his teaching position in England during the war years and joined the British military. After retiring from the military he joined Shamash's faculty. I remember him especially for his clarity and his sense of humor.

One day, when he was teaching in the classroom adjacent to ours, his students walked out of the classroom en masse. They were highly agitated, and paced the hallway arguing among themselves. Clearly, something awful had happened.

It seems that during his lecture, Mr. Rogers had made a remark that the students understood to mean he concurred with Hitler's killing of the Jews of Europe. The story spread like a brushfire. World War II was still fresh in our minds. We were reeling from the horror of the extermination of European Jewry and were shocked to hear what the students next door relayed. My class had a lecture scheduled with Mr. Rogers right after the recess, but we decided to join the others in a boycott. We wanted the school principal to investigate the matter before deciding if we would continue the boycott.

My high School class, 1949-50
Samra Shamash seated in front row, third from left; Daniel in back row, sixth from left.

The principal joined us in our classroom, and reported that Mr. Rogers had denied saying what was attributed to him. The principal told us he felt convinced of Mr. Rogers' sincerity; he thought we should hear him out.

We agreed to listen to his explanation.

Mr. Rogers looked tense, even frightened, when he walked in. He was stooped, his face was red, his hands were shaking, and he avoided eye contact with us. I felt sorry for him. I no longer remember the details of his explanation. But

139

I remember feeling there had been a colossal misunderstanding and that the man might have been accused unjustly. Was I just trying to paper over an unpleasant incident I couldn't deal with? Was I concerned about what a prolonged boycott would do to our education? Or did I really believe him? I don't know. But the class finally agreed to accept Mr. Rogers' apology, and move on.

By June of 1950, my years of Arabic secondary schooling had come to an end. Two months later, the ministry of education announced that two Alliance graduates -- my classmate, Miss Samra Shamash, and I -- had scored the highest in the country in English composition.

Samra and I shared a five-dinar prize, which I accepted without much excitement. My mind was no longer on Iraq. I had already signed away my Iraqi citizenship in return for being allowed to emigrate, and was waiting for the day when I would leave the country.

That was also the time when l'Alliance was forced to shut down. From all I have been able to gather, to day l'Alliance lies in ruins, its doors broken, its windows shattered, its long beautiful walkways dilapidated. It saddens me to think of the fall of the giant. Sometimes I wonder about the portrait of Sir Albert, the nobleman who had made a gift of that building to my alma mater. What happened to that portrait? Is it still hanging proudly where it hung for generations? And the Sasson synagogue? It was opened for services on the Sabbath, kept always sparkling, and it had rolling steel doors to protect it from plunder. Does it, too, lie in ruins?

A HISTORY OF VIOLENCE

THE SWINGING PENDULUM

My parents lived through calm times in Baghdad and through times when Jews were persecuted. My father told me about the peaceful times, and though I drank in his stories, that is exactly what they were for me - stories.

In my experience, whatever peace we enjoyed in Baghdad was shaky at best. We had limited contact with the Arabs around us, although we did pay my father's Muslim friends formal visits on their holidays to wish them joy, and some of them, in turn, visited us on our holidays. I don't remember Shiites being friends with my family. Shiites considered Jews to be unclean and would never eat or drink from dishes used by Jews, no matter how well these dishes were washed. If a Shiite accidentally brushed against us in the street, he cursed us. One Shiite told a school friend of mine: "The clay the Jews are made of is dirty. Nothing can make a Jew clean."

Still, in the history of my community, there was no counterpart to the pogroms that took place against the Jews in Eastern Europe with the open support of those countries' governments. Our more fortunate history was due not so much to the tolerance of the local populace, as to the restraining influence of the Ottomans, who ruled Iraq for four centuries (1534-1918), a period of intermittent peace and persecution for the Jews. The Turks were protective of their Jewish subjects, and the Jews respected the Turks. Though the Turks are Muslims, they didn't particularly trust the Arabs and were often in conflict with them. But they did trust the Jews, who were frequently appointed to high positions in the Ottoman Empire. Iraq's chief s*arraf,* or banker, was, as far as I know, always a Jew during the Ottoman period.

My father cherished his memories of the Turks from his law school days in Istanbul. He taught me Turkish when I was a boy, and shared with me much of what I know about the experiences of Iraq's Jews during his own lifetime at the turn of the century.

In 1917 the British occupied Iraq and, in August 1921, invited Emir Faisal from Saudi Arabia to come to Iraq. In a national referendum held that year under British oversight, Emir Faisal, later King Faisal I, was elected king of an independent Iraq under British mandate. The British mandate expired in 1932, at which time Iraq became an independent country and was admitted to the League of Nations.

King Faisal I (in light coat) at the boys' Alliance Israelite in Baghdad, January 13, 1924.

Faisal I was supportive of the Jewish community. His first Minister of Finance, Sir Sasson Haskell, was Jewish, a graduate of my alma mater - l'Ecole de l'Alliance Israelite. Some refer to Sir Sasson as the Alexander Hamilton of modern Iraq, for his genius in putting the newly independent nation's financial house in order. Faisal I was enamored of the educational accomplishments of the Jewish community, and often took dignitaries from abroad to visit the Jewish schools in Baghdad. I remember from my childhood when we spoke of Faisal I as "mehasidei oummot haolam," or "Righteous Among the Nations."

Faisal I died in 1933, a year after I was born, and his son Ghazi ascended the throne. That marked the beginning of the dark times of the thirties and forties for the Jews of Iraq, the years of my growing up in Baghdad. Ghazi surrounded himself with a group of extremists who were anti-British, anti-Jewish, and pro-Nazi. They were supported and financed by the German embassy in Baghdad and they circulated Hitler's *Mein Kampf,* the *Protocols of the Elders of Zion,* and other rabid anti-Jewish books. Even though I was only seven years old, I still remember how terrified we were when, in 1939, the Mufti of Jerusalem, Haj Ameen al-Husseini, joined the group around Ghazi. The Mufti, interpreter of Islamic religious law, was a Nazi collaborator. In Iraq, he helped engineer the pro-Nazi coup, which culminated in the *farhood,* the massacre of the Jews of Baghdad in June 1941 that my family and I barely escaped.

Iraq's parliament might have had a mitigating influence, but it was a parliament without teeth - pretty much a rubber stamp for whomever happened to be in power. When I was eleven, one of the local papers asked a prominent member of the parliament which direction he thought Iraq should take in World War II. He responded: "Don't get me involved in politics." Even as a child, I was stunned to read his answer. But in time I came to realize that he knew his position was largely ceremonial, not one that could counterbalance or check the king and the prime minister. The most he could do was approve their policies and assist in their implementation.

The government set aside seats in the parliament for a number of non-elected individuals who were heads of tribes. A perhaps apocryphal story about one such member circulated in Baghdad when I was a teenager. When the roll was called in the Iraqi Parliament at the beginning of the session, one of the tribal heads was dozing when his name was called. The representative sitting next to him nudged him to respond. He opened his eyes and declared, "I vote in favor." His neighbor whispered that it was not a vote, just the roll call. The tribal chief opened his eyes and responded

143

indignantly, "I vote in favor and I am also present." Then he went back to dozing.

The enforcement of law was at the whim of those in positions of power. A rule of men, not of law, prevailed. I grew up feeling there was practically nothing on which one could really depend. Everything was volatile and could explode into violence without warning. Rampant government corruption added to the instability and to my feelings of unease. The police, the body that should protect all members of the populace, operated under a system of bribery and payola, as did almost every other branch of the civil service.

Indeed, bribery permeated almost every government nook and cranny: issuance of passports, certification of documents, application for construction work or issuance of business permits. But perhaps the least visible was the annual income tax assessment. There was no estimated quarterly tax payment for business owners, independent professionals, and other self-employed people. Instead, the Tax Assessor calculated the amount owed and sent a tax bill annually to each individual. Those assessments were almost always exaggerated; the burden to show they were excessive was on the taxpayer. Usually this was accomplished with a bribe. The Treasury Department didn't entertain appeals, and taking the case to court was generally more costly than most people could afford. Bribing the Assessor was the path of least resistance.

Because Jews constituted most of Iraq's businessmen and independent professionals, they were the ones hardest hit by the corrupt tax system. One wealthy Jewish businessman enlisted my father to take his case to court. Baba took the case directly to the Appeals Court, where he asked that the Tax Assessor substantiate the businessman's assessment. When it was plain the Assessor didn't have the flimsiest documentation, and the businessman had kept good records of his business transactions, the court ruled in favor of the businessman.

This tangled affair couldn't have been more different than my first experience as a U.S. taxpayer. When I filed my first tax return I didn't know I was expected to declare myself as a dependent and deduct a personal exemption from my income. The IRS corrected the mistake on my return and sent me a refund of $120. The government corrected a mistake I had made in its favor? I could hardly believe it. It wouldn't have happened in Iraq.

It was an open secret that the most lucrative government appointment in Iraq was that of the minister in charge of police. That minister appointed the district commanders and expected a monthly payment, which varied with the district, from every district commander. The district commanders in turn shook down the local station commanders, and those in wealthy neighborhoods had to come up with the largest sums. The station serving areas where wealthy Jews lived was one of those.

Accepting bribes was a favorite way to raise funds for the monthly payoffs. People were frequently arrested on trumped-up charges, which were dropped when the police were paid off. If the bribe was not immediately forthcoming, the detainees were tortured to extract confessions and to put pressure on families and communities to come up with the bribe. Since the payola came due every month, the last days of the month were the most dangerous days to walk the streets of Baghdad. Arrests would accelerate if a station commander had not yet raised enough money to meet his quota.

We collected money within the Jewish community in order to pay off the police and free the people who were wrongfully arrested. My father told me that no one liked to help perpetuate a corrupt system, but the Jewish community felt that it was important to save the lives of innocent people. When the arrested person was wealthy enough, he paid the "fine" himself, but there were many who could not afford the fine, and the community had to come to their rescue.

Those collections didn't always save people from torture. Sometimes not enough money was collected. Sometimes the collection didn't reach the police in time. And sometimes the police just enjoyed the sense of power torture gave them, even though they knew the money was on its way.

Many of the charges were preposterous. Two well-dressed Jews were picked up and accused of engaging in homosexual acts in the middle of the street. When they were brought in front of the station commander, he slapped their cheeks and spat in their faces. The arrested men knew exactly what was going on. This initial roughing-up was typical, and was meant to intimidate. It was a clear message hinting of worse things to follow, if the men didn't pay the expected bribe. And, of course, they did pay.

The police saw no need to cover up these activities. Corruption was built into the system, and inventing an original charge was something a police officer saw as an ingenious accomplishment. The station commander in charge of the "homosexual" case related his part in the story when he was a guest in the home of Jewish friends of ours. He bragged about his ingenuity in intimidating the two Jewish men. Our friends said he chuckled when he told them proudly, "You should have seen their faces when I slapped their cheeks and spat in their faces. They were even afraid to wipe the spittle off their faces."

It didn't matter to him that he was telling the story in a Jewish home. He knew the Jews couldn't do anything about the situation. He held the power and felt no need to conceal his contempt for the powerless Jews. He could visit in Jewish homes and eat Jewish food, and the very next day he could arrest those very same Jews on a trumped-up charge.

NIGHT TERRORS

The local police station in our district was across the street from our home. Every sound from the station seemed to make its way into my bedroom at night, the time when the torture took place. I could hear the sharp sound of the bamboo rod as it hit human flesh.

This initial torture was often done on the ground floor. There was also a room in the basement, where the police would torture their victims to get them to concede or admit guilt. From there, the sounds of people in anguish rent the dark night. At first the victims cried and yelled. After a while, the cries turned to howling, just howling.

The worst time was summer, when we slept on the roof. The windows of the police station were open when the police started their lashings. The police didn't care what their neighbors might think; they knew that nobody would stop them.

I remained glued to my bed on the roof during those summer nights, as I heard the cries of pain coming from the victims and felt waves of helplessness wash over my body. The thought that a member of my family could be the next victim kept knocking at the doors of my mind. I held my hands over my face, trying to keep that horrible thought at bay. But I couldn't shut out the sounds of terror, the sounds that still invade my life.

For seven years—from the age of eleven until I escaped Baghdad—my dreams were haunted by these nightly sounds of human agony. I don't recall speaking with my parents about my fears. In those days, we didn't wear emotions on our sleeves, or talk much about feelings. If my parents sought to comfort me, it was usually with a touch or a hug. There was an unspoken understanding that we were highly vulnerable.

When I was in the transitional camp, *Sha'ar Aliyah*, immediately after my arrival in Israel from Baghdad, several times I awakened in the middle of the night screaming in fear. I was fortunate to be sharing the tent with a wonderful Kurdish family from Northern Iraq. When I woke up the first time, both parents were sitting at my bedside with their arms around me, gently telling me that it was OK, that we were no longer in Iraq. They told me I had been screaming that the police were coming.

Sometimes I still dream I am back in Baghdad sleeping in my bedroom. I hear the voices of the victims screaming in pain. I wake up terrified, look around and wonder, "Where am I?" It takes me a while to realize I am no longer in Baghdad across the street from the police station.

It has been difficult to shake loose from the terror. For years after I left Iraq, I remained conscious of fear sitting on my shoulder ready to spring from its perch, grow before

147

my eyes into full-blown terror, and hold me frozen in its grip. To this day, I cannot bring myself to enter the Moslem quarter of any city. And late at night, an unexpected loud knock at the door or a sudden shout from the street is enough to leave me in a cold sweat and send shudders up and down my spine.

Probably the biggest legacy from my time in Iraq is this fear of torture. In 1956, when I was the sergeant of an Israeli combat unit on the Egyptian border, I worried that we might be taken captive while retreating. I preferred to fight until I was shot and killed in battle, if it came to that, rather than fall into the hands of Arabs who tortured their prisoners.

By law, I was supposed to reveal the line of retreat to the soldiers under my command. Instead, I kept the line of retreat to myself. Perhaps I should not have done so unilaterally, but at the time I felt I was probably the only person in the group who knew the awful consequences of possible capture by the Arabs. I felt protective of the soldiers under my command and couldn't bear to think of any one of them being tortured. I pictured their howls piercing the dark night, as did the howls of the people tortured by the police in Baghdad. I knew I could not let anyone, not just myself, go through that.

THE NAZI TAKEOVER

During World War II, all Arab countries had Nazi leanings, but Iraq was the only Arab country that invited the Nazis to come and make Iraq part of the Nazi axis. The fact that Iraq itself was a violent society only made the situation worse.

In 1941 the King of Iraq was nine-year old King Faisal II. His father, the Nazi collaborator King Ghazi, had been killed in an automobile accident in 1939. At the time Faisal II's maternal uncle was appointed Regent until his nephew reached the age of 18. The Regent himself was only 18 years old, and a playboy to boot.

In April 1941, Rasheed Ali became Iraq's Prime

Minister, backed by a junta of four pro-Nazi colonels, whose aim was to kick out the British and invite the Nazis to Iraq. The Regent, fearing for his safety, fled Baghdad. The city fell under the power of the colonels, and the British made a strategic retreat to Habbaniyeh, some 50 miles to the southwest. With neighboring Syria under Vichy control, the British likely calculated that the Nazis would be able to invade Baghdad from their nearby foothold in Damascus. Indeed, pilots dressed in Nazi uniform were observed in Baghdad not long after the coup was declared. Meanwhile, the pro-Nazi junta held Baghdad's Jewish community hostage. Cries of "Kill the Jews" were heard everywhere, and special youth paramilitary groups roamed the streets. Unarmed and unable to defend ourselves, we couldn't escape, as restrictions on leaving Iraq steadily tightened.

The arrival of other Arab nationalists from neighboring Syria and Palestine further fueled anti-Jewish sentiments. Swastikas were painted on the walls of shops on Rasheed Street. During this period, street attacks on Jews increased, and Jewish shops were often looted. These incidents often took place on Friday afternoons, when people filed out of the mosques. The mob would run in the streets, yelling and screaming, with bulging eyes that exuded hate. They screamed "*Allahu Akbar*," "God is the greatest," with its implication that their violence was perpetrated on behalf of God. They attacked and beat Jewish people unlucky enough to be in their path.

I was nine years old when the 1941 coup took place. But I was overcome by feelings of isolation and despair when I began to realize what was happening to us. Only the fact that England was at war with Iraq gave us some hope.

The stakes were enormously high. We knew that if England fell to Hitler, we were lost. And our dread only intensified when we saw Iraqis jubilant and dancing in the streets, celebrating the imminent downfall of the British. At this low point, Winston Churchill's leadership lifted us from utter despair - he was our idol and inspiration. Uncle Guerji would listen to his speeches on the BBC in our home, and even though I couldn't understand a word, the defiance and resolve in Churchill's voice needed no translation.

Our father's unwavering faith in Churchill was palpable when he gathered us together and read us the British leader's speeches that he had clipped from the newspaper. We felt Baba's faith when he'd pause after reading a promise by Churchill that brighter days lay ahead, that England would win the war and punish Hitler for his crimes. Wide-eyed, he would silently look each one of us in the eye, as if to say, "Did you hear it? Did you get the message? We are going to win." With Churchill's words transmitted this way by our father and ultimate protector, the revered world leader might have been with us in the room. And his speeches from a faraway land became, thanks to Baba's intervention, intimate and profoundly reassuring sources of calm.

In May 1941, the British moved on Baghdad. During the British assault against the Iraqi military, British planes targeted military installations almost every night. One could expect them almost on the dot, at midnight. We waited for the raid to be over before we went to sleep. Bombs rattled our windows, our house shook and we quaked in our shoes. I went to sleep only to have nightmares about the bombs, and about the Iraqis who might break into our house at any time.

The Jewish community's loyalties were with the British, though we could never openly say so. Indeed, the Iraqis coerced us into supporting their war effort against the British. Young paramilitary gangs, neighbors and all sorts of other groups came to our home to collect money for the fight against the British. My parents were afraid that rebuffing them would invite charges of treason and identify us as British sympathizers. My parents were giving money to support the Nazis who intended to kill us along with the British whom we saw as our friends. In effect, we were giving money to bring about our own demise. It was difficult to make sense of what we were going through.

Baghdad's Jews collected large sums of humanitarian aid for the Red Crescent, the Muslim counterpart of the Red Cross. Under Jewish law, Jews are expected to help the wounded and otherwise needy, regardless of religion or nationality. Even beyond that, we were shaken down regularly to help pay for the war against the British.

My family had its own private terror, too.

There was a huge lot for storing scrap metal behind our house. During the day, British planes circled above the lot, no doubt checking whether it was a military depot. The lot, the size of an entire city block, probably looked like military target from the air. The Iraqis often placed military depots in civilian areas to deter the conscientious enemy from dropping bombs on them and inflicting civilian casualties.

Every night we were overcome by anxiety. "Do you think they will bomb the yard tonight?" we would ask each other, our eyes wide as we stared out into the darkness. Nobody was brave enough to mention our worst fear. If a bomb was dropped on the lot, it could hit our home. Even the force of a near miss could destroy our home. We were terrified of being buried alive under the rubble—especially since we knew the authorities wouldn't spend time or effort in digging us out. And so every night we waited and, when the bombs fell on other parts of the city, heaved a sigh of relief and went to sleep when the raid was over. In the end the British never bombed the lot behind our house.

One night, a second cousin of mine who lived a block away from us tried to turn on the radio. The house was in total darkness, as decreed by martial law. Our windows were covered with dark curtains, but we were still not allowed to turn on lights. When my cousin couldn't find the station he wanted, he turned the lights on for a split second just to see the radio dial. The military happened to be in the area. They banged on his door with the butts of their rifles. When he opened the door they arrested him.

"We know you are trying to establish telegraphic contact with the British to direct their air raids," they told him, as they dragged him outside his home.

There was a stream flowing in front of my cousin's home, and the soldiers took him there to kill him. He struggled with them. His brother ran quickly to the police station on the other side of the street. The police had not noticed what was happening, and didn't even know the military were in the area because the night was dark as pitch. To my cousin's good fortune, the police and the military were on bad terms. The police came in force, not so much to rescue my cousin, but to object to the military's infringement on their turf. Under cover of the ensuing skirmish, my cousin escaped.

During the coup period, my brother, my two sisters, and I suffered from stress-related illnesses. My sisters Muzli and Reyna couldn't retain any food. My brother Jacob and I developed symptoms of urinary-tract blockages. Jacob's case was much worse than mine. Only at night, when my father got him out of bed half asleep, was he able to urinate.

It was not always possible to see our family physician because of the disruption. Many establishments were shut down. My father had a hard time practicing law during that period. When he left the house for his office, we never knew if he would return. Terror was palpable in the atmosphere at home. I could even feel my father's worry, though he tried so hard to hide it.

On the surface, my father comported himself as a non-Zionist, but I suspected his heart was with those of us supporting the struggle for a Jewish homeland in Israel. His pretense seemed just that-- pretense. He had much to lose antagonizing the Iraqis. In addition to being an independent lawyer, he was a member of the Governing Council that oversaw the six central--and most important--provinces of Iraq, including Baghdad. Council members were elected pro forma; in practice they were appointed. My father was selected mainly because the Muslim who controlled appointments was an old friend of his, a moderate who eventually lost out to the forces of Arab nationalism. Because of my father's prominence, he couldn't risk being perceived as an enemy of Iraq. As a leader of the Jewish community, it would also have further endangered our community.

FARHOOD

On the last day of May, 1941 rumor had it that the

prime minister, Rasheed Ali, and the Mufti of Jerusalem had escaped to Germany—rumor that later proved correct. That day, my brother and I felt cooped up, and prevailed on Baba to take us for a walk by the Tigris in the early evening.

It was cool, and I was relieved to be out in the open. We drank in the scents of sweet grass and marigolds growing along the riverbank. Flocks of sparrows chirped above our heads. It was reassuring to see life around us, and it was soothing to stroll by the Tigris and watch its peaceful flow.

Then, without warning, a shot shattered the peace of the evening. I clutched my father's hand. His face mirrored the anxiety on mine. Jacob stood stock-still, and I could see that he, too, was alarmed. We didn't give voice to our anxiety, because that would mean admitting that something awful was happening or about to happen, something we didn't want to face. So we walked on, but our peaceful interlude was over. Jacob and I both walked as close to Baba as we could. It felt good to feel his hand enfold mine as we walked.

A few moments later, we heard the sound of a machine gun from close by. We could no longer ignore the potential danger. We turned in the direction of home and quickened our pace. I was terrified that somebody would kill my father. So many children had lost their parents. I didn't want to face my fear or think about what might be happening to cause it. Maybe it was the military causing the disturbance, but it could also be the mob. I didn't know which I feared most.

When we arrived home I could see the anxiety in my mother's eyes, and her relief that we were safe. Once we arrived there, we stayed at home. We didn't say much. We couldn't settle down to do anything. It was the eve of the Jewish holiday *sh'buoth*, but no one felt like celebrating. My father did recite the *kiddush* blessing and my mother and Jamila made half-hearted attempts to get us to eat.

We desperately wanted to believe that what we had heard was just one random shooting. We wanted to believe that with the removal of Rasheed Ali and his cohorts from power the worst was behind us. Yet the tension was thick in the very air we breathed.   On the eve of *sh'buoth* we usually gathered at Uncle Moshe's home to study sacred texts all night. But on that *sh'buoth* night we were afraid to venture out.

The following morning, we didn't attend the synagogue. A close friend of the family, Shlomo Gah'tan-- whom we reverently called Ammu Shlomo--dropped in to pay us the traditional holiday visit. Ammu Shlomo was a short, blond, blue-eyed man in his early sixties, a wealthy businessman who chose his words with great care. We children loved him like a grandfather. While Ammu Shlomo sat and chatted with us, the telephone rang. It was his wife, Amma Rahel. She had sent their car and driver to fetch Ammu Shlomo and drive him home. Violence was rampant in the Jewish areas of downtown Baghdad, she said, and she wanted Ammu Shlomo to come home.

We were all plunged into deep anxiety. No more pretending, no more wishful thinking. The call from Amma Rahel had said it all: The worst was not behind us; most likely it was ahead of us.

The government owned the radio station in Iraq, so we knew that nothing useful could be gleaned from the radio. The truth was never broadcast over the air. Even rumors, as uncertain as they were, tended to be more informative than the official broadcasts.

We lived in the modern part of Baghdad, where some streets were heavily Jewish, but where Muslims and Christians also lived. Downtown Baghdad, the old part of the city, was almost entirely Jewish. It was in that neighborhood that the massacre began. As the day wore on, we began to hear shots, but were still completely in the dark as to what was happening. We did know that when Rasheed Ali and his cronies escaped, they had left a vacuum in Baghdad. We had thought that the British had moved in to fill the vacuum. Instead, it now seemed that the mob was doing that.

We later learned that when the British had defeated the Iraqi army a few days before, they didn't return to Baghdad, but chose to stop at the outskirts of the city. The Muslim mob, joined by the Iraqi police and the military,

154

seized this opportunity to vent their frustration on Baghdad's Jewish community. Because the Jews had quietly supported the British against the Nazis, we were cast as scapegoats. The British had dealt the Iraqis a humiliating defeat and now the Iraqis would settle that account vicariously--by slaughtering the Jews.

Ever since the pro-Nazi government in Iraq had come to power, hatred for the Jews had been simmering to a slow boil. Now it was boiling over. We, however, had no idea that the police, the military, and the mob had joined forces and that inside the city the mob ruled. Some of those who survived the attacks told us later that the police would come to a Jewish house with the mob and shoot out the lock. Then the mob would break in to loot and kill. They would drag children out of the house and force them to watch as they massacred their parents before their eyes.

We could hear the screams as the mob drew closer to our part of town. It was progressing from downtown Baghdad to our part of the city. We remained locked in our home. My father barricaded the house, but we knew the barricades would be useless against the mob.

In Baghdad, on that *sh'buoth* day, we couldn't flee. There was no place to go. But I could feel my young body poised, ready for flight.

The mob didn't reach our part of town that day. Night fell. The mob's noise subsided. It was especially dark because all the streetlights were turned off, as they had been during the entire period when Iraq was at war with the British. But we could see the pale moon in the sky. It was now the second night of *sh'buoth*. That was a dreadful night, and I don't think any one of us slept. We were cut off from any news of what was happening. We tried to act normally. Meals were prepared, but nobody ate much, and we children wandered about aimlessly.

Rumors flew among our Jewish neighbors the next day. The thrust of all we heard let us know that chaos reigned. The previous day the mob had attacked Jewish homes, and there had been enormous massacres of Jews in the older part of the city.

155

By midmorning the fearful noise resumed. It got louder as the day wore on. The mob was approaching our neighborhood.

Mama was overwhelmed. Her way of avoiding acknowledgment of the danger was to take a nap. When she woke up in the early afternoon, her cheeks were red, and she looked so innocent and beautiful. I didn't want her to be killed. She looked at me with sleep still clouding her eyes.

"Do we have any news, any news at all?" she asked.

I shook my head. But we both could hear the sounds of the mob and the whistle of the shots getting closer. They were probably no more than a block or two from our home, and we knew what that meant. Even then we didn't want to think about what was happening. My mother held out her arms and I fell into them.

My father had a book of Psalms open, silently reading from it, as he always did when he sought comfort. There was an overriding mood of helplessness. The mob could easily break the locks on our doors at any moment.

We waited and waited frozen in fear, and when the unexpected happened we couldn't at first take it in. We looked at each other in disbelief as we heard the shouts of the mob diminishing and falling silent. We heard horses outside and rushed to the windows to see mounted troops patrolling our street. We later learned these were military regiments loyal to the Regent, who had returned to Baghdad two days before. The British and the Regent had apparently decided that the massacre and chaos had gone far enough. The Regent had directed the units loyal to him to bring order, by whatever means necessary. The regiments had managed to stop the mob in its tracks. It was late in the afternoon of the second day of *sh'buoth*, but it seemed as if centuries had passed since we had heard the sound of those first shots on the eve of the holiday. We thanked God for our deliverance, for the arrival of the troops.

Years later I read what actually transpired that day. Were it not for a fortunate convergence of circumstances, the Regent's troops wouldn't have made it to our part of town before the mob. Our home might have been invaded, and my family and I might have been massacred along with the rest.

The marauders didn't reach our home because they first spent time returning to their own homes to stash the loot stolen earlier from Jews. They wanted to secure their new riches, and the weight of the stolen goods slowed them down.

It took days before we felt safe enough to venture outside. Only then did we learn the extent of the death and destruction the mob had inflicted on the Jewish community of Baghdad.

Within the next few days we heard from other members of our extended family. My maternal Uncle Guerji had gone to work on the first day of the massacre, not knowing what was taking place downtown. We didn't know he had gone to his office and were too afraid to walk the two blocks to my grandmother's house to check on her and my uncle. Uncle Guerji told us he had left his office and headed home in the early afternoon of that day. The buses were not running, and the streets were chaotic, crowded with looters and gunmen. His office messenger, a Muslim, gave my uncle his uniform and turban, so that he would look like a Muslim. My uncle wore sunglasses to further disguise himself. The messenger escorted my uncle all the way from his downtown office to my grandmother's home.

"I was so grateful for his company," Uncle Guerji told us, "as we walked through Rasheed Street and through the milling crowds. There were bullets flying all around. I shivered as I heard the bullets hiss through the air, but, thank God, no bullet hit either one of us."

He went on to tell how he had been stopped several times by hoodlums and looters, how he had responded to their queries in the Muslim dialect and how they had then allowed him to proceed unharmed, believing he was a Muslim.

"I am lucky to be alive," my uncle concluded as my mother sighed, and I knew she was thinking of the many others who had not been so lucky.

I remember thinking that my Uncle Guerji had served his country well as an honest civil servant. How could it be that his life was now in danger, just because he was Jewish? How could it be that we were all in danger of being killed, just because we were Jews?

Uncle Guerji's messenger was a reliable friend who probably saved his life. Not all of the Muslims who had professed to be our friends were as trustworthy.

Across the street from our home was a public school. A Muslim family who looked after the school lived there. They weren't rich, and we often shared food with them and gave them clothing. Our home was open to them, and we thought of them as our friends.

In the afternoon of the second day of *sh'buoth*, when the mob was getting closer and we could hear their cries of triumph, the Muslim family washed the steps in front of the school and came out to sit there. Among themselves they talked loudly about the neighboring Jewish homes, including ours. They discussed which members of their family would go to which Jewish home with the mob and participate in the looting. They had assigned two members of their family to our house.

They saw us on our second floor balcony, where we had ventured out to try to see what was going on. They knew we could hear every word they said, but that didn't disturb them. They continued to talk openly about their plan to loot our home. To them we were as good as dead and no longer of any account. It still hurts me to remember how Mama used to call them "our good neighbors." I admired her for greeting them with a smile a few days later, when they knocked on our door asking for medicine for a sick baby.

I would like to think the British took back control of Iraq in order to prevent Jews from being massacred. But, if that were their aim, they would have moved on Baghdad sooner than they did. The fact is that the only sure way the British could count on access to Iraqi oil was to control Iraq. But, even though we knew the British acted out of self-interest, we still saw them as our rescuers.

Following their return to Baghdad after the Iraqi coup, the British kept a tight hold on Iraq. They pressured the Iraqis into declaring war against Nazi Germany. The Iraqis complied, but their hearts were not in it, and they cheered whenever the Nazis won a battle.

In our synagogue, I met Jews among the British airmen who moved into Baghdad. They were dressed in their military uniforms when they came to worship with us during the high holidays. They were treated with love and affection and given the seats of honor as treasured sons of the community. They were young and fresh and wholesome and sometimes a little awkward, but they were always respectful and polite.

There was an outpouring of love for the British. They were our friends; but the fact that there were Jews among them standing side by side with the rest of the British people made me very proud. This was a new experience for us—a realization that there were countries where Jews were treated as equal to other members of society. Seeing this first hand strengthened my resolve to leave Iraq one day.

I am not sure if the Jewish soldiers from England recognized how much our lives were circumscribed by living in predominantly Muslim Baghdad. But it was clear to me that their lives were not hindered by living in a Christian society. The seeds of my conviction that the majority in any society should respect minorities were sown, oddly, in Baghdad, a city in which that idea had no credence.

Order was restored as a result of the British presence in Baghdad, but we continued to live uneasily as a hated minority in a Muslim world.

Not long after the big massacre of *sh'buoth*, 1941, it was rumored there was going to be another one, even worse. Some Jews armed themselves. An older friend of mine bought a big handgun. He told me if the mob took over again, he was going into the street to shoot anyone who attacked Jewish homes.

Terrible fears returned. There were intermittent rumors that the mob was coming again. On one occasion, when the rumors held the ring of truth, and Jews wouldn't venture out of their homes, my brother and I started boiling water in the bedroom upstairs near the second-floor balcony, which overlooked the front entrance. We planned to toss bottles of boiling water on the mob when it came to attack our house. I remember the terror that rose in my throat, as we were boiling the water. We knew our tactic wouldn't stem the tide of violence; indeed it would probably further inflame the mob and result in our being tortured before being put to death. But we couldn't sit around feeling helpless; we had to do something to protect our home.

We felt safe pursuing our plan because Baba was downstairs reading the Psalms. We poured the first pan of boiling water into the bottles.

"This will teach them not to mess with the Jews," Jacob said bravely.

I nodded in agreement and began to refill the pan with fresh water.

"What are you boys doing?" I looked up and saw Baba standing in the doorway.

"When the mob gets to our home we're going to toss bottles of boiling water on them. That will stop them in their tracks."

A strange look passed over my father's face. I couldn't interpret it - maybe it reflected a mixture of pride and fear. But then his face settled into a look I more easily identified - one of sternness mingled with sadness.

"As I have told you, children, Jews don't kill."

"But it's self-defense," I protested. "The mob is coming to kill us."

"You can't be sure the mob will kill us. Unless you are one hundred percent sure, you can't attack."

It was a tortured argument, and I guess Baba knew it.

"So we have to wait until we are dead before we can fight back, do we?"

My father didn't reprove me.

"Empty the bottles, son."

I wanted to remind my father that the Maccabees fought back even on the Sabbath, but Jacob was already emptying the bottles.

Was it possible my father was wiping tears from his eyes as he turned to leave the room? No doubt it was heartbreaking to see his sons driven to violence by violence. It took me a while to realize that he was not so much worried about violating Jewish law; rather, he feared that an enflamed mob would torture brazen children who chose to fight back with boiling water—the same fear that tormented me.

NARROW ESCAPE

As I look back, I realize the 1941 massacre was actually an intense manifestation of the terror that permeated our lives before and afterwards. We couldn't ignore the *farhood*. It was massive. But living in Baghdad, we tended to subconsciously bury—perhaps as a defense mechanism-- many of the specific incidents of violence and hatred toward us.

One such incident took place in the spring of 1940, one year before the *farhood*. I was eight and riding the bus home from school with Jacob, Helwa, and Latifa. It was a day when my father's messenger, Saleem, was not able to escort us for protection.

The bus made its way down Rasheed Street, Baghdad's main thoroughfare, dropping off passengers every few minutes. Our stop was the one right after the bus turned left off Rasheed Street, where Rasheed Street met the Tigris boardwalk. On this particular day, we children and one tall Jewish man, perhaps in his early thirties, were the only people left on the bus by the time the bus reached the boardwalk. As the bus turned left, we made sure we had our belongings in hand, ready for our bent-over exit from the bus. We didn't want to get up until the last possible minute.

As the bus approached our stop, the driver braked and we got up to go. Suddenly we were thrown back on our seats as the driver sped up again.

"Stop! Stop!" we yelled in unison, but the driver ignored us. Instead, he went faster and faster. The bus headed toward the deserted section of a very long road past all of the unaware houses, including our maternal grandmother's house. I looked at Jacob in dismay. Where was the driver taking us? Jacob, thirteen years old at the time, looked pale and worried. What would our grandmother think, if she knew what was happening to us? What would our parents do, if we didn't arrive home ever again?

The bus sped past the long park on our left and then, beyond the park, into a deserted part of the road, so dangerous that we had never seen it before. Now we were too terrified to take note of it. I know there were tall trees and lots of undergrowth. We clung to each other, as the trees seemed to race past the bus.

I looked back at the conductor who was sitting on his special seat staring stone-faced ahead. He had to know what the driver's plan was. He held the door handle tightly, probably to make sure no one could open the door and jump out. My heart sank when I realized what was happening.

We were being kidnapped.

Jacob, Helwa, Latifa and I moved closer to each other as we hurtled into the unknown.

Suddenly a voice broke the silence.

"Stop this bus right now!"

It was the Jewish man who was sitting right behind the driver. But the driver didn't even slow down.

The man, who was probably a plumber, took a huge wrench out of a battered bag he had at his feet. He raised the wrench over the driver's head. His face was red and the veins stood out on his forehead, but to me he looked like a protecting angel.

"Stop now or I'll split your head open!" he yelled at the driver.

The bus screeched to a halt, and the man, still holding the wrench, ordered the conductor to unlock the door and get out of the bus. He then watched us get off the bus before he himself got off.

Shaken, we set out on foot, a three-mile walk we had not expected to take when we left home that morning. It was a walk that the bus driver had not expected us to take either.

I looked at my sisters. They were so beautiful. I didn't want to think about what could have happened to them. I glanced behind me. Our rescuer, carrying his heavy bag on his shoulder, was walking slowly a good distance behind us.

"That man was brave." I said.

Jacob nodded and I could tell he admired the man, too.

"He would have killed the driver and the conductor, both. The Jews from the poorer section of town are a lot bolder than we are."

Jacob's remark was borne out just a year later. During the *farhood* when the mob approached our prosperous neighborhood, we found ourselves totally unprepared. We had no idea how to defend ourselves. We were sheep ready to be slaughtered. In the poorer section of the city, however, the Jews fought back. My father's messenger Saleem, a Jew who lived in that section, told us that when the mob came, he and his neighbors tore down a wall in his home. They carried the bricks from the wall up to their rooftop and threw them at the mob. They injured several of their attackers, including one policeman. The mob retreated.

World War II came to an end, the Nazis were defeated and the Jews in Europe who survived the concentration camps were liberated. The Arabs established the Arab League, a postwar pact between Arab nations whose battle cry was "Save Palestine," meaning from the Jews. The United Nations began considering the fate of the Jewish settlement in Palestine. Now, as we pinned our hopes on the establishment of a Jewish state in Palestine, the *Hagganah*, the Jewish underground that later became Israel Defense Force, took on new life.

The *Hagganah* broadcast underground news from Palestine in Arabic, but the Iraqis prohibited us from listening to it. We would hide with our radio in the far end of our basement, way in the back of the house, to listen to the news. We sat ever so close to the radio, so that the volume could be kept as low as possible. Those times with our Jewish brethren in Palestine were more important to us than our daily meals. We were filled with hope at the thought that the one thing we always prayed for would come to pass, and we would join our coreligionists on the other side of the divide in a Jewish state, all our own.

In Baghdad the government-orchestrated mistreatment of Jews reached new heights. Increasingly, we suffered the consequences of the conflict between the Jews and the Arabs in Palestine. The Iraqis were infuriated that the Jews dared to want a homeland of their own, and they organized demonstrations against Zionism. Each time a demonstration was held protesting the so-called Zionists in Palestine, Jewish shops in Baghdad were looted, Jewish gatherings were attacked, and individual Jews were beaten in the streets.

It was evident that it was not in Britain's interest that Israel be established as a state. Britain depended on Arab oil. It suited its purposes to appease the Arabs, and the Arabs were very much opposed to the founding of a Jewish state.

We no longer regarded the British as our saviors; for in the matter of Israel they were taking the side of the Arabs. In fact, when Israel became independent, the British Broadcasting Corporation took its cue from the Arab press and referred to Israel in their Arabic radio programs as "the supposed Israel." We couldn't trust the Arabic news broadcasts, and now we felt we couldn't trust the BBC, which regurgitated the news broadcast by the Arabs. It was a very lonely time.

After World War II, the Jewish community in Palestine had its own battle over British limitations on Jewish immigration into Palestine. The help the Jews in Palestine were receiving from people in the U.S. contrasted sharply with the active opposition of the British government. But would the American help be enough? Were the Jews in Palestine strong and determined? I, like my classmates, quietly contributed money, through the local Zionist underground, to help the Jewish community in Palestine. We wanted to go to Palestine and join our coreligionists in their struggle for independence. But we were not allowed to leave Iraq.

A BEACON OF FREEDOM

I am not sure if many people realize how devastating it is to be deprived of information about what is happening in the outside world.

The news blackout the Iraqis imposed after the establishment of the State of Israel was a dark time. We were deprived of access to papers other than those published in Arab countries. All radio broadcasts, other than those coming from Arab countries and the Arabic program on the BBC, were jammed. Looking back now, I liken the sense of utter isolation we felt then to slow strangulation.

When Iraq and the rest of the Arab countries went to war in 1948 to thwart the establishment of Israel, news came in on the Arab stations: "We have smashed the Jews here, and we have destroyed them there." On the first day of the Arab assault the Iraqi radio announced that the Iraqis had occupied a large part of what was to become Israel. On hearing this, my mother fell apart. She just sat and sobbed. The Arab radio stations reported one victory after another. The thrust of the news was that the Jewish settlement in Israel was being wiped out. We were doomed. The Jews would never have a homeland.

There were families among us who had sons and daughters in Israel serving in the *Hagganah, Irgun Tsvaee Leumi,* and the *Stern* underground groups. The news was so bad that those families prepared to sit *shib'a* for their loved ones in Israel.

Still, some lapses and inconsistencies in the Arab news reports began to make us wonder. One day the news reported that the Iraqi army had occupied Kokhav Aveer, a settlement in Israel. A day later came radio reports that the Iraqi artillery was shelling Kokhav Aveer. When I went to school, I asked my classmate Joshua Ezekiel if he had heard the same two reports as I had.

Joshua just grinned. He, too, had noticed the inconsistency. Why would they bomb Kokhav Aveer if it were in their hands, we wondered. They either never seized it, as they claimed, or lost it in the meantime, but wouldn't say so. We both shook our heads. Maybe the Iraqis weren't doing as well as they claimed.

We needed to know the facts and trusted the *Hagganah* radio to give them to us. But every time my siblings and I went to listen to the *Hagganah* station, we could hear only the first few opening sentences identifying the station. After that, there was nothing but static. We slapped the radio; we moved our heads closer; we changed the location of the radio. Nothing helped.

The Arab news media were telling lies, but we couldn't separate the falsehoods from the truth. Even the news from London was twisted. We wanted to know if our brethren in Israel were being decimated, as the Arab press had reported. We needed to look elsewhere for the truth.

Baghdad had three foreign centers of information: the French, the British, and the American. On orders of the Iraqi government, the British and the French centers shut down. The U.S. Information Center didn't comply with the order, and remained open. It maintained a large library and several reading rooms filled with current issues of American newspapers as well as weekly and monthly magazines. We turned there for honest reporting.

I don't know whether the American people were ever aware of the great service they rendered to humanity by establishing U.S. Information Centers around the world or how grateful we were for the unequivocal stand the center in Baghdad took by refusing to shut down. For people who live in open societies with a free press, our starvation for information must be difficult to grasp.

We knew agents of the Iraqi secret police were planted across the street from the Center, and we worried. If they caught us or took our pictures, that would be the end for us and for our families. We tried to sneak in without being noticed.

In the New York Times and other newspapers in the Center's reading room I read a completely different story from the one the Arab press had been feeding us. The Jews in Palestine were not being defeated. They were holding their own. In fact, they were winning. What a relief!

My friends and I had to be careful leaving the Center in order to avoid being noticed by the Iraqi secret service. Our strategy was to gather together inside the door and then burst through onto the street, running and fanning out in different directions. We felt this way the secret police would be taken by surprise and, before they could gather their wits, we would disappear. It was an adventure that could have had dire consequences. But we were desperate for truthful news.

EXECUTION OF SHAFEEK ADAS

On the day Israel was declared a state (May 14, 1948), Iraq declared martial law and set up military courts. A new government was formed, and Sadeq el Bassam was appointed Defense Minister in charge of martial law. My father was stunned at the news of Bassam's appointment. He told us that Bassam hated the Jews, and that he was known for his virulent anti-Jewish speeches. Under Bassam's leadership, the criminal code was revised, greatly stiffening penalties for those accused of Zionism. Sentences ranged from a minimum of seven years imprisonment to death. Since the military courts judged on the evidence of two witnesses, anyone who held a grudge against a Jew, or was inclined to take revenge on a Jew, could find a second witness to testify that the Jew in question was a Zionist. No appeal of military court decisions was allowed.

Martial law lasted nineteen months. During the intervening months, members of our community were arrested en masse and accused of being Zionist agents for the flimsiest of reasons: a prayer book printed in Jerusalem, a prayer shawl with a star of David sewn on it, or an amulet with Aramaic inscriptions. Arrested Jews were taken away and tortured. Some returned with broken bones. Some returned invalids for life. And some never returned.

Many Jews were sentenced to long-term imprisonment; others were required to pay enormous "fines" to avoid prison. Uncle Moshe was arrested and charged with distributing Zionist leaflets. He was to be tried and sentenced under martial law. My uncle was not involved in any Zionist activity, and no Zionist leaflets or any such evidence was seized or produced as evidence. Had it not been for the intervention of Supreme Court Justice Al Aaraj, at the behest of my father, Uncle Moshe would have suffered the same fate as others who were accused of Zionism. Al Aaraj, who ordered Uncle Moshe's immediate release, was an old friend of my father.

The secret police raided Jewish homes in the early morning hours. The raids would begin with banging on the door with rifle butts. Sometimes the agents simply broke down the door. It was a favorite practice of the dreaded Criminal Investigation Department, or CID, to round up the Jewish children during those raids and force them to watch, as they bludgeoned their father or beat and kicked their mother. I spent sleepless nights worrying. I didn't know how I could stand to see my parents being violated. I dreaded the night for the raid it might bring; I was afraid to leave the house during the day for fear of being noticed by the police.

There was nothing we could do to stem the reign of terror that swept through the country. Every day we heard of new atrocities committed against members of our community. I remember in particular the hanging of a wealthy Jewish entrepreneur, Shafeek Adas, who lived in Basra. His death hit close to home, for he was a man I knew.

Adas was a multimillionaire businessman, the exclusive agent of the Ford Motor Company in Iraq and a partner in a closely held corporation that bought and sold surplus. I had met him a few years before his death at a lunch gathering in a Jewish club in Basra. I remember him as lively and personable; the gathering seemed alive and happy largely because of his presence. My father told me of the great sorrow Adas had in his life. His six-year old youngest son was retarded, but he loved that son as much as the child loved him.

Adas was arrested and accused of selling surplus goods to Israel – goods that he bought from the British and the American military, and sold to Italy for transshipment to

Israel. Mutual friends, who could see the handwriting on the wall, later told my father they had urged Adas to call the Regent and ask for help. Adas was well connected, with powerful friends. But Adas didn't take their advice because, they said, he was unwilling to believe that he was really in trouble.

Fresh rumors began circulating not long after that: Now Adas was said to have sold Israel the tanks that it used to defeat the Iraqi army in 1948. I don't know if Israel possessed tanks during the 1948 war. But the rumor was a manifestation of something I noticed many times among Iraqis during my years growing up: the unwillingness to accept responsibility for failure and the fear of critical self-examination. The tendency was to find a scapegoat or search for a convenient excuse for the failure.

The entrepreneur Shafeek Adas
Hung by the Iraqis in 1948 on trumped-up charges.

Now the Iraqi newspapers and radio latched onto the theme that Mr. Adas was the person who had caused Iraq to lose the war with Israel, and we repeatedly heard the radio commentators demand his head. Adas was tried and convicted of helping Israel win the war against Iraq. He was to be hung on gallows constructed in the front yard of a mansion he was in the process of building. He would never live in that house, and the authorities wanted him to see his unrealized dream house with his dying eyes.

My family and I listened, horrified, to the live broadcast of his execution in gory detail. The radio reported Mr. Adas was remarkably composed as he was led to the gallows, but collapsed when he saw his retarded son brought by the police to watch his hanging. The hanging was prolonged by the soldiers who, several times, pulled him back from the brink of death while the watching crowd screamed its delight.

Adas was hanged on August 23, 1948. All of his assets were confiscated, and his vaunted Ford agency was taken over by a Muslim. Adas owned only 15% of the shares of the surplus corporation accused of supplying tanks to Israel.

In the fall of 1949, a Jewish high school student in Baghdad was arrested and accused of being a Zionist. He was tortured until he agreed to "co-operate" and name his collaborators. The police took him to Jewish schools and asked him to identify his "collaborators" from among the students. Many of those he singled out were known among their classmates to be apolitical. Some in the Jewish community felt he was pointing to people at random, just to save his skin, to avoid further torture. I dreaded the thought of that young man coming to our school. I never knew when he would be brought there and point to me as a collaborator. I don't think I worried so much about what that would do to my life, although I worried plenty about torture. I worried about what my arrest would do to my parents and the rest of my family.

The wave of arrests pushed thousands of terrorized families to seek to leave the country. Jews couldn't legally leave Iraq, so they turned to professional smugglers who specialized in getting criminals out of the country. Several of my classmates and a cousin of mine turned to the smugglers for help.

The escape routes were through Kurdistan in northern Iraq and then across the mountains to Iran. To conceal the Jewish identity of the escapees, smugglers had them wear turbans or Kurdish caps and Bedouin or Kurdish attire. The escapees either walked or rode on donkeys as they crossed through the mountains with the help of their handlers. This was how my two nephews, Rony and Emile, were smuggled out of Iraq. Among my memorabilia, I have a Kurdish cap that Rony's handlers had given him when he hid in the home of a Kurdish family in northern Iraq.

During the late forties, rumors circulated that the Iraqi government was considering an exchange of population - Jews going to Israel and Palestinians moving to Iraq to take their place. If it ever existed, the plan never came to fruition. However, five thousand Palestinian refugees came to Baghdad about the time of the mass exodus of Jews; Jewish dwellings and synagogues, including the synagogue I grew up in, were seized and turned over to them.

The Palestinians refugees were not allowed to work, perhaps out of fear they might compete with Iraqis. The Palestinians had a reputation of being more enterprising than the Iraqis. Somehow, one Palestinian family received permission to open an ice-cream parlor. It became so successful that it captured the clientele of all the ice-cream parlors in downtown Baghdad. Whenever I passed by the Palestinian parlor--which I was actually afraid to visit--it was jammed with customers, while neighboring ice cream shops were deserted. Not long after, the government withdrew the license of the Palestinian parlor and shut it down for good.

PULLING TOGETHER

Through those days my parents showed no outward inclination to leave Iraq. My father, I know, kept hoping for the best, praying that better days lay ahead, with my mother, as always, supporting him. For better or worse, this was the hope that allowed my parents' generation, as well earlier generations, to survive the difficult spells they had lived through – the hope that the storm would pass and a more peaceful life would return. They focused on the good they could remember and tried hard to purge from their mind the harsh treatment they had encountered. It was as if they had been conditioned to see the violence against them as a normal part of life. Jews had to put up with episodes of violence, as if this was all that Jews could or should expect from life.

I realized, too, that as one of the Jewish community's leaders, my father felt duty-bound to remain and support that community as long as it survived in Baghdad. Then too, he was a sixty-one-year-old lawyer practicing under the Iraqi legal system. Leaving the country would have required starting again from scratch – not an easy task for a man of his age.

We could sense our parents' unease, mingled with the tenuous hope that the terror would end, that it would never touch our family. But every night I fell into an uneasy sleep, waiting for that battering knock on the door. Though my father had not visited Israel since the mid-forties, up to that time he had visited Palestine almost annually. He owned a large lot on Mount Scopus in East Jerusalem that he had purchased in 1920 for two hundred pounds sterling. In the years following the death of King Faisal I in 1933, Jewish association with Palestine, including ownership of land there, became grounds for arrest and imprisonment. My father's land had become a liability; there was no telling what would happen if someone were to unearth records of his lot in Jerusalem. I fervently wished my father would decide to leave. Anything was better than waiting for terror to arrive at our door.

I don't know what instinctively drove me to resist the mistreatment we endured in Iraq—or why I didn't accept the situation, as my immediate family and ancestors always had. Accommodation was not my way. I simply couldn't be party to injustice, and couldn't push aside the horrors with vague hopes of better times ahead.

1948 faded into 1949, and Israel had been in existence for a whole year. On the eve of the first anniversary of the nation's birth, the Jewish underground distributed copies of the text of a new *kiddush* text written for the first

172

yom haatsmaout, Israel's day of independence. The day of Israel's rebirth was now a holy day to be sanctified.

It was dangerous for a Jew in Iraq to be caught with any document about Israel, particularly one that sanctified the day of its creation. But I tucked my copy of the *kiddush* blessing carefully in my notebook, and prayed to make it home safely with it. Once at home, I set up the *mady*, laying out the customary loaves of Iraqi bread. I placed the saltcellar beside the bread, covering the bread with an embroidered cloth. Then I filled the *kiddush* cup with grape juice and set it on the table.

When my father came home that evening, he looked serious and was unusually silent. He looked at the table I had prepared and still didn't say a word. It was I who broke the silence.

"I have the *kiddush* ready, Baba," I said, as I handed him the text for the new *kiddush*, ending with the *Shehehiyyanu* blessing that was recited on special occasions.

To my utter amazement, my ostensibly non-Zionist father took the *kiddush* cup in hand and recited the blessing as written in the text I had gotten from the underground. I looked at him with new understanding. He read the clandestine text without a word of protest and in tones that told me he meant every word he uttered.

At the conclusion of the *kiddush* recitation, I went up to my father to give him the customary kiss on his hands before drinking from the *kiddush* cup. He looked at me, I felt, with pride. We didn't exchange words. But our silence spoke volumes. Now I knew. We were both pulling in the same direction. In spite of all appearances, Baba's heart was with our brethren in Israel.

EXODUS

On the eve of *purim*, March 9, 1950, at the peak of a stretch of relentless terror, the Iraqi Parliament decreed that Jews wishing to leave Iraq would be permitted to file an exit petition during the following year. The statute stipulated that those who filed a petition would forfeit their citizenship, but it was silent on other important questions. It didn't state, for example, whether the petitioner would for sure be allowed to leave Iraq. Prior to this, a public declaration by a Jew of the intention to leave Iraq was tantamount to treason, and the community worried that the new law might be a set-up. Could the statute be a ploy by the Iraqi authorities to flush out the "Zionists" for torture or execution?

The statute was also silent on what would happen to the petitioners' assets. Would they be forfeited along with citizenship, or could they be cashed in before departure? While many of us were troubled by what the statute left unsaid, none of us shed tears at the prospect of losing our Iraqi citizenship. But the leadership of the community worried about the legal implications of the loss of citizenship. According to international law, an individual stripped of his citizenship reverts automatically to the citizenship he had before, or to that of his ancestors. But it was a different story with us. We were there from time immemorial and had no other citizenship to fall back on. Without Iraqi citizenship, we became stateless. Where would we go? With the exception of Israel, no country accepted stateless people. Most of us wanted to go to Israel, but Iraq had declared war on our hoped-for homeland.

And so the leadership of the Jewish community agonized about the fate of those who would leave Iraq. The destruction of European Jewry during World War II was on everyone's mind. Did a similar fate await the Babylonian Jews?

The British government offered to permit the airplanes flying the   Jewish émigrés to land in Cyprus, but wouldn't allow the émigrés to remain in Cyprus. We didn't know what would happen next.

Some three months after the passage of the exit statute, the first two British Airways planes carrying Jewish immigrants took off from Baghdad's airport and headed for Cyprus. From there, unbeknownst to the Iraqi government (and to any of us), the planes quietly continued on to Llyda airport in Israel. Later flights, although this was not publicized or officially sanctioned, went directly from Baghdad to Llyda airport.

At Mis'ouda Shemtob Synagogue's registration center, Baghdad -
Jews wishing to file petitions to leave Iraq, waiting in courtyard for the petition office
to open. This center is where my father filed my petition to leave Iraq

You knew something was coming to an end. Our once-vibrant community was disappearing. The long lines that had always formed in front of the bakery on Friday mornings were dwindling. The streets and sidewalks were emptied of life. The light-hearted crowds that had always paraded along the Tigris riverbank on the Sabbath had by now thinned to almost nothing.

For those left behind in Iraq, there was great difficulty learning whether loved ones had in fact arrived in Israel.

Letters couldn't be sent from Israel to Iraq; that would open the recipients to the charge of espionage by the Iraqi authorities. Moreover, since the Iraqis censored all letters addressed to Jews, no mention could be made in any letter about arrival in Israel. So simple codes were devised between those who flew out of Iraq and the families that stayed behind. An example might be the phrase, "I just bought a pair of shoes." People who arrived in Israel communicated with relatives or friends in Sydney, London, Paris, or New York. They in turn wrote to families in Iraq, including in their letter the innocuous sentence "I just bought a pair of shoes." In this way, the recipient in Baghdad got confirmation that their loved one had arrived safely in Israel.

Jews waiting outside Meir Twaig Synagogue petition center, Baghdad, 1950
Meir Twaig was the only standing synagogue found by US invading forces in 2003.

In the fall of 1950, letters containing the prearranged codes began to trickle back to Iraq from France and other countries. At that point, the pace of registrations to leave Iraq accelerated. By March 9, 1951, the date on which the exit statute was due to expire, close to ninety percent of the 140,000 to 150,000 members of Iraq's Jewish community had filed an exit petition. My sisters Muzli, Reyna, Helwa and

Latifa filed to leave a few months after I did. My parents, Jacob, and Valentine came several years later. Jamila didn't emigrate until 1973. So my beloved, motherly sister and I had no face-to-face contact for 22 years.

During the one-year window for exit petitions, the Iraqi authorities allowed very few petitioners to leave the country. This first handful of émigrés was allowed to dispose of their assets before they left the country. Unfortunately, no one saw the trap being set by the Iraqi government, how this liberal policy was designed to lull the remaining Jews into complacency. Most Jews who signed the exit petition were left with the impression that they, too, would be allowed to liquidate their immovable assets and wind up their affairs before leaving. Practically no one disposed of his home or liquidated his business before signing the exit petition. People reckoned that, with the slow pace of flights out of Baghdad, it would take decades before their turn to leave the country would come.

And so it was a shock to all of us when, on the day the statute expired, the Iraqi authorities cut off all phone lines and closed all banks for three days. We didn't understand what was happening. Gradually the plot became clear. When the banks reopened and the telephones hummed again we discovered all assets of the Jews who had filed an exit petition had been seized. Under a new "Decree for the Control and Management of Assets of Denaturalized Iraqis," Iraq's Custodian General was ordered "to lay hands" on all property belonging to anyone who had signed an exit petition and to "administer, dispose and liquidate it." Over one hundred and twenty thousand Jews were left without means. Overnight, millionaires became paupers.

Once they had seized the Jewish assets, the Iraqi authorities accelerated the pace of the flights. Now, instead of one plane leaving every two or three weeks, as has been the practice before the Iraqis seized our assets, twelve planes packed with Jewish immigrants left daily from Baghdad's airport. The flights came to an end in August 1951.

I was on one of those flights. My immigrant number was 14296. I left for Israel on April 1, 1951.

177

The period preceding my flight from Iraq was a time of enormous anxiety for me. How many more weeks or months would it take before I would reach safety? Would I ever really make it out? There was talk among Iraqis that by allowing the Jews to leave the country, Iraq was providing Israel's military with recruits that would turn their guns against Iraq. Might the government decide to call off the exodus? That was not unthinkable; the Iraqis were known to pass laws only to ignore them or to reverse them without notice.

During the three-week period between the expropriation of Jewish assets and the day I flew out of Iraq, I mostly stayed at home to avoid being noticed. On the few occasions I went out, I walked the streets with trepidation. The Jewish "traitors" who had registered to leave Iraq gave the police and the mob an excuse, if any were needed, for a new type of harassment. Ordinary Muslims, not just the police, stopped Jewish men and women on the street, searched them and took what they found in their pockets, on the grounds that the government had seized the assets of those who had filed an exit petition. No one bothered to check whether the person being searched had indeed filed such a petition. And I doubt that anything seized from the pockets of the Jews on the street ever found its way to the government.

My own prize possession was the stamp collection that my father had given me. His collection included stamps from the time of the Ottoman period, as well as from the time when the British occupied Iraq in 1917. For a short while, the British had used the same postage stamps issued by the Ottoman Empire, printed with the added words "IRAQ in British Occupation," along with the new value of each stamp. In a few cases the word IRAQ was replaced by the word BAGHDAD. Those stamps were rare. Baba had a few in his collection, and I wanted to protect his valuable stamps in a safe place, away from our home.

One day, I put these stamps in my pockets and took the downtown bus to my father's office. He had not applied to leave Iraq, and I felt it would be safe to keep his collection in his office. I was relieved when the bus finally reached its destination. I had only a few yards to walk to the office. But my nervousness must have given me away. No sooner had I stepped off the bus than a tall, heavyset Muslim, who had just passed by me, turned and demanded to know what I had in my pockets. I froze, speechless. "My goose is cooked," I thought. The man was going to take the stamps, and then who knows what would happen next – perhaps he would turn me over to the police, and that would be the end of my dream of leaving Iraq.

Stamps issued by the British immediately after their occupation of Iraq in 1917. (The "An" stands for Ana, an Ottoman currency unit, roughly equivalent to one penny)

The man frisked me, but never put his hands in my pockets to see what I had. He then asked if I had any money on me. I said I didn't. I had taken just enough change to pay for a one-way bus fare. I couldn't believe my eyes when he accepted my answer, turned around and walked away.

It was fortunate that the whole incident didn't last long enough for a crowd of curious spectators to gather around and attack me. In disbelief, I headed for my father's office, where he kept the stamps in his safe. He brought them with him when he, my mother and brother came to Israel seven years later and gave them back to me.

My lucky escape with the stamps didn't quiet my feelings of uneasiness. I had trouble sleeping during the weeks that preceded my flight from Baghdad. I dreamed of the police breaking into our home and throwing me in jail for declaring my desire to leave Iraq. I dreamed of being dragged out of the plane by CID agents, just as it was about to take off. My sleeplessness got worse as the immigrant numbers got closer to mine. My pain at leaving my family grew sharper. I wanted to leave, but knowing that I would be cut off from my parents weighed on my heart. I wouldn't be able to communicate with them once I got to Israel. Iraq was at war with Israel, and the Iraqis punished those who received communications from "the enemy" with long prison terms and torture. Sadly, in those times children were forced to choose between their parents and their desire to live as free human beings.

The March 9, 1950 law allowed denaturalized Iraqi Jews to take with them fifty dinars per person when they left the country. Rumor had it that some of the airport inspectors were regularly confiscating these funds before allowing Jewish immigrants to board the plane. That didn't bother me. I didn't care about money. I just wanted to leave the country alive. But it did bother my father; he worried that I might arrive penniless in Israel.

One morning, I was in his room, watching him get ready for work. He put his arm around my shoulder and told me he was worried that they might take my fifty dinars at the airport. I said I didn't care. Without waiting for my answer, Baba took off his wedding ring and asked me to wear it. He said there might be less chance losing the ring than cash. I was aghast. "I can't take it," I told him. He had not taken off that ring since his wedding day. I couldn't entertain the thought of ever taking it away from him. But I also understood his concern and what he was struggling with. Like the rest of us, my father felt helpless in dealing with the organized theft and the inspectors' lawlessness at Baghdad's airport.

I gave him a hug. He put his wedding ring back on. I never forgot the tenderness of that gesture.

The night before I left Baghdad, my aunt Rosa and her two daughters, Grace and Esperance, came to say goodbye. My two cousins and I were close. The thought that I might never see them again was painful. I sang to them as I swung gently in my hammock, "*Faut-il se quitter sans espoir, sans espoir de retour?*" ("Should we be parting with no hope of return?") As, if to reassure myself, I also sang the refrain, "*Ce n'est pas un adieux mes freres, ce n'est qu'un au revoir. Oui nous nous reverrons my freres, ce n'est qu'un au revoir.*" ("This isn't an adieu, my friends, it is only an *au revoir*, yes, we surely will see each other again, this is only an *au revoir*.")

I wanted both worlds: I wanted to leave Iraq, and I wanted to stay in touch with my family. But in the tyrannical world of Iraq, my two wishes were incompatible.

The following day we called the registration center at the Shemtob synagogue. There was a good chance, they said, that my number would be reached within the day. That was it. This would be my last, bittersweet day in Baghdad. It was a relief to know that the suspense was almost over. I wanted to go. But this would probably be the last time I would ever see my parents. I cried, but I didn't want Mama to see my tears. I kept on my big sunglasses. Mama was composed at first, but by midmorning she broke down. She rushed toward me and hugged me tightly, as she broke into tears. "I will miss you, dear Dannu. Will I ever see you again? Why was it decreed that we have to suffer?" A gush of chest pain hit me. I couldn't breathe. The hardest part of my emigration was leaving my mother behind. I pushed her away. I don't know why, except that the pain was too much to bear. Perhaps I didn't want to see my mother in her moment of anguish. I went to my room and sobbed.

The registration center had promised to give us a call when my immigration number was reached. At dinnertime, we sat together to have our usual cup of tea with Feta cheese sandwiches. Nobody said much. I was composed throughout the evening. It didn't look as if I would be leaving that night. Still I felt a sense of inner peace. The wait was approaching its end.

At 10 p.m. the telephone rang. The plane could take one more passenger; I was next in line. Mama, had tears in her eyes. "Please stay one more night," she pleaded. But I was adamant. I wanted to go. I wanted to get it over with.

Baba called a taxicab. Minutes later, Jacob announced the cab had arrived. My parents, siblings and Uncle Moshe stood in line in our courtyard to bid me goodbye. I hugged my mother first, then my siblings, then Uncle Moshe. Baba stood at the end of the line. His eyes glistened with tears. I had hardly ever seen him cry before. I gave him a big hug, and then turned toward the vestibule without looking back. I couldn't bear seeing Baba's tears.

Latifa.

Midway down the long vestibule on my way out, Latifa met me as I passed by the dining room. She didn't say a word, but tears were streaming down her cheeks. She had been waiting in the dining room behind the door to be the last one to say good-bye. She took my right hand and kissed it. I hugged her and rushed out to the waiting taxicab.

Jacob, Baba and Uncle Moshe loaded my trunk on the back seat of the taxicab, and I headed for the airport alone.

The waiting lounge was brightly lit and full of emigrants—a sea of humanity. Some emigrants had been there since the afternoon. Some sat on their suitcases, others stood quietly or wandered around. I was rushed to a room, where I found myself alone with four inspectors and an armed policeman.

A kindly looking older inspector, probably the chief inspector, opened my trunk. He went lightly through my belongings, and seemed to be satisfied that I had nothing objectionable. He asked me to empty my pockets. I took out everything and put it on the table. He glanced at it, said it was fine and left the room.

I began to put things back in my pocket. The policeman stepped forward. My vision glasses and my sunglasses were in my hand ready to go back in my pocket.

"Why do you need two pairs of glasses?" the policeman asked. 'Give me one of them."

I put my expensive sunglasses in my pocket and handed him my vision pair. He put them on, shifted them up and down on his nose, and turned his head from one side to the other. Finally, he threw the glasses down on the table and walked away muttering to himself.

In the meantime the younger inspectors got busy working on the contents of my trunk. They went through item-by-item, and kept for themselves what they wanted. One paunchy inspector sized up one of my dress shirts. It was too small for him. He passed it on to the inspector next to him. It seemed to fit him; he kept it.

I felt detached, totally numb as I watched what was happening to my belongings. I didn't care. I felt as if I were perched high above, looking down with disinterest at what was happening to someone else's suitcase. All I wanted was to go. I was so close to freedom. But these inspectors seemed to take their good time – relishing every piece they kept for themselves. Would it ever be over? Why don't they keep my whole trunk and just let me go? Would I finally be allowed to leave Baghdad tonight? Would I really make it to freedom?

At that moment Israel seemed to be a million miles away.

PART TWO - ISRAEL

OUT OF THE INFERNO, APRIL 1, 1951

When I got on the plane that was to take me out of Iraq, I knew only that I was leaving a country in which I had lived all of my life as a second-class citizen. Nobody on the plane knew our intended destination. We had heard some planes had flown directly to Israel. Other planes had landed in Cyprus. The uncertainty added to our anxiety.

I took my seat on the plane scarcely daring to believe that I was leaving. My fingernails dug into the palms of my hands as I waited for the plane to take off. I shrunk down into my seat. I didn't feel like talking to anybody, and I noticed the silence on the plane was almost unbroken.

I had never flown before, and it frightened me. But I was even more afraid that we would be dragged off the plane before it could take off. We had been stripped of our citizenship, but that wouldn't stop Iraqi officials from taking us into custody at the last moment.

The tension pervading the plane was palpable. Nobody dared to say we were glad to be leaving, not even in a whisper. Nobody dared to greet the sound of the closing doors with a cheer or even with a sigh of relief. When the plane raced down the runway and took off, the silence within the plane was still almost unbroken. As we ascended through the darkness into the night sky, I could see the lights of the airport below, but the only sound was the drone of the engines.

Then the woman behind me whispered to the plane, "May God make you as strong as iron." Amen, I said in my heart. We, too, needed to be strong. We were leaving behind the only life that we had known, a life we certainly wanted to leave, but we faced the unknown.

No matter what lay ahead, I knew I didn't want to live in a non-Jewish society, not even in England where the standard of education was high and where some of our relatives lived. I wanted to avoid repeating our people's miserable experience in Iraq. In Israel, a land owned and governed by Jews, I would be in a country free of discrimination against Jews. There I knew I would be safe.

But my journey was tearing me away from my family, and there was no certainty we would ever be reunited. I blinked back tears. This was my choice. I couldn't live as a Jew among Muslims any longer.

The sleepless, tense nights I had spent anticipating my flight finally took their toll. I let go and, exhausted, fell asleep. When I awoke it seemed to me that the plane was no longer in the air.

"I think we have landed," the woman behind me said to her husband. "I see intermittent lights."

We had indeed landed. The lights were on an airport runway. As we came to a halt the cabin buzzed with word that we had arrived in Israel. Was it really Israel?

I could hear the murmur of voices as I looked around the plane jammed with refugees from Baghdad. Someone was reciting the *Shehehiyyanu*, a prayer of thanks. Many of the passengers just sat quietly, looking apprehensive.

I was dazed and disoriented when I staggered off the plane that early morning of April 1, 1951 at Llyda Airport (later renamed Ben Gurion Airport). I could hardly believe I was out of the inferno that people called Iraq.

I arrived ready to hug and embrace any and every one I encountered in my new homeland. I was in a country where every Jew belonged, where for the first time in my life I would be a part of the majority. In Israel I would be greeted with warmth and outstretched hands.

The other immigrants on the plane had come to this new life with their families. Staying with the family was the tradition among Babylonian Jews. I was eighteen years old, but I was the only one who had come alone.

In fact, this was my first venture on my own outside the boundaries of the sheltered environment in which I had grown up. And there was to be no going back. There would be no contact with my parents, perhaps forever. But the ramifications of my decision had yet to sink in. I could entertain only one idea: I was fortunate to be out of that Gehenna.

It was only later that afternoon when we were dropped off at *Sha'ar Aliyah*, a holding camp for incoming immigrants near Haifa, that I began to get a glimmer of the enormity of the step I had taken, and the radical way in which my life was about to change.

But now, waiting in the Llyda airport, I perceived only that it was overcast and cold outside, though I didn't feel cold. I was wearing several layers of clothing - my best suit, shirt and necktie; a blue sweater that Muzli had knitted for me; a leather jacket; an enormous overcoat, twice my size, that my father had had made especially for my flight to Israel.

Metallic trunk my father had commissioned for me -- airport inspectors often tore apart the cardboard suitcases of Jewish immigrants on the pretext that they needed to search for hidden valuables. The number 14296 is my immigrant number; a shipping clerk no doubt misspelled my last name; I is the initial of my father's name, Ibrahim, as pronounced in Iraq.

I wasn't wearing all these clothes for warmth; I was wearing them to make it harder for the Iraqi customs inspectors to commandeer them, to ensure they arrived with me in Israel. But even the clothes seemed unimportant now. Nothing seemed to matter except that I was in the Promised Land.

When we were led to Llyda's airport terminal, I followed as if I were a robot. Three hours ago I had been in

Baghdad having my belongings pawed over by airport officials; now I was almost too numb to claim an Irish blanket somebody had found on the plane, a blanket I knew was mine. It was one my mother had packed for me, a prized possession she wanted me to have, and I could barely summon the energy to claim it. I walked when I was told to walk and stood when I was told to stand.

A burly sanitation worker with a spray gun in hand stood before me. Maybe because I was ready to embrace everybody I came across, I didn't regard him as hostile, in spite of his grim expression. He motioned for me to pull my pants down, and I complied.

Suddenly he aimed his spray gun at me and proceeded to spray my genitals with a powder that smelled like DDT. I recoiled and coughed. It was difficult to breathe. Why, I wondered, did he spray me with DDT? I thought DDT was used for killing bugs in agriculture. Even so I remained trusting. It couldn't hurt to breathe that stuff, I thought, because if it did, he wouldn't have done it. He was Jewish, and would never hurt me. I was in a Jewish land with other Jews, and whatever was being done couldn't have been done with anything but the best of intentions.

The Hebrew I heard was spoken too fast for me to follow, but the main language spoken by those who met us at the airport, which I later learned was Yiddish, was one I had never heard before. I wondered why the Jews from Iraq who had preceded us weren't here to welcome us. Didn't they know we needed them to explain to us what was happening in a language we understood? I felt a mounting sense of frustration, but choked it down. I couldn't allow myself to feel. Maybe I wouldn't feel anything ever again.

Not one person who met us at the airport had smiled at us. Nobody seemed to understand that we were used to being welcomed by friends with smiles and steaming cups of hot tea. At that moment my family in Baghdad was probably gathered around our table drinking tea together, and here I was alone in a land where I didn't understand one word that was spoken. How could I have imagined Israel was my home? I quickly dismissed such doubts and allowed myself to sink deep into lethargy.

My fellow passengers were bursting with questions. How long were we going to be at the airport? Some people had arrived here almost a full day before me. They were weary and asking when they would be fed. Others asked about relatives who had left Baghdad a week or two before, how they could get in touch with them and where we ourselves were headed. All questions—in whatever language--were met with silence. People tried Judeo-Arabic, English, French - nobody in charge seemed to understand.

I didn't ask any questions. I sat quietly waiting for something to happen, but I had no idea what that something would be.

I felt my wrist and was relieved that my Omega watch was still there. That watch meant a lot to me. I had tutored students in math and physics when I was in high school, and my watch was the first thing I had bought with my own money. When I was being inspected at Baghdad's airport I had it pushed well above my wrist, hoping the customs inspectors wouldn't notice it and ask me to hand it over.

I couldn't tell how long we had been waiting outside the terminal. It had been just after dawn when we left the terminal. Now, it seemed the sun had been out for a good while. People were sitting on their luggage, and one man blurted out, "I knew it, I knew it. I knew this is how it was going to be. We will be left in the fields." Was this true, or had he gone off the deep end? Being left in suspense was beginning to gnaw at me.

Around noon a few open trucks arrived; we were to pile in. I had never ridden in a truck before, much less in the back of one. The journey to *Sha'ar Aliyah* took about two hours. The ride was windy and bouncy. It pained me to see the older people huddled together on the floor, some of them dressed in elegant suits. They looked worried and uncertain.

For me, however, the ride was a novelty. With the cool air on my face and the warm sun washing over me, I felt a new sense of freedom. This was my new country, my new homeland. I held the railings tightly and threw my head back. I felt alive, revived. We passed by orange groves, and the fragrance of orange blossoms triggered a memory of distillers coming to our home in Baghdad to extract fresh rosewater and orange blossom water. Was this home? It smelled like home.

I was impressed and frightened as we turned onto the coastal highway along the Mediterranean on our way to *Sha'ar Aliyah.* I had never seen a sea before. The Tigris was wide, but it was nothing like this endless expanse of water. The waves were high and wild. I remembered Victor Hugo's poem, "Oceano Nox," about the treacherous waves, the drowning people, and the wrecked boats. Here were those waves right before my eyes. They beat the shore mercilessly.

Finally we reached the *Sha'ar Aliyah* camp where we would stay until we were moved to semi-permanent quarters.

CHOOSING MY BIRTHDAY

After we climbed off the truck, we were herded to a barrack for processing. I took my place in a long line that snaked around the room. After a few minutes I pulled myself together as I realized I had moved to the head of the line and the official sitting at the table was addressing me.

"What is the date of your birth?"

"1932," I told him.

"I need the day and month, too."

"I don't have that information."

The official's pen was poised over the paper on the table, but he set the pen down and stared at me.

"You don't?"

" I don't."

He shook his head and picked up his pen again.

"Well, I need it."

Nobody had ever needed it before. Not knowing my precise birthday hadn't posed any practical problem in dealings with officialdom in Iraq. There, it was the year of birth that was important - date and month were irrelevant on passports, school registration documents and the like. Though my father kept meticulous records of the birth dates of each of his ten children, he never shared them with us. Jewish tradition discouraged a preoccupation with birthdays, emphasizing instead one's good deeds and achievements throughout life.

Babylonian immigrants being processed in *Sha'ar Aliyah*

There was little use in sharing all this with the official drumming his fingers on the table. What was I going to do? My father was far away in Baghdad, and in any case he kept our birth records locked in his cupboard. Whenever the subject had come up, he'd assured us he would give us our birth date when we married and left our parents' home—as he had when Jamila, my oldest sister, got married. He had expected to give me my own record before I left for Israel. But in the turbulent days that preceded my flight from Baghdad, my mind was on anything but my birth date. I suspect it was the same for my father.

But here I was. I needed to give *Sha'ar Aliyah*'s bureaucrat a month and a day to jot on his form. There were three hundred and sixty five days to pick from. And I blurted out the first date that came to mind: January sixth. The die was cast. The harried Israeli official recorded the date and moved on to the next person in line.

I would later track down my actual birth date—June 14, 1932—from dates that my father inscribed on a picture of me on my *bar miswah* day.

It never crossed my mind that my phony birth date would stay with me for the rest of my life and would appear on every legal document I possess. In many ways, however, my self-created birthday was fitting. On that first day in Israel I was embarking on a new life, bidding goodbye forever to the country of my birth and to a now-vanished way of life to which I would never return.

SHA'AR ALIYAH

Sha'ar Aliyah was a sprawling camp abandoned by the British military. To the east were the Carmel Mountains, majestic, beautiful against the sky. Baghdad is flat, and I had never before seen mountains. I felt a sense of peace as I drank in the beauty of the surroundings. But the camp itself was a dreadful place.

Sha'ar Aliyah lacked minimal hygienic amenities. The bathrooms were located at the far ends of the camp, and were not well kept. Nor were there enough of them. Even at night, there were long lines. Tempers flared. There were long lines for water, too. Only cold water was available, and people had to carry it in buckets for long distances. It was miserable when it rained, whether one was waiting for water, the bathroom, or the daily ration of food. The tents provided little comfort. They were poorly furnished, and most had gaping holes.

I didn't have to cook for myself, though I did have to do my own laundry. Fortunately, my mother had sent a large bar of soap with me to Israel. The first time I tried to wash my own shirt, I was sparing with the soap, because I had no idea how long it would have to last. I ran the soap lightly over the collar and rubbed it between my hands, but no matter how hard I rubbed, the dirt still clung stubbornly. I had seen the maids in my parents' home wash our clothes, and it hadn't looked difficult. I couldn't understand why the dirt wouldn't be moved.

Close to tears, I looked up and saw a young woman laughing at me. She had a round face and black curly hair. I thought she was beautiful, and, though her dark eyes reflected amusement, they also exuded compassion. She came over and put her arm around me.

"Here, let me do that for you. My name is Violette, by the way."

She not only took my shirt and washed it, but also invited me back to her family's tent. It was every bit as cold as my own, but it was filled with the warmth of love and caring.

When we arrived, Violette's father was sitting outside taking off his *tefilleen*. He reminded me of my father, whom I had so often watched performing the same ritual after morning prayers. Violette's father wore a head covering similar to that worn by the Kurdish Jews, and his accent was that of the Jews of Northern Iraq. I could tell that he was happy to be able to pray openly.

Violette introduced me to her family and then asked me to move into the tent with them. I accepted gladly, happy that I could help the family by carrying water for them. Her parents welcomed me. We were Jews helping one another, and it felt good.

As hard as I had tried to imagine harsh living conditions while leading my comfortable life in Iraq, I had never come close to imagining the hardships of *Sha'ar Aliyah*. Still, I put up with them without complaint. It was a small price to pay for freedom.

But those who had emigrated with young families in tow had it particularly hard. They were destined to struggle with inadequate water and poor hygienic conditions for some time, and were likely to spend years in tents or huts that offered poor protection from hot or cold weather. How and when would they fit into Israeli society? How would they educate their children? The uncertainty surrounding their lives weighed heavily on them. The Palestinians occupied our synagogues and houses in Baghdad. It would make such a difference to these families if they were given the assets left behind by the Palestinians in Israel, I thought.

I, however, didn't have a family to worry about. I planned to join the military immediately, and, even though an immigrant of military age was exempt from military service for the first year in Israel, I had no intention of spending a year in limbo. I would put my military service behind me and concentrate on continuing my education.

I decided to join the Air Force. I was determined to become a pilot for my own reasons. When I left Iraq I knew that, sooner or later, the Iraqi government would seize my parents' home in Baghdad. I had a deep attachment to my home and, as soon as my family was safely out of Iraq, I planned to fly my plane over Baghdad and bomb that house. The Iraqi government wouldn't be allowed to have it. I wasn't sure how I would locate the house or how I would persuade the other members of my crew to fly with me on such a mission. But, when the time came, I would find a way. Nothing would be allowed to deter me.

Something did.

"Your eyesight isn't perfect," the physician who tested me declared. "You can't be a pilot, but you could be a navigator."

Not be a pilot! My world was crumbling around me.

"I want to be a pilot, not a navigator," I stammered.

"But a navigator is also an officer," a member of the examining board explained.

An officer! Who cared about being an officer? I wanted to be a pilot, the one in charge of the plane. I wanted to be the one who ordered the bomb dropped on my home. But if I revealed that, I would kill my chances of joining the Air Force altogether. I looked into the puzzled and implacable faces of the board members and swallowed my dream.

Eventually it was decided I would be transferred to the Air Force ground crew, once I had finished three months of basic training.

Surprisingly, when my plans were thwarted it came as a relief, as if I had been released from a vow I didn't want to fulfill. I didn't want to spend the rest of my life hating the Arabs. I wanted to put the past behind me and concentrate on making a success of my life. The Arabs took our material possessions, I thought to myself. They can have them. I still have my life, and I am going to make a go of it. I would complete my military service and become a productive member of Israeli society.

And, though life was difficult in *Sha'ar Aliyah*, I was no longer totally alone. Violette and her family were my friends, and then I bumped into Nahoom, the receptionist at Ammu Guerji's clinic. I hadn't known he was in Israel and it was wonderful to see him.

Ammu Guerji was a sought-after doctor, and it was Nahoom's job to see that patients saw him in the proper order. I often sat in Ammu Guerji's waiting room and admired Nahoom's tact when he had to tell patients that they were not next in line as they claimed, but would get to see the doctor soon. Nahoom knew me. He knew my family. Here in *Sha'ar Aliyah* he was my family, my connection to home.

One day, an incident occurred at camp that left me shaken, but happy Nahoom was my friend. As I considered the camp's inhabitants and realized that many of them came from Baghdad's working class, I remarked to Nahoom: "Isn't it nice that we are all the same here?" Nahoom didn't get a chance to reply. On hearing my remark, a man twice my size stood up and bore down on me with a snarl. He probably would have made mincemeat of me if Nahoom had not held him at bay.

However, I didn't completely appreciate the depths of Nahoom's skill with people until I saw him strike up a friendship with one of the Hungarian women who served us our food at *Sha'ar Aliyah*'s dining room. It was when I noticed I was being served large portions of food that I understood Nahoom's charm.

"It's not me. It's you," Nahoom explained.

He was friendly with the small dark server, but the tall fair one had told Nahoom that she fancied me. I couldn't quite believe Nahoom, but I appreciated the generous portions of food on my plate.

195

Later I discovered there might have been something to Nahoom's claim.

Every day the tall fair server smiled at me as she heaped food on my plate. Unfortunately, I couldn't eat much of it. It was not food that I or other Middle Easterners were used to, and I generally gave the extra to families with children. My big portions, however, vanished on the day this young woman discovered I was leaving shortly for military service. Then she didn't smile as she served me a miserly portion of food and pointedly requested that I leave the dining room and not linger over my food.

From that day on, my formerly friendly server wouldn't meet my eye as she slapped small portions of food on my plate. I found the situation disconcerting, but I put it out of my mind when I took my leave of Nahoom and of Violette and her family on April 17th 1951 and began my military service in Israel.

IN THE MILITARY

Nahoom didn't join me in the military, choosing instead to defer. I, however, was eager to join up. I wanted to serve my new homeland. I felt also the military would serve as a stepping-stone for entry into Israeli society. I would learn Hebrew, and perhaps a profession, both of which would prepare me to become a productive citizen.

But, though I didn't realize it when I signed up, I was not ready for the military. I needed time to mourn my uprooting and the loss of my family. I needed to allow my spirit to heal. During basic military training there was no time for any of that. It was go, go, go. For three months we trained almost non-stop. Emotionally, this total immersion was a difficult period for me, at least in the short run. In the long run, however, it was probably the best decision I could have made.

For basic training I was stationed in Saraphand, a major camp in Rishon leSion, a coastal town about ten miles southeast of Tel Aviv. I shared a large brick bungalow with some fifty other new recruits. Our beds consisted of mattresses on top of boards positioned over sawhorses. This made it easy for the beds to be overturned if we didn't leap out of bed when the wake-up whistle sounded. It seemed to me that I had barely gone to bed when that whistle sounded in the cold dark hours of the early morning. Almost as soon as our bare feet hit the floor, we were off for our jog at dawn. Dressed only in boots and khaki pants, I shivered as I ran.

Food, or the lack of it, was a problem. I often looked longingly at the fruit of the cactus growing all around us in the fields where we trained, but when I tried to eat it the thorns stuck in my mouth and I didn't know how to remove them. It seemed to me that all we ever got to eat was black bread, rock-hard frozen margarine, and salty, stinky herring, which I hated. The beverage of choice was weak tea, a far cry from the strong black tea with milk we drank in Baghdad.

I could have bought food to supplement my meal, as some did, but our allowance was the equivalent of about one dollar per month. Out of this I had to buy shoe polish, toothpaste and other personal supplies. To save on polish, I shined only the fronts of my boots. One day during inspection I got caught.

"I suppose this means you wash only your face and never your behind," my sergeant barked in biting tones.

We learned to crawl under two-foot-high barbed wire on our backs and on our bellies under a searing noonday sun. The fair- skinned among us often had blisters from the sun, which in this exercise were rubbed raw by the desert sand. Sometimes we were wakened at night to go out on maneuvers. Sleep deprivation was common, but it was never considered an excuse for underperformance. Sometimes we were up until after midnight cleaning our rifles, trying to rid them of sand particles.

Training in the field -. Daniel 2d row, 2d from the left

I remember the first time we trained at night using what we believed to be live ammunition. It was frightening to crawl under barbed wire in the sand while bullets whistled over our heads. All hell broke loose that night. One soldier refused to take part in this exercise. He had a wife and children, and if he were to die fighting the enemy that was bad enough. He was terrified at the thought of facing Israeli fire. He sat on the ground and cried, begging to be excused while the trainers shot bullets over his head, insisting that he participate. I saw what was happening out of the corner of my eye, as I slid along the sand on my belly. Those bullets were scary, but we had to be ready for combat.

Daniel on guard duty

There was a two-week period when I had a respite. Those of us who had gone directly from *Sha'ar Aliyah* into the military were required to attend Hebrew classes for two hours every afternoon during that two-week period, so that we would at least understand some basic commands in our new language. Our Hebrew teacher was a young man who never woke us up if we fell asleep in his class; some afternoons I slept through the whole class. It felt so good to take a nap, and I was grateful to our easy-going teacher.

REUNIONS

Jews celebrate the giving of the Ten Commandments when the *sh'buoth* holiday arrives, and this year my joy in the holiday's arrival was doubled. A couple of weeks before I left Baghdad, Ammu Silman, my father's younger brother, had left for Israel with his wife, Amma Margo, their daughter and two sons. I had finally found out where they were, and I was going to see them.

When I received my holiday pass at *sh'buoth*, I hitchhiked to the Khay'riya *ma'abara*, the tent city where my uncle had been assigned. It was night by the time I arrived, and there were no lights in the *ma'abara*. I wandered around, frightened and lonely. The scent of orange blossoms in the air only intensified my homesickness.

A view of a *ma'abara* – immigrants' tent city

Slits of light gleamed from some of the tents, but it wasn't enough for me to find my way. I wished the moon were full, as I stumbled over the uneven ground and tripped over the ropes holding down the tents. I stopped to listen for a minute, as I heard the noise of a tattered tent blowing in the wind. I hoped my uncle and his wife weren't living in a tattered tent.

I stopped at tent after tent, but no one seemed to know my uncle. What would I do if I couldn't find my uncle and his family?

Finally, I found a man who was able to help. Following his directions, I made my way to my relatives' tent, and their welcoming cries drew me out of the darkness into a warm circle of light where we all kissed and embraced. They boiled the only egg they had and gave it to me. I agonized over eating it, knowing their food was severely rationed. But it was an offering of love, and could not be refused. I savored their love for me, even as I found it hard to swallow the egg.

Ammu Silman and I knew each other at some deep level, which we didn't need to talk about. We just felt it. I sat close to him in the tent and, for the first time since coming to Israel, basked in the warmth of family love. They, too, were displaced, but I envied the fact that at least they were together.

Ammu Silman and Amma Margo always lived in a rented house.

"Silman should buy a house," Ammu Moshe would say. "There is security in owning one's home."

I thought of this as I looked around the shabby tent that Ammu Silman and his family now called home. It seemed as though there was no semblance of security anywhere—not for a Jew in Baghdad, not for a displaced Jew living in a tent in Israel. I am sure that Ammu Silman had felt some sense of security years ago, when he won the lottery and put the money in the bank, but that peace of mind had been fleeting. The day that Ammu Silman had withdrawn the last two hundred dinars from his account, he was standing in the bank counting his money when a thief snatched it from his hands and ran away with it. The police just shrugged when my uncle reported the theft.

Ammu Silman's *ma'abara* was the usual tent city without proper sanitary facilities and almost impossible living conditions, especially for people accustomed to city life. Its one redeeming feature was that it was set in a field surrounded by orange groves. But even that had its drawbacks. Coyotes prowled the groves at night, keeping everybody in the *ma'abara* awake with their howling. As I lay in my bed during the two nights I spent with my uncle and his family, I was glad that I had decided to join the military instead of living in a *ma'abara*.

The uncertainties of hitchhiking worked against me on my way back to camp following the *sh'buoth* holiday. I was a few minutes late, and knew that returning through the main gate meant I would be reported for tardiness. I had, however, done my share of guard duty at night, so I knew the location of the holes in the fence that enclosed our camp. I had also learned to crawl on my belly and move silently when necessary. Basic training, I decided, could be used to benefit me as well as the army.

I sneaked into camp, moving silently through one of the fence's holes, afraid the guard outside would catch sight of me. I felt my heart pounding in my throat, even as I told myself the risk was worthwhile. I slipped into my bungalow minutes before roll call and wiped the sweat off my forehead, scarcely daring to believe in my own luck.

Though it was wonderful to see them, the visit with my uncle and his family intensified my longing to see other members of my family. And then the unexpected happened.

Across the road from our basic-training camp there was a *ma'abara* where new immigrants were placed. One day, about two months into my basic training, I heard that my maternal grandmother, Yemma Aziza, had arrived in the camp with her sons, Khalu Sion and Khalu Guerji, her daughters Khala Nazeema and Khala Toya, and Khala Toya's family.

Khalu Guerji was the prominent member of that branch of my family. When he arrived in Israel, Khalu Guerji was single and in his early forties. Until a few months before immigrating to Israel, he had served as Iraq's Assistant Minister of Finance for Currency. Traditionally, Jews had dominated the high positions in Iraq's Finance Ministry, a carryover from the time of King Faisal I, who was enamored of the Jewish community's commercial and banking know-how. It was also a carryover from the period of the Ottoman Empire, when the Empire's financiers were mostly Jewish.

With heightened Iraqi nationalism and increased hostility toward the Jews, more and more of the ministry's Jewish staff members were let go and replaced by Muslims. Uncle Guerji was one of the few members of the Jewish community left in a high position at the ministry. But life became increasingly difficult for him, too, in the late forties as hostilities against the Jews of Iraq gained momentum. At one point, Khalu Guerji was threatened with court-martial for treason, when he opposed the hiring of someone, whose main qualification was that he was a Muslim and a relative of a cabinet member. In time, my uncle was eased out of the government. The ministry abrogated his pension contract and put him on notice that, if he chose to bring a civil suit against the ministry for breaking the contract, he would be charged as a supporter of the "Zionist Entity" and tried before a court martial.

I remember Khalu Guerji as intense, energetic and hard working. In Baghdad he left home early in the morning to be at work before everyone else. He stayed behind long after everyone in his office had gone home. He was a meticulous, elegant man, dressed in the best of suits, his shoes always sparkling. In spite of his overwhelming commitment to his work, he maintained a great deal of interest in the world around. He followed the details of the war against the Nazis to the minutia. But, unlike my father, Khalu Guerji never involved himself in the activities of the Jewish community or shared the burden of running its affairs.

By the time I reached the age of sixteen, I had attained the same height and build as Khalu Guerji, and so inherited all his elegant castoff suits and neckties. To my delight, that meant that I became one of the most dapper young men around.

Khala Toya, whose name was a diminutive of Victoria, was my least favorite aunt, even though one day she would change my life with a single, highly uncharacteristic act of generosity. Khala Toya was one of my mother's younger sisters. She was a tall and imposing figure, and she carried herself as though she ruled the world. In fact, she was aptly named because she possessed Queen Victoria's regal, imperious air. Everything that pertained in any way to Khala Toya was bigger, better or more desirable--at least according to Khala Toya.

She was forever blowing her own horn and that of her immediate family. Her husband, Shafeek, who worked under Khalu Guerji, never struck me as bright. But to hear Khala Toya talk, the Ministry of Finance revolved around her husband.

"Everybody in the office comes to Shafeek with the difficult problems," she would boast.

Khala Toya filled any environment in which she moved with a deep sense of her own self-importance, and she never saw beyond that. Everybody else existed to do her bidding, in one way or another.

When they went out in public, many Jewish women wore a black silk cloak, called *abayi*, which covered them from head to toe. Not Khala Toya -- she sallied forth into the streets carrying a large handbag and swishing her long skirts as she walked, her hard hazel eyes looking neither to the right nor to the left. Several of my siblings and I had no liking for her, particularly because she stole money from Jamila's trousseau budget, but I don't think she took much account of us. I wonder if she would have cared had she known that we privately called her *baghla*, or mule, because we thought she looked like one. She was not pretty, but she wore her high opinion of herself on her face for everyone to see.

My uncles Guerji and Sion, who worked hard to save for a dowry for their unmarried sister Khala Nazeema, didn't have an easy time providing for the family, but Khala Toya showed no consideration for either one. She, her husband and her three children showed up at my grandmother Aziza's house every night for dinner. Khala Toya never lifted a finger to put a plate on the table or wash a dish. She and her family sat at the table, expecting to be served by her sister, Khala Nazeema, who was living at home with my grandmother and my two maternal uncles.

Worse yet, Khala Toya helped to destroy Nazeema's first marriage. Again, our dreadful marriage customs played right into her hands.

This time, it involved the need to obtain proof of the bride's virginity and the groom's virility. After the marriage ceremony the bride and groom customarily retreated to a room where the woman was to be deflowered and the bloody sheet later produced as proof that she had been a virgin. After the proof was exhibited, friends and family who had waited outside the marriage bedroom rejoiced. This demeaning custom produced enormous anxiety in the man. Some men found themselves unable to rise to the occasion, and at times it took several days before the required proof could be produced. This is what happened to Khala Nazeema, who married a shy and gentle young man.

When deflowering didn't happen on the wedding day, Khala Toya made the situation her business. She advocated divorce, and in the end she prevailed: Khala Nazeema divorced her husband. But when she returned to her mother Aziza's house, she cried for days and refused to be consoled. In time, she reverted to being the unhappy servant to Khala Toya instead of being in charge of her own home.

I thought about all of this as I learned my grandmother had arrived. The separation and vicissitudes we all had endured had done much to soften my feelings toward Khala Toya. After all, she was my mother's sister. I felt my love for my mother rise up to include Khala Toya, and I looked forward to seeing her with the rest of my grandmother's family. I also thirsted for news of my parents and siblings who were still in Iraq. And so I was excited as I told myself I would soon see my grandmother.

But my initial excitement turned to frustration and disappointment. The *ma'abara* was just across the road, but I wouldn't get a pass to leave camp for another two whole weeks. I couldn't wait that long to see my grandmother. I made up my mind to sneak out of camp for a few hours on the coming Saturday to visit the *ma'abara*. Saturday, I decided, was the best day for my escape. The exact time, however, would have to be decided on the spur of the moment.

Saturday was a day of rest when we had no training. We could do as we pleased, short of leaving the camp without a pass, but had to be in our quarters when checks were made. At the conclusion of each check, the time of the next check was announced, and the interval between checks could vary anywhere from one to four hours. The trick was to leave during a longer interval and return in time for the next check, without my absence being noticed. This was not as easy as it sounds.

I picked the best time that I could to leave and removed my military hat so that I would be less easily identifiable as a soldier. Then I made my way down the hill and across the road to the *ma'abara*. I couldn't move too quickly lest I draw attention to myself, and I had to move confidently to give the impression that I was authorized to be out and about. My heart pounded. I ducked whenever I heard the sound of a vehicle on the road.

The welcome from my family when I found them was worth the risk I had taken.

"What has happened to your hair?" my grandmother asked, noticing that my thick curly hair had been reduced to a crew cut.

"You are so thin," my aunts clucked.

I had, indeed, lost weight. In basic training we used to joke that the army made us go for a run after lunch to be sure the mouthful we ate would be melted from our bodies.

But everybody kissed me and held me close. It was a joy to know that some of my family had made it to Israel, and that I had managed to spend a few stolen moments with them. But the joy was tempered with sadness. My grandmother shook her head and, with tears streaming down her cheeks, looked around the shabby tent, which was a far cry from her home in Baghdad.

"Look at what has happened to us."

Khalu Guerji sat quietly on his bed and didn't participate in the conversation. He looked worried, and seemed engrossed in his thoughts. Was he scared that he might be too old to find employment? Gone was the nattily dressed man who had given me the best suits I had ever worn; gone was the confident look and the enthusiasm of the hard-driving uncle I remembered from my younger years. He looked broken. He had suffered the biggest fall of them all, I said to myself. As I bade him goodbye, I wondered what the future held for him, for Khalu Sion, and the rest of the family.

They had to find work in order to survive. It was heartrending to see them uprooted in their middle years.

Grandma Aziza probably suffered the most. She was seventy when she arrived in Israel. She was the elder in the family. Everyone turned to her for reassurance and warmth at a time when she herself was overwhelmed with a sense of loss.

During our Baghdad days, Grandma Aziza had radiated serenity and composure. When we ate at her house she presided over a full table, urging all of us to have "just a little more." Now, the food rations were so small there was hardly anything to serve. Her eyes mourned the brimming bowls of food that had graced her table in Baghdad. In Israel that feeling of plenty and prosperity was gone. Here her face was set in worried lines. In Israel, her favorite son, Uncle Guerji, a former Assistant Minister of the Treasury, was just another unemployed person. In his early forties, Uncle Guerji couldn't hope to ever return to anything comparable to his former position. No one was sure, least of all Uncle Guerji, that he would ever be gainfully employed again. Younger men went begging for jobs. Uncle Sion, who was four years older than Uncle Guerji, was in an even worse position.

"How are we going to make it?" Grandma often asked. She was too proud to live on handouts, and there was precious little of that in any case.

And then there was Aunt Nazeema. She was the youngest in the family. Still, she was hitting forty. In Baghdad my two uncles had worked hard to save enough money to marry her off after her divorce and pay for her dowry. But all that was gone now. The Iraqis had seized everything they had.

"What hope is there for getting Nazeema married off when both Guerji and Sion are unemployed?" Grandma would ask. She knew all too well that there was nothing she could do to help. She had never held a job. She spent her younger years bringing up her children and was the rock on which the family leaned. And now at age seventy she was confronted with a grim and meager existence she could never have envisioned during her life in Baghdad.

Grandma never regained her sense of peace. She didn't live to see Aunt Nazeema and Uncle Guerji get married. She wore an expression of sadness and defeat until the day she died, six years after arriving in Israel.

AIR FORCE

When I completed my basic training I was transferred to the Air Force. During my remaining twenty-seven months of service, I was affiliated with **Wing 4**, the heavy and light bombers unit.

Morning flag-raising ceremony in Wing 4 - Daniel on the right saluting the Israeli flag

I was a member of a team in charge of technical supplies for the airplanes, mostly B-17s and Mosquitoes (two-propeller lighter bombers). It was a critical job. The planes, which flew mainly training and reconnaissance missions, were grounded for repairs as briefly as possible. Whenever we received a request for a part that contained the phrase "Airplane on the ground," the part necessary for the repair had to be available immediately. Somebody from our unit had to be on call twenty-four hours a day, and all airplane parts had to be in stock at all times. I had to be familiar with all the parts, and at times I had to travel from one base to another to pick up parts from warehouses.

The first few months I was with Wing 4 we were based at Tel Nof, a major airfield in South Central Israel, built by the British military prior to Israel's independence. We lived in big tents, four people to a tent. There was space to move around, store our belongings and create a semblance of order in our lives. It was the first time I began to feel I could be happy in a home other than the one I grew up in. But I was still delighted when Wing 4 moved to Has'sore, a few miles south of Tel Nof.

Soldiers who shared the bungalow with me
Daniel – front row in middle

In Has'sore I shared a snug bungalow with two men from India, one from Iraq and an Israeli of Yemenite descent. We lived together in harmony. Soon I transferred my love of my Tel Nof tent to our new bungalow, and grew to think of it as home.

Every morning when I woke up, I gazed at the land stretching out before my eyes in every direction. I could see kibbutz Has'sore up on a hill about a mile away, though its entrance cut through our camp. I could see its trees, lush grass and the red roofs of its houses in the distance.

At Has'sore there were movies, a library and weekly songfests. There was even a well-stocked store and snack bar.

It was tempting to stop at the snack bar in the evening and have a cup of tea or enjoy a wafer or two. But the monthly allowance I received from the military was barely enough to pay for necessities. Those who could afford to patronize the store had family that supplemented their monthly allowance from the military. I didn't feel especially deprived, but when I learned that construction workers were well paid, I arranged to spend my next quarterly vacation -- five days every three months -- working in construction. I had no special skills in this field, for among Baghdad's Jews manual labor was scorned. So I was given the task of hauling bricks from ground level to the upper floor of a large apartment complex under construction. I spent my five days filling a large burlap bag with bricks, tying it to my shoulder and carrying it up to the top floors of the building. I had a weak back, and it hurt at night. But it felt good at the end of the day to receive my pay. The money I saved from those five days lasted me for months.

MORE REUNIONS

My older sister Muzli had married Naim Aslan in Baghdad two months before I left for Israel. They came to Israel a few weeks after my arrival.

During my childhood, my relationship with Muzli had been bumpy—I tried to stay out of her way, because she seemed to enjoy making life difficult for others. She changed for the better after her marriage to Naim.

Naim spent his younger years in Hilla, a town near old Babylon, some fifty miles southwest of Baghdad. He was outgoing, loved to host family and friends, and never failed to offer Turkish coffee with cardamom to anyone who dropped in for a visit.

One of Naim's entertaining talents was telling fortunes by reading the sediment of Turkish coffee. His readings were the highlight of any visit to their home. Sometimes it took Naim five minutes to "unlock the secrets" of the sediment and tell everything there was to tell. At other times, he would ponder a cup for as long as fifteen minutes.

He was such an accomplished storyteller that he swept his listeners along on the tide of his smooth and assured declarations. Everyone, believer and skeptic, listened attentively; you could hear a pin drop.

Muzli sitting in our home in Baghdad, April 22, 1949

When Naim and Muzli came to Israel, they were assigned to *ma'abarat* Brenner in South Central Israel. The *ma'abara* was in an open field with tall eucalyptus trees and many cactus plants. Across the road there was a well-established kibbutz, Giv'at Brenner. The kibbutz hired *ma'abara* residents to help with work in the fields, and this was where Naim found work. About half a mile east of the *ma'abara* was an Arab village that had been largely destroyed during the 1948 war. New immigrants inhabited the village's tumbledown mud houses.

Like other *ma'abara*, *ma'abarat* Brenner lacked a sewage system. The pathway to the outhouses was lined with cactus plants. Walking at night to the outhouses was risky, particularly in the rain. There was no electricity, and flashlights were not available. Even with a kerosene lamp the path was hard to see. A misstep could end in a painful brush with a cactus plant. Cactus thorns, when lodged under the skin, were hard to dislodge. Tweezers were practically non-existent in the *ma'abara*, and medical help was not readily available. The thorns often resulted in swelling and infection.

Naim and Muzli were among the lucky ones who were allotted a canvas hut. The hut was no bigger than a tent, but it had a flat roof that made it possible to stand up straight inside. And, by contrast with the tents' dirt floors, huts had cement floors, which made it easier to keep clean. Naim and Muzli shared their hut with Naim's widowed mother, who had accompanied them on their flight to Israel.

I hitchhiked to *ma'abarat* Brenner in search of Naim and Muzli, and it was a joyful reunion. Naim was a happy man by nature, and his temperament seemed to have rubbed off on Muzli. We hugged and kissed. There were lots of smiles and laughter. It was a beautiful, cool day. The *ma'abara* was bathed in sunshine and a sea breeze wafted over us, ruffling the eucalyptus leaves. We ate lunch together. There were no chairs or tables. We sat on the edges of the beds the Jewish Agency had provided. But no one seemed to mind. We were happy just to be back together under the same roof. Naim and Muzli had cooked a meal on their tiny kerosene stove. It was not the big Sabbath lunch we were accustomed to in the old country, but it felt festive nonetheless. Naim had bought the stove with money he had earned from his work. In a place where there were so few worldly possessions, it was a blessing to own a kerosene stove.

I visited Naim and Muzli many times after that. Naim would come back tired at the end of his workday in the fields. His small physique was not that of a strong laborer, and he suffered from backaches. His fingers were calcified from working with the hoe and shovel, but he was thankful just to have a job.

Most of the time it was dark by the time I reached their *ma'abara*. Naim and Muzli had bought a small kerosene lamp, which hung on one of the posts in their hut. The lamp's faint light stood in marked contrast to the bright lights we were accustomed to in my parents' home. But we knew it was a luxury; many *ma'abara* residents spent the nights in darkness. We sat in the hut and talked, drinking hot tea. Sometimes Muzli sang Egyptian songs, and we all joined in. For a few moments, we seemed to forget our trials in Iraq and the difficulties of *ma'abara* living.

Naim, who felt honored to be a member of our family, couldn't do enough for me. Occasionally, he and I took a walk to the village east of the *ma'abara*, drawn by the bright light of the Aladdin lamps that the merchants had lit to sell their wares. One evening we walked through the village and admired the displays of artifacts and colorful fruits and vegetables. Gentle night breezes caressed our faces, as we walked under the star-studded sky. We were happy to be alive, happy to be together, happy that Naim's marriage to Muzli had made us brothers.

Naim, working now, though not making much money, knew that I had even less than he did.

"Let me buy you something Danny, something you would like – a peach maybe, or a pear."

I looked into Naim's eager eyes and saw how much he wanted to please me. I knew how hard he worked to support Muzli, his mother and himself and how important it was to him to make their home the hospitable place that it was. I remembered my parents' home in Baghdad. I could see it in my mind, ringing with life, a welcoming place filled with light.

Suddenly it struck me. What Naim's home lacked was bright light. Their single kerosene lamp was not enough. Naim and Muzli's home, one of the most welcoming places I knew, was dark, not a suitable atmosphere for Naim, not in the least bit reflective of him.

I looked at the shelves of the store in which we were standing and saw a single lamp there, waiting to be sold.

"Instead of buying me a peach or a pear, which I do appreciate, what I would really like, Naim, is for you to save your money and buy another lamp for your home. That's what I would like."

Naim's eyes shone, as he smiled his pleasure in realizing there was something he could do that would please me.

"I will do that, Danny."

A week later when I arrived there were two lamps hanging on opposite walls of the hut. Naim rubbed his hands together in glee as he noted my pleasure in the amount of light in the hut.

"You like it Danny?"

"It's wonderful, Naim." Then, jokingly, I added, "But three would be better than two."

On my next visit there were three lamps hanging on the walls, and the light they cast into the room reflected not only Naim's happiness at my surprise and pleasure, but also seemed to be a symbol of the turn my sister's and her husband's lives were taking.

On a Sabbath afternoon in a rowboat on the Yarkon River, Ramat Gan, 1955
L to R: Helwa, Naim, Muzli and Daniel

Naim saw his lamps as a way of pleasing me, bringing me happiness. Little by little, they were gaining a foothold in this land. We didn't have to live dreary and dingy lives. We could reclaim the kind of life we had enjoyed in our homes, a life filled with light and love.

Ammu Moshe, his wife Khala Guerjiyi and my sisters Reyna, Helwa, and Latifa arrived in Israel on June 16, 1951.

214

They shared a tent in a *ma'abara* five miles south of Tel Aviv. Two months passed before I got to see them. I was overjoyed, but devastated when I saw their living conditions. When I was in *Sha'ar Aliyah*, the horrific conditions there didn't bother me as much. I knew my stay was temporary. But when I saw my uncle, aunt and three sisters living in a small tent in an open field, my heart turned over. I wanted to rush out, buy them a large house in the middle of a city and transport them there. But I knew my wish was idle fantasy.

Ammu Moshe and Khala Guerjiyi were like second parents to us; they had no children, and they loved us as they would love their own children. After shopping for us every day in Baghdad, Ammu Moshe came to visit us most evenings. He would tell us about his doings in the business world, share gossip about the commodities markets, and listen with us to the evening news.

Any time I stopped by at Khala Guerjiyi's during my younger years there was something stashed away in the closet, waiting for me - a baklava, an almond bar, a quince louzeena, or a small bag of sunflower seeds. And on my way out, there were always a few fils that she would drop in my pocket for an ice cream cone. Now my beloved aunt and uncle looked frail and anxious. I could see the fear of the unknown in Khala Guerjiyi's eyes. It was painful to see how they had fallen.

It was hot when I went to visit another evening that summer. Heat shimmered against the canvas of the tent and the air inside was stifling. Bugs came in and out at will. I remember walking into the tent and seeing Helwa—usually so calm-- shaking with fear at the sight of a centipede scurrying across the floor. She was crying and calling out for Mama, terrified.

In Baghdad, centipedes were believed to crawl in through a person's ear and make their way to the brain and destroy it. Our family didn't believe in such tales, but my sisters' lives had been turned upside down in a short period of time. It probably seemed to Helwa that anything and everything bad could happen in Israel in that open field.

I squashed the centipede with my big military boots. I

put my arms around Helwa and held her until she calmed down. It was all I could do, and it wasn't enough. I couldn't protect my sisters, aunt and uncle adequately.

A view of a *ma'abara*, one of many flooded during the heavy rain in winter 1951-52

I couldn't protect them when they lay in bed and listened to the howling of the coyotes outside, fearful that one would barge into their tent, which had no doors that could be shut securely, no locks. I couldn't protect them from the daytime heat or from the snakes that lurked in their path when they visited the outhouse at night. They were suffering, and I couldn't do anything to help. It tore at my heart to see them living in the open, hostile countryside at the mercy of the elements.

The winter that followed, the worst on record in Israel, brought even more hardship. Heavy winds and rains swept across the land. The field in which my sisters' *ma'abara* was situated quickly turned into a sea of mud.

One winter evening I trudged through the mud to their tent. I was happy to arrive and to be out of the driving rain and the biting wind. Suddenly our exclamations of joy at seeing one another turned to cries of dismay, as the main tent pole lurched dangerously to one side. I could see that the tent was in imminent danger of falling.

"Mama! Mama!" Reyna cried, as she and Helwa sobbed. Latifa just stood there helplessly wringing her hands.

I ran outside and pulled on a slack rope to get the pole back into position, but the peg around which the rope was wound was coming out of the muddy ground and needed to be hammered back into place.

Ammu Moshe came outside.

"I need a hammer, a hammer," I told him.

The wind and rain pummeled me. I was crouched in the middle of a big puddle that filled my boots with water, as I desperately pulled the rope toward me to prevent the tent from collapsing. The raindrops came down diagonally. Driven by the wind, they lashed hard at my face like nails.

As I pulled the rope, I became aware of pandemonium all around me. Ours was not the only tent in danger of collapsing. The next-door neighbor's tent pole was tilting dangerously. There were small children in that tent. Terrified, they came out in their pajamas, crying. Their parents held on to the ropes, as I did, calling for help. I was torn. I wanted to help. But I knew if I let go, the tent would fall on my sisters. I pulled tight. I waited for someone to hand me a hammer. The word came back: No hammer could be found.

I looked around and found a large stone. It would have to do. I used it to hammer the peg into the ground. I hammered and hammered. Was I trying to hammer my frustrations into the ground with that peg? My sisters were living under miserable conditions, and I couldn't do anything to improve their lot. Why did life have to be like this?

My intensity must have scared Ammu Moshe. I heard him repeat over and over again:

"Stop, Daniel, stop!"

I paid no attention. As I kept on hammering, I heard the tent next-door fall to the ground. Next to the fallen tent stood an older woman with long black hair and an embroidered headband holding it in place. She held a kerosene lantern. I don't know why I noticed that the headband was missing the customary pearls. Did the customs inspectors at Baghdad's airport confiscate them? I wondered. Were we to be left with nothing? The few belongings that people had managed to bring with them out of their native Iraq were being destroyed in the rain in Israel as their tents were being knocked down. Would we ever see better days? I continued to hammer as these thoughts rushed through my head.

I could hear babies crying and people screaming all around. I wished I could help everybody, but all I could do was continue to hammer, until I got our tent secured.

We were city dwellers. We knew well-lit city streets and brick houses. We knew that danger lurked in the world outside in Baghdad, but being with the family gave us a feeling of security. Now I had the feeling that there was no safety, no security. Everything familiar had been ripped away, and we couldn't even keep inclement weather at bay.

Inside the tent, my sisters were shaken. It seemed as if every imaginable misery could happen here in Israel in the rain-swept muddy field. Conditions in Iraq had been bad, but on some level conditions in Israel were worse. Why did this country seem so inhospitable?

During the following months, Uncle Moshe managed to put together enough money to buy a 350-square-foot one-bedroom apartment in Ramat Gan, a suburb of Tel Aviv. My three sisters went to live with him and Khala Guerjiyi in their apartment. It wasn't much, but it was better than living in a tent in a *ma'abara.*

In Baghdad my sisters would have lived with our parents until marriages were arranged for them. In Israel they had to work at menial jobs to help support themselves. They were intelligent and found such work boring. There were so many inconveniences, each one perhaps unimportant in itself, but their cumulative effect weighed on my sisters' spirits.

Planting saplings at kibbutz Ein haShofet – L to R: Helwa's friend, Daniel, Helwa's friend, Helwa

Soon enough, Helwa and Latifa had to face the sticky matter of military service. Among Babylonian Jews it was unheard of for women to serve in the military. Here, everybody under a certain age was required to serve two years. Immigrants were given the choice of deferral for one year after their arrival. Married women or women who declared themselves to be religious were exempt from induction, provided they met standards of modesty in dress as well. But the definition of "religious" and "modest" in Israel differed from our Babylonian customs. In Israel, wearing sleeveless shirts and bare legs disqualified a woman from being classified as religious for the purpose of receiving a military exemption. No such strictures prevailed in Baghdad's hot climate.

Reyna, Helwa, and Latifa opted for the automatic one-year deferral. By the end of the year, Reyna was past the age for compulsory service. Helwa, by then twenty-three, and Latifa, twenty-one, had to report for service. They didn't. Neither felt they could in good conscience ask for an exemption from the military on the grounds of being religious in the sense accepted in Israel. Both wore sandals and dressed in sleeveless shirts, but they still believed, Helwa more so than Latifa, that it ran against our traditions to have women serve in the military. From the time they made that decision they became fugitives, just like undocumented aliens. Everyone in Israel carried an ID card showing current military status, and MPs, for security reasons, would often check ID's when people boarded buses. Helwa and Latifa lived in dread of being discovered. They avoided traveling by bus as much as possible. On the road they steered away from the vehicles of military police. Their undocumented status made them ripe for exploitation at work. They had to accept wages below those agreed upon with the labor unions, and which were barely enough for subsistence. There were times when they were cheated out of payment, but they couldn't complain for fear of blowing their cover. "How long should we have to take it?" Latifa would ask tearfully.

Latifa, in training overalls, heading for the mess hall, September 3, 1953   Latifa, left, and two of her friends in the antiaircraft artillery regimen

For Latifa, the answer was "not much longer." She went to the recruiting office and defiantly declared, "I am not religious." She was not penalized for not reporting at the end of her one-year exemption and served two years in the antiaircraft artillery.

Helwa held on for four more years. Her trials came to an end when she got married.

A BOUT WITH PNEUMONIA

No doubt partly because of the foul weather during the winter of 1951-52, I became quite ill. I delayed seeing the camp doctor, hoping the sickness would pass of its own accord, until I could barely stand.

"Why did you wait so long?" the doctor asked me.

" I didn't want to open myself to the charge of malingering," I said.

The doctor shook his head incredulously.

"You have a bad case of pneumonia."

He ordered a vehicle to rush me to Tel Nof's hospital.

The trip to the hospital was not long, but it was excruciating. The motion of the vehicle rattled me. I coughed. I felt as if I were burning with fever, but at the same time I felt cold. My body shook, and I just wanted to lie down and close my eyes. The driver had all windows closed. He turned on the heater, but nothing seemed to help. Finally we reached the hospital, where I passed out.

When I finally opened my eyes, I was lying in bed in a room by myself. Several blankets covered me. My joints ached, and I couldn't move a limb. It was painful to breathe, and things looked blurry. Was I dying? What would happen if I were to die? Would my sisters find out? The military had no address for any of my relatives who had arrived recently in Israel. Would my parents be told?

When I joined the military, I was asked for the address of my next of kin. I gave my parents' address in Baghdad. But I worried how word would reach my parents if something happened to me. Iraq was still at war with Israel— it had never signed the armistice treaty after the 1948-49 war of independence. So I didn't expect the military to send my parents a notice of my death. But I wondered if anyone I cared about would be told if I died.

A nurse walked in. She had a needle in hand, ready to give me an injection. She smiled, patted my hair and asked me how I felt. I couldn't muster the energy to answer. I just nodded. I wanted to know how long I had been there, but I couldn't talk. She lifted the covers to expose my arm, and gave me the injection. It felt like an eternity before the needle finally came out of my arm. The nurse covered me and left. I lay in that room for two weeks. Eventually I gained strength and sat up in bed.

One bright morning, the nurse walked in with a smile.

"The doctor said we can wheel you out this morning, and you can have breakfast on the patio."

Outside, the sun shone brightly. It was a beautiful day. It felt so good to be out in the open. Other patients sat around the table and ate their breakfast. There were several food trays and bowls on the table. I was feeling disoriented, and was too weak to reach out for what I wanted. But I noticed a bowl of boiled eggs right in front of me. They reminded me of the brown eggs of the Sabbath days in Baghdad. I reached for an egg, peeled it and dropped the shells into a big metal bowl that contained what looked like garbage.

"What are you doing?" the young nurse asked, her eyes crinkling with laughter. "Why are you throwing eggshells into the bowl of herring?"

I explained that I hadn't done it intentionally.

"Now we know what you think of herring," she teased.

I could only smile weakly. I had given away my true feelings about herring, something I wouldn't have done normally. I made no distinction between garbage and herring.

Indeed, to me herring signified all that was wrong with the Israeli diet. In time I learned to tolerate East European foods like potatoes and black bread. But the one thing I never got used to was the dreadful, salty "*dag maloo'ah,*" as herring was known in Israel. I still remember the barrel of herring wheeled around the mess hall during breakfast. The cook would move from table to table, stick his fat, filthy hands in the barrel and throw handfuls of herring into metal bowls, as the salty water from the barrel dripped from his hands all over the table. The herring smelled and looked repulsive.

"Eat it. *dag maloo'ah* is good for you," he would say.

The first time I witnessed this nauseating ritual I had to rush from the table and go outside to throw up.

After spending three weeks in the hospital, I was taken to a convalescent home in Mount Carmel. Most of the time I spent in bed, happy to sink into the peace and serenity surrounding me. Some of the patients had been wounded in training or in border skirmishes. Others had been seriously ill and needed, as I did, to regain their strength. But, as I recovered, I could finally notice my surroundings and reflect on all that had happened to me. I could mourn my separation from my parents and the dispersion of my family. I could drink in the beauty of the valley below and of the Mediterranean at the foot of the mountain. For the three weeks I was there I could be quiet and heal my spirit.

During that time, my thoughts seemed to flow constantly to my parents and the life I had left behind in Baghdad. My parents didn't know that I had made it safely to Israel. In the rush getting out of Baghdad, I didn't make arrangements to send them any coded message. But two months or so into my basic training I had written to them at our home in Baghdad. I must have written something innocuous, hoping that my parents would have no difficulty identifying who had written the letter. I knew it was risky, but I was desperate to communicate with them. But the military returned the letter to me with a note warning that the Iraqis opened letters sent to Jews and might harm them if they discovered the letter had come from Israel. I never tried to communicate with my parents again.

I loved my parents, but I needed to face the fact that I might never see them again. I felt I had to sever my ties with the past to move forward into my new life in Israel. In order to become part of Israeli society, I felt I must adopt its values and customs as my own. At the time, I didn't foresee the devil's bargain I was striking: how much of my essential self I'd be giving up.

"STOP YOUR ARABIC!"

Hebrew was the official language of Israel, but many other languages that European immigrants brought with them were used and treated with respect. My native language, Judeo-Arabic, was not. The unmistakable message was that there was something intrinsically unacceptable about being a Jew from an Arab land. An older immigrant from Poland, who worked with me in Wing 4, invariably addressed me as "*attem haSh'horim*", or "you the blacks," when referring to immigrants from Arab lands. Other soldiers would loudly mimic Arabic songs in a denigrating way as soon as they learned I was from Iraq. In the Wing 4 lounge, it was common for soldiers who were immigrants from Eastern Europe to shout back and forth to one another in Yiddish. But when Babylonian soldiers spoke Judeo-Arabic, there were usually cries of "Shut up!", "Stop your Arabic!" The pervasiveness of this prejudice was driven home to me during a planning meeting of Wing 4, which I attended.

A number of soldiers didn't understand much Hebrew and if they spoke Romanian, Polish or Yiddish, directives were readily given in those languages. This particular meeting was being run by a young second lieutenant called Battat who was Israeli-born, but whose family hailed from Iraq. Battat was the only soldier of officer rank on campus with a Middle Eastern background. I knew that he spoke and understood Judeo-Arabic. There were about a dozen soldiers at that meeting, and they were mostly from Iraq. It quickly became obvious to Battat that one young man wasn't following the discussion.

"What language do you speak?" Battat asked.

"Judeo-Arabic."

There was a long silence. Two European soldiers in the group were looking fixedly at Battat, who was clearly uneasy. Battat shifted in his seat and a flush rose from his neck to his forehead. The thoughts running through Battat's mind seemed to echo in mine, but I remained silent and looked away.

How could Battat admit to knowing Judeo-Arabic, a language deemed unacceptable in Israel? How could he associate himself with a despised minority? How could I? Even as the thought crossed my mind that Battat and I should be able to speak in any language we chose to, I pushed the thought away. In spite of myself, my mind strayed to the time I went to see the Muslim doctor when I was a boy and defiantly spoke to him in Judeo-Arabic, even though Muslims expected to be spoken to in their own dialect.

What had happened to me since then? Now I was careful to lower my voice when speaking Judeo-Arabic in public. Ours was a language that, in Israel, had been dubbed Arabic, the language of the enemy. And Battat obviously felt the same way. The fact that he was an officer who outranked the two Europeans in the group made no difference, just as it made no difference that the Jew in Baghdad was a professor and the Muslim he spoke with was a garbage collector. The Jew was expected to defer, to hide his Judeo-Arabic and speak in the Muslim dialect instead.

I wished that Battat would take a stand, but he couldn't bring himself to do it. He didn't translate his instructions into Judeo-Arabic. The young soldier from Iraq was on his own.

I DON'T WANT TO BE A PHYSICIAN

My time in the military was drawing to an end, and I realized that I would need skills in order to survive. I enrolled in an evening accounting course in Tel Aviv. I had no clear direction yet, but I liked the subject and figured that if I were to make it to college, a job in accounting might pay my way.

At the same time I was preparing to take the entrance exam for Hebrew University Medical School. There were five physicians in my family, and becoming a physician was considered the height of accomplishment in my family.

I was not enamored of becoming a doctor. Unlike the rest of my family, I didn't hold physicians in awe and couldn't -- I still can't -- stand the sight of blood. One time my sister Latifa needed treatment for Leishmaniasis, a tropical disease common in Baghdad. I accompanied her to Uncle Guerji's clinic and stayed with her while he injected a needle into a painful boil on her finger. The sight of the bloody procedure and her writhing in pain was enough to make me pass out. When I opened my eyes, Latifa was standing next to me, holding a wet cloth to my forehead.

In spite of this phobia, I still felt I should apply to medical school. Though I was living far away from my parents and the community in which I grew up, I still felt their influence. Looking back, I can't imagine what I thought I was doing. Perhaps I was hoping that I would be turned down, so that I could say I had at least tried.

I hitchhiked to Jerusalem and took the medical school entrance exam. When I finished, I heaved a sigh of relief. I had done my duty, and now I could get on with my life.

Not long after, I received a letter from the admissions office saying that I should report to the university in Jerusalem for a preparatory meeting for entrance to the medical school.

I panicked.

"My God. This is getting serious. I don't want to be a physician!"

I wrote immediately to the admissions office saying that I didn't have money for the bus fare to Jerusalem, which was true, and as I expected I never heard from them again. If the school had offered to pay for my travel fare, I am not sure what I would have done. Whatever my future held, I knew it wouldn't involve medicine.

TWO CONSCRIPTS

As my discharge date approached, I began to feel regrets about leaving. I had gotten used to life in the Air Force, and had come to think of the conscripts in Wing 4 as my family. The camp at Has'sore had been my home for over two years, and during that time I rubbed shoulders with a number of memorable characters.

At Wing 4 we didn't have daily formation or inspection, as was the practice in the infantry or the artillery. The only exception was the sanitation crew. They mustered every morning, carrying their brooms, brushes, buckets, hoses, shovels, hoes, and rakes. Dressed in blue work overalls and berets, they stood in line for roll call and their assignments for the day.

Without fail, a spindly young conscript from Algiers stood at the head of the line. His name was Gilbert. He had dark skin, curly black hair, and the color of his eyes matched his blue overalls. He held his tall broom against his right shoulder, like a rifle. He beamed with pleasure, turning his face right and left as if to ask every passerby: Did you notice me? Can you see my enormous broom?

Gilbert spoke French. At times each word came out broken in pieces with quick breaths in between. At others, four or five words tumbled out at once. He spoke little Hebrew, and his speech all sounded like unintelligible French. But the broad smile of wonder and amazement never left his face even when he realized people couldn't understand what he was saying. On the contrary, he seemed exhilarated when people asked him to repeat what he said.

Gilbert loved to hear his name, particularly when it was pronounced the French way – Jilbegh, with the guttural French GH for R. I used to call him "Monsieur Jilbegh," and that always elicited a bigger smile than usual, a straightened body, and an uplifted head.

Gilbert's favorite work assignment was cleaning the camp's bathrooms. Not surprisingly, he had no competition for this assignment.

When I was promoted to the rank of sergeant, I was moved to new, more spacious living quarters, closer to the Wing's entrance. Gilbert's face lit up when he saw my three stripes, and he pledged to come every day at the end of his shift, to sweep my bungalow. I declined the offer gently. I was not particularly thrilled at the prospect of having my bedroom swept with the same broom used to sweep the camp's toilets.

On the day of my discharge from the Air Force, I saw Gilbert and the rest of the sanitation crew for the last time. I yelled my usual, "Salut, Monsieur Jilbegh" and stepped forward to the parade and shook Gilbert's left hand, as he continued his march with the rest of the sanitation crew.

Daniel, shortly after being promoted to the rank of sergeant

I often thought about Gilbert and wondered how he managed in society at large. Was he able to deal with the rough and tumble of civilian life? He seemed to be so innocent, so vulnerable. Did he continue in sanitation? Did he choose to return to Algiers to be with his family? Maybe his family too was displaced. Where could he have ended up? And to day, as I write my memoirs, I wonder about him, as I wonder about the rest of the conscripts of Wing 4 who made up my little family while I served in the military.

Zari Salloomee was quite a different character. Zari came from a poor Muslim village in Iraq. He was short and muscular, had black hair that stood up in spikes, a thick moustache, and dark skin. He was cross-eyed, adding to his fierce look and menacing appearance. Zari bore a close resemblance to a vulture, the type of person one would be terrified to bump against on a dark night.

Before coming to Israel, Zari had served two years in the Iraqi military. Jews in Iraq served at most three months in the Iraqi military; most were well-educated enough to qualify for shorter stints. Zari was the first Jew I ever met who had served the full tour of duty.

By all indications, Zari was a misfit. He didn't have the staying power to hold down a job, and there were few jobs for which he was qualified. Those who had dealings with him described him as unpredictable, driven by impulse. He would erupt at the slightest provocation. Some wondered if he was mentally stable. Others went so far as to say he was schizophrenic. But I had a hunch that Zari was a shrewd bully who knew exactly what he was doing. The reputation he had was precisely the one he had cultivated. He liked being able to behave exactly as he pleased and, because most people were afraid of his outbursts, he would do just that – blow up.

Whatever his personality disorders, the collective wisdom was that Zari was stupid. And Zari took full advantage of this perception. He was always ready to flex his muscles, and he got into fistfights frequently. He landed in the Wing's jail several times. Nothing seemed to help.

Zari treated me with deference, and would stop by my office to talk. I didn't particularly want to see him, but I never told him that. During our visits, he lashed out at Israel's military for what he sarcastically called the princely treatment of its soldiers. He maintained that the rough treatment he had received in the Iraqi army had enhanced his stamina.

"In the Iraqi military," Zari would tell me, "we all ate from the same big plate, and we felt we were sharing with our brothers. How do you create the sense of brotherhood when everyone has his own food domain?"

(I did know that conditions in the Iraqi military were deplorable: Cold showers, lice, floggings. Most Muslim conscripts were illiterate. It was said that because few of them could tell right from left, during training they were each given a tomato to hold in their right hand and an onion for the left hand. They were ordered to "turn tomato" or "turn onion" until they learned to tell left from right.)

The day arrived when Zari was talked into working in the officers' dining room as a server. After I was promoted to sergeant, I was entitled to eat in the officers' dining room. Zari was ecstatic when he saw me enter the officers' dining room for the first time.

"Welcome, Areef Khazzoom," he said with a smile, using the Arabic word for sergeant.

He took my hand and seated me at one of the tables. I was flattered, but embarrassed by the special treatment. Still, who would dare question Zari's actions? He brought me a tray full of food. He had selected the kind of food that was closest to our daily diet in the old country.

At first I was very happy to get the kind of dishes I'd eaten in my parents' home. In time, however, my excitement gave way to discomfort. Zari brought me a lot more food than he brought the rest. I was embarrassed, and couldn't eat it all. Zari wouldn't listen to my pleas to bring smaller portions. Worse, he insisted that I eat everything he brought. I thought that he would be offended if I turned back the tray, and worried that he might turn on me.

I was beginning to feel helpless. And then it occurred to me that I was not obligated to eat in the officers' dining room. I could go back to the mess hall if I wanted to, and then I wouldn't have to deal with Zari. And so I did.

A couple of days later, there was a knock on my office door. It was Zari. He looked grim, and he had a forbidding look on his face. He didn't say a word. He closed the door slowly and sat on the floor with his back against the door, as if to make sure nobody could come in.

I felt a stab of fear. Why had he come?

Finally he broke the silence. Zari told me he was getting married the following week. He had applied for a wedding leave, but was granted only two days. He complained that it took him a whole day to hitchhike from Has'sore to his *ma'abara* in northern Israel. He was furious that he was not granted adequate time for his wedding celebration.

"So now I have decided to escape from the camp for my wedding. Would you, Areef Khazzoom, look it up in your law books," he asked, "and tell me how long they would imprison me if I were to escape for, say, two weeks or three weeks?"

I checked the rules and gave him the answer. But it was not what he wanted. He hesitated a minute and came straight to the point.

"How many days of unauthorized absence would

230

bring a maximum of three weeks in jail?"

"Eighteen days."

Zari's face lit up. There was a shrewd look in his eyes.

"That's good, Areef Khazzoom. For the information, I thank you."

The rule was that when a soldier was imprisoned for up to three weeks, the days he spent in jail would count toward his military service. But if his imprisonment exceeded three weeks, his discharge would be delayed by the same number of days he sat in jail.

Now it was clear what Zari was after. He wanted to escape from the camp for a period of time that wouldn't extend his date of discharge. A week later Zari vanished from sight. He showed up exactly eighteen days later to turn himself in. The man was no fool, I thought to myself. He was a shrewd, calculating person who knew exactly what he was doing.

DAY OF DISCHARGE

October 2, 1953 was the day of my discharge from the military. Even though I had looked forward to it for a long time, I remember it as a bittersweet day. I felt sad, as though I were separating from a close friend.

I had grown a lot during the months I spent in the Air Force. I learned Hebrew, acquired new skills working in a large organization and received excellent care when I convalesced after my bout with pneumonia.

But there was a time to be weaned. And that time had come.

I rode down to the airfield where our shops were located to bid farewell to my coworkers. Hanan Landau came out of his office to greet me. Hanan, a major in the Air Force, was the head of our unit. I had worked with him during the last twenty-five months of my service. Hanan was German-born, and had immigrated to Israel when Hitler took over. Prior to his arrival, a native of Israel had headed our unit.

I was still new to Israeli ways when Hanan arrived, and was not aware of the historical tensions between Jews of Eastern European background and Jews of German background. For weeks beforehand everybody talked about the misery of having this "*Yeke*" in our midst. When I asked friends in camp why a "*Yeke*" would be so bad to have around, I was told horror stories about how demanding, rigid, intolerant, and arrogant "*Yekes*" were. I took the stories seriously, and was terrified to think of what lay ahead, since I was supposed to work directly with the head of our unit.

But it was the surprise of my life when Hanan Landau came on board. Right from the outset, we had a close working relationship. We synchronized admirably. Hanan wanted everything above board, and so did I. He expected commitment, and so did I. He insisted on transparency and didn't tolerate fudging, and so did I. He abhorred favoritism - protectsia, as it was known in Israel- and so did I. In time, Hanan and I became good friends, and I learned to be wary of derogatory characterizations applied to entire groups.

I left Hanan's office and turned to what used to be my office. A coworker – my successor -- was already occupying it. We hugged warmly as I entered. I lingered for a moment taking in the scene. I ran my hand slowly over the top of what used to be my desk. I thought to myself I was so much more fortunate than those immigrants who had to live in a ma'abara.

Finally, I visited my bedroom, the most difficult place to part with. It was my refuge. I paused to take one last look through the window. There was the kibbutz that greeted me every morning when I woke up, as beautiful as ever. I said a prayer in my heart that the kibbutz and its members would never have to separate from each other. A separation from one's home was heart-rending.

I left my bedroom, kissed the Mezuzah at the doorpost, and closed the door behind me for the last time.

DETOUR IN THE NEGEV

I was discharged from the Air Force on October 2, 1953. The military gave me fifteen liras (about five dollars), a bus pass good for free travel and a voucher for dormitory-style lodging during the following two weeks.

I now had my sights set on attending college and majoring in science. In high school I was a top student in math, physics and chemistry, and math was my love. But courses in the sciences were offered only at Hebrew University in Jerusalem and at Israel's Institute of Technology (Technion) in Haifa, and I couldn't afford the tuition at either school. Reluctantly, I decided to postpone college. I would find a job and save money first.

I had two choices. I could stay in Ramat Gan with Ammu Moshe and Khala Guerjiyi and look for work in nearby Tel Aviv. My other choice was to go to Bersheba, an arid, sparsely populated Arab town in the heart of the Negev desert in Southern Israel. Most of the Arab population in that area was nomadic. Almost all the Jewish inhabitants were recent immigrants from the Middle East. I was not anxious to live in the desert, but I felt I owed it to my new country. Israel was striving to convert the Negev into productive farmland. But the Negev's arid climate and its distance from population centers discouraged people from moving to Bersheba. It was incumbent upon us, the younger generation, to do our share and help realize the dream of making the desert bloom.

I chose to go to Bersheba. The bus trip took five hours. As we pulled into town, we passed a few run down houses. One building stood out. It was Bank haPoaleem, the only bank and, as it turned out, the only solid building in town. A dilapidated hotel stood a few yards away from the bank. There was no bus station– only a bus stop. As far as I could see, Bersheba's sprawling *ma'abara* dominated the town.

I got off the bus with no idea of where to go or how to find a job. My voucher for lodging was good for twelve more days, so I knew I wouldn't be left out on the street. My aunt had packed food for me, and I had my fifteen liras in my pocket.

"Why put off the job search till to-morrow?" I figured. "Why not just go to the bank right now and inquire? What could I lose?"

The bank manager was a well-dressed, slim man in his late thirties with thinning hair. He had been born in Israel to parents who grew up in Iraq, I learned later. He had a poised manner and impressed me as a kind person, eager to help. He smiled and motioned to me to take a seat.

"My name is Daniel Khazzoom. I have just completed my military service, and I'm looking for work."

The words were out of my mouth before I knew it. I was terrified. "What have I done? Why so fast? I blew it!" But the manager seemed unruffled. He actually seemed to be pleased with my directness.

I told him I was a graduate of l'Ecole de l'Alliance Israelite in Baghdad, and briefly explained my work and responsibilities in the Air Force. But I dwelt mostly on the accounting course I had passed with distinction.

This seemed to interest the manager less than my earlier schooling.

"You are a graduate of l'Alliance Israelite?" he said, beaming. "That is a top school. This is just wonderful. We need people like you."

Obviously delighted, he shook hands with me, and hustled me off to meet the assistant manager, who was also the bank's accountant. In glowing terms, the manager went on about my education at l'Alliance. The assistant manager, a Mr. BenBassat, suggested that we have a chat over tea.

A soft-spoken, stocky man in his early fifties, Mr. benBassat had been born in Sofia, Bulgaria. He had immigrated to Israel at the end of World War II, and joined the Hagganah. He walked with a limp, the result of an injury during the war of independence. Mr. benBassat had a fatherly look, and when he smiled, one scarcely noticed the lines deeply etched into his face or his thinning hair, which he smoothed down with his large hand.

I told him about wanting to help settle the desert and about my plans to go to college and make something of myself.

"It is so good to meet a young man with your sense of purpose."

When the manager returned, Mr. benBassat said he would like to have me work with him.

The manager motioned to an unoccupied desk next to Mr. benBassat's.

"Here is your desk. It is all yours. You can start working now, and I want to welcome you to our family."

I was on the verge of tears. I could scarcely believe I had landed a job.

That evening I found a bed in the hotel and settled in. I sat at the edge of my bed and looked around. I had had nothing to eat since that morning. But I didn't feel hungry. I felt pumped up, exhilarated; I was on my way. The people I had met in the bank seemed like caring, warm human beings. It would be a pleasure to spend the next year or two working with them. Who knows, maybe by then a university would spring up here. Israel had grand plans for Bersheba.

That night I turned in early, but was awakened at midnight by loud voices in my room. A crowd of truck drivers had come in to occupy the other beds in my room, switched on all the lights, began smoking and sat discussing all that had happened to them that day. It was hours before they turned off the lights and settled down to sleep.

This became the pattern for my entire stay at the hotel. During the following few nights, I probably was more sleep-deprived than I had been in basic training.

"This can't go on much longer," I said to myself. I had to find a different place to stay. But where? There was no other hotel in town, and I couldn't afford to rent a private room. Sadly, I had to concede I was at a dead end. I realized I couldn't stay in Bersheba if I wanted to save money for college. I needed to go back to Ramat Gan and move in with my sisters and Ammu Moshe.

It was a painful day when I told my colleagues at the bank what I needed to do. In the ten short days I had been with them, we'd grown quite close. The manager and Mr. benBassat didn't try to stop me from leaving, though I knew they didn't want me to go.

The manager accompanied me to the bus on my way back to Ramat Gan. He put his arm around my shoulder, as I was about to board.

"I wish you well, Danny. If ever you need a reference, you know where to come."

Bersheba is now a sprawling modern city; Bank haPoaleem is part of "Old Bersheba." Whenever I go there, I walk to "Old Bersheba" and spend a moment or two in front of the old building, remembering the first time I walked through its doors, suitcase in hand. Bersheba has many more bank buildings now, all modern and impressive. But this old building holds a special place in my heart.

I felt sad and discouraged as I rode the bus back to Ramat Gan. Would I ever find such marvelous working colleagues again? Would I ever be able to save enough money to cover the expenses of attending Hebrew University or Technion? Would I ever realize my dream of majoring in science? My short experience with living expenses in Bersheba had undermined my self-confidence. I was beginning to have doubts.

The salaries in Tel Aviv were higher than in Bersheba. I was beginning to wonder if I shouldn't postpone college until I had saved enough to live on my own in Jerusalem or Haifa. But by the time I managed to save enough, would I be too old for college? What other choice did I have?

I wanted to borrow money for college and pay off my debts after graduation. But in Israel, educational loans were out of the question. Banks wanted collateral, and I could offer none.

By the time the bus reached Tel Aviv, I had decided to compromise on my choice of major. Tel Aviv had an evening school, the School of Law and Economics, which offered degrees in economics, law, political science, and auditing. None of these fields was my calling. But whatever I would be doing in Tel Aviv would involve work with a business establishment. Studying economics or auditing while I was working might enhance my performance and earnings. If I managed to save enough in the meantime, I could then leave for Jerusalem or Haifa to major in science.

It was cold logic that led me to economics as a stopgap measure. Inertia and lack of adequate funds kept me permanently in a field that failed to ignite my imagination the way math and science always had. In Iraq, the social sciences were disparaged, and reserved for the least talented students. As a result, I lacked even the basic fundamentals of economics when I began studying it in college, and carried with me the tendency to look down on the field as well.

Today as I look back, I wish I had not been so cautious. I wish I had gone to Jerusalem or Haifa and taken the plunge. During my lifetime I took many gambles, and against all odds, things eventually fell into place. I wish I had adopted the same determined attitude toward my education.

In terms of accomplishments, I can't complain. I did well as an academic in quantitative economics, and my published research work has influenced thinking and policymaking in the U.S. and Canada. But in spite of all those achievements, my heart remains in the sciences.

COLLEGE YEARS

AN UNLIKELY BENEFACTOR

Tuition at the School of Law and Economics was one hundred and twenty liras, the equivalent of forty dollars. I had twenty liras, altogether – my original allowance from the military plus what I had managed to save from my work at Bank haPoaleem.

"May I give you the twenty liras I have and sign a promissory note for the balance?" I asked the school's Academic Secretary.

"No, I am sorry. The full tuition fee must be paid in advance."

"Is there a scholarship I can apply for?"

"No, there isn't."

"Could I borrow the money from a bank?"

"Banks don't lend money to pay tuition fees."

The Academic Secretary suggested that I send letters to several places, including the ministry of education and the office of the Prime Minister, inquiring about the availability of a scholarship or loan. No one responded.

The night before the start of the fall term, we had a family gathering at grandma Aziza's apartment. I told my relatives of my plight. Everyone sympathized, but it was Khala Toya who took me by the hand and led me to the bedroom, where she took down a suitcase she had brought with her from Baghdad.

"What are you doing, Khala Toya?"

She didn't answer. She opened the suitcase and tore between the two layers at the bottom, exposing to view a few banknotes she had hidden there before leaving Baghdad. I knew she had been holding on to the money for dear life, but she gave it to me to pay for my tuition. I was stunned, elated and grateful that this difficult woman, of all people, would be the one to rescue me at a time when she and her husband had such bleak prospects.

I wish I could say that Khala Toya became a different person after she made this magnificent sacrifice on my

238

behalf. She didn't. She still had nothing good to say about my father whom she had defrauded when she helped to buy Jamila's trousseau, and she constantly belittled others when they weren't present. But even Khala Toya felt that family members should come to one another's aid in time of need.

I thought about that the next evening as I attended the first lecture of the semester.

My book of Histadroot membership, issued in November 1953

To find a job, I registered with the Labor Exchange, an arm of the Histadroot, the powerful labor union in Israel. The long arm of the Histadroot reached into the government, healthcare, banking, industry, and the inner recesses of the private sector. Practically everybody who wanted work had to be a member of the Histadroot. Every employer had to deal with the Histadroot.

When I was not actively looking for work, I roamed the streets of Tel Aviv getting to know the city. I noticed how many middle-aged and older Jews from Iraq were sitting alone on the park benches along Rothschild Boulevard with a look of despair and resignation on their faces. Many of these men were entrepreneurs who had owned businesses in Iraq. They were used to being contributing members of society. Now they had nothing to look forward to. They were cast aside.

Among the faces, I saw one that I recognized: a French teacher from l'Alliance Israelite, Monsieur Bonfils, a stocky, gentle-looking man.

Monsieur Isaac Bonfils, my Alliance teacher

"Monsieur Bonfils," I called out.

I saw the familiar face light up.

"Joseph! *Comment vas-tu mon fils?*" he replied.

"I just came from the Labor Exchange. I am looking for work. How about you, Monsieur Bonfils? How are you doing? Are you working?"

The smile on my teacher's face faded into gloom as he shook his head in resignation.

"They have no work for me in this country. They say I am too old for what they have," he replied.

Monsieur Bonfils was not much older than fifty. He was not a wealthy man. He lived on a teacher's salary. He had a big house in Baghdad, but it was confiscated when the Iraqi government froze the assets of the Jews who left the country. How was he supporting himself and his wife?

What had happened to the members of the wonderful Jewish community from Baghdad? I wished we could have transported the community in its entirety to Israel. But things were different now. The community was scattered, and who knew what would happen to the people who had left or to those who remained behind? If my parents, my brother Jacob, my sister Valentine and my sister Jamila and her family ever managed to get out of Iraq and make it to Israel, I wondered if they too, would sit, despondent, on park benches. I remembered my old French teacher as a lion, exuding energy and a love of learning. He was a walking dictionary, and I looked up to him. It was shocking to see how fast and how far the mighty could fall.

My uncles were enduring similar humiliations.

A couple of years after our arrival in Israel, my maternal uncle Guerji received a small sum of money that he had stashed away in a Swiss bank years before he left Baghdad. He used it to buy the privilege of renting a small store in a Tel Aviv slum, where he opened a restaurant. I stopped by the restaurant one evening. It startled me to see this once-elegant and powerful man wearing a white apron. Still, he seemed happy to have something that kept him busy. That evening, the restaurant was practically empty. Water was boiling in the pot for tea, but because of stringent rationing, he had run out of food. There was not even a piece of bread in the store. A tired-looking man in his sixties walked in and sat at one of the spotlessly clean tables. Uncle Guerji set down a glass of water in front of the man, who ordered a plate of mashed eggplant. Uncle Guerji, inexperienced and apparently afraid of losing a potential customer, launched forth into a recitation in heavy, Babylonian-accented biblical Hebrew. He ticked off all the items on the menu: "And we had mashed eggplant, and we had fried eggplant, and we had Baba Gannoush, and we had crispy rice, and we had boiled eggs, and we had ..." The man's eyes bulged, as he grew increasingly impatient with this litany of "we had." He finally lifted the glass of water and brought it down hard on the table, shattering the glass. "Tell me what you have that I can eat," he howled. Poor Uncle Guerji sheepishly had to admit, "We don't have anything." With that, the irate customer stalked out of the restaurant. Sadly, Uncle Guerji took his chef's towel and swept the broken glass. A month later, he closed the restaurant.

I had great sympathy for displaced workers of my father's generation. But setting out on my life's journey was not all that easy either. I told my friend Yarmiyahoo Halperin of my frustrations landing a job. He was Russian-born, a former captain in the British navy and a staunch proponent of free enterprise. He told me that he had mentioned me to a Mr. Weinberg, the General Manager of Bank Leumi, Israel's largest bank.

"Mr. Weinberg told me the bank has open slots for young people like you, and would like you to apply," he told me. "Why don't you fill out an application?"

I presented myself to Bank Leumi's personnel manager, a man with gray curly hair, and glasses with metallic rims. I was struck by how small his eyes looked behind his thick lenses.

"No, no, young man. You can't come in here on your own looking for work," he said. "First you must go to the Histadroot labor exchange. We hire all of our people from there."

I was puzzled. But I needed work, and if that was the accepted way of doing things, I wasn't going to point out that I was already registered with the Histadroot labor exchange or that the bank's General Manager had said I should apply.

The man at the Histadroot labor exchange was about as helpful as the bank official had been.

"What do you expect me to do?" he snapped. "We need a letter from the bank telling us there are open positions for someone with your background."

As the days went by, I wore a path between the bank and the Histadroot. Each needed a letter from the other before anything could be done about employing me, but neither one was willing to make the first move.

The next time I visited the Histadroot labor exchange, there was a kindly, soft-spoken Syrian gentleman behind the desk. I explained my problem to him.

"With your permission, I am going to go through our files and examine the record," he said.

"With your permission?" These were the first courteous words I'd heard in all my dealings with the Labor Exchange up to that point.

When he came back to his desk, he apologized profusely. It turned out that a letter from the bank had been languishing in their files for some time.

He wrote a letter of referral to the bank, shook my hands warmly, and apologized again for the runaround.

On my way to the bank, I stopped by Rothschild Boulevard to look for Ammu Moshe. He had been worried about me and wanted to walk with me to the bank. Several of his friends, who were also anxiously following the saga, decided to join us in the march to the bank. I was touched. Perhaps they viewed my success as theirs, too. If they could no longer participate actively in life in Israel, as they had in Baghdad, perhaps they could do so vicariously through me.

Everyone waited outside the building, as I went up to the personnel office. I felt more confident this time; much of my anxiety was gone. I was surrounded by love, protected by the shield of caring that Ammu Moshe and his friends had for me. My spirits were high.

This time, the meeting was brief. The personnel manager looked at the letter of referral, perused my school transcripts and declared:

"It is all go."

When I emerged from the meeting, Ammu Moshe and his friends were all anxiously waiting for me.

"What happened? Did you get the job?"

Hearing my good news, they grinned and pumped my hand warmly.

"You're on your way, Danny. Congratulations!" a distant cousin in the crowd exclaimed.

Daniel (r) training with bazooka, reserve service, October 27, 1955

My college career didn't run a straight course. It wasn't easy to work a full day and go to college at night, but it was especially difficult when my studies were disrupted by repeated calls for service in the reserves. Every year I was called up for four to six weeks, and the call could come in the summer, midwinter, or during final exams. No less problematic were the many shorter calls at odd times. My cell leader would show up at my office, or late at night at home, with orders to appear within hours at a certain camp. I, in turn, had to drop everything and notify the half-dozen members of my cell. Sometimes, the call was an exercise in preparedness, and we went back home once we all showed up. But sometimes the call was for real, and we ended up staying in camp a few days.

Without telephones or cars, these roundups were tiring. Some members of my cell lived miles away from my home. Running from one place to another to notify people was particularly difficult late at night when the buses were no longer running. Often I was too exhausted to attend classes the following day.

And there was my problem with the professors.

Almost all our economics professors held high positions in government, Histadroot or the private sector. Most viewed teaching as a sideline and dragged to class tired after a full day's work. Their lectures were stale, and some read verbatim from their notes of years before.

Our lectures were conducted in Hebrew, but only two or three members of the Faculty were native Israelis. Almost all the rest were Eastern Europeans, and their command of Hebrew varied widely. Generally the students were better versed in Hebrew than the professors. Sometimes this was a source of discord; at other times, it was a source of hilarity.

Our young instructor in psychology was a dynamic lecturer, one of the few who loved his topic, but his command of Hebrew left a lot to be desired. Once he devoted a whole lecture to the importance of setting realistic goals. Our good instructor confused the word "Hazitot," meaning "goals" in Hebrew, with the word "Haziyot," which means "bras." The class went wild during the lecture. Oblivious and entirely engrossed in his presentation, the professor plodded through his detailed exposition of "Haziyot," and how they should be tackled as conditions changed.

Most of our textbooks were in English, and they were expensive. The school had a   library, but it rarely carried more than one copy of each textbook. We could not study in the library – it had no desks or chairs.

There was no place to study in my uncle and aunt's apartment, either. My sisters and I slept in the hall, and there was no space for a desk. The point was moot anyway. By the time I got home from school my sisters were in bed. I couldn't turn on the light to sit and study.

Sometimes I went to coffee shops to study after class. Occasionally I managed to do good work, but most of the time it was difficult to do serious thinking or concentrate on writing a paper in a coffee shop. On a few occasions I was kicked out for staying too long. To stay longer, I had to order more drinks. Sometimes I felt helpless. Where do I to turn?

Life consisted of non-stop work and study. More than once during my second year in college, I felt it was time to call it quits. I didn't get enough sleep. I was often hungry. I longed for free, unrestricted evenings.

One of the many happy gatherings at Naim and Muzli's home in Tel Aviv
On the eve of the *Brit Mila* (circumcision) of Reuben, Naim and Muzli's firstborn son. Seated, l to r: Albert benHayeem; Daniel; our cousin Sami; Helwa; (friend); Latifa; Reyna. Standing in the back: Saleh (Naim's cousin); seated in the front Naim's grand cousin.

At such times, visits with Naim and Muzli cheered me enormously. They lived in a cottage in Tel Aviv's Montefiore neighborhood, not far from school. On one visit I was feeling exhausted, dispirited, and unsure about continuing in college. I was not challenged, and I missed terribly my Alliance and Shamash days when I would be so engrossed in my physics, chemistry, and math classes that I didn't need to take notes. I was not getting much from college, felt I was a misfit in economics, and on top of that my instructors were mostly dull.

When I saw Naim's welcoming smile I knew that here I would be sheltered, if briefly, from the doubts that had been tormenting me. As usual, the aroma of the Turkish coffee brewing in the kitchen filled the air. We had our demitasse, and when Naim picked up my cup for prognostication I didn't resist.

Naim must have detected my sense of loss. He stared pensively at the grounds, turning the cup around.

"It looks confusing. I see something dark, heavy."

Naim paused a minute.

"These are clouds, gray clouds hanging over your head. But here—something very good, Danny. Very good."

I didn't believe in his prognostications, but Naim saw clouds hanging over my head. That was exactly how I felt. And then the good signs. Could something good lie ahead? Naim took his good time, peering into the cup.

"They are thick and gray," he said. "But they are moving. They are getting thinner. I see the sun at the other end. There is a boat, a big boat. It looks like you will be taking a long journey. Here are the stars."

I needed the stars. I needed the sun.

As it turned out, less than a year after that, I took the boat to France as an exchange student. But, whether Naim could see the future or not, just listening to him lifted my spirits. I walked away from his house with a lighter step. Naim had given me hope. I would continue on toward the stars.

I compared my situation with most of my Babylonian classmates, *ma'abarot* residents who, through no fault of their own, dropped out in their first semester of college. Their living conditions were not conducive to study, and, even worse, they had to miss the final two hours of classes every night in order to make the last bus to their *ma'abara*. The cumulative effect of missing so many lectures finally took its toll. They dropped out.

I recalled how my father had finished law school despite adversity. My life was certainly not as bad as his. I should expect no less from myself.

AFTER HOURS

My classmate Albert benHayeem and I studied together frequently. I admired Albert, who had escaped from Baghdad at the height of Jewish persecution in Iraq. We met on the first night of the school year and became friends for life.

One evening, after classes, Albert and I went for a walk on Allenby Street, Tel Aviv's main thoroughfare. We were both hungry. We passed by a small hall where a wedding was being celebrated, and stopped to watch. Wooden boards mounted on sawhorses served as tables, and people sat on benches around the tables. There was food on the tables. A small band played Israeli music. People sang, some clapped, others tapped their feet to the tune of the music. Not much pomp. But everyone seemed to be having a good time.

Retreat for college students at Beit Berel, April 23, 1955.
Daniel seated, 2d row. Behind, Albert standing (bent)

Albert suggested we move closer to the entrance to watch the goings on. He didn't stop at the door, but kept going. I followed him. A chubby middle-aged man, neatly dressed in a white open-collar shirt, stood at the other end of the vestibule. Albert extended his right hand and warmly shook the man's hand. He apologized profusely for arriving so late, and explained that it was all because of that darn professor who had a habit of going past class time. The man assured Albert not to worry, but Albert insisted that he still felt awful for barging into the celebration so late. And before I knew it, Albert had managed to engage his new friend in an animated conversation.

I stood at Albert's side, marveling at his ability to churn up so many subjects so effortlessly. From where did he unearth so many topics to talk about?

Then, Albert turned to me and with a big smile, introduced me, explaining that I was a classmate he had invited to attend the wedding. What chutzpah, I thought, squirming with embarrassment.

I doubt that the man believed a word of what Albert said. He must have known we were fakes. But it was a wedding, the atmosphere was jovial, and no one seemed to be in the mood to embarrass anyone else. And I guess Albert knew how to capitalize on that. We carried our books with us, and the man probably knew we were desperate college students looking for something to eat.

He took us to a table in the back, invited us to eat and wished us an enjoyable evening. Without hesitation, Albert turned to the food in front of us; I hesitated, but not for long. We ate our fill and joined in the celebration. We clapped and sang with the rest, and I felt invigorated to see happy faces around us. And for a few happy moments, I even lost sight of the fact that we were intruders.

Bank Leumi had a tradition of holding lavish *purim* parties for its employees. In 1956, the party was held in Bat Yam, a seaside town in central Israel, south of Tel Aviv. Today, Bat Yam is a resort town with 150,000 inhabitants, but in the mid-fifties, its population numbered ten thousand and it was notable for one thing: its large lunatic asylum. Among Israelis, the popular expression "Send him to Bat Yam" meant "he is insane." On occasion, inmates escaped from the asylum and caused panic in nearby communities.

Because Bat Yam was isolated and somewhat inaccessible, the bank chartered buses to shuttle its employees to and from the party.

My date that evening happened to live in Bat Yam, not far from the hall where the party was held. We had a wonderful time. The food was good, the prizes fantastic, and the band outstanding. I danced till I was about to fall off my feet. Half an hour before midnight, the announcement came over the PA system that the last shuttle would leave in half an hour. We had time for one more dance, we decided. I didn't allow extra time to find my way back on dark, unfamiliar streets after escorting my date home.

We danced our last tango and left for her house, ten minutes away.

On the way back, I got lost and missed the bus.

I was tired and had no money for a taxicab. But it was moot anyway. There was nothing in sight, not a soul was around.

The hall was not far from the main road. If I stayed on the main road, I reasoned, I could walk to Jaffa, the next town. From Jaffa, I would do the same —stay on the main road until I reached Tel Aviv. From Tel Aviv I would head for Ramat Gan. How long would that take? Hours. But I had no other choice.

It was a moonless night, and the street lamps, few and far between, didn't do much to dispel the darkness. I began to worry. It was a period of incursions into Israel by *fedayeen*. These guerilla fighters, supported by Egypt, Jordan and other Arab states, could very well be in the vicinity. The road was dark and deserted - ideal for infiltrators. My head was heavy and my feet were getting sore, but I trudged along.

A police car whizzed by. Suddenly it stopped, turned around and directed its spotlight on me. Two policemen got out of the car and approached me carefully.

"What is your name?"

"Daniel Khazzoom." The name meant nothing to them, and why should it?

"Where are you coming from?"

"Bat Yam."

"Bat Yam!" The two policemen glanced at each other quizzically.

"And where are you going?"

"To Ramat Gan."

"Hum, you are walking from Bat Yam all the way to Ramat Gan, right?"

"Yes."

"What were you doing in Bat Yam?"

"I was at a party."

"At a party! And what did you do at the party? Were you dancing?"

"Yes, I was."

"You were, were you? You like to dance?"

"Yes, I do."

I remember one of the policemen raising his bushy eyebrows and the other shaking his head, as they looked at each other, as if to ask, "What do we do with this lunatic?" And then, all of a sudden, it hit me, "Bat Yam's lunatic asylum! These policemen must be thinking I am an escapee." It was too late. I was too slow to grasp what was happening. But I was so exhausted I couldn't begin to explain what had happened with the shuttle. I remember thinking maybe it was all for the good. Maybe they would decide to take me to city jail. I wanted to lie down. A night in jail would bring welcome relief.

But the law didn't cooperate. The two policemen checked my ID card and verified my address. Then they turned their backs and drove away, taking with them my chance of spending a restful night in jail.

I didn't arrive in Ramat Gan until early morning, when the city had come awake and the buses were rumbling through the streets. I found my sisters, my uncle, and my aunt up, worried and waiting for me.

"Where have you been, Danny?"

Seeing how exhausted I was and the way I tumbled into bed, my sisters didn't find it hard to believe I had walked the twelve long miles from Bat Yam to Ramat Gan. And they didn't let me forget the night I was taken for a lunatic.

DEFENDING ISRAEL

In 1956, infiltration from Egypt into Israel intensified, and the *fedayeen's* sneak attacks on border communities grew in ferocity. Kibbutzim and moshavim -- agricultural co-operatives -- along Israel's borders were forced to divert most of their residents to guard against attacks, leaving practically no one to attend to farming or the daily needs of the community. There was an urgent need to shore up those communities and prevent their collapse.

Volunteers to help kibbutz Sa'ad, May 1956. Daniel seated first row second from left

A volunteer program was put in to help these communities. I volunteered to work for Kibbutz Sa'ad.

Sa'ad was a modern Orthodox kibbutz founded in 1947 by Jews from Germany and Austria. It was a green oasis surrounded by desert stretching as far as the eye could see. Not long ago, this oasis was a desert like the rest, nothing but sand.

During my stay, I helped build a fence around the kibbutz, and dug ditches around the fence. At night, I did guard duty.

I spent much of my spare time around the kibbutz' livestock enclosures. I loved to watch the cows showering their calves with affection. As a child, I had watched cows being milked, and I remember how touched I was to see how cows stood motionless when the calf drank its milk.

Daniel erecting a barbed wire fence ...   digging a ditch around outer fence

Hammering with a post hole-digger before installing a barbed wire fence, Kibbutz Sa'ad, May 1956

But perhaps the most rewarding part of my volunteer work was watching Sa'ad's community--men, women, and children--as they sat in their dining room and ate peacefully. It was gratifying to think that I might have had something to do with restoring a sense of peace to that embattled community.

A few days after my return from Sa'ad, I received a notice for my annual service with the reserves, and was stationed on a small hilltop on the border with Egypt. The Egyptian military was stationed across from us on three hilltops in a horseshoe formation, and a narrow valley separated us. Occasionally, when the wind blew in our direction, I could hear the Egyptian soldiers talking to each other.

Bolstered by a flow of new Czech ordnance, the Egyptian soldiers rarely missed an opportunity to flex their newly armed muscles.

At night our group descended into the valley and lay on the ground to intercept infiltrators and thwart beachhead advances by the Egyptians. Our location changed every night. We returned to our position atop the hill just before dawn.

One night, a shot came flying from one of the Egyptian positions. Soon more shots began to fly in all directions, echoing in a frightening cacophony. The shooting could have been a ploy to discover our location, and I worried that someone in our group might be tempted to return fire and reveal our location.

That did not happen, and soon the shooting died out. An Egyptian informer we were expecting to cross to our side that night never showed up. Was he captured or killed by the Egyptians? Could that have caused the commotion? I never found out.

Then there was the chain smoker under my command, a feisty man in his early forties. We were past midway in our service. By then, the long days of sitting guard and the sleepless nights spent lying on rocky terrain down the valley had taken their toll. Nerves were taut and tempers flared. The group grew increasingly edgy.

One night while we were down in the valley, the chain smoker covered himself with a blanket and lit up. The blanket was thin, and, although he was a good distance from me, I could clearly see the light.

"I sympathize with your need to smoke, and I wish I could help," I told him the following day. "But there isn't much I can do, given that we are where we are. I must ask you to refrain from smoking when we are in the valley."

Grabbing his rifle and pointing it at me, he yelled,

"You better lay off, if you want to return alive to your family."

I reiterated that I expected him to obey the rules.

I was anxious when we went down to the valley that night. If he lit up, I would have to initiate a disciplinary action against him. He would be prosecuted and probably jailed. Nonetheless, he seemed hotheaded enough to carry out his threat. But I couldn't give in.

He surprised me.

He didn't light up – neither that night, nor the following nights, and all was quiet on the Egyptian border.

NEW VISTAS IN EUROPE

In the spring of 1956, I was among a group of Israeli economics students chosen to travel to France on a student-exchange program. The purpose was to give us exposure to the management of major business establishments in France. I was paired with a brick factory, les Tuileries de Marseille, and a bank in Marseilles and received a stipend from both institutions.

At sunset, Daniel standing on the deck of boat, on the way to Marseilles

I left by boat for Marseilles that July. The trip took seven days. During that time the tensions that had built up during my time on the Egyptian border dissolved. In the daytime I stood at the deck's railing, watched the wake, felt the breeze on my face, and let my eyes roam over the endless expanse.

At night, as total darkness surrounded the boat, I lifted my eyes to the stars and was reminded of the summer nights in Baghdad when I had slept on the rooftop.

On the first night of our trip, I met Nissim Tal, a student at Hebrew University who was part of the exchange program and was also being sponsored by the brick factory.

256

Born in Jerusalem, Nissim was of Babylonian descent, and could speak a few words of Judeo-Arabic.

Nissim told me about his family's struggle during the long siege of Jerusalem by the Jordanian army in 1948, before independence. No food or medical supplies could get through during the six-month ordeal. People tried to manage on whatever they had and shared with their neighbors as much as they could. Nissim's father, a grocer, had his storage room filled with cans of sardines, which sustained the family and their neighbors throughout the siege. Nissim told me that he could no longer stand the sight or smell of sardines, and had not touched them since.

Nissim (left) and Daniel on their way to Les Tuileries de Marseilles

I spent four weeks at les Tuileries de Marseilles, rotating through several departments. It was a big company, with shipments all over France. On my first day, I was invited to meet Les Tuileries' chairman. He was awe-inspiring, correct, but very human. He said he was happy to have his organization sponsor students from Israel. "*Nous sommes des amis*," "we are friends," were his words.

We worked long days with a three-hour siesta break. Every time we came to work, morning and afternoon, and every time we left work, we made the rounds and shook hands with everyone in the department. This was a ritual I had never seen before, but in time I came to see that it injected a human dimension into the workday, allowing me to meet and get to know my coworkers.

At the end of four weeks at Les Tuileries, I transferred to my second sponsor, a bank in Marseilles's financial district. In the bank, as in the Tuileries before, I was rotated through different departments. Those rotations gave me a panoramic view of the bank's workings, and I appreciated that a lot.

I was surprised to discover how much hostility my coworkers at the bank felt toward Germans and Germany. The memories of the Nazi occupation of France were still fresh, and my coworkers seemed to be resolute in their rejection of any reconciliation with Germany. In Israel I had met survivors of the concentration camps and so tended to see the bitterness toward the Nazis primarily through the Jewish experience. Yet none of my French coworkers were Jewish. Their bitterness and aversion to anything German surpassed much of what I had heard from Jewish survivors of the concentration camps.

One of my newly made friends in Marseilles took me one evening for a walk to show me around. We passed by seafood restaurants at the beach. There, for the first time in my life, I saw people gulping down clams and eating crabs. I had seen crabs only in pictures before. To me they looked like big scorpions, and I never thought people would want to eat them. My friend took me inside one of those restaurants. There I saw a lobster being taken from the midst of ice cubes and thrown into a large pot of boiling water. The lobster was alive when it was thrown in the boiling water. I was aghast. I never saw a lobster before, and did not like the looks of what I saw. But I could not get over the fact that it was being boiled while still alive. This is inhumane, I screamed. My friend did not seem to think much of it. The sight of a live lobster being dropped in boiling water plays back in my mind to this day.

Marseilles boasted one synagogue, founded by Jews from Tunisia.

Nissim and I went there for services on a Sabbath day. A few minutes into the services, I heard organ music and noticed a large organ high above the sanctuary entrance. I wondered if we had stumbled into a church by mistake.

A congregant seated next to me explained that the membership felt that the organ music helped them focus and communicate their prayers to God. But since observant Jews were not allowed to play a musical instrument on the Sabbath, the synagogue engaged the services of a young Catholic musician to play. That confused me too: If music was intended to help communicate our Jewish prayer to God, why did it need the intercession of a Catholic to help it reach its destination?

Nissim and I walked out to the courtyard. We noticed a small gathering in a chapel at the far end of the courtyard. The synagogue made the chapel available every Sabbath day to a group of postwar immigrants from Central and Eastern Europe, who followed the Ashkenazi rites. We joined in. The services were traditional, but I couldn't understand a word. Even so, it was a relief to be in a traditional milieu.

During my sojourn in Marseilles, I vacillated between the Sephardi and the Ashkenazi congregations. Neither was satisfactory. The hardest day was *yom kippoor*. I struggled the whole day as the organ blared, at times drowning out the cantor and everyone else. When the day came to an end, and people began to disperse, I stepped up to the *hekhal*, put my hands on the *sefer Torah* and recited quietly my own prayer of atonement. I asked God for forgiveness and prayed for my parents' welfare in Iraq. I remembered the days of *yom kippoor* in my parents' home when we lived under the same roof, and I intoned quietly the beautiful poem of *yom kippoor*, one we sang in unison in our synagogue, "*Hatanoo lefaneikha, rahem aleinoo*," or "we transgressed, dear God, have mercy on us."

I hugged the *sefer Torah* and headed home to break the fast.

My work at the bank in Marseilles was drawing to a close, and my thoughts began to turn towards Paris. During my time in l'Alliance, I had heard a lot about Paris, and now I was going to see it with my own eyes. Nissim had already left for the French capital and I planned to meet him there.

I would journey to Paris by truck, a mode of travel that was commonly used by French students at the time. By custom, the students paid for the trucker's meals and, in theory at least, provided him with company on a boring ride.

When I first met with my trucker to arrange for the ride he seemed to be a pleasant fellow, dressed neatly in a suit and tie. It was a shock to see him wearing baggy overalls on the evening we left Marseilles. His stomach stuck out, and his bald head glistened in the fading daylight, giving him a sinister look. He was short and swarthy, and looked ready for anything. I marveled at how clothes can make the man.

I climbed into my seat beside the driver and we were off. Before long, night fell, and all I could see were lights shining here and there through the darkness. I put my head back on the seat and dozed off.

I was jolted awake by the sound of tires squealing and the truck rocking dangerously from side to side. I saved myself from going through the windshield by slamming my hands against the dashboard. A small red car was stopped at the side of the road in front of us. The truck driver got out to confront the tall, thin well-dressed young man getting out of the car. By the time I joined them, two young women in dresses were standing behind the driver of the car. They looked as if they had just come from a party.

"I must insist that I see your driver's license," the tall man said. "You should not be allowed on the road. We were almost killed."

The young women were silent, as indeed I was. I surmised that someone had gone through a stop sign, and from what I could gather, it probably was the truck driver.

The trucker's face was red, his eyes almost closed, and the words sputtered from his lips.

"Just because you decided to have fun, does that mean you should deprive me of my livelihood?"

The trucker turned around and climbed back into the cabin. I did too. The young man's face darkened.

"Your license, if you please."

The trucker shook his fist at the young man.

"Do you want me to cut off your head? Just say the word. I would do it whenever you want me to."

The young man hesitated for a moment. Then he turned and got into his car, followed by the two young women who scurried across the road and almost tumbled over one another in their haste to get away.

I watched the taillights of the red car disappear into the darkness.

"Insolent young puppy," the trucker said.

I was silent, not wanting to have anything more to do with him. I had seen too much violence in the streets of Baghdad, where every argument and disagreement seemed to be settled with physical combat. I didn't like the violence on the French country road any more than I had liked it on the streets of Baghdad. From that moment on I didn't allow myself to doze off.

Shortly after this encounter, the trucker abruptly pulled off the road and climbed into the bed behind his seat. I sat in the darkness nervously playing with my fingers, listening to his snores, afraid to fall asleep. I longed for the bright lights of the restaurant where we had stopped earlier and I had bought the trucker coffee and a sandwich. I wanted people around me talking and laughing. I didn't want to be sitting in the truck alone with a violent man. I wondered if saving the cost of a bus ride to Paris was worth it, if it meant driving all night with a man who couldn't control his temper.

In Paris, I was able to make the first contact since leaving home with a member of my family still living in Baghdad. While in Marseilles, I had learned, through relatives in Liverpool, England, that my brother Jacob was in Turkey on a short trip. I had written to him, asking for news of home, and his reply arrived when I was in Paris. I opened the envelope with trembling fingers.

I learned that both my parents were still alive, but that Ammu Shlomo, the beloved family friend who had paid us a visit during the farhood, had recently died. The loss hit me hard; Shlomo had been our surrogate grandfather. My cheeks were wet as I read Jacob's letter and saw the travelers' check he had sent me. What money he had remaining before heading back to Baghdad he had sent to me. I decided to spend it on what became a six-week trip to England.

Nissim and I got to see many shows in Paris. We had student ID's that allowed us to buy tickets to performances at very cheap prices. Of course the seats were not the best. Once I remember sitting on the side in the front row of a theater where the lights from the stage shone straight into my eyes obscuring my vision of what was happening on the stage. But it was wonderful to be able to go to the theater, as it was wonderful to walk through the streets of Paris at all hours of the day and night. At every hour the streets pulsated with life, with the music of human voices, with the sound of guitars playing in coffee houses, with the swirling crowds and the sounds of happy laughter.

One night as we were wandering through Paris we stopped in a coffee shop where a crowd of young people was singing and playing instruments. It was there that I met Christine from Vienna. Christine was a medium built woman in her early twenties. She wore a colorful Slavic apron, which stood her out in the crowd, and she seemed to exude a sense of tranquility and composure. I felt a sense of peace just looking at her clear, unaffected gaze and beauty. Christine was not a student, but a tourist who had hooked up with a group of students. I introduced myself to her and we went out for a walk along the Seine that night. Christine and I began to hang out together, enjoying our walks, our visits to the theaters, and each other's company. We both knew our relationship had no future.

One night as we held hands and watched the

glittering reflections of the moon on the Seine, Christine turned to me and her blue eyes looked sadly into my brown ones. "I am Catholic. You are Jewish."

There was nothing to add. We were as deeply committed to our religions as we might have been to each other if things were different. But it wasn't to be and we knew it.

VENICE'S JEWISH GHETTO

Before we parted ways—Nissim back to Israel and me to England—we decided to visit Rome and Venice. I admired the historical sites in Rome, but I fell in love with Venice at first sight.

Nissim and I wandered through the alleys of Venice and took the ferries from place to place. But the area that tugged at my heart was the Jewish ghetto. The ghetto square had five synagogues, but they were now all museums. I walked toward the Spanish and Portuguese synagogue. It looked beautiful from the outside, but it was closed. I managed to get into the Oriental Synagogue, a gorgeous building with stained glass windows. Alone inside, I touched the *hekhal's* velvet curtain and ran my hand over the seats. If that synagogue could talk, what stories would it tell? In the eyes of my mind I saw congregants flock in for the Friday night services, a *bar miswah* being called to the Torah, a young couple standing under their wedding canopy. What had happened to all those people? Where were they now? How did this synagogue feel with its children all gone?

When I left the synagogue I paused again in the silent ghetto square. I closed my eyes and pictured a Sabbath morning in Venice before the war, before the Nazis steamrolled through, flattening the Jewish community. I could see people, old and young, streaming out of the synagogues and filling the square. I could hear the laughter of children, see youngsters running and chasing each other, and I could hear the cries of babies and the greetings of "Shabbat Shalom" filling the air. The savory smells of

Sabbath lunches wafted through open windows, carried on the summer breezes. I reveled in the scene for a few moments and then I opened my eyes. Only stones and silence and empty houses remained.

I went to visit with the rabbi of Venice. He was a soft-spoken older man who spoke Hebrew fluently. He told me about the history of the community and its tribulation during the war years. When the Nazis occupied Venice, they called in the head of the Jewish community and ordered him to submit a list of the names and addresses of all the Jews in town. Knowing this would consign them to deportation to death camps, he refused to do so, and chose death over cooperating with the Nazis. He went home and committed suicide. The rabbi's sadness at the decimation of his community was palpable.

"Still I am glad there is a country like Israel where people can go," he said.

Venice was a beautiful city, but its Jewish community had been destroyed, just as our community in Baghdad had been destroyed. A cloud of mourning seemed to hang over the Jewish Ghetto, as the few families that were still there sat on their suitcases poised for flight to the Promised Land. I wondered what awaited them there. I wondered what memories they would carry with them.

In 1998 I revisited Venice and found a burgeoning Jewish community in what used to be the Jewish Ghetto. I looked at the Jewish bakery and stores and at the Jewish children playing in the alleyways. It was late Friday afternoon. I stopped first at Habbad House to light the Friday night candles with the community, and then headed for the Spanish and Portuguese synagogue to attend services. I was overcome with emotion when I lifted up my eyes and, for the first time in more than four decades, saw the Spanish and Portuguese synagogue before me. Its door was now open, and worshippers were streaming in. I couldn't contain my emotions. I broke down and wept.

A LESSON IN DEMOCRACY

Back in France, I crossed the Channel to Dover from Calais. It was a rough voyage, and my stomach felt it. There were, however, some quiet moments during which I thankfully turned to my book, which was written in Hebrew. As I turned the pages from right to left, I glanced up occasionally to meet the puzzled eyes of an older man sitting opposite me. Several times he seemed on the verge of speaking to me, but sighed and leaned back in his chair when my eyes returned to my book.

Finally he leaned forward and tapped me on my shoulder.

"Young man, what are you reading?"

"A book in Hebrew."

"Do all Hebrew books start from the end?"

"No. We read Hebrew from right to left, unlike English, which is read from left to right."

His mouth dropped open, but he continued to sit and stare as I continued to sit and read. It was my first encounter with an American in Europe. I wondered if he were astonished to discover that things were done differently in different parts of the world. It was a lesson that was to be brought home to me in spades when I met the English in their own country.

At the University of London's Hillel House, where I stayed, it cost one shilling a night for bed and breakfast. I guarded my little store of wealth carefully, making my pennies last. Breakfast was a substantial meal, and it became my main meal. For the rest of the day I subsisted on bread and the strong, sweet English tea, similar to what we always drank in Baghdad.

The London underground was a great novelty, just as it had been in Paris. Riding the subway, I'd daydream about the streets opening up so the pedestrians would see us riding below them. That was pure fantasy, of course. But I had not counted on my entire life opening up in London. Yet open up it did.

My stay in London coincided with the Suez Canal crisis. Many of the English felt their country had no business being in the Suez; others supported their country's involvement. We had many discussions on the topic at Hillel, and a student there suggested that I visit Hyde Park to hear more.

When I got to the park there were knots of people gathered here and there around men who stood on low boxes or stepladders, which raised them above the crowd. Everyone was engaged in debate. I stopped at a gathering where the speaker spoke in favor of the British involvement in the Suez campaign. The debate with the crowd heated up, and tempers began to flare. I watched the speaker's face grow red and spittle begin to form at the edges of his mouth. A man from the crowd with whom he was arguing was equally involved. I held my breath as the man stepped forward toward the box. He shook his clenched fist as his voice went up and his face turned purple. "My God, someone is going to be killed; someone is about to be stabbed," I thought. That was what happened on the streets in Baghdad when people disagreed. I turned my back on the scene. I didn't want to see blood. I couldn't bear to look over my shoulder, but I was waiting to hear the first scream of pain. It never came. Sheepishly I turned back to look. The speaker was still there. The man who had moved forward to the speaker's box was walking calmly away.

Amazing! I couldn't believe my eyes.

The same scene repeated itself later with another member of the crowd. And still nothing happened. There was no gunfire, no exchange of blows. People seemed to agree to disagree and walk away from one another without laying as much as a finger on one another. What was going on?

I stood in silence drinking in the scene. It was drizzling, but I scarcely felt the rain on my face. I remembered the American on the ferry who was puzzled watching me read from right to left. I could explain to him that Hebrew was read that way, but who would explain to me what was happening in Hyde Park? I didn't even know what questions to ask. Suddenly it hit me. "This is democracy."

The following Sunday I went to Hyde Park again, this time at dawn. I was there as the speakers were setting up their platforms and launching their speeches. There were debates and sharp exchanges. But again, there was no violence.

During my remaining two weeks in London, I went faithfully every Sunday to Hyde Park and stayed there until almost everyone had left. Those visits to Hyde Park were a turning point in my life. I began to realize, for the first time, that there was more to democracy than voting for a parliament. Not every place in the world was like Iraq. I could turn the pages of my life from left to right or from right to left. It was up to me, and nobody would deny me my right to do so. Better still, in a democracy nobody would want to. I wanted to run though the streets shouting "Eureka! Eureka! I have discovered democracy in Hyde Park in London."

THE REMARKABLE PENNY

I knew my time in London was running short, and that I'd soon have to return to Israel, for my carefully hoarded funds were running low. And then fortune smiled on me.

I used the public telephone in Hillel House to make local calls, which then cost three pence. One day my third penny, a well-worn coin, didn't make the required ping, and I didn't get a dial tone. I pressed the coin-return button, but nothing happened. In frustration, I slapped the telephone box hard. Six pence fell out of the telephone. I repeated the operation using my lucky penny and slapping the phone box. This time it spat out five pence. Now I almost had the twelve pence I needed to pay for another night at Hillel.

In the following days, I used my private system to fund a longer stay in London. Each morning, the lucky penny and a firm slap to the telephone box would produce the necessary change. I was careful not to take more than my required twelve pence. Then I went downstairs to the dining room, paid for another breakfast and one more night's lodging. My luck held out for about ten days. Finally one morning my treasured penny remained within the telephone and I knew it was time to leave London.

In the scheme of things, that telephone windfall was modest, just as my stay in England was relatively brief. But the benefits were enormous. I returned to Israel a much different and more perceptive young man than the one who had sailed for France several months before.

MY EUROPEAN EPIPHANY

LIVING IN DENIAL

My sojourn in France and England was the period of my awakening to the cold truth about my place in Israel as a Jew from an Arab land. I had closed my eyes and made myself accept or overlook the fact that my people were second-class citizens in Israel. I had ignored the situation because this truth was so difficult to accept—and I had so much wanted it to be otherwise. During my stay in Europe I gathered the strength to acknowledge that I had been leading a double life.

Outwardly I was a normal, perhaps ambitious, young man forging ahead, fitting into Israeli society. I served in the military, attended college while working to support myself, voted in elections, and did many of the things a civic-minded young man would do.

But there was another side – a subterranean side, a life parallel to my outward life. It was the life of a Jew from an Arab land - a life of pain and confusion; a life in denial; a life of struggle with identity, disappointment, and shattered dreams. I managed to contain that life during most of the time I lived in Israel. It bubbled to the surface and took over following my trip to France and England.

In Iraq we had never talked about German Jews, Polish Jews, or Russian Jews, but rather about Jews from Germany, Jews from Poland, Jews from Russia or Jews from Iraq. The distinction is a fine one, but we believed that Jews were first and foremost Jews. That they happened to be born in one country or another was incidental. Our real homeland was the land to which Moses led our ancestors when they left Egypt, and all Jews, no matter where they were born or where they lived, belonged there equally.

I was a Jew who grew up in Iraq and I viewed myself as a human being, entitled to live in peace. As far as I was concerned, all peoples including Arabs and Jews should be treated with dignity. But though Jews had lived in what is now Iraq for centuries before Islam came into being, the Jews of Iraq were branded as the enemy and singled out for mistreatment by the Muslim majority.

I chose to leave Baghdad because I was no longer willing to subject myself to persecution. Nor did I want to live as a tenth class citizen with far fewer rights than the Muslim majority. Leaving my parents' home before marriage was a wrenching break with Babylonian Jewish tradition and a traumatic change in my own life, but I was completely clear about my desire to live as a Jew among Jews. Nothing was more important than that.

When I got off the plane at Llyda airport I was euphoric to at last be in a place where everyone else was Jewish. No more would I be a member of an ethnically despised minority. No more would I be pushed around. And no more would I endure discrimination.

But the reality didn't match my dream.

Jews from Arab lands faced hostility and discrimination in Israel, where the dominant attitude was that Europeans had built the country, entitling them to priority treatment.

It was not easy living in this climate and enduring derogatory stereotyping. When a Jew from Iraq, Egypt, Morocco or other Arab land committed an offense, the newspapers were sure to print the criminal's country of origin. This reinforced the perception of rowdy, uneducated, and violent Jews from Arab lands. It was the opposite when one of those Jews had an achievement to his credit. When I became the first graduate of a college in Israel to be admitted to Harvard, the haArets newspaper headline read: "A Young Israeli Broke the Barrier to Harvard." Nowhere did it mention that I was an immigrant from Iraq, as it probably would have had I robbed a bank.

At first I brushed off the hostile attitudes, believing that an integral part of assimilating was to go along with the majority opinion. At the time, I didn't realize how much I was hurting myself by living in denial.

I even accepted the argument that blamed immigrants from Arab lands for their own problems. Conventional wisdom had it that the problem was a conflict of cultures: the western culture of the Europeans living in Israel versus the primitive culture of those of us who came from Arab lands. Moreover, this conflict was said to reflect differences in education, between those who were educated and had a tradition of education on one hand, and immigrants from Arab lands who were uneducated and lacked a tradition of education, on the other. Nothing could have been further from the truth, but I refused to let myself acknowledge that.

I didn't allow myself to dwell on the fact that all of my sisters, all of my cousins, three of my four aunts and I were all educated in French schools in Baghdad, that French culture, literature and poetry were ingrained in us, that we treasured educational achievements. Nor did I boast, even to myself, that in my immediate family we had five physicians, one nuclear physicist, two pharmaceutical chemists, or that my father was a distinguished lawyer. Instead, I conceded that there were Babylonian Jews who were ignorant and uneducated. In doing so, I failed to acknowledge a critical cause of the educational disparities: Palestinians who came to Iraq were given Jewish homes and synagogues, while their vacated properties were nationalized by Israel. Israel refused to process Middle Eastern Jews' claims against those Palestinian assets. Had we received compensation for assets seized when we fled our homelands, like reparations given to most refugees from the Holocaust, Jews from Arab lands would have had the funds to start anew in Israel and educate their children. In my case, for example, even the relatively small sum of a hundred and twenty liras I received from my aunt made such a big difference in my life. Without it I might have missed out on higher education.

The sweeping nature of the stereotype, and the derogatory way in which it was almost always expressed, was distressing. No less troubling was the flip side of the dictum, which left the impression that there was a college on every street corner in Eastern Europe. Still, I swallowed it whole, because I didn't want to shatter my long-held illusion of Jews living together in harmony in Israel.

But even in those days when I was so eager to accommodate, I had great difficulty dealing with the epithet that was often hurled at us: "Attem Aravim" – "You are Arabs." In Iraq we had been persecuted by Arabs for being Jewish. In Israel, all of a sudden we became Arabs. That hurt.

True, we were not the same as European Jews, but we were Jews nonetheless, with a proud history of maintaining our identity in the face of adversity. Although we didn't live in ghettoes and no brick walls separated us from our Arab neighbors, we did maintain our distinct Jewish life. We lived by Jewish Law, and had our own governing institutions, schools, hospitals, and courts.

But it was also true that my people had lived in an Arab milieu for generations, and there was a lot of Arab in us. It would be silly to say Jews in America are not American, just as it would be silly to say that the Jews of Iraq had not picked up traits of the Arab culture. But in Israel, when they said, "You are Arabs" they were calling us the enemy.

As a case in point, our native tongue, Judeo-Arabic, was mimicked as the language of the Arab enemy.

Judeo-Arabic, one of many Jewish languages, is a mixture of medieval Arabic, Hebrew and Aramaic with a smattering of Turkish and Persian. It is an outgrowth of Aramaic, the language my ancestors spoke and used to write the Talmud. Yiddish, or Judeo-German, as it is known linguistically, is the native tongue of most East European Jews. It is medieval German with a mixture of Hebrew and other local European languages. Like Judeo-Arabic, it is written in Hebrew characters, though the characters are different from the Hebrew characters used in Judeo-Arabic.

The notion that Judeo-Arabic was the language of the Arab enemy is no less absurd than the corollary, which would equate Yiddish with German, the language of the Nazi enemy. And while Judeo-Arabic was ridiculed as Arabic, Yiddish was exalted as the epitome of Jewish; Judeo-Arabic was derided as cacophonous, Yiddish was hailed as music to the ear.

Indeed, any differences with the East European outlook, practices, and traditions were treated as inherently inferior.

Unlike observant East European Jews, Babylonian Jews didn't wear skullcaps all the time. We were viewed as lax for that and, like our level of education, our level of religious observance was seen as needing to be "elevated."

In Israel's religious-school system, which is part of Israel's public school system, every teacher had to be observant according to the tenet of East European Jewry. When a woman who taught in the religious school system married an observant Jew from an Arab land who didn't wear a skull cap all the time, she was fired on the grounds she had married a non-observant Jew. Such dismissals, over differences in ancestral religious practices, were still occurring a few years ago, according to my friend, the late Abraham ben Yaacob, a noted author and historian of Babylonian Jewry.

A rabbi from an Arab land who sought to serve in a religious capacity in government had to abandon his own traditional rabbinical robe and don the black hat and long black coat of the East Europeans – otherwise he would be denied a rabbinical position. It was troubling to see the venerable Rabbi Silman Hougy, an old family friend from Baghdad, dressed in the East European attire. The religious practices of Jews from Arab lands are being swallowed up bit by bit, I thought to myself.

When my sister Latifa married Felix Aknin, his father, a learned Jew from Cairo, wanted to officiate at the wedding ceremony. But he was not allowed to do so. An official from the Ministry of Religion had to officiate or the marriage wouldn't be recognized as legal. The official came dressed in long coat, black hat, and long forelocks –anathema to our practices. None of us could relate to the ceremony he conducted. When he left, Latifa's father-in-law, with a shaven face and wearing white, repeated the ceremony in the way it would have been conducted in Egypt.

Living in Baghdad, I found it relatively easy to recognize that Arabs hated me just because I was a Jew. It was unjust, but frankly I didn't care what the Arabs thought of us. It was much more difficult to face discrimination by fellow Jews.

Celebrating Latifa and Felix's wedding
L to r: Latifa, Albert benHayeem, Daniel, Muzli

I had not expected my chosen country to be a place where "All Jews are equal, but some are more equal than others," as Levi Eshkol, a former prime minister of Israel, once put it. I was wearing rose-colored glasses, glasses I had designed for myself that clouded my vision. I was unable to see clearly that the difficulties we were experiencing in Israel were not isolated incidents, but part of a pattern.

When I first arrived in Israel it was extremely disheartening that no one assigned to help us settle in spoke our language. There was no welcome awaiting us, no hugs, no smiles, and no handshakes to ease the impact of the sudden change in our lives.

Instead we were greeted by stone-faced sanitation workers armed with spray guns.

Later I learned that immigrants from East European countries were greeted upon arrival in Israel by bands and delegations of dignitaries. It was then that I began to view our experience at the airport through a different lens. My shift in perspective was sharpened further when I noticed how cabinet members and members of Israel's parliament fell all over themselves to welcome the immigrants from the Soviet Union as they arrived at the same airport at which we arrived. The contrast to our chilly reception was so pointed, so stark.

GOVERNMENT COMPLICITY

What was particularly insidious about the discriminatory practices was that they were not so evident to people of goodwill and to Jews in the Diaspora, particularly America. I believe American Jewry wouldn't have stood idly by had they known what was truly going on. But the problem was well hidden under a veneer of institutional authority.

The price of rice was one example.

The staple of the European diet was potato, while rice was the staple in the diet of Jews from Arab lands. The government subsidized potatoes heavily but did not subsidize rice. The result was that potatoes were dirt cheap, while the price of rice skyrocketed. Because the immigrants from Arab lands had a higher unemployment rate, earned less than their European counterparts, and had larger families than the Europeans, the escalating price of rice hit hardest those who could least afford it.

The same was true of other food items. For a long time, the government subsidized only the black bread "*lehem shahor*" favored by East European Jews. The price of pita bread, which was part of the diet of Jews from Arab lands, was a multiple of the price of black bread, pound for pound.

I puzzled over these price disparities during my stay in London. It was only after returning to Israel later that year that I realized the invisible hand of a culturally insensitive government had been responsible.

DUSTY BYROADS OF JEWISH HISTORY

My sudden loss of social standing hampered my adjustment to Israel. Within the Jewish community in Iraq I had been admired for my distinguished family and my own intellectual abilities. Now, in Israel, I was lumped in with the uneducated and the ignorant. In my eagerness to shake off this stigma, I intentionally distanced myself from my heritage.

In my heart I knew my heritage was important and respected within the wider Jewish community. I was proud that Babylonian Jews had written the Talmud, the cornerstone of Jewish life and learning. But in Israel, I pushed these facts to the back of my brain. I couldn't let myself admit that the accepted Israeli view of Jews from Arab lands sprang solely from prejudice.

The notion that my people belonged to the dusty byroads of Jewish history and civilization permeated every aspect of Israeli society, including universities.

The obligatory course on the Economic History of the Jewish People, which I took in my junior year in college, was typical. As the semester wore on, it became clear that that course was limited to the economic history of the Jews of Central and Eastern Europe. It had nothing to say about Jews from Arab lands, or the Sephardim in general: Nothing about the contributions of the Cochin Jews of India or the international business and philanthropic empires of the Babylonian Sasson, Kh'doury or Hardoon dynasties. Nothing about the Pereira brothers, who were instrumental in propelling the industrial revolution in France but whose risky lending practices ultimately led to their downfall. Nothing about the sixteenth century international banker and businesswoman Dona Gracia Nasi, who also rescued thousands of Jews from the Inquisition. I was flabbergasted that such a big chunk of Jewish history was being ignored.

I considered trying to set matters straight by writing my term paper on the economic contribution of Babylonian Jewry. But my background and heritage had already been called into question too many times. I couldn't muster the courage to invite another rebuff.

Instead, I wrote a paper about the Jews of England. I now know that my conflicted feelings about this course were part of my journey toward reclaiming myself. My hunch is that if I had taken that course after my visit to France and England, I would have written the paper about my own people.

THE AWAKENING

It had been enlightening to realize how much more comfortable I felt while traveling in Europe. Away from Israel, I saw that I'd been walking on eggshells. In France I could relax and be myself for the first time since leaving Baghdad. But then I wondered: Could that be because I was educated in French schools and was fluent in the language?

The real breakthrough came during my stay in England. It was then, standing away from the dazzling influence of Israel, in a totally unfamiliar foreign culture, that I had the courage to confront the question directly: Could it be Israel's problem rather than ours?

At the University of London's Hillel House I met several Jewish and non-Jewish families, Jewish leaders, and community activists. And I felt at home, no less than I did in France. Here, too, I found that I didn't have to guard my tongue. I could express myself freely without fear of ridicule. It was a heady experience.

I talked with the English about controversial subjects, but the conversations never degenerated into personal controversies or name-calling, as had happened so many times in Israel. At no time during my six weeks in England was I cut down or derided for my ethnic background, dress habits, skin color, or political views. It was refreshing to be treated with courtesy.

Walking through the streets of London, I asked myself, how much more western could one be than being British? Or French? In western cultures I seemed to have no difficulty. Indeed, I had the time of my life. Why was it not so in Israel? Could it be that what Israelis called the clash of western versus "primitive" cultures was just a smokescreen for a need to dominate, to put us down?

I found it striking that most European Israelis knew very little, nor cared to know, about the history, culture, living conditions, and aspirations of Babylonian Jewry. Many refused even to entertain the notion that we had a culture or decent living conditions in the countries from which we came.

In fact, I had enjoyed a life of physical comfort in Baghdad. Yet because people in Israel considered Levantine the equivalent of backward, they scoffed at my story about being called from the Baghdad airport at midnight to get the last seat on the plane to Israel. They simply didn't believe my family had a telephone.

The Israeli establishment openly expressed eagerness to keep the State of Israel from being afflicted by "Levantinization." More than once, I was told, "Don't be a Levantine." What else was I supposed to be? What is a Jew supposed to be when he is told, "Don't be a kike"? When the legendary Ben Gurion warned that Israel was running the risk of Levantinization, he was, in effect, ratifying the notion of European superiority. And when the same Ben Gurion said, "We got rid of some good Arabs and got bad Jews in their place," he was talking about me and other Jews from Arab lands. Had Ben Gurion made that statement in the U.S., there would have been an outcry from American Jewry. But he made the statement in Israel, where it was accepted as true.

In England, I saw for the first time the similarity between those slurs and Nazi master-race arguments. It was cold comfort that Jews themselves had voiced them. Most distressing of all was the realization that we ourselves had internalized them.

I recalled how contemptuous I had become of the elders in our community, whom I saw as the epitome of "Levantines." Not even our family elder, Uncle Moshe, was spared: I was impatient with his opinions and ideas, which I saw as springing from an inferior way of thinking and viewing the world. I was deeply chagrined to realize how unwittingly I had absorbed the supremacist attitudes surrounding me.

I thought about the time Uncle Moshe had approached me to write a letter of recommendation for a middle-aged immigrant from Iraq who had applied for a managerial position at Bank Leumi. The man had been a manager at a bank in Baghdad, but because of his age had not been able to find a comparable job in Israel. Uncle Moshe felt that because I had established myself at Bank Leumi, a letter of support from me would be helpful. I didn't know the man, but Uncle Moshe swore by him, saying that he would attest to the man's competence and declaring that, if hired, he would put to shame many managers at Bank Leumi. What I remember is my utter disdain for Uncle Moshe's judgment. How could someone from the backward Iraqis surpass a manager of the big Bank Leumi? What did they know about banking in Iraq? Yet the truth was that while Iraq had an underdeveloped economy, it had a highly developed commercial banking system. The scorn I felt for my uncle, and for his high opinion of another immigrant from Iraq, was symptomatic of the problem.

I chided myself for what I now saw as self-destructive efforts to merge into Israeli society. I had socialized mostly with young Ashkenazis from Eastern Europe. I was drawn to them even though I knew I was not fully accepted by them. One afternoon as my friends and I sat together and shared stories from our past, I was telling about the time I had gone to an upscale shop in Baghdad to buy a velvet jacket. The store was on the first floor of the Semiramis Hotel, a three-story luxury building on the banks of the Tigris.

As I described the building I overheard one member of my group mutter, "As if there are any three-story buildings in Baghdad."

My pleasure in reliving a happy experience vanished. I didn't respond to the comment. I lapsed into silence and didn't finish my story.

Such incidents were disturbingly common. Yet, if I took exception to a derogatory comment, I was chastised for being too sensitive, and asked why I couldn't take a joke. Now, from the vantage point of England, I saw that those frequent jabs at my culture were, indeed, no joke. Each incident in itself didn't amount to much, but the constant barrage had worn me down and made me feel less than acceptable.

I longed to share my new insights with some of the other students living in Hillel House. Undoubtedly, many of them had encountered anti-Semitism, but did they know much about the plight of Israeli Jews from Arab lands? Yet I kept mum, out of loyalty to Israel. If British Jews learned about our situation, I was afraid they might not support Israel.

Nonetheless, in my own mind I was no longer sweeping the problems under the rug. I couldn't change the way Jews from Arab lands were regarded in Israel. But I could see it for what it was and stop identifying with it.

CHANGING DIRECTION

By the time I returned to Israel, I had decided that I needed to find a home elsewhere. As a college senior, the end was in sight. Graduate study abroad seemed to offer a solution.

In the short term, meanwhile, my work at Bank Leumi in Tel Aviv had become unsatisfying. I was doing repetitive work in the Foreign Exchange department that offered few professional challenges while cutting into the time I could devote to study.

When I decided to leave the bank, its workers' union negotiated an agreement with management that allowed me to receive in one lump sum my three-year accumulated pension. These funds helped greatly with living expenses. At last I could concentrate exclusively on my studies and attend classes feeling fresh and rested. There was a new spring in my step.

Less than three months after quitting the bank, opportunity knocked again.

Yits'hak Guelfat, one of my economics instructors, was on the board of directors of a nonprofit organization, the Consumers' Cooperative Society, Israel's largest retailer. Now the Society was recruiting an economist, and Professor Guelfat recommended me for the job.

During my interview with the Society's president, Yisrael Sh'pan, I could feel his hesitancy to hire a Middle Easterner battling with his respect for Professor Guelfat's opinion. But as our discussion continued, he grew increasingly interested in my background. In the end, he hired me. I was elated.

The job at the Society gave me the practical experience I wanted in applied economics, but my commute to work in Tel Aviv from Ramat Gan cut into my study time and the cramped family apartment was no place to study. Because I could now afford it, I rented a room in an apartment house in North Tel Aviv. It contained only a bed, a folding table and a folding chair, but I could close the door and concentrate.

As time went by at my new job, I felt Yisrael Sh'pan's respect for me grow. He trusted the reports I wrote and appreciated my analytical ability. The other members of the Society also respected me, though some appeared to do so grudgingly. The only other Middle Eastern employee was our middle-aged elevator operator. As I rode the elevator every day up to my office, I could feel the operator's pride in me—a situation that was as sad as it was heartwarming.

Instead of slavishly attempting to assimilate into Israeli society, I was finally becoming comfortable with my identity as a Jew from an Arab land. It was good to realize that at least some of my coworkers at the Society saw me for who I really was, and also as a person worthy of their respect.

Of course it wasn't as simple as all of that. When I was in the military I was also respected by my fellow soldiers and officers for the person that I was, for my skills and for my abilities. But there were civilians who worked on the military base who treated me as if I were the lowest of the low and did not hide their disdain for me. I tried to ignore their slurs and their jibes about "the dark skinned people", and "You the blacks", but it wasn't always easy. And now, though I was respected at work, I still had to deal with put-downs on the street and in fleeting encounters. To the casual observer in Israel I was the black one who did not belong in Israel. The people who hurled insults at me did not know me, but that did not make the insults easier to handle. Couldn't they see that I a person, albeit different from them in lots of ways, but deep down basically the same?

I had a good relationship with my landlords, Joseph and Miriam Schlezinger. I believe Joseph in particular was interested in all Jews coming together from all over the world and forming one society. I remember one evening in particular when he came home from a meeting very upbeat and excited. His eyes danced and his arms flailed the air as he tried to tell Miriam about the meeting. I thought at first that he had discovered some wonderful new knowledge at the meeting. However, when I could cut through the excitement that laced his words to discover its source, I found that what he was excited about was the fact that the attendees at the meeting were "Amkha" - Jews from many, many countries. He had loved being with them all, feeling that all of these Jews were part of his people.

I grew fond of my landlords, Joseph and Miriam, but they, too, had their prejudices. They despised Romanians. I never told them that I had dated a Romanian-born woman.

Every Friday night during my senior year, as well as the following year I spent in Israel, I attended the lectures and discussions that were held in the building of the Zionist Organization of America. Those discussions were informative. They opened my world to wider horizons and broadened my views. People from other countries, members of the K'neset, members of the Cabinet and others lectured there and discussed topics of interest. I remembered one program in particular, a round table discussion.

The topic under discussion was the election of members of the K'neset by the varying parties instead of directly by the people. Direct election, of which I am in favor, still does not happen in elections to the K'neset, though the Mappai party, the party in power at the time, was in favor of it at that discussion in the mid 1950's. People who spoke in favor of the concept were listened to, but the speaker who got the loudest round of applause spoke against direct election by the people.

"If I am elected by the people in a district," the speaker declared, "my view of Israel would be a narrow one, focused on the people in that particular district. If, on the other hand, a party selects me, I have a more national perspective and am focused on the good of the whole country. Would the Negev desert ever have blossomed if we had direct election by the people in Israel?"

His words and the ensuing applause disheartened me. In focusing on what the parties saw as the whole country, whole segments of that country were overlooked or deliberately ignored. Jews from Arab lands were very easily lost in the shuffle even while the desert bloomed.

Still I remained determined. I would rise above whatever biases that existed and make my way in the world.

I graduated from college in November 1957. The commencement ceremony was utterly lacking in pomp and splendor: no caps and gowns, no stately procession of graduates and faculty, no outdoor reception on a campus lawn. We assembled in a drab lecture hall at night -- everyone had already put in a full working day.

Still, spirits were high. Every one seemed relaxed and in a good mood. Graduates were called to the podium, one by one, to receive their diplomas.

It took a good while before it was my turn. I didn't think I would feel excited to receive my diploma. It was only a formality, I felt. Yet when I stepped up to the podium, I was elated when I held that document in my hand.

I missed my parents' presence that evening. I remembered how my father had sat me down not long before I left Baghdad, and told me that I should not think of college as the be-all and end-all, that it would be all right if I didn't attend college. Baba's observation puzzled me. It ran counter to my entire upbringing—and to my father's own history of going to law school despite his poverty. Could it be that he was worried I might fall into despair if I couldn't make it to college in my new homeland? I was not sure how to react. But on the night of my graduation, all that had faded away. I only wished my mother and father could have been there. I felt they would have been proud to see their son among the graduates.

Receiving my hard-won college diploma from the school's dean

During my senior year, the School of Law and Economics joined with other academic departments that had sprouted in Tel Aviv, to form a new university, Tel Aviv University, which has since rivaled Hebrew University. My class was the first to receive diplomas with the new insignia - Tel Aviv University – School of Law and Economics.

I graduated with a Bachelor of Science in Economics. But I always regretted my lack of a liberal-arts education. In Israel people attended college in order to acquire a profession, to learn a trade. Attending college to acquire knowledge for its own sake was unheard of. The dominant attitude was that there was insufficient time or money to spend discovering oneself or learning about the finer things in life, which might not have immediate applications or contribute directly to one's ability to make a living. Viewed through that prism, accounting was considered fine; economics was OK; philosophy was a waste of time!

A LONG SHOT

FLOODING THE MARKET

Even if I had wanted to stay in Israel, Hebrew University was not a viable option for graduate work. To protect its hegemony, Hebrew University had practically declared war on Tel Aviv's School of Law and Economics. It didn't recognize the Tel Aviv diploma and expected Tel Aviv University graduates to start from scratch as candidates for a bachelor's degree at Hebrew University before applying for graduate school. The antagonism extended to job openings. Hebrew University graduates dominated the top echelons of the Central Bank and the Ministry of Finance, Israel's two leading economic institutions, and they effectively blocked the appointment of Tel Aviv graduates as economists at both.

I decided to focus primarily on the U.S. in my search for a graduate school. I had a great admiration for the US, its democratic institutions, and its freedom of the press. And I remembered with gratitude the courageous stand of the US Information Center in Baghdad when it defied the Iraqi government's order to shut down.

At the U.S. embassy's library in Tel Aviv I unearthed a goldmine: Voluminous guidebooks to American graduate schools and financial aid.

Every day after work I combed those guidebooks for schools offering programs in my field, scholarships and loans. I rented an Underwood typewriter, and every evening I sat at my folding table and typed letters to graduate schools and financial-aid organizations. I flooded the market. I wrote to top schools and to schools I had never heard of. Sometimes I was drawn to a marginal school simply because it was located in a region with a balmy climate.

The workload mounted as the responses began to come in. Sometimes I stayed up until two o'clock in the morning and got up at seven to go to work. The number of letters of reference that my former college instructors had to send on my behalf mounted too. Some accepted the burden cheerfully; others were not so happy about it.

I remember that period as one of utter exhaustion, mixed with a sense of determination. On the Sabbath I would stay in bed all day to catch up on my sleep. The mounting pressure energized me. Giving up never crossed my mind.

Some of the responses were disappointing. One financial-aid institution advertised that it specialized in scholarships for first-year graduate students indigenous to the Middle East. I was thrilled; I was as indigenous to the Middle East as they come. This was one application that would bring sure-fire results, or so I thought. But the response to my application made it clear that only Arabs were eligible; Jews were not.

All the other financial-aid institutions I contacted turned me down.

But there were pleasant surprises, as well. While I was turned down by several lesser schools, such as Alabama State University, I was admitted to a number of elite schools. I held off responding to any offer until I heard from the prize I sought: Harvard.

A DREAMER?

When I told friends I had applied to Harvard, they thought I'd taken leave of my senses.

"No graduate, even from Hebrew University or Technion, is known to have made it to Harvard. You graduated from a dinky little school that no one ever heard of. You are setting yourself up for disappointment," my friends told me, sometimes gently and sometimes disparagingly.

Others pointed out that Harvard was expensive. The annual tuition fee for the Graduate School of Arts and Sciences was $1,000 - among the highest in the U.S. It was a staggering sum by comparison with the annual per-capita income in Israel at the time, which was around $500, as I recall.

"Are you out of your mind? How are you going to pay for it?" people asked.

I didn't have an answer. But I was not deterred. I clung to my longstanding conviction that lack of money need not be--and should not be--an obstacle to education. But I had no idea how was I going to implement that lofty principle. I would cross that bridge when I came to it.

Each of my university applications involved a series of hurdles in the admission process. I never allowed myself to become overwhelmed by the mounds of difficulties that lay ahead. Instead, I focused on one hurdle at a time, the one that lay immediately at hand. Only when I got over that hurdle did I turn my attention to the next.

I departed only once from that rule, with near-disastrous results.

When I began applying to graduate schools in July 1957, I had also set in motion an inquiry about getting a visa to the U.S. Obtaining a sponsor's affidavit for a visa was likely to take time, I figured, and it would be wise to have that out of the way in case I was admitted to a school.

I wrote to David Bassoon, asking for his help getting the necessary affidavit. David was the manager of the Baghdad branch of Shasha Trading Company, an international company headquartered in New York and owned by the Shashas, a Baghdadian Jewish family. David and his wife, my cousin Grace, had joined my brother Jacob on the trip to Turkey when I was in Marseilles. I had reestablished contact with them at that time, before they had all returned to Baghdad.

I had to be discreet to evade the censors in Iraq. In my letter to David, I was careful not to reveal my identity— while providing enough hints to let him know who the letter was from and what I was asking.

I sent my letter to the Liverpool branch of the Shasha Trading Company, with instructions to enclose it in one of the company's official envelopes and mail it on to David in Baghdad. It never occurred to me to ask the company's secretary to discard my envelope—carrying Israeli stamps and my return address-- before forwarding my letter. I assumed everyone in the Liverpool office knew it was dangerous for Jews living in Iraq to receive correspondence from Israel. I should not have taken anything for granted.

The secretary in Liverpool tucked my envelope and letter into one of the company's envelopes and mailed it to David. Like all mail addressed to Jewish residents of Baghdad, the letter from Liverpool went first to the censor's office. Something fortunate happened this time. The censor stamped the envelope "Approved for Delivery" without ever opening it.

When David opened the envelope he was terrified to find inside the incriminating envelope from Tel Aviv. He couldn't destroy the evidence without being noticed at the office, or without leaving traces that his Arab employees would discover. So he put the letter in his pocket, walked matter-of-factly out of his office, and headed home. There he burned the envelope.

Everyone in the family was shaken when they heard the story. My parents, too, would have been implicated had the censor opened the letter.

David was magnanimous about that awful incident. Though I had put him at great risk, he went immediately to work on my request. Less than six months later, I received an affidavit for a U.S. visa from the company's headquarters in New York. The company's president, Maurice Shasha, had pledged his company's assets as a collateral. This gesture moved me to tears. I had never met Maurice Shasha, yet he was willing to go to such lengths on my behalf.

Now there was nothing to do but wait. Harvard's answer came a few weeks later. I was qualified to enroll in the PhD program, without going through the Masters program.

But there was one big hitch. Before granting me admission, Harvard needed evidence that I had at my disposal $4,800 to cover my first two year's tuition and living expenses. I barely had the equivalent of $30 in my bank account. How was I going to come up with the rest?

Israel's foreign exchange controls made matters worse. Even if I had had the money in Israeli liras, I couldn't just walk into a bank and buy dollars. I needed to apply first to Israel's Treasury for permission to purchase dollars. That involved extensive paperwork, and it took weeks and months before the Treasury rendered a decision. The Treasury was particularly tight-fisted with hard currency -- dollars and pounds sterling -- and it was guided by a list of priorities, in which graduate work abroad in the social sciences was at the lowest rung.

Everything seemed to militate against meeting Harvard's $4,800 requirement.

A BIT OF SUBTERFUGE

While working for Bank Leumi, I had learned the intricacies of foreign- exchange controls, the mechanics of applying to the Treasury, and the Treasury's approval process. I also became familiar with how the bank processed foreign-exchange applications once the Treasury had approved them. All this came in handy when I needed to show Harvard evidence of financial responsibility. But, even today, I feel uncomfortable about the devious way I put that knowledge to use.

This is how it worked.

When the Treasury approved an application for foreign exchange, it sent a notice to Bank Leumi, authorizing the bank to sell, say, $5,000 dollars to the applicant. The notice didn't obligate the applicant to buy all or part of the $5,000. It merely approved her right to do so.

Upon receipt of the Treasury's approval, Bank Leumi mailed a one-liner to the applicant, addressed to " To Whom It May Concern," stating, "This is to certify that the Treasury has allotted to so and so the sum of $5,000."

That one-liner might work for me if and when I could convince the Treasury to approve my application for $4,800, I figured. Reading the one-liner, Harvard might conclude that the "allotted" dollars were actually sitting in my bank account, and accept the bank's letter as evidence of financial responsibility.

It was worth a try. If it worked, it would give me breathing time until I had to face paying my tuition and living expenses. Maybe I could borrow money from an

American bank. What basis did I have for expecting that to happen? None, really. The truth is that I had no idea how to finance graduate school, any more than I knew how to pay for my airfare to the U.S.

Harvard had given me only five weeks to give my answer. I appealed to the Treasury committee for urgent consideration, and asked to be present when it took up my application. With trepidation, I traveled to Jerusalem and hand-delivered my application.

The committee called a few days later to say that they expected to consider my application on the following Friday afternoon, and that I would be allowed to attend.

I was tense the day I received the call. I continued to fret about how to anticipate questions, stay alert, be at my best while I awaited that all-important interview. What if some committee members were graduates of Hebrew University? How would they react to the application of a graduate of Tel Aviv University? There were civil servants prejudiced against Middle Eastern Jews. What if one or two of them were members of the committee?

By the end of the day, I realized I would crack if I didn't stop worrying. There were just too many things to worry about. I had done the best I could. It was time to let go. I would just be myself at the meeting. If I failed, I would learn from the experience. Maybe I could try again later.

I was at peace with myself.

THE BEST-LAID SCHEMES

On the eve of my meeting with the Treasury committee I went out with Louise Clayton, whom I had met in London at an a cappella concert in a synagogue. Louise was one of the singers: then twenty-one years old, an only child, and the apple of her parents' eyes. She took me to corners of London that I might never have found on my own. With her, I learned to appreciate good theater and acquired a sense of British history. In the spring of 1957 she had come to Israel for a visit.

We walked along the beach in Tel Aviv before stopping in a coffee shop. I wanted to be rested the next day, so we cut the evening short and flagged a taxicab.

The driver took a shortcut through a pitch-dark street in a section of North Tel Aviv under construction. I thought I saw something strange near an apartment building, something that flitted across my line of vision and vanished suddenly.

"Did you notice anything?" I asked the driver.

"I think I saw something."

I looked back as we stopped the car. I could see nothing out of the ordinary, but it was so dark I couldn't be sure. Something eerie was in the air.

"Shouldn't we back up to the apartment building and see?" I asked the driver.

" Sure."

We stopped the car by the building's entrance. Our headlights threw light on the entrance, but we couldn't see past the thick hedge in front of the building. The car windows were open, but I couldn't hear a sound.

"Does anyone hear anything?" I asked.

No one did. I reached for the door handle.

"Maybe I should go out and look."

Before I got the door open, two men emerged from behind the hedge. In the headlights I could see they were wearing suits and ties. The taller of the two carried a briefcase. They brushed their suits with their hands as they proceeded to walk briskly. If these men were as respectable as they looked, I wondered, why did they have to hide behind the hedge?

The cab driver slowly followed them. Suddenly the taller man turned to face the taxi. He pulled a gun from his pocket, and pointed it at us. It was a small gun, much smaller than any I had seen in the military. The driver stopped the car. The man didn't approach us or say anything. He just stood and stared at us, gun in hand.

The sight of someone pointing a gun from such close range sent chills up and down my spine. Armed violence was not common in Israel, and I couldn't believe this was happening. The figure standing in the pale light, surrounded by darkness, didn't seem real. Were we watching a clip from a Western movie?

We decided it was safer not to confront the pair and stayed in the car. The tall man put the gun in his pocket, and the two resumed their brisk walk. We drove past and headed for a small movie theater nearby, where the driver said we would find a public phone.

The outside lights of the theater were off, but the door was open and we could see light inside. We walked in, and were startled to find a man lying motionless on the floor. I was afraid to touch him to find out if he was dead. Drawers were pulled open, a chair was overturned, and papers were strewn everywhere.

I ran to the phone and called the police. They asked us not to leave the scene.

No sooner had I hung up than the man opened his eyes, groaned and reached a hand behind his head. He blinked at us and shook his head, grimacing a little.

Bit by bit he told us his story. He worked at the theater and was alone, closing the accounts of the day, when two men wearing suits and ties walked into the theater and demanded that he hand over the cash. He refused. One of the intruders struck him on the head with a sharp object. He couldn't remember what happened next.

"Those two men were obviously leaving this place when we ran across them," I exclaimed.

The taxi driver and Louise nodded in agreement.

It was close to midnight when the police finally showed up. I was worried about my next day's meeting in Jerusalem. I needed a restful night. But now that the police had arrived, it should not take us long to report what we had seen and head home.

The police had a different plan.

"We can't release you yet," one officer said.

Release you? Were we under arrest? What was going on? We were only doing our civic duty when we reported what we had seen.

It was close to 2 a.m. when the police finally finished taking the report from the theater's employee, inspecting the drawers, tracking the footprints, and taking measurements. We could go home, but were told to show up the next morning at police headquarters downtown to identify the suspects from a line-up.

"How long will that take?" I asked.

"We don't know. But you should plan on being there the whole day."

"I have an important meeting to attend in Jerusalem tomorrow afternoon," I explained. "Couldn't it wait until Sunday?"

"We don't know. You'll have to show up at 9 am and talk to the station commander. He's the one to decide."

I was worried and angry that this snag would put an end to everything I had been trying to piece together. "The best-laid schemes o' Mice an' Men Gang, aft a-gley," I thought. I was an innocent citizen and had committed no crime, yet the police were restricting my freedom of movement.

I tossed and turned in bed. By the time I fell asleep, I had made up my mind. I wouldn't let this new hurdle stand in the way. If the station commander wouldn't permit me to leave for Jerusalem, I would just take off and worry about the consequences later.

I was at the police station at 9 a.m., tired, incoherent, and tense-- everything I didn't want to be on the day of my meeting in Jerusalem. The station commander was reluctant to postpone the line-up until Sunday, but, realizing he needed my cooperation, he compromised. I would leave for Jerusalem when I had to, but return to the station immediately after my meeting.

In the meantime, one line-up was ready. I joined Louise and the driver in the line-up room. The scene shocked me. I shuddered at the thought of mistakenly accusing an innocent man without an airtight alibi.

About a dozen young men stood in the lineup. Except for one who looked defiant, all seemed tired and broken. They must have been yanked out of their beds in the wee hours of the morning. Several avoided eye contact. One had his eyes fixed on the ground the entire time. I tried to remember the features of the two we had encountered the night before. I was never good at recalling facial details. Still I struggled to find any shred of resemblance between them and the men who had threatened us the night before. Finally, I told the station commander I couldn't in good conscience identify any as a suspect. Louise, on the other hand, pointed out two people without hesitation.

Weary with stress, I finally untangled myself from the police and boarded the bus to Jerusalem. I had a short nap on the way and woke up refreshed.

THE LINCHPIN MEETING

I was alert and focused when I walked into the committee's room. Gone were the tension and disorientation I had experienced that morning. I needed to concentrate on the critical business at hand.

The committee was made up of five men and one woman. I only knew the chairman was a Treasury official, a gruff man probably in his mid-fifties. The rest were middle aged, too, and looked tired. My case was apparently the last on the agenda for the day.

From the start, the question was: why spend dollars on funding graduate work abroad when the same could be accomplished at Hebrew University in Jerusalem? I explained the problem with Hebrew University and challenged the committee members to put themselves in my place. Would they choose to start over from scratch as freshmen at Hebrew University rather than go on to graduate school at a top institution in the U.S.? As I spoke, the woman on the panel kept nodding in agreement. She was, I thought, on my side, and I drew strength from what I perceived as her empathy. One committee member seemed to be in deep thought. The chairman was stone-faced. He proposed postponing the decision until a later date. I said I couldn't wait.

"Why are you pressuring us?" he growled, raising his voice.

I remember those words to this day. They still ring in my head.

"I am not pressuring you. I am under pressure to meet a deadline," I said.

I saw sympathetic looks on the faces of the rest of the interviewers. The chairman asked me to wait outside.

I felt serene as I sat outside. I had done the best I could and was reconciled to whatever might happen. But deep inside, I had the feeling I had made it.

Finally, the chairman called me back in. His demeanor had changed; he was smiling and actually looked humane. The committee had been impressed with my credentials and the way I had defended my application, he said. With a grin, he told me my application had been approved.

I had made it! I was ecstatic. Of course other hurdles lay ahead. But I didn't care. All had to do with money. I wanted to go out and announce my success to the skeptics, to those who had urged "realism," to those who had counseled against aiming high and to those who had exhorted me not to risk disappointment.

There was one detail to work out, the chairman said. The Treasury would authorize me to purchase $4,400, instead of the $4,800 that Harvard required. But in order to formally satisfy Harvard's requirement, the chairman would notify Bank Leumi that the Treasury had authorized $4,800, on condition I sign an agreement not to purchase more than $4,400 from the bank.

"Would you sign off on that?" the chairman asked.

This was the least of my worries. At that point I couldn't put my hands on $50, much less $4,400. It made no difference whether I were authorized to purchase $4400 or $4800. I couldn't acquire either amount.

I readily agreed to the chairman's terms.

Then I walked outside, sat on the steps of the Treasury building, put my head in my hands and sobbed.

THE MIRACLE

Bank Leumi was ready with its one-liner: "This is to certify that the Treasury has allotted to Mr. Daniel Khazzoom the sum of $4,800." The director of the bank's foreign-exchange department, Yits'hak Avital, looked happy when he handed me the letter.

"I hope to be able to call you Professor Khazzoom next time I see you," he said.

I express mailed the bank's authorization to Harvard. There was nothing else to do but wait. Would it work?

In short order, Harvard sent me its letter of admission.

I wrote to Mr. Shasha in New York to share the news with him and thank him for his magnanimity. Even though I didn't make use of his affidavit, his willingness to vouch for me had been a source of hope and strength.

I expected to be in Cambridge, Massachusetts in mid-September 1958 for the start of the school year. I had 100 liras in my bank account, but needed 950 liras ($320) to pay for my airfare.

When my friend, Albert, learned I had been admitted to Harvard, he gave me all of his savings: 200 liras. Other friends and members of my family chipped in. The Consumers' Co-operative Society came through too, but I was still 150 liras short. There was one other possible benefactor: the Fund for the Education of Immigrants from Iraq, which had been established by Babylonian educators and leaders at the start of the exodus from Iraq to Israel.

Several times before, I had been tempted to ask the trustees of the Fund for help, but I didn't have the audacity to approach them, having let them down in the past.

During my college years, several leaders of the Babylonian Jewish community ran for election to the K'neset and worked hard to convince us that raising the issue of discrimination in the K'neset would contribute to a change for the better.

I, like many other young Babylonian immigrants, had not only disavowed our traditional leaders and their agenda, but actively campaigned against them. We argued that electing Babylonian representatives to parliament would be divisive-- even though the ethnic division was glaring, and was there for everyone to see. We proclaimed we wanted one Jewish people, not Jews with ethnic tags.

But perhaps the real reason why the young people of my generation had opposed our elders was our reluctance to admit we were the people who were tagged "Second Israel," the ones that the press called "Laggard Israel." It was too embarrassing, too painful, for us to stand up and be counted among the laggards. Better to pretend they didn't exist.

We prevailed. None of the Babylonian candidates were elected.

Later, I came to regret what we had done. Those leaders were honest. They had the courage of their convictions. They saw discrimination and tried to wrestle with it.

Several board members at the Fund for the Education of Immigrants from Iraq were part of the same Babylonian leadership I had opposed during my years of denial. How could I now turn to them for help? That Fund was the embodiment, the quintessence of the traditions of Babylonian Jewry. It reflected the worldview of the Jews of Iraq, their values and societal priorities. Having been so hostile to the preservation of those traditions, how could I justify benefiting from those same traditions, just because they now happened to serve my needs? I finally concluded that honesty and logic required me to stay away from the Fund.

As I wracked my brain trying to think of sources of financial aid, it occurred to me to write to Bekhor Shitrit, the minister of police and the lone Sephardi member of the Israeli cabinet. He was the scion of an illustrious family that had lived in Israel for generations.

I had written letters to other cabinet members asking for help, but my letters were ignored. Mr. Shitrit responded promptly, assuring me that he would be back in touch, as soon as he had time to think of a way to help me.

Then my life took an unexpected twist.

Paying for the tuition and living expenses for my first two years in graduate school was, I knew, something I would have to face eventually, but I planned to tackle this problem once I had the money for airfare. But when I learned of a chance to get tuition assistance, finding the 150 liras suddenly became a pressing priority.

Harvard notified me that I was eligible for a Ford Foundation grant to attend The Economics Institute, an experimental program established that year. The Institute was intended to provide remedial instruction in English and economic theory to first-year foreign grad students. Classes, beginning the second week in July 1958, were to be held on the campus of the University of Wisconsin, Madison. The program included extracurricular activities to familiarize the foreign students with life in the U.S. -- trips to the countryside, tours of factories and farms, meetings with scholars and dignitaries, and weekends with American families.

I was excited about the chance to improve my English and become oriented to my new American environment. There was also an advantage to being in the U.S. some two and a half months before beginning the semester at Harvard. While attending the Institute, I could contact American banks about getting a school loan.

Even as I worried about my 150-lira shortfall, I rolled up my sleeves, sat in front of my Underwood typewriter, and filled out the Ford Foundation application for the Institute.

I had no idea what my chances of getting the grant were. But that didn't prevent me from daydreaming about what I'd do with the money if it came through. I'd pay the $400 tuition fee for the Institute, but would scrimp on meals and save on my other living expenses. Maybe I could get on just one meal a day. Maybe I could also share a room with other students to save on rent. If so, I'd need to borrow less, and maybe that would enhance my chances of getting an education loan from a bank. Maybe. Maybe. Maybe.

The response was not long in coming. The Ford Foundation approved a $1,000 grant for tuition and room and board, a $250 allowance for a round-trip flight from New York to Madison and a generous sum for a four-night stay in a hotel in New York.

"This is a miracle," I said when I read the Foundation's letter.

I considered hitchhiking instead of flying from New York to Madison and back. I could then save the airfare allowance. I was adept at hitchhiking. I did a lot of that when I was in the military. Maybe I could do it in the U.S. too. Why not? I might be able to save enough to pay for my first-term tuition at Harvard. That would lift a big burden off my back. Maybe. Maybe. Maybe.

But my immediate problem was coming up with the 150-lira airfare to the U.S. I couldn't use the grant money to pay for my airfare. I had to first get to New York to get the grant. Otherwise, I'd lose my chance of attending the Institute, lose the Ford Foundation award and, with it, the dream of saving enough to help with my Harvard fees. So much hinged on closing that 150-lira shortfall.

Then, unexpectedly, I received a letter from the Fund for the Education of Immigrants from Iraq. Minister Shitrit had asked them to help me cover my 150-lira shortfall. The letter pledged the Fund's assistance. That would do it, I said to myself. But I was still plagued by guilt about accepting their help. How could I face them?

Two weeks later, another letter arrived. The Fund had a check for me to pick up. They had sponsored a benefit dance party and had set aside my 150 liras out of the proceeds.

When I went to pick up the check, a middle-aged man at the Fund smiled and said, "We're so proud of you, Danny," as he handed me the check.

I wanted to tell him how much their forgiveness meant to me, but I could only murmur my thanks while fighting back tears. When the chips were down, this community that I had dismissed for most of my time in Israel had come through with magnanimity.

I gazed at the check, and was pleasantly surprised to notice that Minister Bekhor Shitrit had countersigned it.

I thought back on my efforts to get to graduate

school, on the struggle to put the pieces together, one at a time – piece, by piece, by piece. That check was another of those pieces, arguably the most important. But it had more than monetary value. It was part of my history. It epitomized the generosity of the Babylonian community and its willingness to come to my rescue, in spite of what I had done.

Photograph of the 150-lira check from the Babylonian Educational Fund

It signified my effort to continue my education, even without the wherewithal, and it symbolized what I was and what I had been through. It carried a message that I wanted preserved as inspiration for immigrants, the poor and the downtrodden: "Don't give up on education for want of money, and don't get discouraged before you have tried. Take a risk. It is true that even if you try, you might not make it. But if you don't try, you will never shine."

I had to cash the check to pay my airfare. But before I did I paid to have it photographed. It was expensive, but I was not going to scrimp. That check had too much value. Without it, the whole endeavor might have failed.

To this day, the framed photograph of that check hangs proudly in my study.

I lost contact with the Fund, but I never forgot its mission. For years I donated to organizations in Israel dedicated to preserving the cultural heritage of the Babylonian community and educating its children.

When my friend and fellow economist, Vivi Darweesh-Lecker, of Bar Ilan University passed away in 2002, her husband Eddy told me about a fund that had established a fellowship in her memory to support doctoral and post-doctoral work by members of the Babylonian community. I was electrified. It was none other than the Fund that had given me the 150 200

I sent the Fund a check in Vivi's memory, and renewed my links with it.

A DESPERATE PLOY

Late in April 1958, while I was engrossed with my Harvard application, Uncle Moshe handed me a letter smuggled out of Baghdad. I immediately recognized my father's handwriting. Ammu Moshe had established communications with Baghdad through covert channels that the Babylonian Bank in Tel Aviv maintained with remnants of the Jewish community in Iraq. I learned later that he had kept my parents up to date on our activities in Israel through this channel.

My father wrote that he had acceded to my mother and brother's insistence that they leave Iraq immediately. Further, he stated that he expected me to cancel my plans to go abroad and stay in Israel to support my parents. Should I choose to stick to my plans, Baba continued, he would have no choice but to let my mother and brother leave by themselves, while he would stay behind and face whatever fate had in store for him. He ended his letter with a Judeo-Arabic saying, "Whatever is written on the forehead, the eye can't escape witnessing," a Babylonian saying that conjures up misery and destruction.

It was a devastating letter. Was everything I had been working on to go down the drain? How could my father make such demands on my future? He was casting me as the villain, responsible for his threatened separation from my mother. Blood surged through my veins, my heart pounded and I had difficulty breathing. At no other time in my life do I recall a surge of emotions such as I experienced that day.

I tried to calm down and sort through my feelings. If my father came to Israel I knew he would suffer a terrible drop in social status. I imagined he was still practicing law. But he would need a license to practice in Israel. At sixty-eight, he was almost certainly in no shape to go back to law school and start over again. His message clearly sprang from fear of what the future might hold. Maybe he imagined himself jobless and friendless in a new country, where he would no longer enjoy the prominence he had once enjoyed. He was a drowning man who would latch onto anything he could grab, even at the risk of sinking his rescuer. He must have been driven by panic, I said to myself. I should be more understanding.

Still, I despised him for maneuvering to make me responsible for the breakup of my parents' long, happy marriage. I treasured that aspect of their life, and my father knew it. During all my years in Israel, I had dreamed of the day when my parents would make it out of Iraq, alive and whole. I looked forward to welcoming them and helping them resettle. I owed that to them. But I didn't owe them my life. And that was where my father and I parted company. It was also where I had parted company with other oppressive Babylonian practices.

In Iraq, it was customary to expect sons to take care of their parents and support them in their old age. That was why most Babylonian Jews, like other Middle Easterners and Asians, preferred to have sons and not daughters. Sons were the social security for old age. My parents had five daughters and one son – myself -- living in Israel. My father wrote to me, but not to any of my sisters, asking that I dedicate my life to my parents. This was not an unusual request for a Babylonian Jew. Many "good" sons gave up the opportunity to have careers or get married and have families of their own, because they were expected to devote their lives exclusively to their parents. People were pilloried for bucking those practices.

As I thought through the implications of my father's letter, I realized he had no power over me. I would still go ahead with my plans; he had no claim on my life. I knew that my father had no compunction about tormenting the conscience of others, if that was what it took to get his way. It was a weapon I had seen him use before to bend Ammu Moshe to his will.

In 1950, the year that Jews were given the opportunity to register to leave Iraq and relinquish their citizenship, I was the only one in my family to do so. Later on, when Uncle Moshe decided to register to leave Iraq with Aunt Guerjiyi, he and my father discussed the matter. I was the only other person present during their conversation.

My parents had had a hard time finding suitable spouses for Jamila and Muzli, and paying off their dowries had drained their resources. Marrying off my other sisters was expected to be even tougher because so many eligible bachelors were planning to leave in the big exodus. Reyna, Helwa and Latifa were in their late teens or early twenties, which in Iraq was considered a marriageable age.

"When you go to Israel, Moshe," I heard my father declare, "take Reyna, Helwa, and Latifa with you and see that they get married there."

Ammu Moshe's eyes widened and his jaw dropped. He thought for a while.

"It's a big responsibility," he replied.

Ammu Moshe was in his early sixties. He had no children of his own, and he no doubt dreaded the prospect of being saddled with this unwelcome burden at his advanced age.

" It is up to you, Moshe," my father continued. "If you don't take care of this, the retribution for the miserable lives they would end up leading here will fall on your head."

I looked at Ammu Moshe. He was foaming mad. His mouth was working, though no words were coming out. He finally let out a curse and left the room.

I don't know what further was said, if anything. I do know that when Ammu Moshe and Khala Guerjiyi came to Israel they brought Reyna, Helwa and Latifa with them.

As I thought through all of that, I realized that I couldn't just ignore my father's letter and go on with my life as if nothing had happened. I needed to get word to him that he couldn't threaten me into submission, that I had no plans to change course.

I also felt that even though my father had written to me and not to my sisters, his threat to stay behind in Iraq had implications for my sisters, as well. They needed to know about his letter, as well as the consequences of what I was about to tell him. It would affect their lives, too. Mama and Baba were the parents of us all. I thought it might do us good to hold a family meeting and exchange views on the subject.

I was uncertain how my sisters would react to my intention to stick to my plan, knowing that my parents might arrive anytime soon. My sisters knew practically nothing about my effort to gain admission to Harvard or the hoops I had been through to piece things together.

I know my sisters were proud that I held the most prominent job in my family. But judging from occasional comments I heard from them, they probably wondered why I would want to abandon the big catch I had in hand in favor of the less tangible rewards of graduate work. Nor do I believe it would have mattered much to them whether I was admitted to Harvard or to a dinky school in Timbuktu. In fairness, I don't think many in Israel knew the difference either. To most people in Israel, a university was a university. That there was such a thing as first-rate university and a third-rate university was beyond the ken of most Israelis.

I was agitated when I told my sisters what had transpired with our father. I told them I felt awful that I might have to leave at a time when our parents would be arriving in Israel, but I assured them that I had no plans of shirking my responsibility to help, even when I was abroad. I noted I was not our parents' only child and didn't feel I was the only one who had the responsibility to support them. I shared with my sisters my sense of outrage at my father's machinations. I told them I planned to give Ammu Moshe a letter for my father, informing him in no uncertain terms that I didn't plan to change course. I asked for my sisters' reactions.

There was a long silence, as well as sad faces. Latifa proposed that we write a letter to our father, telling him that we looked forward to having him join us with Mama and Jacob, that although I would be abroad all of their children would be there to help. Latifa proposed that we put our initials to the letter. We agreed this was the way to go.

I drafted the response in code form.

"SON, YOU LOOK SO DIFFERENT"

In May 1958, my parents and my brother Jacob left Baghdad on a tourist visa to Turkey. (Valentine had arrived eight months before through Turkey). From there they boarded a plane to Israel. Jews by then were normally barred from leaving Iraq. But depending on the whims of the regime, some were allowed to go on short visits abroad, but had to leave their assets or family members behind as collateral. The exit doors closed for good in 1958, with close to 15,000 Jews remaining in Iraq.

As I sat in the airport awaiting my parents' arrival I was still stewing over my father's letter. Maybe it was all to the good that we wouldn't be together for very long. At the same time, I was struggling with my own guilt.

Maybe my father was right. Maybe I should stay. But if I did, what would that do to my future? My preoccupation with my parents' resettlement might not leave me time to put the pieces back together. I might fall into the same trap that other "good" sons had fallen into. They watched their life go by, while they were absorbed in taking care of their parents. I didn't want that to happen to me. But I still didn't want to see my parents suffer.

It seemed doubtful that our conflict would be resolved without pain and sorrow. But the least I could do was to spend as much time as possible with them during the short time I had remaining in Israel. The first few weeks and months would be the hardest for them. But at least I spoke Hebrew, and could serve as a buffer between them and Israel's bureaucracy.

As I sat absorbed in my thoughts, the announcement came over the public address system that their flight from Turkey had landed.

I was allowed to go on the tarmac outside the waiting area when people began to disembark. The passengers had a good distance to walk to the customs area. I was not sure my parents would be able to walk that far on their own.

From the distance, I could see my mother, followed by my father. As I got closer I could see she was beaming. I rushed to her and gave her a hug. She hugged me and kissed me on both cheeks, but didn't recognize me. She asked if I was Naim, Muzli's husband. When I told her it was Daniel, she rushed to put her arms around me. Then she pulled her head back to take a closer look at me.

"You look so different, my son!" she exclaimed.

I guess I did. I was eighteen when I had left. More than seven years had passed. My father approached slowly. He looked worried, and his eyes seemed to have sunk deep in their sockets. His steps were heavy, and he had aged much more than I had expected. I gave him a big hug and held his hands to my chest, as if to reassure him that in spite of it all, I was still his son and that I would do what I could to stand by his side.

Jacob trailed behind. I went to meet him. I put my arms around him and told him I was glad to see him.

"My goodness your voice has changed. It is so different now," he remarked.

A lot of things were different now, I thought to myself. A long separation takes its toll. Still, nothing could change the fact that they were-- and remained-- my own flesh and blood. I felt a surge of joy; at the same time I felt overwhelmed with sorrow over the pain of separation that we had all endured. I couldn't respond to Jacob's observation. I was choked with emotion. He embraced me and we both broke into tears.

My parents had managed to take with them some photographs and other items of sentimental value – possibly by paying a bribe – and were allowed to take enough money to pay for their expenses during their stay in Turkey, where Baba made a sentimental visit to his law school in Istanbul. Even before we left the airport, my father reached into his pocket and handed me travelers' checks in pounds sterling that he had brought from Baghdad. I was familiar with these checks. The Iraqi authorities had stamped them "Not Negotiable in Israel." Banks in Israel did redeem them, but at a fraction of their face value. There was also a thriving black market in Tel Aviv, where "Not Negotiable in Israel" checks were redeemed at close to their face value. The difference between what the banks and the black market paid was substantial.

Jacob, September 28, '1957

My parents left the decision about what to do with the checks to me. I was uneasy about breaking the law by redeeming the checks in the black market. On the other hand, I felt protective of what little my parents had salvaged from their wealth. Those checks were all they had. Nothing else would be coming to them in the future. How could I justify advising them to turn them over to a bank, knowing that the bank would take advantage of them?

Ultimately, I followed my instinct to obey the law. The loss my parents incurred was sizeable, and I wished I had the money to compensate them for it. They used their greatly reduced nest egg for the down payment on a one-bedroom apartment they bought in Ramat Gan shortly after they arrived.

My parents and my brother spent their first weekend in Israel at the apartment of Ammu Moshe and Khala Guerjiyi, and our first Friday night *kiddush* was a memorable experience. There were hugs and tears of joy. At long last, we were reunited. We had been so accustomed to thinking of our parents as living in danger that it was hard to believe they were now safe. But it was also painful to see the fall they had suffered—from our big house in Baghdad to makeshift accommodations in my uncle's cramped apartment hallway. None of us had the wherewithal to provide them with anything close to the physical comfort we had enjoyed growing up. We worried also about their age and endurance. It was easier for my sisters and me to adjust to a lower standard of living. We were young, and there was always hope for a better future. But what future was there for a man in his late sixties and a woman in her late fifties?

I was moved when we chanted "*shalom aleikhem, mal'akhei hashalom*," "peace be unto you, angels of peace," that first Friday night. It had been over seven years since we had last chanted the *kiddush* hymn together. Then it was the Woman of Valor, which we always chanted for my mother. We congregated around Mama, and some of us replayed what we used to do in our younger years - playfully pushing each other to snuggle close to her.

Then it was time for the leader of the *kiddush* ceremony to hold the *kiddush* cup and recite the sanctification over the fruit of the vine. My father, who had always presided over this part of the ritual, insisted that Ammu Moshe do us the honor this time. At the end of the sanctification, Baba bent over and kissed Ammu Moshe's hand. I was startled. I had never seen him do that before. Maybe he wanted to express his gratitude to Ammu Moshe for taking my three sisters with him to Israel and relieving my parents of the responsibility of finding husbands for them.

My parents, April 12, 1961

Before the week was over, my parents found their apartment in my sisters' and Ammu Moshe's neighborhood. In settling close by relatives, they were following the pattern of the old country, where all our homes were within a short walk from one another. Their new neighborhood in Ramat Gan was sought after by immigrants from Iraq. It had many features reminiscent of Baghdad's parks: tall eucalyptus trees, a river, and rowboats.

During the month we overlapped in Israel, Baba and I

never spoke of the letter he had sent me. But he never dropped his insistence that I abandon my plans to go to Harvard and stay in Israel to support him and my mother.

We were at my parents' apartment one day when he again began to badger me. It seemed he would never give up until he had worn me down and gotten what he wanted. I reiterated my decision not to change course. He looked defeated and sad. Helwa looked at him, and then turned to me.

"It hurts his feelings, can't you see?" she exclaimed.

I didn't know what to say. It was useless to carry the conversation any further. But that incident left a heavy burden on my heart, haunting me long after I moved to America.

Jacob, who had a degree in pharmaceutical chemistry from Baghdad's Royal College of Medicine, was eager to find a job, and came to me for advice. I had anticipated this request, and had already compiled a list of healthcare centers that had job openings. I suggested that we start with the prestigious Belinson Hospital, the prize on my list.

I set up an appointment for the following day and accompanied Jacob to the interview. The interviewer was so impressed with Jacob's credentials that he cut the interview short and told Jacob he could start work the following day.

This was beyond my wildest expectations. I felt relieved - a big burden was now off my shoulders. My biggest worry had been that, because of the language barrier, it might take Jacob a long time before he could find a job. Jacob was all smiles.

Mama was ecstatic. Baba was pleased with the news, but hardly effusive. He had difficulty cheering up.

Not long afterward, my father asked if I could help him find a job in the legal profession. I didn't know what to say. I had not done the groundwork for a job search. After writing him that I planned to leave for the U.S., I had assumed he would carry out his threat to stay in Baghdad. There was also the age factor. Immigrants much younger than him were unable to find jobs, particularly in law. But Baba was an active person, and the thought of being shelved and removed from the center of activity was foreign to him.

Having no idea where to start, I suggested that we broach the subject with the Jewish Agency.

We met with an agency official, a middle-aged, kindhearted woman. My father was tense; he looked as if he was facing the fateful test of his life. The official tried to put him at ease, speaking to him slowly in Hebrew.

My father's law diploma, written in the old Turkish alphabet

My father opened a cylindrical container he had carried out of Baghdad and lovingly unfurled his law school diploma. It was written in Turkish. That was the first time I had seen his diploma. It was only then that I began to fully fathom the depth of his fall. My father had never needed to prove himself to anyone before. He had never had to brandish his credentials for anyone. His reputation preceded him. I remembered him as a highly respected professional, a leader of our community. But here he was – a broken and frightened man. He looked anxiously at the agency official to weigh her impressions, as though a defendant waiting for the jury's verdict. His humiliation was heart-rending.

The official seemed touched. She looked at the diploma closely. I don't know if she knew Turkish. With a sad look, she turned to me.

"I can't think of any place to refer your father, in light of his age. He is entitled to rest after a long life of work."

She turned to my father and shook his hands warmly. He seemed to have gotten the gist of it: that this was the end of his illustrious career.

My father never pursued the subject of work again. Not long after the interview, he embarked on a project to compile a Judeo-Arabic/Hebrew dictionary. Recently, while searching through his files, I came across a pile of neatly written pages of Judeo-Arabic words, listed alphabetically, with their Hebrew counterparts written next to them. It was Baba's unfinished dictionary.

LEAVING FOR THE U.S.

I planned to spend the night before my flight to the U.S. with my parents in Ramat Gan. I took my time packing the few belongings in my room in Tel Aviv, lingering as though I had all the time in the world. How could I face my parents? Would I ever see them again? How could I leave them? I had worked so hard to reach my goal—how could I not leave? I remembered how I had felt leaving Baghdad for Israel: uncertain about the future and heartbroken to part with my family. But in Baghdad my father still had his career. In Israel he and my mother were refugees.

It was late in the evening before I arrived at my parents' apartment. The bedroom was dark; my father was already asleep. Mama sat on the balcony waiting for me. Jacob had summoned my sisters to bid me farewell, and we all gathered in the bedroom where Baba slept, undisturbed by the lights and our chatter. I felt that my mother very much wanted to gather me to her and open her heart to me. But I was determined not to let her. I was distant, haughty. That intimidated her. She kept her distance.

A photograph Mama managed to get out of Iraq
She is in our home in Baghdad, my photograph in hand, a few days after I left
Baghdad in 1951

Our seven-year separation, and the constant worry whether I was alive, had been an enormous strain on her. When we were reunited in Israel, she told me that she had cried her heart out when I left home, and that for a while she had kept my picture with her wherever she went. She had a hunch, she said, that if I had made it to Israel, I was serving in the military. So every time there were clashes on Israel's borders she was sure I was in mortal danger.

Now, there were no tears, but her anguish was obvious. I wanted to go to her, hug her and tell her I loved her, that I was sorry to be leaving and that I had missed her during our long years of separation. She had nothing except her children, and the journey out of Iraq had been to reunite with me especially. But something held me back. I suppose I was afraid if I gave in to my emotions, I might decide to stay. Then the intricate plan I had constructed for my future would unravel.

I slept fitfully that night.

The next morning, we all rose early, though no one said much. Our hearts were heavy as we faced yet another separation. Most painful for me was to watch my mother. She sat on a chair and just looked at me. Her eyes spoke of a deep sense of loss.

Mama had set the table for breakfast, but I couldn't force myself to eat. It must have been disappointing for her not to be able to nurture me one last time. But she didn't complain when I walked away from the table.

When it was time to leave, Baba and Jacob said they would escort me up the street to catch a taxicab to the airport.

"Will I ever see you again?" Mama asked.

"I will be back," I said coldly.

"You are lying," Mama replied.

In Judeo-Arabic that expression just connotes doubt, as in "It may never happen." I chose to interpret my mother's remark literally.

"Don't call me a liar," I retorted sharply.

My poor mother couldn't apologize enough. To this day, it pains me to remember how I treated her that morning. Tears streamed down her cheeks. She lifted the bottom of her dress to wipe away her tears, and she asked through her sobs:

"Why were we destined to be dispersed?"

It tore my heart to see Mama's anguish. I wish I had found the courage in that moment to open up to her and make amends for my harsh words. Instead, I just hugged her and kissed her good bye.

Throughout the years, I looked forward to the day when I would return to Israel and apologize to Mama, face to face, for my heartlessness. But death intervened and that day never came.

My father and brother escorted me to the main street where we would find a taxicab. I hugged Jacob. He was my friend; I had shared so much with him in our younger years. I told him how much I would miss him.

I then turned to my father and hugged him. He was standing silently, his eyes filled with tears. He looked at me sadly. How could I leave him? He was my father who loved me and had cared for me when I was a child.

"May God bless you, Baba," I said, as I choked up.

Then I turned away, got into the taxicab and slammed the door. The driver edged into the traffic and sped up.

I didn't look back.

PART THREE: US – Unedited

EN ROUTE TO THE UNKNOWN

On the morning of June 30, 1958, I flew from Tel Aviv to New York via Brussels and Liverpool. As a bonus for purchasing a Sabena ticket, my travel agent arranged for a free overnight stay for me in a hotel in Brussels.

Located in the center of Brussels, the hotel was a massive structure with a large beautiful garden. It reminded me of pictures I had seen of the sprawling mansions of the European nobility in the middle ages. I had never enjoyed so much luxury before. My room was large; it had gorgeous paintings, a large bed, and the most comfortable armchair I ever sat on. There was a large bathroom, a bathtub, and most amazing of all – twenty-four hour hot water. I wondered, "How could I enjoy so much luxury all at once?" I had only twenty-four hours to spend in that hotel.

I treated myself to a long hot shower. At dinnertime, I went downstairs to the dining room - a stately room with paintings of bucolic scenery all over the ceiling, enormous chandeliers and prisms of all sizes flashing their rainbow reflections on the walls, large round tables covered with richly embroidered cloths, and beautiful china plates of all sizes and shapes neatly laid out on the tables.

I sat myself at a table waiting to be served and was delighted when a middle aged American couple asked if they could join me. They were farmers from the Midwest who had flown to Brussels to attend the fair.

When the waiter came to take our orders, I was surprised to hear my friends order iced tea for one and iced coffee for the other. Iced tea? I never heard of iced tea before. We always drank hot strong tea with milk, and the only time I knew of coffee taken cold was when we had coffee-flavored ice cream. My friends noticed my puzzlement.

"It is common in the states to drink iced tea and iced coffee, particularly during the summer time," the lady explained.

That was the beginning of my excursion into the world of foods I knew so little about in the Middle East.

My stopover in Liverpool was long enough to board another propeller plane to New York.

By any rational accounting, I was headed pell-mell for disaster when I boarded the flight for America. I had accepted a place at one of the world's finest universities without a clue how to pay for my tuition and living expenses. I had neither family nor friends in the strange new country where I would spend the next few years. I had prepared at a mediocre undergraduate college and was not at all proficient in English. Worst of all, my yearning to make a new life in a free society was being gnawed at by feelings of guilt at leaving my parents in Israel just when we had been reunited.

On the morning of July 2, 1958 I got my first glimpse of America.

As the plane flew over New York harbor, I caught sight of the Statue of Liberty. I had seen pictures of the statue and had read the inspiring Emma Lazarus poem, but still was unprepared for the size and majesty of the original. It seemed as though she was standing in the harbor waiting for me to arrive. I wanted to put my arms around her and hug her. On the other hand, I was disappointed that the huge skyscrapers that outlined the city skyline dwarfed the statue. Perhaps, I thought, this was a symbol of things to come. My problems, too, might seem smaller once I arrived in America.

"Where in the United States are you going?" the customs official asked as he inspected my passport.

"To the University of Wisconsin, Madison for the Economics Institute and then on to Harvard in Cambridge, Mass., for graduate work."

The official smiled.

"Do you know what a great school Harvard is? It is the best university in the whole of the United States. May you have a wonderful stay. Welcome to the U.S."

I still remember his smile and his firm handshake—his genuine good will. As I walked off with my suitcase, I couldn't help but contrast this complete stranger's welcome with the indifference, even hostility, surrounding my arrival in

Israel. Nor could I forget the many doubters in Israel who had discouraged me from applying to Harvard.

As soon as I arrived in Manhattan, I called on Maurice Shasha, the businessman who, sight unseen and knowing no more than I was a Jew from Baghdad who wanted to do graduate work in the U.S., had been willing to sponsor me, pledging the assets of his company as security. Considering the enormity of his gesture, I wanted to tell him in person how grateful I was. As I looked into his dark, smiling eyes and felt his firm handclasp, I knew he was no longer a stranger, but a friend. I asked him why he was willing to vouch for me when we had never even met.

"My roots are in the Babylonian community, and I love that community," he told me. "It pains me to see the disaster the community has suffered. I would do anything to help revive it. What better way than to help one of its children attend a top institution of learning."

Now Mr. Shasha went a step further.

"I would feel so much better if you would let me send you a check for $100 each month," he said. "Put the money in the bank if you like and don't use it unless you have an emergency. For my part I will rest easy knowing you have it. You can pay it back to me when you graduate."

I shook his hands, but I was too choked up to put my thanks into words.

I stopped at the office of the Ford Foundation in Manhattan, where Mrs. Owens, the managing director, greeted me. She was a tall, slender, chestnut haired woman, who immediately put me at my ease. Soon I was busy signing papers and forms. I inquired from her about the procedure for getting an education loan from a bank or other agencies. She suggested several leads I could pursue. I was glad that I discussed the subject with her.

When Mrs. Owens understood that saving money was important to me, she made the money for my airfare available to me instead of purchasing a plane ticket for me, thereby allowing me to save the larger part of the travel stipend. She warned me that it was not practical to hitch hike, and suggested I consider taking the bus instead.

Traveling by bus to Madison was much cheaper than flying. I also got to see some of the country that was to be my home for the next several years. Things were falling into place.

There were so many things in America that were new to me. Even the taxis' two-way radios were something I had not seen before. I marveled at the fact that the taxis did not have to return to headquarters before going on to their next assignments. Economics was my field, and I admired not alone the efficient organization of the taxicab company, but was impressed by the savings such a system generated. A two-way radio would not help me, but I did need to be organized and very careful with my funds.

In addition to a generous allowance for air travel, the Ford Foundation grant included an additional sum to pay for a four-night stay in a single room in a small hotel in Manhattan. When I went to the hotel, I found out that if I elected to stay in a dormitory style room instead of in a single one I could save myself more than half of my hotel allowance. I called Mrs. Owens to inquire if it would be OK with the Foundation, if I were to stay in a dormitory style room instead of a single room and save the rest of the hotel allowance. Mrs. Owens seemed to be thrilled to see that I was so careful with money and said the Foundation had no problem with my keeping the saving on my hotel allowance.

I did not stay in New York the full four nights. Once the celebrations of the fourth of July were over, I felt it was time to head for the Economics Institute at the University of Wisconsin, Madison and get a head start. There I was going to attend classes to improve my English language skills and learn something about life in my new country.

I took an overnight Greyhound bus to Madison. I vividly remember the bus trip. I was so impressed with the comfortable ride and with the air conditioning on the bus. I was also very impressed by the lighting, cleanliness, air conditioning and the employees' courtesy at the Howard Johnson's at which we had stopped on the way. I was enthralled by the expanse we traveled through and could not get over traveling so far without encountering a single traffic light.

AT THE ECONOMICS INSTITUTE

The summer of 1958 was the first time the Economics Institute went into operation. The Institute occupied one of the buildings on the campus of the University of Wisconsin, Madison, which housed the Institute's administrative offices and lecture halls. The basement housed the language laboratory.

Economics Institute – Faculty, Students and Staff Members, 1958
1st row 1st on right - Mrs. Owens of the Ford Foundation; Wynn Owens Director of the Institute -(unrelated to Mrs. Owens) 2nd row 1st from left; Daniel, 2nd row, 2nd from right

I took full advantage of the lab's resources. Most days I was in the lab from seven in the morning until seven at night, leaving only for lectures and lunch. The lab's various devices helped me with my vocabulary. But there was one interactive device for accent and intonation, which I loved and worked with intensively. I remember sitting for hours in front of that machine, reading a word or a sentence and listening back to the contrast with my accent and intonation, as a native repeated the same word or read the same sentence on the pre-recoded tape. It was a thrill when I could duplicate the native's accent and detect the subtlety in his intonation. During the two-month I spent on campus at Madison, I chose to stay at the YMCA instead of at the University dormitory. That saved half of my lodging allowance. I scrimped on food too - I ate one meal a day at lunchtime. On those days when I was invited to a family for dinner or when the student body was invited to an evening reception, I skipped lunch. But I always felt torn when I did that. Lunch was a wonderful break. The dining room looked out on a grassy yard, which sloped down to Lake Mendota, where I could see white sails skimming over blue water and watch the birds circling over the water.

There was a sense of openness, and I felt lucky to be there.

Even though I worked hard, I think of my time at the Economics Institute as a pleasant one. The Institute took us on trips to factories, a steel mill, and other work places. We also visited the brewery, where Milwaukee beer was made. Gradually a whole new world was opening up to me. Now I was an old hand at going out on Saturday night and walking into bars and coffee shops where the atmosphere was one of ease and conviviality. I was beginning to feel at home.

This feeling was enhanced by a visit one Sunday with an American family that lived on a farm about twenty miles from campus. They were Catholics, and had just returned from Sunday mass when I arrived. Having grown up in a Moslem society, I had learned a good deal about the Moslem practices and beliefs. But I knew much less about the Christian observance, and was curious about the practices and the observance of the family I was visiting. My hosts were open and gracious in answering my questions. The woman of the house explained to me also that she did only essential work, such as light cooking on Sunday, the Sabbath day. I was glad to be in a home where the Sabbath was celebrated, though on a different day from mine. I was learning so much about cultural differences, and I was drinking it all in avidly.

Economics Institute – On a bus trip, heading for a major factory in Milwaukee.
The student sitting in the front row on the left is an Iraqi Kurd. He spoke out against
the 1958 coup in Iraq, which took place while the Institute was in session. He
received threats on his life from Arab students on campus. The authorities took him
into protective custody

In my host's backyard, on a farm outside Madison
In Baghdad I took my afternoon nap in a hammock during the summertime

A Dance Evening at the Economics Institute - Daniel with polka-dotted shirt

324

And while in Madison, I learned also an important lesson in punctuality.

Professor Selig Perlman, Emeritus Professor of Economics at the University of Wisconsin, Madison, who had made major contributions to labor economics was one of our speakers at the Institute. I was very interested in labor economics, and had a long conversation with Professor Perlman after his talk. He invited me to his home for dinner on the following Sunday. The time at which I was supposed to arrive was 6:00 pm. In Israel, however, an invitation for 6:00 pm could mean any time from seven to eight. I thought I was being rather punctual when I showed up just a little after seven to find the house in a bit of an uproar. The family was worried that something untoward had happened to me.

Mrs. Perlman shook my hand.

"I have heard so much about you and am happy to meet you. Welcome to our home. But if ever you are held up like this again, please call and let us know so that we will not worry."

I understood immediately that in America six o'clock meant six o'clock and vowed to myself to be punctual, if ever I received another dinner invitation. At the same time I let out a sigh of relief, realizing that there was to be another time even after I had ruined their dinner plans. And, indeed, that was the beginning of a wonderful friendship. I visited with that family several times after that.

When I left for Harvard, Professor Perlman, who was a Russian Jew, gave me an introductory note to a friend of his on the Faculty at Harvard's School of Business. The note began with "I would like you to meet my friend Daniel. He and I were separated two thousand years ago, and we have finally been reunited." I remember those three sentences verbatim. I had tears in my eyes when Professor Perlman showed me what he had written. I felt his note described my own feeling too. It capsulized what was ingrained in me as a child, that we were all "One Jewish People". I felt as if I had known Professor Perlman from way back. We hugged as I left. I did not really want to leave. It was the last time I saw

Professor Perlman. He died not long after I had left for Cambridge, Mass.

Even though I did not have much money, I resonated to the sense of abundance I encountered in Wisconsin. It was so different from Israel and it brought me back to my childhood in Baghdad, where the same sense of abundance had predominated. We were a large family, but there was always enough of everything. Water flowed from the mountains into our plain, and the market stalls overflowed with foods of all kinds.

The hospitality I experienced in Wisconsin also reminded me of my life in Baghdad, where our homes were always open to friends and to strangers. Some evenings I, along with other students in the Institute, was invited to have dinner in the homes of families who lived in the area. I felt welcomed and a part of everything. I connected with my fellow students, my professors and my new friends. I taught Israeli folk dance at the University of Wisconsin's and at the invitation of Hillel's director, Rabbi Max Ticktin, I led services at Hillel on the first Friday night of my arrival on campus. All of the students who attended the services that evening were Ashkenazi, that is, descendants of Jews who immigrated from Eastern and Central Europe. I was the only one present who hailed from the Middle East. One would think that the two thousand year dispersion of the Jewish people would take its toll on their practices and observances. And it did. Yet, it was amazing how close the prayers had remained. That night I felt as if I was conducting the services in the synagogue in which I grew up in Baghdad. And it felt good to feel at home, even though I was so far away from home.

As I look back on my life history, I think of the two-month time I spent with the Economics Institute in the summer of 1958 as heaven-sent. It was a period of personal growth and a period that opened new horizons in me. My time with the Economics Institute had been also a hiatus, a wonderful introduction to college life in the United States. But above all, it was the period in which I made my biggest strides in learning the English language.

I realized, even while the Institute was still in session, that my hard work on my English was paying off. I noticed that my English skills had improved, that I was able to express myself more easily. I understood more of the lectures than I did upon my arrival, including the guest lectures given by prominent people who were invited to address the students in the Institute. I felt confident when I appeared on TV with a number of my fellow students. When I was asked to comment

Students of the Economics Institute on Graduation Day
On the steps of the Building that housed the Institute at U of Wisconsin, Madison
Daniel front row 4th from left with book in hand

on the recession in the US and its impact on the Israeli economy, I was able to respond with relative ease. I no longer had to go through the agonizing process of "chercher les mots", as they say in French - searching for every word - as often as I did when I arrived in Wisconsin. I knew I still had much to learn, but it was gratifying to see tangible results.

Because of my course of study with the Economics Institute, I arrived in Harvard with a better knowledge of the language than I had when I left Israel, even though I still had to sit with a big dictionary, ever at the ready, as I ploughed through the reading assignments. I do not know how I would have managed at Harvard without the knowledge of the language I acquired during my two months with the Institute. I certainly would not have managed to get through those interminable reading lists, were it not for my intensive work at the Institute.

I feel ever so grateful to the Ford Foundation for having conceived the idea of the Economics Institute and for choosing to make me part of it.

HARVARD

I took the bus from Madison to Boston and arrived a few days too early for the opening of the dorms at Harvard. A scientist who lived on Commonwealth Avenue in Boston and to whom I had received an introduction from a graduate student in Madison, kindly put me up until the dorms opened. During these days I had the opportunity to explore Boston on foot. My education was broadened in several unexpected ways, too.

I remember wandering one day into a Unitarian Church in my host's neighborhood and asking myself what is Unitarian? What does the Unitarian Church stand for? While growing up in Baghdad, I was taught that there were only two Christian denominations: Catholic and Protestant. In 1956, while in France, I learned about divisions and orders within the Catholic Church and later, while in England, I became aware that there were several denominations within Protestantism. But I never heard of Unitarianism before.

Entering the church, I met an earnest young man who explained to me who the Unitarians were, their history, what they stood for, their universal worldview, and their negation of the divinity of Jesus. I was fascinated. He gave me a book about Unitarianism, which provided an extensive background about the Unitarian Church. I read the book with great interest and felt a sense of identification with much of what I read about the Unitarians and what they aspired and stood for.

I learned something about appropriate rain gear during that short time, too. I had picked up a throwaway shower cap at the hotel in New York and, when I was wandering around Harvard Square in a drizzling rain, I used this wonderful cap to protect my head from the damp. The turning heads and the looks ranging from astonished to disapproving told me that there was something wrong with me. I looked at my jacket, checked my trousers, inspected my glasses– I could not find anything wrong. But the heads kept turning and the astonished looks kept coming. That night I told my host about my bafflement at what had happened at Harvard Square that day. When I told him it was drizzling, he asked me, apparently just out of curiosity, where did I get an umbrella, since he knew I did not have one. When I told him I was wearing my throwaway shower cap he doubled up in laughter. I finally caught on. And I guess I learned my lesson.

HARVARD WON'T LET YOU DOWN

I moved from Boston to Cambridge the first day the dorms opened. My effort at economizing on my expenses during the summer had paid off handsomely. When I arrived in Cambridge, I had $600 in my pocket - all money saved from the Ford Foundation grant. I felt fortunate to have something to start with, something I could use to cover my expenses in my initial days in graduate school. I went to the Bursar's office and paid $500 for my first semester's tuition and $45 for the first month at the dorm. I was left with $55. It was not much to be left with even in those days, but I was glad to have one major hurdle behind me: the tuition for the first semester. I knew I would need to find a way to pay for the rest of my time in graduate school. There were books to buy and food to pay for and monthly installments to make on the dorm. By that time, I had compiled a list of sources to contact for an educational loan.

At my first meeting with Seymour Harris, the Chairman of the Economics Department, I told him that I planned to apply for an educational loan, and confided that if I didn't get it I was uncertain about my ability to continue my graduate work.

Professor Harris turned and looked straight at me. His words were measured. "Harvard would not let you down after admitting you. At Harvard you never have to give up your education for lack of money. We would not let that happen."

I was moved by Professor Harris' words. I felt also a sense of vindication. Harvard's stand ratified what I had felt all along – that lack of money should not be an impediment to education. That conviction was the driving force behind my effort to get into graduate school, even though I did not have the means to follow through. I thought of the people who had told me it was plain temerity to apply to Harvard. I felt thankful the doomsayers had not swayed me, and I felt fortunate that I had one role model who was no less audacious than I - my own father, who was fatherless, lived in abject poverty, but managed to get to Law School.

My step was lighter as I left the chairman's office that day. I was to receive $100 a month for a ten-hour-a-week research assistantship in the computing center. I didn't know anything about computers and programming, but Professor Harris did not seem to think that was a problem. I wasn't sure I concurred on that point!

The director of the computing center was an affable individual, and he soon put me at ease. He took me around the center. We stopped by the punch-card machine and scrutinized a few punched cards. Then, as we continued our tour of the center, we stopped in front of the IBM 650, a huge machine with a forbidding appearance. The director explained that IBM 650 was one the most advanced IBM computers around. Its front panel was covered almost from top to bottom with tiny bulbs that blinked incessantly as the computer performed its operations. I stood in front of that panel, totally mesmerized by the speed of those blinking lights. It was incredible that computations could be done at such an amazing speed. Then we turned to the back panel of the computer. The director pulled open a huge board with hundreds of apertures and tens of wires of different colors that connected pairs of apertures. He explained that every time a new program was written the board had to be rewired, so that the electric pulse would follow the dictates of the programming commands.

In the past, I had seen IBM computers in Israel. They did simple operations, such as sorting of punched cards. But I had never seen a computer of this size - one that did complicated operations. That machine had to be programmed in order to do the computations. I did not know programming and had no idea of where to start. But I wanted to stay at Harvard, and if that meant dealing with the computer monster and learning how to write programs and wire that awful board, that was what I would do.

A picture dear to my heart
I took this picture of Widener Library - spent many days and evenings in this library.
Built in 1915, Widener housed close to three million books of Harvard's collection

I asked the director if there was anything I could read that would give me the background I needed. "Yes, sure", he responded, and in a matter-of-factly way he proceeded to tell me I could find some in the main library. For me, that was not much of help. I did not know where to start, if I were to go to the library. Widener, Harvard's central library, was endless, and there were several other large libraries. I had no experience working with large libraries. Where should I begin? How could I find the material I needed? I had no idea.

But that was the first lesson I learned about Harvard, one that was repeatedly confirmed throughout my days in graduate school. At Harvard you are not babied. You are left to your own devices, and you either swim and make it to the finish or sink. The director of the computing Center was not being heartless or uncaring. That was the attitude on campus.

It was tough getting the help I needed, but I finally managed to get hold of several publications. I studied the material and managed to squeeze by, but never had enough time to do my class work and at the same time invest the time I wanted to invest in order to feel in command of computer operation. I hated that, and it left a bad taste in my mouth about programming. All of the research work I did during my academic life involved extensive computer work, but I never wanted to do any of the programming work myself. I delegated my programming work to my research assistants.

But there were beneficial side effects from my association with the computing center. One of those was a project I worked on with one of my instructors, Robert Dorfman. Professor Dorfman was doing applied work in linear programming, a branch in the field of optimization, and he asked me to do the programming for his project. The work I did for Professor Dorfman gave me insights beyond what I learned in his course. I saw black on white the kind of results linear programming produced. It was a rewarding experience.

My work in the computing center also helped me establish friendships and gave me an opportunity to learn about people and practices in this country. It was there that I learned about Christmas family gatherings and their similarity with Passover family gatherings. Before coming to the US, I was familiar with Jewish and Moslem holidays, but Christian holidays were new to me. Christians were a small minority in Iraq, and I didn't even know when Christmas fell, much less about the role Christmas played in the life of many Americans. There were no outward signs of Christmas celebrations in Baghdad.

It was mid December, when one of the employees of the computing center, a native Bostonian, asked where I would be for Christmas. I told her I would be in the dorm studying as usual,

"Oh, that's awful. You mean you have nowhere to go for Christmas?"

I tried to reassure her that I did not feel I would be missing anything. I told her Christmas was not my holiday and that in Baghdad, where I grew up, and in Israel, where I lived later, we never celebrated Christmas.

"Oh you poor thing. I feel so bad you will be spending Christmas all by yourself."

I do not think I succeeded in reassuring her that while it makes me happy to know that she would be having a good time celebrating the holiday in the warmth of her family, I myself did not feel deprived. Nor did I tell her about the Israeli child who, on seeing a picture of Santa Claus, wrinkled her forehead in puzzlement and asked,

"Daddy, who is the rabbi in the red suit?"

As I look back on my life at Harvard, I remember the period of my research assistantship in the lab with mixed feelings. I was grateful for the financial support, the practical experience in research work and the opportunity to make friends and learn about the people in this country, but felt torn because I could not learn everything I wanted to learn about programming the IBM 650. I was fortunate that by the end of the first semester, Harvard offered me a fellowship for my second year. That made it unnecessary for me to continue with the research assistantship in the Computing Center past my first year in school.

HILLEL

During my first year in graduate school, *rosh hashana* fell just before school started. I went to Harvard's Hillel House to meet with Rabbi Morris L. Zigmond the director of the New England Hillel. Rabbi Zigmond had warm feelings toward the Babylonian Jews, and we hit it off from our first meeting.

Rabbi Zigmond's kindness made a big difference in my life during my first High Holidays period. A huge wave of loneliness swept over me as we approached *rosh hashana*. I remembered how we used to gather together and sing *rosh hashana* songs and hum the High Holidays' beautiful melodies, weeks before the start of the holidays. Almost everything we did during that period revolved around the coming holidays and an aura of excitement and liveliness permeated the air. Here in Cambridge, I was so far away from all of that. I thought of my parents who had just lost their home in Baghdad. They were probably suffering as much or more than I was. It saddened me a lot to think of that.

Then Rabbi Zigmond invited me not only to attend the High Holidays services but also to have lunch and dinner at Hillel during all holidays. I was touched by his caring and very grateful for the kindness of Hillel, the institution that stood behind him. The edge was taken off my sense of loneliness by this invitation, by the anticipation of spending the holidays with the community at Hillel.

A few weeks later, Rabbi Morris L. Zigmond, the director of the New England Hillel, designated me the recipient of a $200 scholarship that an anonymous donor had set up for a deserving graduate student. I set it aside to pay the monthly installments on my dorm, secure in knowing I'd have shelter at least through January.

I was grateful to be able to eat well during *rosh hashana*. Small things helped, too. At the end of our meal on the eve of the first day of *rosh hashana*, Rabbi benZion Gold, Harvard's Hillel director, asked me to lead the grace after meal. That got me off to a good start. It made me feel very much a part of the community.

I was at first disappointed with the *rosh hashana* services. Unlike the Sabbath services that were similar in the Sephardi and Ashkenazi rites, the High Holiday services were vastly different. Still it was a wonderful experience to be sitting with my coreligionists and experience the sense of our common roots. By the end of the services, I was humming some of the new tunes that I had heard during the services

I made new friends during meal times on *rosh hashana*. One of those was David Feldman, a Brit who had taken a leave of absence from his job at the United Nations' headquarters in New York to attend graduate school at Harvard. David and I formed a close friendship. We studied together very often during the following two years. I remember many Friday nights I spent with him and his wife, Rose, celebrating the Sabbath together.

David and I had religious concerns in common. I remember one spring day during our second year in graduate school when I bumped into David as I was crossing Harvard Yard on my way to Widener library. We were approaching the time when we had to take the comprehensives. Those were written exams given once a year in two consecutive days, and they were required of all PhD candidates in economics.

David looked glum when we met that day. He was so upset that he did not return my greetings.

"What is the matter, David?" I asked.

"You don't know. It is awful. I just found out that the day the comprehensives are scheduled to begin falls on the first day of Passover. I can't take the exam during Passover."

"Neither can I," I said. "But what is the big deal?" I added. "Let us just go to the chairman of the department and tell him about the scheduling conflict."

I felt the whole thing was probably nothing more than an oversight.

"Do you really think that will help?" David inquired.

"Why not?" I responded.

David did not answer. But it was clear he doubted seeing the chairman would accomplish much. I realized there was no point in pressing him to join me and decided to go by myself.

I headed for the office of Arthur Smithies, who was then the chairman of the Department of Economics. Professor Smithies, normally a gruff individual, could not have been more gracious or more accommodating. He immediately told me he would reschedule the comprehensives to the third day after the beginning of the

Passover, when it would be permissible for observant Jews to do regular work.

Kippoor services at Hillel, like *rosh hashana's*, were vastly different from the Sephardi services. But as the day wore on I began to feel more comfortable with the recurring tunes. The day I spent attending those services was also a day when I met more of my coreligionists at Harvard. In particular, I remember Shlomo and Leah Eckstein. Shlomo had left Germany at a very young age to live in Mexico. Leah had emigrated from Czechoslovakia to Israel at a young age. Leah and Shlomo exuded compassion and friendship.

As *Kippoor* day was drawing to a close and as the services were winding down, I began to feel piercing spasms of loneliness. I remembered the breaking of the fast with my family at the end of *yom kippoor*. It was an occasion for celebration. We spent hours relaxing together and enjoying food and drinks my mother had prepared several days before *yom kippoor*.

Now I imagined myself walking back to my dorm. I would be in my room all by myself. There would be no tables full of tantalizing food and drinks, and there would be no crowd to celebrate the end of *Kippoor* with. It would be back to books and to endless work. No respite in sight.

Then as the services ended and the crowd began to disperse, Leah walked to me with a warm, smile on her face.

"Daniel, would you please join me and my husband in celebrating the breaking of the fast? It would give us a great pleasure to have you celebrate with us".

I was moved to tears, and felt a close sense of kinship with Leah and Shlomo. Those people grew up so far away from where I did, and yet we shared the same tradition of "celebrating" the break of the fast. I felt as if life had been pumped back in me.

"How kind. I would be delighted to join you and Shlomo," I said.

That night was the beginning of a long and ongoing friendship with the Ecksteins. I remember the Friday nights I spent with Leah and Shlomo celebrating the Sabbath. I remember in particular Shlomo and Leah's delight in their young son, now a grown man serving as a rabbi. It was wonderful to feel I was a part of that family, sharing in their life.

Shlomo and Leah left for Israel toward the end of my second year in graduate school. Two years later, when Shlomo returned to Cambridge to defend his thesis, he stayed with my wife, Joan, and me in our apartment in Cambridge. It was a pleasure to be able to host Shlomo. I felt I owed him and Leah so much for their kindness and hospitality. Shlomo went back to Israel to become the President of Bar Ilan University.

THE INTERMINABLE READING LISTS

When I settled into life during my first semester I worked non-stop to keep up with the enormous amount of required reading. In spite of the strides I had made, I still couldn't read English quickly. My vocabulary was still limited, and I didn't want to just skip over unfamiliar words. With a dictionary always beside me, I looked up every word I didn't understand. While this habit built my vocabulary, it greatly slowed my reading speed and disrupted my concentration.

To compensate, I decided to cut out time spent on anything other than classes or study sessions with fellow students. I drew up a chart on which I recorded my daily activities, looking for "waste" that I could redirect to my reading lists. "Waste" could mean a 15-minute rest on my bed, or a 10-minute break to watch the news in the dorm's common room. I went to bed later and got up earlier, finally paring my sleep down to five hours a night. I was beginning to feel so exhausted I could not keep my eyes open. I discovered the stimulating effect of coffee. I bought a coffee pot and used coffee to keep myself awake. That began a process of dependence on coffee that I could not wean myself from for a long time afterwards.

In time, I discovered there were fewer distractions in the library than there was in my room. I tried that new saving avenue. I resolved to study in Widener, Harvard's central library. There I continued to work hard on increasing the time I spent on my reading list. But many times, I could not keep my eyes open. I needed coffee to keep myself awake, and that required going to the restaurant outside the library. But that "wasted" time; moreover, a cup of coffee cost 5c - money I could not come up with easily. In my room, making my own coffee cost less and it took less time to drink a cup of coffee and go back to study. I wavered constantly. It was a struggle.

Studying at the dorm, Perkins Hall

My dorm sofa doubled as a bed

I realized I was in a tailspin - the harder I tried to save time, the more I found I was getting nowhere and the more desperate I became to find more time to spend on my reading list. I could no longer think of enjoying the simple things in life that my classmates seemed to be able to find time for. I began to look back with nostalgia at the few things I had enjoyed during my college days. In Madison I had felt relatively free, in spite of my hard work in the lab. At Harvard, I felt as if I was doomed to a life of constant work and no rest.

Was I ready to give up? No, I was not - giving up was not in the cards. Deep down inside me, I was convinced there was a better way of doing things, and my task was to find that way. What was that way? I did not have the foggiest idea, but

I was convinced it was only a matter of time to find it. I just had to keep my eyes open for it.

My language handicap showed up in another area: class lectures.

When I was at the Economics Institute, I became aware that American English accents were quite varied. At the beginning of the Institute, I had to struggle to make sense of things, as I listened to our instructors who came from different universities all over the country. But all of them had one thing in common: they always spoke slowly and clearly, knowing that we were all foreigners.

At Harvard, the Faculty added a couple of layers of difficulty for me. There was not always that emphasis on clarity in lecture delivery. Some lectures were practically incomprehensible. For a toddler in the language, such as myself, that was a problem. Additionally, Harvard's Faculty came from many different countries, and some spoke with heavy foreign accents.

I understood very well the lectures in economic theory, the basic course every graduate student in Economics had to take. The instructor, Edward Chamberlain, spoke slowly and clearly. By contrast, our lectures in Money and Banking were a disaster. The instructor, who was visiting from the University of Michigan, Ann Arbor, sounded as if he had a hot potato in his mouth. I could not understand a word of what he said. In some of the lectures I sat in, I found it helpful to watch the lips of the instructor. But our Money and Banking instructor never stood still. He paced briskly, back and forth, along the platform, which stretched from one end of the lecture hall to the other. He never stopped to face the class for more than a second or two, before resuming his brisk strides on the platform, all the while looking at the floor as he continued mumbling. My head moved constantly from right to left and left to right as I followed his movement on the platform. I wanted to take notes, but the page in my Money and Banking notebook was as empty at the end of his lecture as it was at its beginning. Those lectures were the most frustrating I remember, particularly because Money and

Banking fascinated me, and I wanted so much to know what our instructor had to say.

Harvard Yard
Daniel standing next to the statue of John Harvard

It was another story with Gottfried Haberler, who was Austrian and who spoke with a very heavy Germanic accent. But his lectures had one virtue - he spoke very slowly and he looked his students in the eye. Slowly I began to understand his lectures and enjoy them. In time I became one of his admirers. His work on "Prosperity and Depression", a classic in the field of business cycles, is the most lucid book in economics I ever read. It cleared much of the confusion I had in my own mind about the operation of the macro economic system, and it helped me understand the subtleties in some of the basic concepts, such as the difference between saving and hoarding, that no other book was able to explain as well.

My appreciation for Haberler's depth and contributions increased as I listened more to him and read more of his writings. He served on my dissertation committee. Years after my graduation, I went to visit him in his office at the American Enterprise Institute (AEI) in Washington, DC, which he had joined after his retirement. It was an emotional meeting for both of us. Professor Haberler was in his mid eighties. He looked weak and shriveled, and he moved very slowly. We talked about AEI and we reminisced about Harvard. In his ever-slow speech and with sadness in his eyes, he confided to me that a difficult task lay ahead for him. He was to take his dog to be put to sleep that afternoon. I was touched. He was attached to his dog and did not want to see it die. Maybe he was thinking about his own old age, maybe he was thinking about his own death. But in spite of his old age, his drive for research and discovery did not dull. He dug up two articles he had published that year and gave them to me before I left.

There was also a great deal of variance in the extent to which the instructors at Harvard came prepared for their lectures. Several Faculty members did not put much time into preparing for their lectures. They left a lot for the students to fill in on their own.

A group of classmates and I used to get together regularly after our lectures every day. We dissected the lecture, examining what had been said from several angles, drilling deeper into the lecture, filling gaps in the instructor's presentation, and clarifying the obfuscated parts of the lecture.

Harvard provided ample space for those gatherings. There was never a shortage of rooms with blackboards, chalk, conference tables, and comfortable seats. Sometimes our group discussions lasted half an hour, sometimes they went over three hours. Faculty did hold office hours, but we rarely ever turned to Faculty for help.

I feel fortunate that I had such bright peers. Our gatherings were the most educational of any forum I remember from my days in graduate school. That was where I did most of my learning and gained most of my insights. That was also what kept my sanity in the Money and Banking class, in spite of my recurrent frustration with the lectures in that course. I had an A in the finals of that course, and the credit goes to the insights I gained during those group discussions.

It was wonderful to see how we pulled selflessly together in that group. But it was not all milk and honey. There was also rivalry and a great deal of cutthroat competition among Harvard's students. I remember one time walking to a classmate, Larry Schwartz, who lived down the corridor in the dormitory. We had a reading assignment in economic history, but all library copies were out. I asked Larry if he had read the assignment. He said he had.

"May I borrow your book until to-morrow morning?"

"No," Larry said.

I was taken by surprise. Seeing my puzzlement, Larry continued,

"Why should I let you have the book and give up my advantage?"

Knowing that the letter grades at Harvard were determined on a curve, I thought that maybe that was behind Larry's refusal to lend me the book. And maybe that was indeed the case. But, during my years at Harvard, I saw many other instances of cutthroat competition – destroy before he gets ahead of you.

MONEY THROES

My Spartan existence was worsened by perpetual worries about money. The research assistantship and the grant from Rabbi Zigmond helped, but didn't stretch far enough. I was sending my parents $35 a month to help with their living expenses. I was importing my textbooks from England, where they cost less than half as much as in the States. My diet consisted of boiled eggs, bread, coffee and iceberg lettuce. I used my hotplate to boil the eggs and make coffee in my room. Most of the time I did not feel I had my fill. I tried to ignore the hunger pangs. Sometimes I just stuffed myself with bread. Once or twice a week I went for lunch to Harkness Commons, the graduate dorm's dining hall, where I could eat as much as I wanted for one dollar.

It got increasingly cold in Cambridge as we got closer to the winter months. It snowed for the first time one day in early November. The whole area was covered with a white blanket. I felt conflicted as I watched the snow come down. It was a gorgeous sight. But how was I going to manage? The university kept the dorms heated, and it felt warm and cozy in my little room. Walking outside in the snow and cold to attend lectures or to get to the library was another story. I was not used to the cold, and I did not have warm clothes to wear.

At Harvard Yard, on a cold day
John Harvard statue covered with snow

In Baghdad it never snowed and never got too cold. Only once during my lifetime in Baghdad did the thermometer drop to freezing level. I remember the day that happened. I was walking on Rasheed Street on my way home from school when I noticed a big crowd gathered in a circle, watching in amazement something I could not see from the distance. Several pointed with their fingers to something on the ground. When I got closer I could see a thin crust of ice on a puddle of water. I was astonished. That was the only time in my life, before coming to the US, that I saw frozen water on the ground. That afternoon, the Ministry of Education announced the closure of all public and private schools in Baghdad until further notice.

Harvard's Littauer Center covered with snow, on a sunny day
I took this picture during my last year in graduate school. Littauer housed the
Departments of Economics and Government as well as seminar rooms and a library

When I emigrated from Iraq, my father had an
enormous overcoat made for me. I never felt comfortable
wearing that overcoat. It was twice my size, and I was
relieved that I never needed to wear it in Israel because the
weather was temperate. I did not take the overcoat with me
to the US, something I came to regret. I bought earmuffs,
when it got cold in November, and they were wonderful when
it was windy. I needed gloves too, but they were beyond my
means.

One day I carried my books from my room to
Widener Library across Harvard Yard. I did not have a book
bag, which would have made carrying so many books a lot
easier. The books were heavy, and it was intensely cold
outside. Soon my fingers began to hurt from the cold. It was a
long way across Harvard Yard. The ground was snow-
covered, and I could not stop and lay the books on the
ground to give my fingers a respite. When I finally reached
Widener, I lay the books at the entrance to the library. My

fingers were crippled from the cold. The pain was excruciating. After using lots of hot water, I managed to bring my fingers back to life. I was lucky they weren't totally frostbitten.

LONGING FOR FAMILY

As winter set in, my thoughts turned repeatedly to my parents and the difficulties they were having adjusting to their new life in Israel. I yearned just to hear my mother's voice, and late one night I felt so desperate that I threw myself at the mercy of the overseas operator.

"I need to talk to my parents in Israel, but I am a student and I don't have the money to pay for the call. Is there any way you could help me?" I pleaded. "Is there any way we could work out the cost of the call?"

"You don't have the money and you want to make a transatlantic call?"

"Just for two minutes."

I fought back tears as I felt a flush of shame rising on my face. This was totally humiliating. I, who had never begged for anything, was asking a total stranger for a free ride.

"There is no way, sir. AT&T wouldn't allow us to do that."

I replaced the phone on the hook and walked blindly out of the telephone booth, sunk in the pain of rejection and humiliation. It was hard to ask for anything and harder to be turned down. But the hardest of all was the longing to hear my mother's voice, knowing that longing wouldn't be satisfied. I had done this to myself. I had chosen to come to Harvard instead of staying in Israel.

I was in touch with my father and brother by letter, but my mother didn't know how to write, so she could only communicate with me through their correspondence. I had been away from her for so many years while I was in Israel. And now we were separated again.

Even as I thought about it, I struggled with my sense of guilt. I had left Israel not long after my parents' arrival in Israel. I left at a time when they were in greatest need of help. But if I had not come to Harvard when I did, I probably would have lost that opportunity forever. I was flying in the face of traditions by not staying in Israel with my parents. But I wondered also if any member of my family realized how difficult it had been for me to leave and how I still suffered pangs of conscience for choosing to leave.

A LETTER FROM MY FATHER

My worries about my parents and my sense of guilt for having left them at their time of greatest need never left me. At the same time, I was receiving disturbing letters from my brother, Jacob, which did not help either. Jacob's letters were full of complaints about his difficulties in Israel - there were no decent cigarettes to be had; there was no time to go out; he just hated being in Israel. Curiously every one of Jacob's letters ended with an exhortation not to worry about him. They stated something like, "But don't you worry about me. I just wanted to give vent to my frustrations. I have no one to talk to. Don't fret. You just go on having a good time in America."

Those letters made me feel miserable. None of the things Jacob complained about sounded as bad to me as what I had lived through. Still I was tormented to read of the hardship his letters portrayed. I had to concede that it is difficult to adjust to a new environment, a new country. I had to concede also that Jacob's tolerance for change might be lower than mine. I was eighteen when I went to Israel. He was thirty-one. At the same time it was hard for me to believe that Jacob really had no audience but me to which he could relate his miseries. Why was he unloading all of those complaints on me? Maybe he just wanted me to feel sorry for him. Maybe he resented my going on with my life, but did not feel free to say so. Maybe this was his way of expressing his resentment less overtly.

Jacob was living with my parents and helping to support them. I was in the United States pursuing a graduate education. To him it probably seemed that I had the better deal.

What did Jacob think I was doing at Harvard? What "good time" was he talking about? Evidently Jacob knew nothing of how difficult my life really was. All he knew was that I was in America and he was in Israel living under conditions that he did not find tolerable.

I suspect Jacob might have been complaining to my parents, too.

A week or two after the AT&T operator had turned me down, I received a letter from Jacob, alerting me that our father was writing to me to ask me to come back. "Ignore what he says," Jacob said. "Don't pay attention to what he asks of you."

Looking back at the situation I suspect Jacob was feeling guilty. He probably had created a commotion that got out of hand, provoking my father to action. Baba probably felt that, since he himself had no way of lightening the burden on Jacob, his only alternative was to ask me to come back to help.

Jacob's letter put me in a tailspin. I had trouble concentrating on my studies in my agitation awaiting my father's letter and fearing the kind of pressure he might bring to bear. I wished his letter would just come and put an end to my anxiety.

Some two weeks later, I heard again from Jacob, noting that my father was taking a lot of time finishing his letter, and to ignore it. I was both relieved and apprehensive when our father's letter finally arrived a week or so later. He said that I should come back to Israel and help support the family. The inducement he offered was that I could then "enjoy Mama's delicious cooking."

I shoved the letter in my pocket and walked through the campus with my mind in turmoil. Was there never to be an end to it? Was my father going to continue to torment me through all my years at Harvard? Would he stop even after I graduated? I was doing what I could. I was sending money to help with my parents' expenses. To bolster my resolve, I reminded myself that my father had paid for Jacob's college education but had been unable to contribute to mine.

At the same time, my heart was heavy as I thought about the tragedy of my parents' uprooting. Had life worked out differently, Baba might now have been imploring me to come back to Baghdad. He could have offered to share his prestigious position in that society with me. He could have told me that he would open doors in Baghdadi society for me. Now he was a broken man living in Israel. He had nothing left to offer me but my mother's cooking. It broke my heart to think of how he had fallen. I pictured him as a drowning man clutching at straws. Writing that letter must have been a bitter pill for my father to swallow, just as it was heart breaking for me to read it. But I had to get on with my life as I had planned it. I could not accede to my father's request, whatever the motivation behind it might have been, and return to Israel.

I ignored Baba's request. He never broached the subject again.

In spite of my feelings about Jacob's complaining letters, I felt I should do something to help him get out of the mood he was in. While in college, I had read Dale Carnegie's book "How to Stop Worrying and Start Living" and had found particular passages in the book very helpful. I wondered if some of those passages might not help Jacob feel better, perhaps help pull him out of his gloom. I had brought the book with me from Israel. Would it not be nice if I could share some of those passages with Jacob? But how would I do that? Calling him over the phone and reading those parts to him would be prohibitive. I knew the alternative of just recommending to him to buy the book and read it on his own would not work with him. He would not buy the book. Moreover that would be impersonal. I wanted to do something that had a personal touch.

A friend in the dorm suggested that I make a recording of those passages and send them over to Jacob. He gave me the address of a recording company in Boston. I called the company. I was pleasantly surprised to learn that it was not an expensive operation. I felt I needed to do whatever was necessary to round up the money to pay for it.

During the winter break, I traveled to Boston and cut an LP in which I talked to Jacob and read to him selected passages from Carnegie's book. The company was very nice. They even packaged the LP for me. I sent the package to Jacob by registered mail. I felt good to be able to do at least that much for my brother. I had no other way of helping, short of abandoning my graduate schooling and going back to Israel. But I did not want to sacrifice my life.

I sent to Jacob a separate letter and told him about the LP I had mailed him. I told him I hoped he would find the recording helpful and urged him to listen to it and let me know his reaction.

Jacob made no mention of my recording when he responded to that letter. He did not acknowledge the receipt of the LP either. I do not know if he ever bothered listening to it.

A THERAPY SESSION THAT CHANGED MY LIFE

I was fortunate to have attended a university that viewed emotional sickness the same way it viewed physical sickness. Harvard was one of the very few schools that offered free psychiatric treatment to its students. I had several therapy sessions during my first year in graduate school. Sometimes I talked with my therapist about my sense of guilt in leaving my parents behind in Israel. Sometimes I talked about my sense of exhaustion at the unrelenting pressure I was under to keep up with the demands of an intensive study program, all in a language that was not my native tongue. But all of these problems paled in the face of my continuing turmoil over my disillusionment with life in Israel. No matter how and where the session started, it always came back to my inability to deal with the ethnic problems in Israel.

In one session I talked about my feelings of being pulled in opposite directions: On one hand, my experience in

Israel as a Jew from an Arab land and my shattered dream of making Israel my homeland; on the other, my sense of duty to settle in Israel at the end of my graduate work.

Speaking slowly and with his blue eyes fixed sharply on me, my psychiatrist asked, "Daniel, why do you have to go back? Why don't you just stay here?"

I bristled at his question. How could I do that? I would be a traitor. For ages, Jews had prayed for the ingathering of the exiles; during my childhood in Baghdad we prayed for that goal every day. It was ingrained in me. How could I turn my back on it? I cried uncontrollably.

But, as I dried my tears, a sense of peace stole over me. I felt relieved. Suddenly, my life looked a whole lot brighter.

My psychiatrist's pointed question forced me to confront reality head on. My psychiatrist was not an anti-Semite; he was not trying to undermine Israel. His question sounded reasonable. Why did I have to return? Why live in a place where my life would be a roller coaster? I liked my friends at Harvard. I liked the warmth and courtesy I had been shown by Americans everywhere, Jews and non-Jews alike: I felt at home in America. Why feel guilty about that?

Yes, I was an exile, an outsider with foreign customs and a shaky command of English. But for the first time in my life, no one seemed to hold my differences against me. Indeed, all these positive impressions had struck a deep chord with me, seeming to speak volumes about the sensitivity and character of the American people.

That therapy session was the most critical turning point in my life. *Why do you have to go back? Why don't you just stay here?* Whatever emotional conflict had tormented me up until then about leaving Israel vanished. The psychiatrist's questions freed me from my shackles. I was entitled to live where I was at peace with myself.

I found home in the US.

In time several events occurred both in the US and Israel that reinforced my sense that choosing to stay in the US was a wise decision.

A LESSON IN GEOGRAPHY

I studied and studied, always feeling that I was never doing enough. But when the lighter moments came I relished them.

One day I stopped by the office of the Department of Economics. The Department's secretary was chatting with the building janitor and a graduate student. When we finished clarifying the question I came in for, the secretary casually asked me if I knew where British Columbia was.

"She's asking me where some place in the World is located?" I thought. I was brought up in French schools. How would I know? In school we studied the geography of France in detail and knew almost every little town in France, but we were given superficial exposure to the geography of the rest of the world. It was the same with history and literature. We studied French history in minute detail and we memorized speeches of France's historic figures. We were drilled in the writings of the great French writers and poets. But we had practically no exposure to the history, literature or poetry in the US, England, or the rest f Europe. Although it was not stated openly, the message that the pitch of our French education instilled in us was that the world began with France and ended with France. In time I came to resent that as I realized how France-tilted our education was. From reading the papers, I learned about the major cities in the US. I knew also about Toronto and Montreal in Canada. But I never heard of British Columbia. Yet here I was. I wanted to help the secretary, but I did not know what to say.

I turned to the graduate student. He was a US native. But he said he did not know where British Columbia was. I turned to the janitor. He was picking up the wastebaskets. He was a very friendly older person with a cheerful, chubby face. He stopped, put down the wastebasket and scratched his head thoughtfully before he shook it.

"You got me on this one, Dan," he said

I wished I knew the answer. I wanted very much to help the secretary. It occurred to me that the Australians were very friendly with the British. I had seen Australian soldiers during WW II in Baghdad with British flags on their uniforms. It was clear to me that the Australians had a high regard for the British, maybe enough to include "British" in the name of one of their cities. I shared those thoughts with the Department secretary and wondered out loud: "Could it be that British Columbia is a town or perhaps a city in Australia?" I turned to the graduate student. He said that it was likely. He felt my hunch made sense. The janitor said he went along. The secretary was happy. We placed British Columbia squarely in Australia. And on that note we left.

Years later when I was a member of the Faculty at McGill University, Montreal, my department colleagues and I were having a departmental lunch together, and I shared this story with them. They did not think it was funny. Some were visibly upset by the story. Like many in Canada, they believed that the US looked down on Canada and that Americans never felt they needed to educate themselves about Canadians. They felt this story confirmed their view of the condescending attitude of the Americans.

Luckily my colleagues at McGill did not hear the sequel to the original story, which happened about ten years later when I was teaching in Stanford and trying to reach a colleague at the University of British Columbia (UBC). My colleague at UBC and I were working on related research projects and we frequently exchanged ideas about our work. One evening I needed to get in touch with him, but I had left my little phone book behind in my office at Stanford. I needed to call the information in British Columbia to get his home phone number. But first I needed the area code for British Columbia.

I called the AT &T operator.

"I need the area code for Vancouver, please."

I was put on hold for a good while. When the operator finally came back on the line, his voice over the wires sounded puzzled.

"I can't find a listing for Vancouver"

"It's in British Columbia", I said.

I was put on a long hold. After several minutes the operator came back on the line again.

"There is no listing for British Columbia in California".

NO MONEY TO PAY FOR ANTIBIOTICS

Not long before I left Israel for the US, I started treatment on a back tooth, but did not have time to complete the treatment before I left for the US. I was having severe pain in that tooth when I went to see the dentist at Harvard's clinic.

The dentist determined the tooth had to be removed but, when he tried to pull it, it just would not budge. He was forced to use a dentist's hammer and chisel, but because the tooth was in the back it was difficult for the dentist to hold the chisel steady. The chisel cut my gum as it slipped from position. I bled a lot. The hammer's pounding resonated in my head. I felt dizzy and nearly passed out. Finally, the tooth came out, but by then I was too weak to stand up.

The tooth must have been abscessed, since the dentist gave me a prescription for a ten-day dose of antibiotics. While Harvard provided its students with full medical insurance, including dental insurance, it did not provide prescription coverage. I did not have enough to pay the $2.50 for the antibiotics dose prescribed by my dentist. We were almost at the end of the month, and I had only twenty-five cents left. I asked the pharmacist what he thought we should do. He said he would sell me two pills for the quarter I had. He felt it would be better to have two pills than have none. I bought the two pills and prayed that everything would be okay.

Two days later I was running a high fever. I was weakened, and I could not get out of bed. One of my fellow students in the dorm rushed me to Harvard's hospital on Mt. Auburn Street in Cambridge. The doctor was amazed at my condition. He shook his head in anguish when he learned I had taken only two pills instead of the twenty prescribed by my dentist. He had me stay in the hospital, where I was pumped full of streptomycin and put on the road to recovery. Here, too, I was told that my nutritional needs were not being met, that I was very run down. I shrugged and explained I was eating as well as I could afford to eat. When I left the hospital, the physician who attended to me when I arrived gave me a supply of pills, not a prescription. I was grateful for that gesture.

I was back to my class work immediately after my return from the hospital.

FIRST THANKSGIVING DAY

November was drawing to a close and people were getting ready to celebrate Thanksgiving Day. I had never heard of a national thanksgiving day and was impressed by the idea. It is common for observant Jews to offer a prayer of thanks when eating or drinking and to recite a special prayer of thanks for the beauty of nature, for the rebirth of the moon and for the blossoming of trees during springtime. The *sukkoth* holiday, which falls around the middle of October, is a holiday in which the Jewish community as a whole offers thanks to God for the bounty of the harvest. I appreciated the idea of giving thanks individually and collectively. Though years later I learned about the Canadian Thanksgiving Day, up to that point I had never heard of a modern country setting aside a day to remember its blessings and offer thanks for the riches and prosperity bestowed on it. To see a whole nation give collective thanks struck a deep chord in me. I thought it spoke volumes about the sensitivity and the character of the American people.

I fell in love with Thanksgiving Day from day one. Even though I stayed in the dorms on that day, I thought of the day as a festive occasion. I felt I had a lot to be thankful for, and took a break from my studies to reflect on my blessings. I thought of my parents and my brother. I was so grateful they had come out alive from Iraq. I thought of Harvard and how fortunate I was to be associated with such a venerable institution. I thought of my airfare to the US and how miraculous it was that it got pieced together. I thought of the wonderful grant from the Ford Foundation. It not only made my life at Harvard easier by offering me an opportunity to improve my English, but also allowed me to save enough to pay for the start of my graduate work. I thought of the research assistantship that enabled me to buy books and bread. I remembered the grant from the anonymous donor through Harvard's Hillel, which ensured I had a roof over my head during the rest of the semester. I felt thankful for my friendship with Rabbi Zigmond; I remembered my time at Hillel and the wonderful friends I made there. I thought of the friendship with my fellow students at the dorm. I looked at the bright sun shining outside. It was such a beautiful day. There was so much to be thankful for!

Just remembering my blessings made me feel energized. I felt happy. I felt enamored of the beauty of the occasion and I resolved to celebrate Thanksgiving Day every year in the future. When I got married to Joan two years later, we held our wedding on Thanksgiving Day. We celebrated that day every year after that.

And maybe there is something to the idea that giving thanks begets more occasions for thanks.

A day or two after Thanksgiving Day I received a check from my father. I do not remember the exact amount, but it was around $300. The check represented a payment closing out my account in a program called Hissakhone leBinyan (Savings for Building). The program, which was very popular during the time I lived in Israel, was intended to encourage young individuals and families to purchase their own apartments. Individuals diverted to the program any amount they could set aside from their monthly paycheck. (I had managed to put about $50 a year in the account during the five years I worked at Bank Leumi and the Consumers' Cooperative Society) When there was enough in the individual's account, the money was used as a down payment on the purchase of one of the apartments built by the program. To discourage people from using their accumulated savings for purposes other than the purchase of an apartment, the program's bylaws stipulated a waiting period, before the accumulated savings could be withdrawn. That meant that I had been unable to use the money for my airfare to the US. Now, six month's later my father had collected my money and sent it to me.

I jumped from joy, when the check arrived - one more thing to be thankful for.

WAVES OF LONELINESS AND THE MAGIC OF MUSIC

As the instruction period was coming to a close, I could not help but notice that my class was growing smaller and smaller. Students, some graduates from other Ivy League schools, could not take the pressure and dropped out. It was frightening to watch that happening. Seeing the attrition, I began to wonder. How much longer would I be able to withstand the pressure? I was laboring under several handicaps. I was still not fully at ease reading English and the fact that my constant companion was a dictionary gave me little comfort. My undergraduate education left much to be desired. What hope could I have, coming as I did from a rinky-dink school, when graduates from top colleges were falling by the wayside? What would happen if I too could no longer take the pressure of constant work? The devastating prospect of dropping out loomed in front of me, a large black cloud on the horizon of my hopes. Would I succeed, when others with stronger background and mastery of the language were unable to make it?

Those were anxious days. I worried a lot. But then I resurrected my determined self. Giving up was not a choice. I would keep at it.

Winter break began in the third week of December. No sooner had the last day of instruction ended than the graduate dorms emptied of students, all heading home to be with their families.

Looking out the window of my dorm on the deserted yard

I told myself that staying at Harvard during the winter break did not matter to me. I did not mind being alone in the dorms for a few weeks. The reality, however, was different.

Everyone from my floor, the first floor of Perkins Hall, was gone. There was only the guard who sat at the entrance and the hollow sound of my footsteps echoing through the empty hallway. One other graduate student from Greece, who lived on the third floor, remained in the building. The corridors that had teemed with graduate students coming and going were now lifeless. It was depressing. It felt as if those buildings had been transformed overnight into a ghost town.

I realized I was ill prepared for the waves of loneliness that swept over me in that empty dorm. I fled to the library. On my way to Widener, I crossed Harvard Yard. It was empty of any life. I walked through Harvard Square. Except for the area around the entrance to the subway, the Square was nearly deserted. Even Widener seemed lifeless. There were people in the reading room, but I could count them on my fingers.

I returned to the dorm to cook and eat my lonely meal of boiled eggs-and-lettuce sandwiches and coffee. I had not anticipated the feeling of dejection and did not know quite how to deal with it.

I pulled myself together. I had a lot of reading to catch up with, I had a term paper to write on Mercantilism, and I needed to study for the coming exams. I hit the books and tried to push aside the thought that it would be more pleasant to be studying with others or with some semblance of life around me. I tried to concentrate, but could not accomplish much. My thoughts kept wandering, and I kept disconnecting from the material I was reading.

Finally I went out for a walk and wandered into a bar. It was dimly lit, which was not particularly uplifting, but there were people there. Some were watching television, some were engaged in conversations among themselves, and one or two were just staring into space smoking cigarettes. I didn't really care; it was enough for me to just see life again, and be back among people.

My acute loneliness seemed to be way out of proportion to what had happened. My Greek friend in the dorm seemed happy as a lark. When I asked him if it bothered him to see the place so empty, he said he didn't care one way or another. Why was my reaction so intense? I decided that the deserted campus had kindled memories of the last days of Baghdad's Jewish community, when it was on its deathbed. I know when people ask me whether I want to make a return visit to Baghdad someday, the question always conjures up in my mind an image of a ghost town: empty houses, deserted streets, death and destruction. My memory is of Jews driven from their homes, our neighborhood emptied of its inhabitants, and the destruction of the community in which I grew up. Those images replayed in my mind when I saw the empty dorm and the deserted streets in Cambridge.

My brief foray into the bar failed to assuage my loneliness, which persisted for the next several days. It occurred to me that listening to familiar music might restore my sense of balance. Music had a soothing effect on me, but

I had not heard any for a long time. I had brought with me from Israel my favorites -- Beethoven's Chorale Symphony, Pastoral Symphony and others that touched my soul and carried me off to a world of peace and serenity. But I didn't have a record player, and there was none in the dorm.

I had the $300 that Baba had sent me. Could I use some of that money to buy a record player? But I already had plans for that money. I had earmarked it to pay for the monthly installments on my dorm during the second semester. Would it be right to use the dorm money to buy a record player? I was torn. I debated with myself. Which was more important? As much as I wanted to hold on to that money to pay for my dorm, I realized the problem facing me was urgent. I had to get music back in my life. That could not wait. There was a good chance music might help.

This was when stereophonic records and record players were just coming on the market. The manager of the Harvard Coop's music department suggested I would enjoy the music much more if I were to buy a stereophonic player, one he had in stock, the very latest in stereophonic sound. As an inducement, he offered a free stereo LP of "Malaguena" played by the 101 Strings Orchestra.

I bought the stereo player and played some of my LP's. It was amazing. My muscles relaxed and my mood brightened. I calmed down. I was not alone anymore. My friend, my music, was back with me, working a miraculous transformation. Before I knew it, I had my book in hand, and I was studying, as the music played. I was focused. I could concentrate. I was happy to get back to work.

I played "Malaguena," over and over again, turning to it almost every time I started my player in the weeks and months that followed. Even now, I can't hear that record without being transported back to my student days at Perkins Hall.

One day, I detected some distortion of high notes when playing my records. When I reported this to the music manager at the Harvard Coop, he exclaimed, "My goodness! A young man with an ear! You are just what we need."

So began a period when I got to test all the new stereo

players the Coop ordered, listening for sound distortion. I learned a lot about the subtleties of stereo recording while soothing my soul with music. It was a heaven-sent opportunity, and the music manager assured me I was a godsend to his department, too. Fate had smiled—or rather sung--to me, when life had seemed bleakest.

The students returned from winter break chattering about ice-skating, parties and family get-togethers. They described life, love, and laughter, and my neighbor from Chicago enthused about a game of Frisbee he had played with his brother and high school friends. I was genuinely awed that people still enjoyed a life of ordinary pleasures with friends and families. Was it really still possible to do those things, I thought wistfully? That kind of life seemed so far away from me, as though it existed only in dreamland.

Then exams began, and my classmates began to voice regret about lost study opportunities. That sounded foreign to me, too.

I stayed up late at night before every exam, took a scalding hot shower in the morning and went to the hall where the exam was administered. The exam in Money and Banking was the last in my series of four finals. The night before that exam, one of my friends in Perkins Hall gave me a pill to keep me awake. That pill did more than keep me alert. All night I was euphoric, enveloped by a sense of peace and serenity, such as I had never experienced before. I felt I was above it all – nothing could hurt me, nothing could touch me. Everything was just the way it should be. It was a wonderful sensation.

I didn't sleep that night, and I didn't feel the need for sleep. "Malaguena" and Beethoven's Pastoral Symphony played repeatedly all night long, as I reviewed the material for the exam.

It was early that morning when I looked out the window. The yard was covered with snow and dawn was breaking. Feeling a deep sense of gratitude for being alive, I washed my face and hands, covered my head and recited the prayer I had recited every morning since childhood – *Modei*

Anee Lefaneikha ... "I am grateful to you, God, for restoring my soul to me ..."

My euphoria continued through the exam. I was focused, confident and felt rested. At noon when the exam ended, I walked back to my dorm. By then, I couldn't keep my eyes open and collapsed on my bed. I didn't wake up until the afternoon of the following day.

SHEDDING THE OLD

I had been working non-stop, but had not been keeping up, and I was convinced something was dreadfully wrong. When classmates invited me to join them at the movies or for a walk, I invariably declined for lack of time. It always troubled me that I was constantly pinned down, and my friends were not. Intellectually, I felt I was a match for them. Nor did I think my language handicap fully explained my problem. So when Harvard announced a three-week intensive "How to Study" course between semesters, I decided to enroll. Minimally, I hoped it would help me understand what was holding me back.

The grades in my finals gave me additional motivation. I made top grades in my two quantitative courses, but didn't do nearly as well in my other two courses. Yet I felt equally prepared in all four. I hoped the study classes would shed light on this problem, too.

That short course was probably the best investment I ever made in myself. It freed me from the shackles of a life devoid of anything but incessant work. As we explored study habits, I was struck by how my upbringing had colored my approach to assignments.

Growing up, my tutors had stressed that every single word in the Torah text carried a wealth of meaning, and not one word should be overlooked or skimmed over. The trouble was, that was exactly how I was reading my Harvard assignments: Doggedly probing for meaning in every word and sentence.

Instead, I learned the importance of concentrating on

themes and ideas, rather than getting bogged down in minutiae. I found I was able to gain a better understanding of material and retain facts and complicated details more readily than before – while spending less time doing it. What a relief to finally be able to occasionally break free of homework drudgery. The cover of darkness was beginning to lift from my life.

It didn't come without a struggle. A tug-of-war raged inside me. I felt that by skipping over words and sentences I was cheating. But I kept reminding myself it was not the Torah that I was reading, only a book written by a mortal.

I was delighted that during second-semester finals instead of staying up all night to study for an exam, I actually took the evening off to attend a reception at the home of Rabbi Roland Gittelsohn, spiritual leader of a large congregation in Boston. I had never done such a thing before, much less on the night before a final exam. Best of all, I scored A's in all finals I took after the study course.

I learned speed-reading in the course, and bought a kit with which to practice. The kit came in a box with a window in front. When I pulled a rubber band, a flash card, inscribed with one word, which I was supposed to read, moved in front of the window at the speed of lightning.

The first day I got the box, I spent hours pulling the rubber band. Words flashed across the window, but before I could recognize any of them, they disappeared. I thought I had made good strides in my speed-reading during the remedial course, but this gadget told me otherwise. Still I did not give up. I kept pulling.

Finally, out of curiosity, I opened the box to see what these elusive words were. All were humongous words I had never seen before - some did not even appear in the abridged dictionary.

What I acquired in the "How to Study" course stayed with me for the rest of my life, and in time I learned to extend it to areas we didn't cover in the course. But it was a zigzag road. I was unwavering in applying, in every final exam I took, the golden principle I learned in the course - you must take a risk if you want to shine. In my case, this meant deciding exactly what a test question asked and replying in a focused way—rather than dumping everything I knew into my blue book in hopes some of it would be satisfactory. But when it came to the Ph.D. orals, where the stakes were higher than in a final, I let my fears get the better of me. I vacillated between my old habit of dumping everything I knew and the more disciplined approach I had learned about in the course.

It was the same story when I began writing my dissertation. But by the time I was midway through, I managed to get hold of myself and let my originality come through. That earned the second half of my dissertation the acclaim of one international institution, the International Monetary Fund (IMF). In 1963, a year after I had completed my dissertation, the IMF invited me to come to Washington, DC and lead the effort to deepen and extend the second half of my dissertation. In 1966, Praeger published my work at the IMF as a book titled "The Currency Ratio in Developing Countries".

The second half of my dissertation was just the beginning of my breakthrough to realizing I could trust my originality and take risks with it. Still it was not until my next project that I came into my own and surged fully ahead. The project was sponsored by the US Federal Power Commission (FPC) and took four years to complete. I felt honored that, on its own initiative, the prestigious Bell Journal of Economics and Management Science offered me a generous sum of money as an inducement to prepare my study as an Invited Paper, which appeared in 1971 as "The FPC Staff Econometric Model of Natural Gas Supply in the US", pp. 51-93.

That study survived the test of time, and it outperformed studies published years later on the same subject. Federal agencies in the US and Canada used the study in policymaking. Several universities, including my own Alma matter, used it as part of their reading list in seminars and courses in energy economics and energy modeling.

I never reverted to my old ways in any work I engaged in later.

TRADITION AND CONTINUITY

No small part of my growing contentment at Harvard was connected to its venerable history. This, the oldest college in the U.S., reeked tradition and continuity with the generations of students who had come before. So it was during my boyhood, within the shelter of Baghdad's Jewish community. Tradition and ritual reminded us of our ancient roots there, since the time of the Babylonian exile in 586 BCE. This history was integral to my identity, to my sense of belonging. It was inextricably connected to the idea of home. I didn't make this connection until I attended Harvard's commencement at the end of my first year on campus. There was pomp and ceremony, with music that had echoed and re-echoed in the halls of Harvard for centuries. Long columns of alumni marched in a procession in Harvard Yard at the beginning of the ceremony. An alumnus marched at the head of each column, holding aloft a sign identifying the class that followed him. Those columns told of a long history; the classes went back to the 19th century.

A short, shriveled man marched slowly and tentatively ahead of the rest of the pack. He was the sole member of the class of 1879! Later on I learned he was 101 years old. He moved his head from side to side as he marched. I wondered about the memories he had of the old Harvard buildings. Was he thinking of his classmates who were no longer around to march with him? People stood up and applauded as he passed by. Was he happy to have lived long enough to receive such an ovation? I locked eyes with several of the alumni, young and old, as they passed. Maybe one day, I thought to myself, I would be among those marching in the procession. Then it would be my turn to watch the young faces as I passed by and remember the days I sat in those old Harvard buildings and struggled to decipher what some of my professors had to say in a language I had not yet fully mastered.

My appreciation of Harvard's history and traditions deepened when, two years later, I worked with Professor Seymour Harris on his book "Harvard's Economic History". There I learned of the difficulties Harvard had faced, but managed to survive against all odds. I marveled at how the school managed to make it at a time when money was not even known. There was that student whose parents paid for his tuition, room and board with eggs produced on their chicken farm. I remember reading in Harvard's records about the conundrum when most of the eggs the student had brought in with him at the beginning of the term were broken. Should the school count him as being all paid up? The school depended on those eggs (and other food items it bartered in exchange for education) to feed the students. And then there was the student whose father paid for tuition, room and board with shoes he made. But no two shoes in the pairs he had sent with his son seemed to be of identical size. What was the school to do?

I remember how fascinated I was when I read about those early times. Harvard's early history took me to a world of dream and wonder. As I delved into that history, I grew increasingly fond of the traditions that developed around that venerable institution, and I never ceased to marvel at how Harvard managed to make it in spite of all the adversities it encountered in those earlier days.

Toward the end of the summer of my first year, I moved out of the dorms and rented a room in the apartment of Mrs. Schertzer, an elderly widow born in Vienna. Mrs. Schertzer was a woman of great warmth, and she treated me as a son. She was meticulous and very correct, especially about table manners. Everything had to be just so, and implements had to be used only for their intended purpose. Mrs. Schertzer's correctness never bothered me; in many ways, I shared her leanings.

But when she returned from a trip to Israel later that year I discovered the full extent of her persnickety nature. As she was recollecting her trip, I asked what had struck her as pleasing or annoying in Israel. She said she found the way tea was served in Israel's coffee houses to be very annoying.

"Every time I tried to drink tea from those tall glasses, the spoon would get in my eye," she explained.

During those years, it was common for coffee houses in Israel to serve tea in a regular water glass and without a saucer. Usually tea was served with a spoon in the glass to stir the sugar.

"Why didn't you just take the spoon out of the glass before drinking?" I asked.

"They never brought a saucer with the glass," lamented Mrs. Schertzer, who could never have stooped to set a dripping spoon on the table.

Word got around quickly in Mrs. Schertzer's neighborhood that an Israeli student had rented a room in her apartment. Less than a week after moving in, I got a call from the lady across the street asking me to lead the High Holiday services at a conservative synagogue in Marlborough, Mass. My caller explained that the synagogue had been closed all year because the Jewish community there had shrunk in size and could no longer afford a permanent rabbi.

"I can't lead the services-- I am not a cantor," I told my caller.

"It does not matter. You are Israeli, and you speak Hebrew."

"I do speak Hebrew," I said, "but I have never led High Holiday services before. Besides, the tunes I know for the Sephardi services are different from the tunes Ashkenazi congregants are accustomed to."

"Don't worry. People will love your tunes," my caller assured me. "We are only two weeks away from the holidays. If you don't come, chances are that the Jewish families in Marlborough won't be able to hold the High Holidays services this year."

If I were to lead the services the way I knew how, they would be unrecognizable to this congregation. Nor would the rites help them recollect their days of growing up, as many people like to do on those occasions. Still, how could I turn my back on a whole community, when there was no one else in sight?

"I will do my best," I finally agreed.

My caller sounded relieved, and told me I would be paid $200. I didn't expect to be paid -- I merely wanted to help.

School would start in two and a half weeks. I decided to spend that time learning as much of the Ashkenazi High Holidays services as I could. I bought five cantorial LP's for High Holiday services, all according to the Ashkenazi rites. I spent several days listening to those records until I felt I had learned the music well enough to conduct the services.

During the High Holidays I stayed in Marlborough with an observant family whose fourteen-year old nephew happened to play the trumpet. This was a godsend. I taught him the sounds of the *shofar*, and had him practice on the congregational s*hofar*. To the delight of everyone, he blew the *shofar* without a hitch during the services on *rosh hashana* and at the end of *yom kippoor*.

When I chanted the Ashkenazi tunes I had so recently learned, people couldn't believe I had not grown up with them. When I didn't know the Ashkenazi melody, I substituted the Babylonian melody, and was pleased to see the congregants join in enthusiastically. It made me happy to see the happy faces around me, and to know I had helped keep the doors of that synagogue open. The congregation's receptiveness to my tinkering with Ashkenazi traditions reminded me again how open and tolerant American society was. Factions, hatred and strife, so endemic in the Middle East, were by comparison, a rarity here.

At the end of *yom kippoor*, our neighbor's son drove me back to Cambridge. He handed me a check for $400. That was a lot more than what I'd been offered.

"Isn't there a mistake?" I asked.

"No, " he said. "We just liked the services."

My second year at Harvard was easier than my first. I was more relaxed about studying and taking exams, and I had fewer financial worries. Living in Mrs. Schertzer's apartment helped remind me that there was life beyond the walls of lecture halls and libraries. My landlady's placid pace of life had a salutary effect on me -- confirming that people could live and function without having to be perpetually on the run.

I often joined Mrs. Schertzer and her guests for the *kiddush* ceremony on Friday night -- a soothing and uplifting tradition I had dearly missed when living in the dorm. These gatherings helped banish the pangs of longing and loneliness I had experienced the year before.

I took my comprehensives and the orals in the spring of 1960, and became eligible to start the work on my dissertation. I received a teaching fellowship for my third year, and my tuition fee for the third and following years dropped to $200.

I felt I was doing well financially, and could afford to take two months off to rest and rejuvenate, before turning to the dissertation work. I wanted to catch up with reading I had wanted to do in philosophy, Judaism and psychology. I also looked forward to reading Joseph Schumpeter's monumental work on The History of Economic Analysis. I admired Schumpeter's intellect and breadth of knowledge. Many had written books before on the history of economic thought, but no one had been able to focus his exposition on the history of analysis, rather than history of thought, as Schumpeter had done. Joseph Schumpeter was a Faculty member at Harvard. I had read one of his books before coming to Harvard, and I always regretted that I did not make it to Harvard soon enough to sit in his class and learn directly from him. He passed away in 1950.

The two-month break was a wonderful period. I managed to do a lot more reading than I thought I would. It was also a time when I reconnected with nature. It was the time of the year when the trees came to full bloom, and the sun shone brightly. Sometimes I took a leisurely walk by Charles River; sometimes I just sat on a bench at the river's bank and watched the waves, just as I did in my days of childhood when I sat on a bench at the Tigris' bank. I breathed the air and watched the lush green around me, as I wandered around Cambridge. I felt life pumped up in me.

I loved music and I enjoyed listening to my stereo. I bought Purcell's horn concerto and listened to the horn ensemble. I fell in love with that record. As it turned out, that record was also a favorite of the woman to whom I was married for the next thirty-four years. She loved the French horn. We sat and listened to that record many times together.

WEDDING BELLS

One Saturday night, Harvard's International House held an evening of international dance. Attendance was free. I loved dancing, and I thought it would be fun to spend the evening at the International House.

I had a wonderful time that night. I learned new international dances, and it was on that night that I met Joan.

After a few weeks Joan and I decided to get married, and we picked Thanksgiving Day as our wedding day. Thanksgiving Day was my favorite secular holiday, and it seemed fitting that I should get married on that day. That would ensure that we would celebrate Thanksgiving every year from then on. Joan, having no particular preference of her own, thought it was wonderful to get married on Thanksgiving Day and went along with the idea.

Joan studied Judaism intensively with Rabbi Miller of Boston and Rabbi Joseph S. Shubow of Brighton, Mass. At the end of a three-month period, she officially joined Judaism.

My in-laws, Marjorie Hansen-Hicks and Lawrence Hicks, drove down from McHenry Shores, Illinois to be with us on our wedding day. My father-in-law was a soft-spoken, affable individual. I liked him from the first day we met. His uncompromising political views contrasted sharply with his easygoing attitude toward other things in life. Mr. Hicks stood for absolutely unfettered capitalism. He was not sure he would be casting a vote in the presidential election, when Senator Barry Goldwater ran for President - he felt the arch conservative Senator was too soft on communism.

My mother-in-law's temperament was the opposite of my father-in-law's. She was assertive, dominant, and combative.

Joan and I wanted to offer a special welcome for my in-laws, and we decided to treat them to a dinner in a *kasher* restaurant in Brookline, the only *kasher* restaurant in the Boston area. Neither one of us had ever been to that restaurant before. It was an expensive place. The restaurant served meat products.

Since Jewish law prohibits the mixing of meat and milk products, *kasher* restaurants that serve meat never serve dairy products, and vice versa for *kasher* restaurants that serve dairy products. Mr. Hicks was a Quaker, Mrs. Hicks was Catholic, and neither one was aware of the restrictions on what can be served in a *kasher* restaurant. But that was not a problem for my father-in-law; it turned out to be a problem for my mother-in-law.

Our Wedding Invitation

When the waiter came back with Mrs. Hicks' order, she asked him to bring her butter. The waiter explained that the restaurant did not serve butter, because Jews were not allowed to eat butter with meat.

"But I am not Jewish," my mother-in-law protested. "I can eat butter with meat."

The waiter did not know what to say. That did not make my mother-in-law any happier. I felt bad for her, but there was nothing I could do to fulfill her wishes. She was upset the rest of that evening. I was sorry that neither Joan nor I had foreseen the snag. We wanted to honor our parents the best way we could, but our well-intentioned effort backfired.

We were married at Temple B'nai Moshe on the following day, Thanksgiving Day, November 24, 1960. All the acrimony of the preceding night was gone by then. My mother-in-law could not be more loving. My father-in-law was as warm as ever.

Exchanging Rings under the Huppah (Wedding Canopy)

Rabbi Shubow who officiated at our wedding was one of the most caring human beings I ever met. He came to the US as a child from his native Poland, attended Harvard, and earned a PhD in Jewish Studies. Rabbi Shubow took personal charge and made sure that everything had been taken care of in anticipation of our wedding – including the snacks and refreshment that were served on our wedding day. He paid for all expenses from his own pocket, and refused to be reimbursed.

Three years later, Rabbi Shubow lent me his velvet three-striped Harvard-crimson gown for my Harvard

Joan on our wedding day   L to R Mr. Hicks, Joan,
Daniel, Mrs. Hicks

Rabbi Shubow chatting with Joan

Joan with Mom and Dad

Enjoying a quiet moment
with my father-in-law

Waltzing

Helping my Best Man do Israeli Hora

At the reception: Members of the family
who hosted me when I led the High Holiday Services in Marlborough

graduation. When I joined the Faculty at Cornell, I bought a gown identical to the one Rabbi Shubow had lent me and wore it in the graduation ceremonies of my students.

In the spring of 1964, the New York Times reported on an incident in which young men broke into a Yeshiva and beat up the students. The perpetrators happened to be black. The incident brought back memories from the days of anti Jewish violence in Baghdad. In Iraq, beating Yeshiva students was the method of choice for expressing contempt for Torah and Judaism. I did not want to see the same thing that happened in Iraq repeat itself in the US, and perpetrated of all things by members of the black community in the midst of the civil rights movement, which we were all rooting for. I wrote to the New York Times expressing my distress at the incident and urging the Black leadership to condemn such acts and work to prevent their recurrence.

Not long after the publication of my letter, I received a letter from Rabbi Shubow praising my stand and telling me how he initially thought that an Arab had written the letter, until he noticed "the good name J. Daniel".

That was the last time I heard from Rabbi Shubow. He passed away in 1969.

Two days after our wedding, Joan and I drove to New York City to spend our honeymoon. A US relative of one of my co-workers at the Consumers Co-operative Society in Israel invited us to stay with his family in Brooklyn. We planned to spend five days touring New York City and return home.

On our first day, Joan and I went for a walk in Central Park. We were taken with the beauty of the park and the diversity of life in it. A hackney carriage drove by. I had ridden in hackney carriages many times in Baghdad. They drove up and down Rasheed Street, Baghdad's mains street, alongside buses and cars. But I noticed Joan's yearning look at the carriage as it approached us.

"AND THEY SHALL BUILD FOR ME A SANCTUARY AND I SHALL DWELL IN THEIR MIDST." — *Exodus, XXV, 8*

בית הכנסת בני משה

Temple Bnai Moshe

1845 COMMONWEALTH AVENUE — BRIGHTON, MASSACHUSETTS 02135
ALGONQUIN 4-3600

1934   בע"ה   **1964**

Thirtieth Anniversary of Our Temple
—— Mortgage Redemption Year ——

April 30, 1964

Professor J. Daniel Khazzoom,
Department of Economics
Cornell University
Ithaca, New York

Dear Good Friend Daniel:

Moshe and I and Mrs. Shubow were thrilled to see your courteous, sensible and incontrovertible letter in the New York Times, in regard to the reticence of Negro leaders in the matter of anti-Semitism in general concerning the attack on the little youngsters of the Lubavitch Yeshivah in New York. Our family are delighted that you spoke up like a man. When I first saw the name Khazzoom, for the moment I thought it might be some Arab speaking in behalf of our people, and suddenly I saw the good name of J. Daniel and I felt like saying, in the words of Shakespeare, "A Daniel Come to Judgment" (See Shakespeare' unfortunate and fortunate play, Shylock.

We are all proud of you, we are honored by your friendship and delight to learn that you stand up like a Maccabee of old in defense of our people. God keep you and your dear wife and your darling baby in the best of good health and may all be blessed with long life and great distinction in academic service and in the service of our faith and our people.

With the fondest regards and sincerest best wishes from Moshe, Mrs. Shubow and myself, I am

Ever faithfully and gratefully yours

Rabbi Joseph S. Shubow

"Wouldn't it be nice to celebrate our honey moon with a ride in a hackney carriage? I never rode a hackney carriage before".

" Sure," I said.

I did not ask the driver how much the ride cost, before getting on the carriage. I was so happy that I found something that Joan liked and was eager to please her.

The ride lasted a few minutes. Joan was beaming when we got off. I was so happy to see how she had enjoyed the ride. I asked the driver how much I owed him, thinking that we probably owed no more than thirty or forty or fifty cents - a ride in Baghdad would cost a tenth of that. He asked for $5. I was stunned. Five dollars for such a short ride? We had $6.50 between us, and it was all we had for our five-day tour in the city. I looked at Joan and she looked at me.

We always giggled whenever we remembered our extravagant ride on our honeymoon in New York.

Joan and I were married for thirty-five years. Our interests began to diverge when our second child left for college. We divorced amicably in 1994.

GRADUATION

KEEPING FAITH

I defended my dissertation in November 1962 and graduated in June 1963.

On Graduation Day
With Joan at the entrance to our apartment building on 1 Gray Street, Cambridge

Prior to my graduation day, Joan and I talked about what I should do when all present remove their caps for the invocation at the beginning of the ceremony. As a sign of reverence, Jews pray with covered heads, and both Joan and I felt it was inappropriate for me to stand with head bared at that point. We both agreed that I would keep my cap on. We did not want to break those ties to Jewish traditions, even if that meant I would stand out during the invocation with the cap on.

And that was what happened.

When the time for the invocation came, everyone stood up. The Marshall waited for everybody to remove his cap for the invocation. I kept mine on. The Marshall signaled to me from the podium to take off my cap. I shook my head in negation. He signaled again, now with a more emphatic hand motion to his head. I shook my head again, more emphatically this time. He tried one more time, and I shook my head one more time. He finally got the message and our pantomimic exchange came to a peaceful close.

With Rabbi Joseph S. Shubow
Rabbi Shubow lent me his PhD Harvard-crimson gown to wear on my graduation day

I turned my head back, and I turned around to look. Sure enough, I was the only one in the crowd who had his head cover on.

The Chaplain proceeded with the convocation, and the ceremony began.

Joan smiled approvingly when I told her later about my pantomimic exchange with the Marshall.

VNIVERSITAS HARVARDIANA

CANTABRIGIÆ IN REPVBLICA MASSACHVSETTENSIVM SITA

Quoniam

IOSEPHVS DANIEL KHAZZOOM

studio diligentiore et specimine eruditionis idoneo adhibitis Professoribus Artium et Scientiarum persuasit se penitus pernoscere

OECONOMICA

Praeses et Socii Collegii Harvardiani Ordine Professorum illorum commendante atque consentientibus honorandis et reverendis Inspectoribus ad gradum PHILOSOPHIÆ DOCTORIS eum admiserunt. In cuius rei testimonium nos Praeses et Decanus Academiae Superioris auctoritate rite commissa die XI Martii anno Domini MDCCCCLXIII Collegiique Harvardiani CCCXXVII litteris hisce Vniversitatis sigillo munitis nomina subscripsimus.

Nathan Marsh Pusey PRÆSES

Iohannes Petersen Elder DECANVS

PhD Diploma
Harvard maintains its old practice of writing its diplomas in Latin

When I completed my dissertation, I transferred to the Math Department at Harvard for a two-year stay. Math was my first love, and I always wanted to go back to it. I intended to do work in math I had always wanted to do, but could not while I was in graduate school, partly because of time and financial constraints and partly because of Seymour Harris's opposition. Professor Harris argued that it was undesirable for economists to be too mathematically oriented. He felt that economics did not lend itself to a mathematical treatment without a loss of substance.

During my last year in graduate school I was imitated as a member of Omicron Delta Epsilon Honor Society in Economics

I arranged for a loan from the Harvard Trust Company to finance the two years I planned to spend with the Math department. Joan supported my desire to pursue work in mathematics. It was during that period that John Dunlop, chairman of the Economics Department, offered me a full time teaching position for the following year with the Department. I was tempted by the offer not only for academic but financial reasons, as well, but felt I should turn down the offer, as tempting as it was. Math was always my love, and now I had an opportunity to follow my heart.

It was in early spring of 1963, during my first post-doctoral year, when the International Monetary Fund offered me a grant to fund continuing work on my dissertation. I decided to spend the summer with the Fund to launch the effort, and return to Cambridge for my second year with the Math Department.

As it happened, I did not return for my second postdoctoral year. Opportunity knocked. I went to Cornell to teach Mathematical Economics.

REFLECTIONS ON MY HARVARD LEGACY

I feel fortunate to have had a Harvard education. I am grateful to that remarkable institution for the doors it opened for me and for the opportunities it gave me to transform myself into who I am and break the ties that held me back. I take pride in my doctorate degree, particularly because I earned it from scratch —without money, or English proficiency, or family support - material or moral. And I did it while fettered by the crippling inhibitions of the traditions in which I grew up. I struggled for many years to reconcile new ways of looking at the world with antiquated customs and ideas. The pull of the old was strong but in the end, the new triumphed, though not without cost.

Harvard exposed me to professors who didn't merely rehash the work of great scholars, but who themselves were stars in their fields. They instilled in us, their disciples so to speak, the notion that innovating and pushing the frontiers of knowledge were well within our grasp as well. By example and by osmosis, we became convinced that we ourselves had within us what it took to achieve greatness.

It was an outstanding research faculty, but it was in general not a teaching faculty and had otherwise little time for students.

In a New York Times Op Ed of November 27, 2003 (How Much for that Professor?) David Kirp of UC Berkeley discussed the relationships between the "luminaries" of research universities and their students, arguing that the relationship is essentially non-existent. "Since the standing of top-rung professors ...depends on what they write, not what they teach," Kirp pointed out, "their main loyalty isn't to their students ..." and that "trophy professors are wooed with ... the promise that they'll rarely encounter an undergraduate".

That was what I saw at Harvard and what shaped my academic career.

I remember my thesis advisor at Harvard, the late Seymour Harris. He was a prolific researcher, and he employed three full-time secretaries, who could barely keep up with his writings. He was also a senior advisor to the US Treasury, spending a lot of time in Washington DC. Once he told a seminar I attended about a young woman who came to his office to see him.

"Professor Harris, it is so nice to see you again," she said as she walked in.

"You look familiar," he responded. "Where did we meet before?"

"You were my thesis advisor," she replied. "I finished my PhD thesis with you last year."

I bought into the supremacy of research work and assumed much of the practices and attitudes I saw at Harvard. During a 37-year academic career, I taught at top universities, including Cornell, Stanford, University of California Berkeley, and McGill in Canada. But I spent most of my time and energy on research work. I made contributions to scholarship in the fields of energy modeling and economics -- research that was influential in shaping American and Canadian government policy. It was exhilarating to attend a conference and meet strangers who recognized me through an article I had written or who expressed appreciation for an insight they gained from a book I had published. It was gratifying to see an idea I proposed put into practice by a public agency or a model I developed being used in formulating public policy. On academic matters, I was happy to interact with my students, but I avoided as much as I could teaching undergraduate courses. I didn't have time to spare from my research work.

As for my wife and children, the toll on them of my round-the-clock preoccupation with research was no less detrimental. But sometimes I wonder - was it all Harvard's legacy or was it my own temperament that made me so receptive to that legacy?

GLIMPSES OF MY MARRIED LIFE

Joan and I found ways to break the monotony of work.

We took Saturdays off to rest and rejuvenate, and we celebrated the Sabbath in our little apartment in Cambridge. I grew up observing the Sabbath, but during my first two years in graduate school I worked seven days a week. When Joan and I decided to observe the Sabbath day, I was nervous about "wasting" a whole day. But gradually I learned to enjoy the break and look forward to it. With my tendency to work incessantly, observing the Sabbath has probably saved my life.

We recited the traditional *kiddush* on Friday night and sang religious paeans of the Jews of Babylon. Sometimes we spent the day reading, sometimes we just puddled around. Many times we sang along, as our LP played songs from the Civil War - those were beautiful songs and they told touching stories. I remember them fondly.

We budgeted $8 a week for our food, but we ate a lot better than I could have ever imagined during my first two years in graduate school. Every Saturday night, we drove to Hay Market Square in downtown Boston and made our food purchases for the week. Hay Market Square was a sprawling collection of carts, stalls, and shops that sold fruits, vegetables, fish, meat, poultry and household appliances. The market shut down on Sunday, and on Saturday night the price of perishables came down to a fraction of what they were in the supermarkets.

I liked those "outings" on Saturday night. I could never take my eyes off the sparkling lights atop of the antenna of Boston's tallest, as we drove by the John Hancock Building, and I loved to watch the reflections of the city's lights on the Charles River, as we approached downtown. I looked forward to the hour or two we spent in Hay Market Square - walking leisurely between the carts and stands, gazing at the many wares on display, shaking hands with new acquaintances we made, and exchanging banter with

Our Apartment on 1 Gray Street, Cambridge
kiddush table, two end-of Sabbath candles and third-night *hanukkah* candles

A peaceful corner on 1 Gray Street, Cambridge
Below, bookshelf in our living room – boards and bricks

merchants we knew. It was a world so different from our world of daily work.

In the winter months, we filled our large thermos bottle with hot coffee before we left for Hay Market Square and served coffee to our merchant friends. It got very cold in Boston, and we could see that the merchants were uncomfortable standing in the freezing-cold weather for so long. Our friends loved the hot coffee, but no one appreciated the gesture more than the fish man. He looked forward to his hot cup of coffee, and he got two cups. I took several pictures of him. He was a charming individual and sheer delight to chat with.

Our friend, the fish man in Hay Market Square, chatting with Joan

On Saturday night our fish man sold his fish five pounds for a dollar. But with us, he never seemed to pay much attention to how heavy the fish got on his scale, as he weighed the five pounds for us. It seemed as if he was only going through the motion of weighing the fish. He never stopped adding fish before his scale's pointer went over eight or nine pounds. Joan asked him several times to accept payment for the extra fish he packed for us, but he would not hear of it.

"I am glad you like my fish. I want you to eat well.

God bless you", he used to say.

As I look at the pictures I took of our fish man, I see him through the eyes of my mind - the gentle middle-aged person I have known in those days. I feel as if the things I am writing about are happening here and now. It is hard to imagine that he is now an old man, painful to think that he might even no longer be around.

We looked forward to our weekly routine after returning from Hay Market Square. Joan fried the fish. We curled up in our corner around the television and watched Saturday Night Movies, as we munched on our sandwiches of crispy fried fish.

In the summer of 1961, we bought a pup tent for two and headed for Niagara Falls on our first camping trip. We arrived at Niagara around three o'clock in the morning and stopped to watch the Rapids of Niagara River. It was breathtaking. I was in awe as I stood in the quiet of the night and listened to the roaring sound of the raging rapids.

Joan and Daniel behind the mist in   Joan wading in the rapids of Niagara River
alcove under one of Niagara's biggest waterfall

We passed by a camp. We were tired, and we decided to stop at the camp. We popped our little tent on a spot in the camp close to the road and curled in to sleep, not realizing that the spot was part of an occupied site.

We felt awful when we woke up in the morning and realized what we had done. We went to apologize to the campers for our encroachment. They were gracious about it.

I often thought about that first camping experience of ours, and wondered how startled the people must have been when they found our tent in their backyard.

But in time we became better informed and more seasoned campers. We also graduated to a more comfortable tent. We took regular camping trips over the weekends to Miles Standish camp on the shore of a crystal blue lake outside Boston. It evokes a sense of peace in me just to think of that camp. It was the most gorgeous camp I have ever been to. We bought a two-person rubber boat and we took it with us whenever we went to Miles Standish.

In front of our tent, Miles Standish, 1963   Our two-person rubber boat

Joan was in her sixth month of pregnancy, when we had a big scare. We had just returned from a wonderful weekend at Miles Standish when Joan started bleeding. I was terrified. I remember Joan looking at me with tears in her eyes. " I feel as if I know him. We have been together for six months", she said. I felt so guilty for going camping when Joan was in her sixth month of pregnancy.

I draw a blank when I try to remember what we did at the time to take care of Joan's bleeding. Fortunately Joan had no more bleeding after that time.

We never went camping after that incident until long after the birth of our child.

One day, I received a call from the minister of one of the local churches in Cambridge, inviting me to join him and his congregation in a dinner celebration. He asked if I would also speak to his congregation about my life experience in Iraq. I told him that I would be happy to speak to his congregation, but I explained that it was not necessary to plan on dinner for me, as I would be having dinner with Joan at home before coming to speak. He asked that I bring Joan with me and that we both join the congregation for dinner. I thanked him again, but this time I had to explain that we both kept *kashruth* and did not eat meat outside.

"Don't worry about it. We can arrange it".

I did not want him or the congregation to go through any trouble for us, and told him so. I reiterated that I would be happy to come to speak.

That evening Joan and I had our meal at home before heading for the church. The church's social hall was full. The atmosphere was one of a family gathering. Congregants milled around, chatting with each other, looking happy. The minister introduced Joan and me to several members of his congregation. They received us warmly, and they seemed to be happy to have us in their midst. I felt as if I, too, was part of that family.

Dinnertime came. The congregants sat at their tables. The minister took Joan and me to the head table. There were two big plates sitting on the table in front of us. They were in a plastic seal and they had "Kosher" printed in big letters on their seal. I turned to the minister. He had a smile on his face.

"We had them ordered for you and your wife. We wanted you to know how glad we are to have you both with us".

I was moved by the gesture. I shook hands with the minister. But I could not say a word. I was choked up with emotions.

That was not the only instance I can remember when people went out of their way to accommodate our (and, later, our children's) observance of *kashruth* laws.

When I was in Washington in the summer of 1963 on a research grant from the International Monetary Fund

(IMF), my colleague in the IMF's research department, Shakkour Shaalan, and his wife Saeeda Shaalan, invited Joan and me for a Friday night dinner in their home in Washington, DC. Shakkour is a Moslem born in Egypt, Saeeda is a Christian born in Syria. Saeeda and Shakkour are wonderful people, and we liked them very much. I told Shakkour and Saeeda that we kept *kashruth* and did not eat meat outside, but that we would love to join them over desert and refreshments. I pleaded with them not to go out of their way and prepare anything special for us. They agreed. But Saeeda had other plans.

Saeeda Shaalan

Shakkour Shaalan

Unbeknown to us, Saeeda went to the kosher butcher shop that Friday afternoon to buy meat for a kosher dinner she had planned for the four of us. She bought a whole new set of pots and pants to cook in and serve the kosher dinner she prepared that evening.

I was overwhelmed by the Shaalans' gesture. I felt a tremendous sense of friendship and appreciation for what they had gone through for us.

On February 3, 2004, I spoke with Shakkour for the first since I had left the IMF forty years before. We reminisced over that Friday night. Shakkour promised that if we visit them in Washington, they would have another dinner with kosher meat served for us. I pleaded with him not to go through the trouble, but this time for a different reason: We had become vegetarian.

My talk to the church community went very well. The audience was fascinated to hear about life in a land so far away. But they were amazed most by the stories I told them about the Tigris River. I drew gasps when I relayed to them that, during the summertime, my father, brother, and I swam daily across the Tigris River. To my audience the Tigris and Euphrates were relics from a far away past, way way back. They existed only in the Biblical world. But to hear that they were still alive and kicking, that people lived on their banks, swam in them or drank their water was too much for many to contain.

IN THE HEART OF WASHINGTON'S GHETTO

The day after my graduation, we packed our belongings in a pile atop our Hillman's rack and headed for Washington, DC to start work on my project at the International Monetary Fund.

On our way to Washington, DC
with belongings atop our Hillman's rack

In Washington, we rented an apartment in the heart of the district's ghetto. We did a lot of soul searching about our racial attitudes before settling on that location.

We had narrowed our search down to two efficiency apartments - one in a new and clean building in the heart of the black ghetto, and the other in an older building two blocs away from the black ghetto. The apartment in the older building cost twenty-five per cent more than the apartment in the newer building inside the ghetto.

We came close to renting the more expensive apartment, and then we caught ourselves. Why were we willing to pay more for an apartment that was no better than another located a few blocs away in a newer and cleaner building? Could it be that we were prejudiced against the Blacks and did not want to live in their midst?

I was stunned to even think that either one of us was driven by prejudice. Joan grew up in Atlanta, Georgia, at a time when Blacks were restricted to sit in the back of the bus. But whenever she took the bus, she sat in the back. At times she was dragged from the back of the bus and beaten. But she stuck it out, and I appreciated her courage and commitment. How could we possibly think of her as prejudiced against the Blacks when she had taken risks to defy the bigots? And I wondered about myself. I did not grow up in the US, and did not feel prejudiced against the blacks. Were we just blowing things out of proportion?

But the fact remained. We were not well off, yet we were willing to squander money on an apartment that cost more than another located in a newer and cleaner building.

We went back home to our hotel to think things over. It was true I did not grow up in the States. But I had attended an elite school in the US and, like it or not, I was a member of the white upper middle class, even though I might not have had the material possessions to show for it. I might have come to identify with the prejudicial tendencies of some members of that class, without being aware of it.

I thought of my Texan classmate at Harvard, the scion of a famous family in Texas. He was the embodiment of gentlemanliness and the epitome of courtesy. I liked him very much and enjoyed talking with him. He never rushed to express an opinion, except on that one occasion when the issue of racism came up in one of our after-class get together. Then I noticed the change in his demeanor. His face grew red and he looked agitated. He opened his briefcase and took out his copy of the Bible. He opened it to Noah's section and pointed with his finger to a passage in that section,

"Here is the proof. It is in the Bible," he exclaimed.

Then he read from the passage that Ham was cursed to be the slave of Shem and Japheth's descendants. I had read that passage several times before when I studied the Bible with my Hebrew tutor in Baghdad, but I never thought that it had any bearing on the Blacks of the world around us. Then why did I not challenge my Texan friend? Why did I continue to be friends with him? That troubled me a lot when I thought about it.

The following day, Joan and I agreed that what we were about to do was evidence of our prejudice against the Blacks. We decided that the right thing to do was to confront our prejudice head on and rent the apartment in the Black ghetto.

I remember only one instance of unpleasantness we encountered during the three months we spent in that apartment. Joan was in her ninth month of pregnancy when we drove home one night. She needed to get to bed quickly. I stopped the car in front of the building to drop her off. A tall heavy-set man leaned with his back against the car door just as I stopped the car and would not let Joan open the door. She rolled down the window and asked him to move over so that she could open the door, but he would not budge. I was furious. I opened my door and walked determinately toward him to pull him out her way. Strangely he chose to move just as he saw me walk angrily toward him.

He was not black. He was a white man.

We never regretted our decision to live in the midst of the ghetto. We felt we did something good for our souls. We felt also that, in our own little way, we had done something that contributed to integration. For me it was also an educational experience. At the beginning I was conscious of the color of the people around us. Gradually, appearances, as in other relationships, receded from the forefront. Increasingly I began to relate to the Blacks around me just as I related to other people.

I remember my time with IMF as an exciting period. I was surrounded by professionals from IMF's Research Department who were world-renowned in their fields. I met with Finance Ministers and other top government officials from many countries, and I learned a lot about the less developed countries and their effort to pull themselves by their own bootstraps. I gained a great deal of insight by talking with them about my research effort and the direction to which I was taking my project.

IMF assigned staff members to help me with my work. I felt fortunate to have their assistance. I remember in particular one of them – Althea McDonald, a New Englander who doggedly worked with me on data construction.

IMF planned on using my initial results in the annual meeting of central bankers and finance officers from countries around the world. I was excited to know that the work I was doing would be used in international policy discussions. I never dreamed of that when I started working on my dissertation.

I must have spent twelve hours a day working in my office, and I enjoyed every minute of it. I never felt what I was doing was work. So much was going on in my mind. I bubbled with ideas. Sometimes I was so geared up I could not get myself to fall asleep. Sometimes I got up in the middle of the night to jot down ideas that occurred to me while in bed.

The grant I received from the IMF was generous. For the first time in years, I felt I had enough on hand to live comfortably.

I took a break from work one day and went with Joan to visit the Capitol. I had seen pictures of the Capitol before, but never had a chance to visit it. I had a soft spot in my heart for that place. To me, the Capitol was a living symbol of democracy in action. I was awed as I stood that day in front the Capitol Building. I stopped to touch the pillars and wondered what stories they would tell if they could speak. I walked to the pictures hanging on the walls to see them from close. I walked around the yards, stopped to look at the dome high above, and thought about its history. I filled rolls and rolls of movie films with everything I could lay my eyes on, in and around the building. I wanted to keep alive everything I saw that day. I still have those movie pictures. Just recently I had them transferred to DVD along with movie pictures we made of our family as our life was unfolding

During my stay with the IMF, Cornell's Department of Economics called about an opening they had in Mathematical Economics. I was torn between responding in the affirmative and sticking to my original plan of returning to Harvard's Math Department. Joan and I talked it over. Cornell's offer was a very good one. I would have an opportunity to teach in my favorite field. We were expecting our first child and I worried that it might prove difficult for me to keep us afloat on borrowed money, I decided to accept Cornell's offer. We made plans to leave for Ithaca, NY, soon after the birth of our child.

BIRTH OF AZIZA

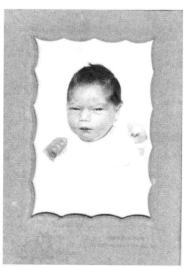

Aziza, minutes after her birth

Aziza was born on Friday afternoon, September 13,

1963 in Washington Hospital Center. It was natural birth. Joan and I had attended natural-birth classes. When I saw little Aziza for the first time, I could not believe I was now a father. Was it true? What was a father supposed to do? I wanted to hold Aziza in my arms and hug her. But I was so scared to touch her. I looked at her. Her eyes were wide open, and she seemed to be staring at me. At the same time it seemed as if she was dazed. I could not resist it. I took her little arm and kissed it, and I said a prayer for her health and well-being.

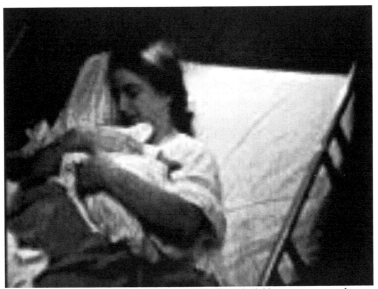

Joan looking lovingly at little Aziza the first time she laid eyes on our newborn

The day after Aziza's birth, I opened a bank savings account for Aziza's education. The bank gave me two silver dollars in return for opening that account. I saved those two dollars for Aziza in the family scrapbook. They are still there.

Gradually I became less afraid to touch Aziza. On the fourth day after Aziza's birth, while waiting for Joan to get ready for me to drive her and Aziza home, I held Aziza in my arm and gently brushed her hair with a little baby hairbrush.

On the first Saturday after Aziza's homecoming, I went to the synagogue to announce the birth of a daughter to Israel and pronounced her name in front of the open Torah Scroll.

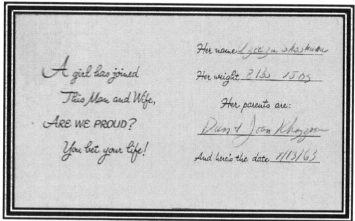

Aziza's Birth Announcement

We named our newly born daughter Aziza, after my maternal grandmother. Aziza is an Arabic name common among Babylonian Jews, and it means dear or precious. We added a Hebrew middle name, Shoshana, which means rose, in the hope that the combination of Hebrew and Arabic would presage reconciliation between Arab and Jew in the Middle East.

The choice of the Arabic name Aziza for our daughter was for me a major step forward in my struggle to reclaim my heritage as a Jew from an Arab land. Joan wholeheartedly supported me in this choice. Jews from Arab lands in Israel who treaded on eggshells for fear of being ridiculed as Arabs, learned to be vigilant. Most shunned any outward connections to their heritage, including giving their children Arabic names. Some went to extremes and adopted, at least outwardly, a hostile attitude toward anything Arabic, as a demonstration of their allegiance to the new order. Their behavior brought to mind the behavior of the Chueta conversos, Jews who were forcibly converted to Christianity in medieval Spain The Chuetas made a public show of their allegiance to the new religion by demonstratively eating pork, the height in Jewish abomination, in full view in public places.

When we went to visit Israel ten years after Aziza's birth, we came face to face with a manifestation of this problem. Latifa, my sister, who avoided any outside identification with the "old" order, chose to call Aziza by an unrelated Hebrew name, Aviva, instead of her real Arabic name. Aziza, a bright little girl whom we brought up to be conscious of the Babylonian heritage, accommodated her aunt for a while. But when Latifa persisted with her misnomer, Aziza put her foot down.

"If you call me Aviva again, I will not answer".

That took care of things. Latifa began to call her niece by her real name, Aziza.

CORNELL

Ten days after Aziza's birth, my family and I left Washington, DC and headed for Ithaca, New York. I gave my first lecture at Cornell two days after our arrival in Ithaca.

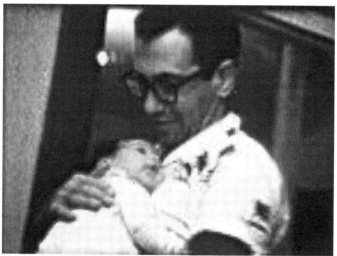

Aziza shortly after arriving to Ithaca

Ithaca is a small college town. Geologists view Ithaca and its surroundings as a geological wonder. Expeditions of geologists visited Ithaca regularly from all over the world. Ithaca had natural attractions for the average individual, as well. It had beautiful hills, breathtaking waterfalls, a gorgeous lake -- Lake Cayuga -- parks and camping sites in Robert Treeman Park. We camped many times in Treeman Park.

Cornell's campus is the most beautiful campus I have ever seen. It commands a scenic view of the valley and Lake Cayuga. Whenever I think of Ithaca and Cornell's campus, I see stretches of pictorial landscape in my mind's eye. It brings a sense of peace to just think about it.

Life in Ithaca had a lot of firsts. Cornell was my first full time teaching appointment. There were many lectures to write from scratch and lots of new grounds to cover. It was the first time Joan and I got settled and began to experience parenthood. Every Friday night when Joan lit the Sabbath candles, we stood together as Joan held Aziza in her arms and recited a prayer for the well-being of "our little bundle".

"our little bundle", age three months, on her first *hanukkah*

It was also the first time we lived in a town that had practically no organized Jewish life. There was no Jewish bookstore and no *kasher* butcher shop. We imported our *kasher* meat from Elmira, NY. Hillel had a presence on campus, but it did not hold regular services. There was one medium-size conservative synagogue in town, but it was more often closed than open. My greatest disappointment during my first year at Cornell was *purim* day. I had rescheduled my lecture for that day so that I could take the day off, and I looked forward to celebrating the holiday with my family at the synagogue. It was a letdown when we went to the synagogue that morning and found the doors closed.

We lived a short walking distance from campus, which was a blessing, particularly during the winter months.

During the snow season, ice covered the streets, and cars could not climb up the steep roads leading to campus.

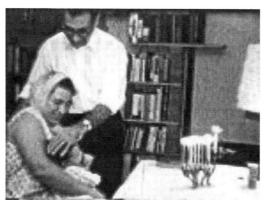

Blessing Aziza on our first *hanukkah* as parents

Our home on 105 College Avenue, Ithaca, on a snowy day

Cornell held classes six days a week. That could have posed a problem for me, because we observed the Sabbath. I remember a conversation I had with Mickey Falkson on the subject. Mickey was one of my contemporaries in graduate school, and for Mickey too it was his first year of teaching at

THE JOURNEY OF A JEW FROM BAGHDAD

Cornell. It was Mickey who told me about Cornell's practice of scheduling classes on Saturday. Mickey was raised Jewish, but was not observant. When I told Mickey I would not teach on Saturday, he was stunned.

"You would tell them you won't teach because you observe the Sabbath?" he asked incredulously.

When I discussed with Frank Golay, my department chairman, the potential for a conflict between my class scheduling and my observance of the Sabbath, Frank could not be more supportive. I never had a scheduling conflict with the Sabbath.

Mickey's comment brought back to mind David Feldman's reaction when I suggested that we ask the chairman of Harvard's Economics to reschedule our written comprehensives so that they would not conflict with the Passover day. In my conversation with Mickey, as in my conversation with David, I had faith in the goodwill of people around us. From day one, I felt that the Christians in the US should not be confused with the Christians of the Inquisition days. And I was never disappointed.

Teaching fulltime was a novelty, and I felt a whole new world had opened up to me. I was teaching exactly what I wanted – mathematical economics. My students were sharp. My teaching load was light. During my first year, I stayed up all night and worked on my lecture notes. My stereo played background music all night. One record I remember from those nights played selected performances by a young soprano, Leontyne Price -- then at the beginning of her career. I loved her rich voice and was delighted when Ms. Price went on to become a famous international opera star.

Joan used to bring Aziza to campus on my lecture days, and we had lunch together at the Faculty Club. But it was hilarious when one day Joan and Aziza arrived early and stood outside my lecture room. Aziza was a little over a year old. She heard my voice and called out "Abba, Abba". I stopped for a moment, but as I resumed, Aziza resumed her call "Abba, Abba". I stopped, and when I resumed, Aziza's voice came back again, "Abba, Abba". The class was in an uproar. Some called out "He is here, he is here. Come in". I opened the door, picked up Aziza and put my arm around her, as I walked back into the classroom. Aziza waved to the class triumphantly. I introduced Joan and then I introduced Aziza as the new student addition to the class. I remember one of my students remarking, "I knew the age of college students has been dropping. But this is ridiculous".

I look back with nostalgia at the times when I stayed up all night, happily working on my lectures. It was cold outside; sometimes it snowed. But inside, it was warm and cozy. It was exciting to experience the novelty of our new life and to see a whole new world opening up.

It was difficult for me during my first year at Cornell to focus on the research work I started at the IMF. I had shared with the IMF my preliminary results before leaving for Ithaca. But I was planning on completing the analysis while at Cornell. To make it easier for me to do my research work, Cornell assigned to me a spacious study in the main library. I assembled all my research material in the study. But now that I was away from Washington, it was difficult for me to get excited about work I had to do in seclusion. I no longer had the interaction with my former colleagues at the IMF. That was what kept new ideas bubbling in my mind and had given me the stimulus to keep focused on my research work. At Cornell, I had lively interaction, but of another kind –with my graduate students. That kept me bubbling, too. But it was removed from the field of my project.

It was then that I realized I was so blessed that when I was working on my dissertation, I had resisted all temptation to accept a faculty appointment before I had completed my dissertation. While at Cornell, struggling to keep alive my research project, I realized why so many who had accepted teaching appointments at universities while they were in the midst of writing their dissertations, never finished their theses, and ended up losing their faculty appointment. Two of my young colleagues at Cornell suffered that fate.

But in spite of the difficulties in keeping the momentum of my project going, I kept at it, if for no reason other than the fact that I had to publish my research results in order to stay in first-rate institutions. My reasons for publishing changed in time. As I matured in my field, I was driven to publish because I had something innovative to say. But at the beginning of my career, I felt very much the pressure of "publish or perish".

My IMF project appeared as a Praeger book three years later.

AN ABORTIVE ATTEMPT AT VEGETARIANISM

I grew up keeping *kashruth*. It was explained to me during my childhood that, aside from the religious aspect of *kashruth*, the *kasher* method of slaughter was a humane method of killing the animal. This found confirmation later in my life when, during my days in graduate school, I read a 1939 report by a British commission set up to evaluate the available slaughtering methods and recommend to the British military the most humane method. The commission, made up of a zoologist, a physician, and another whose profession I no longer remember, recommended the *kasher* slaughtering method. It was noteworthy that none of the commission's members was Jewish.

I was impressed that so many hundred years ago, when people did not think about being humane to other human beings, Jewish traditions concerned themselves with being humane to animals. Still I felt there was an inherent contradiction in the concept "humane slaughter" -- if we wanted to be humane to animals, why slaughter them in the first place? Pushed to its logical conclusion, I felt, *kashruth* required us to be vegetarians. I always had also in the back of mind the sheep that my family slaughtered in the days preceding *rosh hashana*, and the pain I experienced at seeing our lamb being slaughtered.

When I got married, I talked with Joan about becoming vegetarians. We settled on a hybrid diet, retaining fish as part of our diet, but abstaining from eating meat or chicken. Joan felt fish had a less developed nervous system than mammals. I felt killing fish was still taking life, but it was a compromise.

When we lived in Ithaca, the pediatrician said that our one-year old daughter needed the protein from meat. We decided we would serve meat for Aziza, but that we would remain vegetarians. But we did not. What made it hard was that neither Joan nor I knew many vegetarian dishes and our diet became monotonous. With meat on the table, it became tempting to join in with our daughter. We did try to broaden our menu of vegetarian dishes, but vegetarianism was not in vogue, and we did not get much help from our friends either. Gradually we reverted to carnivorousness.

When I told Joan that my Teaching Assistant (TA) at Cornell was Indian, she came up with an idea. Indians respected the cow, and some worshipped it. So it must be that the Indians were vegetarians. Why not ask my TA where we could find a book on Indian cooking?

I thought it was a brilliant idea.

I broached the subject with my TA. He had brought a small cookbook with him from India, he said, and would lend it to me. I told Joan. She was ecstatic.

It took several weeks before my assistant finally brought his small cookbook. At home, I happily waved it at Joan. Joan leafed through it.

"How is this going to help?" she asked with great disappointment, as she handed the book back to me.

I began to thumb through my to-the-rescue cookbook. All of the recipes included meat, and a good deal included pork, of all things.

"I thought the Indians did not kill cows and were vegetarians," I said to my TA, as I handed him back his cookbook.

"Yes that is true," he said.

"So how come your cookbook has pork and other meat dishes?"

"Well, you see, we are Catholics," he said.

ATTACKING THE MESSENGER

While at Cornell, I became friendly with Rabbi Morris Goldfarb, the Director of Cornell's Hillel House. During one of our lunches, Rabbi Goldfarb and I talked about my life in Israel as a Jew from an Arab land and about what led to my decision not to stay in the US. The Rabbi asked me if I would be willing to give a talk at Hillel about the life of Jews from Arab lands in Israel. I hesitated, and told him I would think it over.

I had never spoken before to any audience about the treatment of Jews from Arab lands in Israel. In Israel, we were filled to the brim with the notion that there was an anti-Semitic world out there waiting to pounce on anything it could use to vilify Israel and the Jewish people. I suppose this might have been true of Central and Eastern Europe. But it was depicted as if it were true of the whole non-Jewish world. Even though I never believed that was true of the people in the US, I suppose I was still inhibited by what I had learned in Israel, as well as by our own miserable experience in Iraq.

But what would be wrong with speaking to a Hillel audience? Why did I hesitate? Hillel was after all a community of Jewish Faculty and students. I guess I worried that the audience might become upset with Israel. The American Jewish community was the major supporter of Israel, and, if they got angry with Israel, they might withhold their support. That would hurt Israel. I did not want to hurt Israel, even though I wanted the American Jewish community to know about what had been happening to Jews from Arab lands and come to their help.

Regrettably, the fear of Israel bashing, even though intellectually I did not believe it, had got me one time to tell a lie, which pains me to this day. It happened in the spring of 1959 during my first year in graduate school. I was then a guest at the home of Rabbi Ronald Gittelsohn, the spiritual leader of a reform synagogue in Boston. The Gittelsohns had invited a large crowd for dinner that day. Two of their guests were ministers in local churches.

At one point, Rabbi Gittelsohn turned to me.

"Daniel, is there discrimination against Jews from Arab lands in Israel?"

There was silence. Everyone was listening. I was tongue-tied. I did not know what to say. Yes, of course there was, and plenty of it. But how could I say it? Not only were there other people present, but at least two of those present were not Jewish. How could I say something negative about Israel in their presence?

As hard as it was for me at the time and as painful as it is for me to this day to relive that moment, I lied.

"No, Rabbi Gittelsohn. There is no discrimination against Jews from Arab lands in Israel".

When Rabbi Goldfarb of Cornell's Hillel called me a week later to inquire if I had made up my mind, I was still hesitant to accept his invitation, I shared with him my concerns. He assured me that my fears were unfounded and that it would be educational for the rest of the community to hear about one aspect of life in Israel, which they were not familiar with. With a lot of qualms, I accepted the invitation. We chose one Sunday afternoon for my talk.

I could not sleep the night before my talk. I tossed and turned in bed. How could I go through with it? What if the rabbi was wrong in his assessment? What if my talk was leaked out to media hostile to Israel? Should I call and cancel?

Joan noticed how agitated I was. She got up and made us a hot cup of tea. We talked. Joan pointed out to me that there was no way I could alert the Jewish community in the US to the plight of the Middle Eastern Jews in Israel without risking a leak to the outside world. At the same time, she reminded me of the faith I had in the fairness and decency of the American public. She told me also that she felt that even under the worst scenario, Hillel was still the safest place to talk about the subject in public.

I felt reassured.

By that time it was daylight. I went out to get the Sunday papers and curled up on the sofa to read the news. I began to feel at ease.

Hillel did an effective job of advertising the event. There was a large turnout. I recognized the faces of several colleagues. There were also quite a few Israelis in the crowd.

In my talk I tried to debunk the notion that the ethnic conflict in Israel was a conflict between primitive and western culture or that it was caused by a clash between the educated and those that had no tradition of education. I argued that it was due more to the clash with the monolithic view of the world - where there was only one way of dressing, one way of praying, one way of eating - which characterized the worldview of the leadership and much of the East European public in Israel.

The audience seemed to be interested in what I had to say and was eager to hear me out, but several in the Israeli crowd greeted my talk with catcalls. One Israeli student interrupted me repeatedly with hostile interjections. A tone of "how dare you?" seemed to underlie the remarks of those in the Israeli crowd who spoke out. I felt as if the Israeli crowd viewed me as an enemy for daring to puncture a hole in the dearly held aphorisms about the root causes of the ethnic conflict in Israel. Several of the questions from the Israeli crowd seemed to be more intended to attack me than address the issues I raised. It was a classic example of attacking the messenger instead of tackling the message.

That afternoon was a trying experience for me.

The following Saturday Joan and I put our daughter in the stroller and headed for the home of an Israeli couple who had a daughter of Aziza's age. The couple was our age, and we visited each other regularly on the Sabbath. We knocked on their door several times. There was no answer. It was strange, we thought, because we did hear someone in the house. As we turned back, we noticed through an open window that our friends were, indeed, in the house. We suspected we were no longer welcome in their home. As it turned, our friends never came to visit us after that either. We got the message.

I felt that little experience with our Israeli friends at Cornell was probably a miniature of what I would have encountered had I chosen to settle in Israel and speak my mind about the ethnic conflict in Israel.

Following my experience with the talk at Hillel, I resolved that I would no longer remain silent about the treatment of Jews from Arab lands in Israel. But to avoid being subjected to unpleasantness, I decided to write instead of giving talks. I felt that would not only spare me hostile treatment, but would be a good way of reaching a wider audience.

Over the years, I published several articles on the subject.

WATCHING AZIZA GROW

I watched with love and amazement every new move our newborn made, any new awareness she developed and every little skill she acquired. Aziza was three months old when, for the first time, she responded to our cooing with a smile. We were ecstatic. We bragged to our friends about that.

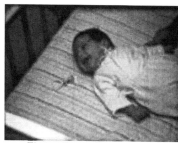 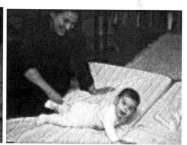

First smile caught on camera - Aziza three months old | Aziza trying to lift herself as Joan proudly proudly looks on

Joan had breast-fed Aziza during her first year. But Aziza was eight months old when, for the first time, we started feeding her solid food, as well -- Gerber's mashed apples. That was a special event, and I remember it tenderly.

Aziza seemed to like the taste of the mashed apple and evidently was eager to get some more. She kicked her legs, flapped her hands and shook her head right and left every time Joan brought the feeding spoon close to her mouth. But in her excitement, she managed to spill much of what the little spoon held. I do not think much made it into her mouth that evening. The mashed apple splashed all over her face and cheeks. With layers of mashed apple dripping all over them, Aziza's cheeks turned into bright reflectors of our living room lights. I rushed to get our movie camera and took pictures to commemorate Aziza's first solid-food-eating event. Those pictures are vividly etched in my mind. Aziza is now forty-three. But as I watch those pictures to day, I feel as if it all happened only yesterday.

Joan tried a new strategy. Instead of using a spoon to feed Aziza the applesauce, she poured the applesauce into the feeding bottle, cut the bottle's nipple wider, and fed Aziza from the bottle. It all went through.

Aziza was a strong willed little girl. I remember the first time when Aziza and I crossed the street together. She was almost two years old then. I extended my hand to her and asked her to hold it before we crossed the street. She refused. She decided she would be

Joan feeding Aziza her first solid food

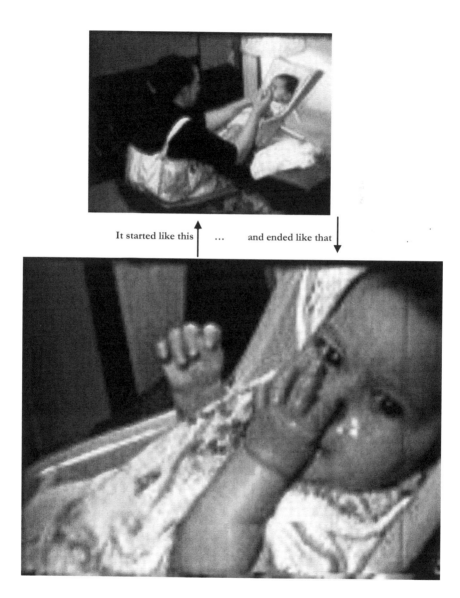

It started like this ↑ ... and ended like that ↓

Aziza with Daniel in our home on 105 College Avenue, Ithaca

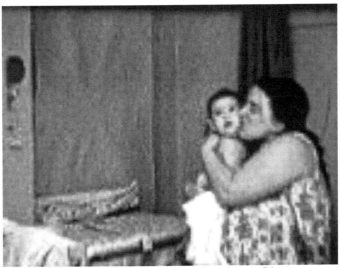

Aziza with Joan in our home on 105 College Avenue, Ithaca

the one to hold her hand. She crossed the street holding her two hands together, with me walking closely next to her.

But glimpses of that trait showed even earlier.

Aziza was nine months old when, on the advice of her pediatrician, we moved her crib from our bedroom to a separate room adjacent to ours. She did not like the change. She protested strenuously. She refused to lie down. She stood up in her crib, held on to the rails, and cried at the top of her lungs as we left the room. She cried for a long time. The pediatrician had already warned us that might happen. We sat in our bedroom, hearts torn. We looked at each other and wondered. Could she be feeling we had abandoned her? Would it damage her to let her cry all by herself? Could the pediatrician be wrong? Should we go and comfort her? We felt it was heartless to just sit there and listen to our daughter cry without lifting a finger to comfort her.

Finally the crying stopped. Joan tiptoed into the bedroom next door to see if Aziza was all right. She came back with tears in her eyes.

"Come see", she told me.

I went to Aziza's bedroom. Aziza had fallen asleep standing up, as her hands held to the crib's railing. Her head, bent forward, rested on the railing. Joan picked her up and tenderly laid her down in her crib. Aziza looked exhausted.

The next day I called our internist and asked to see him urgently. We were both worried about what had transpired the night before and about the effect that might have had on our child. I asked our internist if what had happened could have damaged Aziza in any way.

"Do not worry. Babies are resilient. What happened last night would not affect Aziza in any way".

But unlike our pediatrician, he did not feel it mattered much whether Aziza's crib was in our room or in a separate room. Joan felt that we should get Aziza's crib back to our room. I was happy to move the crib back.

Aziza looked happy. That night she went to bed peacefully.

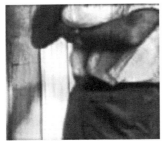

Sleeping perched on my belt

happily taking the first steps

Banging on the glass in my study to let her in …

I open the door …

Pick her up and give her a big kiss … then she engages in her favorite: rummaging

Rummaging some more in the kitchen…

and doing some vacuum cleaning.

We bought a house at 108 Grandview Avenue and had a separate bedroom for Aziza. She slept quietly in her new bedroom. Our bedroom was next to hers. It did not seem to bother Aziza to sleep by herself in a separate bedroom.

We bought intercoms and placed one in Aziza's bedroom, and one in my study in the basement. I watched over Aziza, using those intercoms. A small red bulb lit up whenever the intercom was on.

The intercom we used to watch over Aziza
Red bulb ("the eye") in front in middle

One time, I was caring for Aziza while I was working in my study in the basement. As she woke up, I heard her voice over the intercom saying something that sounded like "I, I, I". I went up to her bedroom and held her in my arms. It felt as if she was agitated about something. But I could not tell what it was. She kept repeating "I, I, I". I tried to think of what she might be saying, but nothing came to mind. I rocked her to sleep and went back to my study. When Joan came back that night, I told her what had happened. She had no idea what the "I, I, I" meant.

The following nights the same thing happened. Aziza would wake up and we would hear her repeat "I, I, I". We were puzzled and we felt helpless. What could she possibly be trying to say?

This went on for a while, until one night Aziza stretched her arm toward the intercom's red light, as she kept repeating, "I, I, I". Could it be that she was scared by the intercom's red button, the "eye" of the intercom, we wondered? Joan had an idea - move the intercom from where it was and place it under Aziza's crib.

That did it. Aziza could no longer see the intercom, and we never heard about the "eye" any more.

Months later, it happened several times that, while I was caring for Aziza, I heard her call over the intercom.

"Pacifier fell! Pacifier fell!"

Every time I went up to her room, I found the pacifier on the floor, but at quite a distance from Aziza's crib. I would wash the pacifier, give it back to Aziza and lay her down in her crib. But the location where I usually found the pacifiers on the floor was puzzling. Pacifiers do not roll easily. If the pacifier had slipped from Aziza's mouth while she was sleeping, it should have fallen on her crib or on the floor close to her crib. How did it get that far away from her crib?

One night I heard Aziza's call over the intercom:

"Pacifier fell! Pacifier fell!"

I went up to Aziza's bedroom, went through the usual routine of washing the pacifier, giving it back to Aziza and laying her down in her bed. I had hardly turned my back to leave the room when Aziza called.

"Pacifier fell! Pacifier fell!"

I turned around. It was hilarious. Aziza did not expect me to turn back so fast. She had her hands still on her mouth pulling out the pacifier, as she prepared to toss it on the floor. Once she had tossed it, she stared at me and sheepishly repeated "Pacifier fell". I doubled up in laughter. I finally got it. It was not the pacifier that she wanted back. She wanted the company. I loved her shrewdness. I took her in my arms and hugged her tightly. I took her with me downstairs to my study and sat her on my lap.

We had a wonderful time together. She rummaged through everything on my desk and pulled my drawers open. I sang to her and we clapped together. Finally she got tired. I took her back to bed and sang to her until she fell asleep. She did not call out again that night about the pacifier.

In Backyard, 108 Grandview Avenue, Ithaca and New York Harbor

In Daddy's arms

Appropriating mommy's hat and daddy's socks

Riding on daddy's shoulders

Aziza's first ride on the bicycle
in front of 108 Grandview Ave, Ithaca

On the ferry boat in New York's harbor, reaching for mommy

On the Beach at Lake Ontario

Stepping into the cold 58-degree water

Back ride

Hop in the air

Sand, shovel and pale

Tugging on the straps of mommy's purse

LULLABIES, FRENCH SONGS, BABYLONIAN SH'BAHOTH

I was usually engrossed in my work. But I was home every evening to have dinner with my family, play with Aziza and put her to bed. I went back to work at night in my study at home. Rarely did I ever go back to my office or the library in the evenings.

I fell asleep as I rocked Aziza to sleep. Joan captured the moment on camera

When I put Aziza to bed I sang to her until she fell asleep. I did not know many lullabies to sing. Harking back to my own childhood, I usually sang to Aziza the French songs I had learned in my Kindergarten days in Baghdad. On occasion, when Aziza did not fall asleep readily, and I had exhausted my repertoire of French songs, I supplemented it with Babylonian Sh'bahoth, religious paeans that we sang in Baghdad on the Sabbath and other Jewish holidays. Aziza did not complain when I switched from French to Hebrew. Hebrew put her to sleep just as easily as French. As for me I was just singing the songs I knew to put my daughter to sleep. I continued to sing my daughter to sleep and then one day, when she was three years old, something wonderful happened.

One Friday night, Joan and I were sitting at the *kiddush* table in our apartment in Yonkers, New York. At the end of the *kiddush* ceremony we began to sing " *yom hashabbath ane kamohoo...*" -- the Sabbath day, there is nothing like it..., a song in honor of the Sabbath. We could not believe our ears when all of a sudden a halting but strong little voice chimed in. It was Aziza! Aziza was singing with us! We were astonished. We stopped singing and just listened to Aziza in utter amazement. Where did she learn the melody, the lyrics? She could not have learned it in the nursery school. They do not teach those songs in this country. Joan and I looked at each other in amazement. Then it dawned on me. *yom hashabbath* was one of those songs I had sung occasionally to Aziza when I put her to bed. She must have learned it effortlessly from those times when I had sung it to her. I expected to have to teach her the Babylonian Sh'bahoth when she grew up. But serendipitously I had hit on a perfect method of teaching her those Sh'bahoth even when she was so little, and without having to work hard at it.

From then on I made a point of singing the traditional Babylonian Sh'bahoth as lullabies. Whenever I put Aziza to bed I sang Sabbath songs to her, and made sure to sing also the songs we sang on each coming holiday. I did the same with our second child, Loolwa. They both learned the Babylonian Sh'bahoth during the times when I put them to bed.

Joan used to say she could tell what the next holiday would be by the songs I sang to the children when I put them to bed.

SCARY TIMES, HAPPY TIMES

One time Aziza, barely a year old, came out of the kitchen with a bottle of liquid cleaner in hand. The top was gone and the bottle was half empty. Joan had used that bottle once or twice before, but she did not use much of it. Where did the rest go? We checked the kitchen floor and we checked the floors in the rest of the house. We checked the toilet. There was trace of spilled cleaner. Where could it have gone? The cleaner had a nice smell. Could Aziza have drunk it? We were petrified when we thought of that. Panic reigned!

We called the pediatrician. He was not in his office. His receptionist would take a message and have him call us back. We waited. A minute passed. It felt as if it were eternity. What if he did not call back for another hour? We had no time to waste. We had to act quickly. We were at our wits' end. What do we do? Should we call the emergency line? We had only one telephone line. What if the pediatrician called in the meantime?

We decided to take our chances.

I called the emergency line. They took the information as fast as I could relay it to them, but I must have been incoherent. I felt as if it was taking them ages. Why couldn't they just get going! Finally they told me the ambulance was on its way. I felt relieved. I hung up. The telephone rang. The pediatrician was on the other end. He was an older man and it was reassuring to talk with him. Calmly he inquired if Aziza was acting normally. I said she was.

"She could not have drunk the cleaner," he assured me. "Even though they smell good, cleaners taste awful".

Besides, I would have seen symptoms of poisoning by now, he told me.

"Do not worry. She is all right. But next time when you leave a message for the pediatrician to call you back, make sure you keep the telephone line free", he advised.

"I will", I promised.

I breathed a sigh of relief, hung up and slumped in the chair.

There were other scary times. Neither Joan nor I had any prior experience with raising children and anything unusual that happened to Aziza was a first for us. But we had also many happy times together. Many of the things we did together were not fancy, but they brought us a lot of pleasure.

I remember fondly the many times when we took Aziza in her carriage, late on Saturday afternoons, and walked to the Faculty Club for a vegetarian meal. I remember those occasions as peaceful times. We looked forward to them.

Joan pushing Aziza's carriage in deep snow, on our way to Cornell's Faculty Club

When Aziza was a little over a year old, she began noticing the traffic lights and their changing colors. Whenever we stopped for a red light, Aziza would make circles in the air with her finger as she kept repeating in a soft voice "round and round and round..." She seemed to be sure that those rounds would change the red to green. And lo and behold, they did. She would clap her hands and triumphantly exclaim, "Tsange to green!" That became family tradition. Whenever we stopped for a red light, the three of us would make circles in the air as we kept repeating "Round and round and round..." When the traffic light had finally changed, everyone would happily exclaim "Tsange to green!" Sometimes, when Aziza was already in college, Joan and I would remember what we used to do when Aziza was little, and would do the same when we had to stop for a red light, "Round and round...".

During my first year at Cornell, Joan and I never went out together without Aziza. We worried about leaving her with a babysitter. But during my second year, one of my colleagues and his wife offered to baby-sit with Aziza. We were very good friends with them, and we agreed.

Joan took me out that night to a big, beautifully lit bowling club. I had never been to a bowling place before. We had a wonderful time that night. Probably not many would think of going to just sit and watch people bowling as an outing. But it was for me. It was wonderful not to have to have to think of lectures that night. Joan seemed as happy to see me relaxed, as I was to see her relax. I loved to watch the players roll those enormous balls and listen to the clicking sounds they made as they hit the pins. Simple pleasure! Even so, I remember that night warmly.

NYU: A LETDOWN

Steve Rousseas, an economist and a native of New York City, had left Cornell's department of economics a year before I arrived to return to his native city and join the faculty at New York University (NYU). When we met on one of Steve's visits back to Cornell, he told me of a $100 million matching grant that NYU had just received from the Ford Foundation. It was one of the largest grants at the time. Steve indicated that he expected the grant to give a major boost to research at the university and suggested that I consider moving to NYU.

It was a tempting idea. I was at the beginning of my career and the pressure of "publish or perish" was ever present. The thought of joining a university awash with research funds was enticing.

Joan thought it would be worthwhile to explore the possibility of joining the faculty at NYU. She felt that it would be easier to raise a Jewish child in New York City than anywhere else in the country. She felt also she would be happier in New York City. Although she never complained about it, Joan was having a hard time in Ithaca. The move from Cambridge to Ithaca was a big drop in our social and intellectual milieu. There were many universities and many choices in Cambridge and the vicinity. There was nothing comparable in Ithaca, and the winter months were particularly confining. Even TV was a problem. There was only one local station, and no TV signal could reach Ithaca from any major center.

I had a long and lively meeting with NYU's economics faculty at the annual meeting of the American Economic Association in December 1964. When I returned home to Ithaca, I told Joan I felt confident I would receive a good offer from NYU. The following day I fell sick with the flu and was in bed for a little over a week. NYU's offer came before I had recovered from the flu.

In August of 1965, we packed our belongings and headed for NYU.

It did not take me long to realize that I had made a

426

mistake in choosing to move to NYU. As to the City itself, there were things I liked, but there was a lot more that I felt I could not live with. Even while we were on the road on our way from Ithaca to the City, I began to have my doubts about whether we had made the right decision. I could feel the difference in the air we breathed. The sky did not look as clear as the sky in Ithaca, and I could see the pollution hanging over in the air. Drivers tailgated me. They honked, they weaved, and they zigzagged around. It was scary. Aziza was sleeping in the bassinet in the back seat, and I worried about being rear-ended. I shared my concerns with Joan. She said she, too, was wondering whether we had made the right decision.

We rented an apartment in a nice part of Yonkers, far away from the congested area of the City. That made us happy and helped calm down our concerns. A magnificent park, Tibbett's Brook Park, was just across the road from our apartment building. It had a beautiful lake, lots of ducks and a variety of birds. We spent many happy Saturdays at that park with our little girl feeding the ducks, watching the birds, flying kites, and scrutinizing every little flower we passed by.

Child ID necklace of Aziza with name and address in Yonkers

Our arrival to Yonkers coincided with a period of increased awareness in the US about the suffering of Russian Jewry under Soviet regime. Not long after our arrival, a demonstration was organized on one Sunday morning in Yonkers to publicize the plight of Russian Jewry. It was one of the first demonstrations to be organized in the US on behalf of Russian Jewry, and there was concern about violence. I had to be out town that day, and could not join in the march. Joan was firm in her resolve to participate in the demonstration.

Feeding the ducks at Tibbett's Brook Park, Yonkers

Teaching Aziza to swim

As Joan described it, the turnout was large and the demonstration orderly. Joan marched in the second row of the demonstration, as she pushed our two-year old daughter in the stroller. It was gratifying for me to learn that many of the participants were non-Jews, including two Yonkers nuns in habit, who marched in the first row of demonstrators.

A Sabbath family walk on a cold day in Yonkers
Our apartment building on Ramsey Rd. in background

Sometimes Joan and Aziza came to visit me in my office in NYU's campus in Washington Square, and we spent time strolling in the Lower East Side of Manhattan before the start of my evening seminar. The little gatherings of Jews in the Lower East Side reminded me of the Jewish gatherings in coffee shops, grocery stores and bakeries in Baghdad during my days of growing up. It evinced in me a mixed sense of sadness and happiness to walk in those neighborhoods and mingle with the people. Sometimes the gatherings merged so much in my thoughts with the gatherings I had seen in Baghdad that I came close to feeling that my community had never died out, that we were never uprooted. Then I would catch myself. Alas, my community was gone!

Even so, it was nice to see that something so close to what I had witnessed in the old country was still alive.

We had our dinner together in a *kasher* restaurant in the Lower East Side - corned beef sandwiches. Joan loved them, and we all joined in.

At other times, Joan and Aziza met me at the end of the Bronx subway line, as I returned at night from my seminar in Washington Square. I felt so happy to see my family at the end of that long day. We would go to a *kasher* restaurant near the subway station and have our usual dinner of cold cuts on rye bread. The owner knew the routine. He no longer asked what we wanted for dinner. He just made the sandwiches and brought them to our table.

At NYU I taught econometrics, a branch in economics that deals with measurements. NYU had two campuses - one in the Bronx and one in downtown Washington Square. I taught one course in each campus.

Although I taught in a field I loved, I was not happy with what I saw at NYU as a university, particularly in Washington Square, the largest constituent of the university. I had a hard time convincing myself that the buildings scattered all over in the midst of bustling Washington Square were anything like a campus. There was no organic tie, no sense of a community of scholars. Wall Street dominated the economics department. Most faculty members were busy with their consulting work on Wall Street, away from their offices. The building that housed the faculty offices of the economics department felt more like a ghost town than a university department. Faculty offices were mostly empty. Professors came to give their lectures, held their office hours and left. I missed the intellectual stimulus, the interaction with colleagues. I missed the sense of community, of collegiality. Often I was the only one in my office on that floor. It was depressing.

I was still relatively new to life in the US when I explored with NYU the possibility of joining the faculty. I did not grow up in a society with the variety of universities that we have in the US. I had heard about good universities and not so good universities. But I had no realistic idea of what that meant. Up until then I had been to two universities,

Harvard and Cornell and I had spent a short two-month period at the University of Wisconsin in Madison. All three were outstanding institutions of learning. In my own mind, I thought of other universities as an extension of what I had seen, with some differences here and there. Hard as I tried, I could not realistically imagine the differences between the various institutions. It never crossed my mind that just as human beings differed significantly in their manner of behavior, their sense of dignity, genteelness and their sense of tradition and history, so did the universities.

There was a sense of class, a sense of dignity and mutual respect that permeated much of the relationship among the faculty and student body at the two universities I had been affiliated with for an extended period of time. I was taken aback to discover how different it was at NYU. The relationship among faculty members, and the relationship between faculty and students hardly exhibited any of what I had experienced at Harvard and Cornell. It was disturbing to see faculty members building themselves up by knocking down colleagues instead of elevating themselves by their own achievements. At Harvard, at Cornell I heard faculty members speak highly of their colleagues or take pride in their colleagues' accomplishments. During the two years I spent at NYU I never heard a faculty member take pride in the breakthrough or the achievement of a colleague. Instead there was a lot of backbiting.

And the hardest thing for me was the fact that NYU was governed autocratically, more as a corporation than a University. The administration called the shots. Faculty was ordered around, often disdainfully. Faculty involvement in university governance was practically non-existent, as was the faculty's role in making the vital decisions in their respective departments.

I was turned off by what I saw and experienced. I submitted my resignation during my first year at NYU. I had no back up University to turn to. But I knew I did not want to be part of that environment. The Department chairman, Manny Stein, prevailed on me to withdraw my resignation, promising a change for the better. I agreed to stay on. But I

431

saw no tangible improvement and no end to what seemed to have been a tradition of backbiting.

My disillusionment with NYU was aggravated by my difficulties in getting used to the way of life in New York. New York was densely populated. There was so much energy radiating all around. The pushing and shoving at the subway stations during rush hours was horrific. At first I used to stand aside and let people go ahead of me, just to avoid jostling them. But I often ended up left behind on the platform as the subway closed its doors and left the station. In the end, what distressed me most was the realization that gradually I was slipping into the same methods I had tried to avoid, just to survive in that environment. I felt that was not what I wanted from life.

I decided I would leave at the end of my second year at NYU. I submitted my resignation, and this time for good.

I joined the faculty at McGill University in Montreal in the fall of that year (1967).

THE DRUNKEN LITTLE TODDLER

Aziza was three years old when on a Saturday night during our second year in Yonkers, the three of us prepared to go out for the evening. Aziza walked ahead of us as we left the apartment. We noticed that she did not seem as steady as usual. Twice her head brushed against the wall as we made our way through the front corridor. Joan asked her if she was feeling OK. Aziza said she was. We put Aziza in her child seat in the back seat of the car and drove off. Aziza was an active little girl. She would normally make observations about places we drove past or play her round-and-round game with the traffic lights whenever we stopped for a red light. That night she was unusually quiet. We wondered if she was OK. It did not take long for the answer to come. Aziza began to throw up. We pulled over and rushed to her in the backseat. Aziza was throwing up violently, and the vomit had a strong smell of wine. What could it be? Aziza could not talk. She was dazed. We were terrified. We sped home to call the pediatrician. Fortunately we were not far from home at the time.

By the time we made it home Aziza was out of it. She did not respond to anything we said to her. Her eyes were closed. She felt like limp meat when I carried her in my arms and laid her in bed. Seeing her in such a condition was frightening.

Aziza sleeping peacefully

While I was on the phone waiting for the operator to page the pediatrician, Joan went to the refrigerator to check. She came back with an empty bottle of wine in her hand. That was the bottle from which we served wine for *kiddush* on the Sabbath. There was almost a quarter of a bottle left when we said the *kiddush* that morning.

We realized what must have happened. Before we had left, Aziza said she was thirsty. She went to the refrigerator in the kitchen to get a drink. Instead of drinking water she must have drunk whatever wine there was in that bottle. Aziza loved the taste of the sweet wine we served for *kiddush.*

In the meantime, the pediatrician was on the phone. He said it was good that she threw up and got the wine out of her system, but that chances were that she would be feeling the effect for a while. He asked that we watch her vital signs until she woke up, and stay in touch with him regarding any irregularities.

Aziza was in deep sleep. She did not wake up for over twenty-four hours. Those were scary hours. Joan and I took turns sitting next to her and watching her vital signs until she awakened.

We were elated when Aziza finally opened her eyes and was back with us after those long scary hours. We could not hug her enough and tell her how much we had missed her. She did not seem to be aware that anything unusual had happened.

BEGINNINGS OF A REWARDING ASSOCIATION

During my second year at NYU, the Office of Economics at the Federal Power Commission (FPC) asked the Brookings Institution for help in finding a qualified econometrician to evaluate an econometric model that the FPC had developed for depicting the relationship between the price and the supply of natural gas in the US.

The Brookings Institution is a Washington-based non-profit organization devoted to research and education. It was established in 1927, and is named after an American philanthropist, Robert Somers Brookings. The FPC is a former independent, five-commissioner regulatory agency. It was established in 1935 by the Federal Power Act. Its responsibilities included, among other things, setting a ceiling on the wellhead price of natural gas sold by oil and gas producers to interstate gas pipelines companies. The FPC was officially abolished in 1978. The Federal Energy Regulatory Agency (FERC), which was established on October 1, 1977, has since replaced the FPC.

FPC's natural gas model was developed under the leadership of Haskell Wald, FPC's chief economist, and Harold Wein, originally a faculty member at the University of Michigan, Ann Arbor's department of Economics, with the support of FPC's Office of Economics. FPC was the first Federal agency that attempted to make use of econometric methods in regulatory decision-making. The model itself was the first in scope and size in the field of natural gas economics. It was intended to help FPC's commissioners evaluate the impact of alternative ceiling prices on the supply of natural gas in the US and determine the optimal choice of a ceiling price that would elicit an adequate supply of natural gas.

Producers of oil and gas argued that that particular model suffered infirmities that invalidated its use in FPC's decision making. They took their case to the US Supreme Court. The court ruled in their favor.

Bill Capron, Senior Fellow at the Brookings Institution recommended my name to the FPC. The FPC asked to do an evaluation of the FPC's model and make a recommendation to either abandon the FPC's modeling effort altogether or outline a path of research that would lead to the development of a defensible model the FPC could use in decision making.

I had no background in the energy field. But the idea of working on evaluating an econometric model that was on the frontier of knowledge appealed to me. The staff that worked on that model helped me acquire quickly the background I needed in the field of natural gas and assisted me in my research work.

My family and I left New York for Washington, DC at the end of May 1967 and rented a garden apartment in Prince George County, Maryland. I was very happy to be back in Washington. I loved the hot weather in Washington, even though at times it got muggy. Joan and Aziza loved the outdoors life too. Aziza felt much freer to play with the children in the neighborhood than she did in Yonkers.

Joan had been training Aziza in Jewish practices. When it was time to light the candles on Friday night, Joan would call Aziza in to join her in lighting the candles. But before coming in, Aziza would turn to her friends and eagerly ask each one of them to go home quickly and light the Sabbath candles with their mommy. Finally Joan had to explain to Aziza that it was not necessary for her to remind her friends of the Sabbath candle lighting, since they were not Jewish, but that she was welcome to invite them to be her guests and watch her light the Sabbath candles.

The first day I arrived at the FPC, I was taken around and introduced to several members of the FPC staff. It was during that first day that I met Sy Wenner, an FPC Administrative Law Judge who had presided over the hearings on FPC's natural gas model. Sy and I had a very productive meeting that day and we became close friends. But our first meeting had a hilarious side, as well.

With Aziza on the way home in Prince George County, MD

We had arrived to Washington during the week when the 1967 Six Day War broke out in Israel. We were all worried for Israel's future, for its very existence. I first heard the news from Joan one afternoon, just as we were getting ready to leave for Washington. When I went home that afternoon she greeted me with tears.

"War broke out! War broke out!" she cried.

Visions of people lying in pools of blood on the ground floated into my mind.

It was lunchtime when Sy and I met in his office. Sy had a transistor radio glued to his ear. We shook hands and exchanged pleasantries. At first, though, Sy kept retreating to a corner with his radio, wanting to hear the news and, at the same time, not wanting to offend me. It turned out that from my last name he deduced I was an Arab and his inherent good manners dictated that he not offend me. After all, Israel was winning and as an Arab that would make me unhappy.

Sy Wenner posing with my (second) daughter Loolwa
February 25, 1979

Eventually, Sy and I cleared up that misunderstanding and discovered we were on the same wavelength on many other aspects of life, too. He was an ardent Zionist and was also extremely interested in the history of the Babylonian Jews, their culture and their pronunciation of the Hebrew language. In fact I made several tapes for him reading articles from a Hebrew newspaper he used to send me regularly to Montreal and, later, to San Francisco so that he could become familiar with the Babylonian pronunciation.

I spent the three months in DC working intensively on the project. I let loose my creativity and originality, but I had also the help of four dedicated staff members of FPC's

Office of Economics. I was given access to all the files, data and computer facilities I needed. The amount and quality of work I was able to do during those three months with the help I received from the FPC and with the assistance I received from the oil and gas industry while in Washington was not anything I could have accomplished anywhere else. It was an exciting period. It was also the period when I began to blossom as a researcher.

By the end of the three-month period, it was clear to me that FPC's model, like any other ground breaking effort, did suffer from limitations but that it had many attributes that were overlooked in the litigation process. I had thoughts on how the work could be designed in a way that would lead to the development of a resilient model that did not suffer from those limitations and that had attributes not possessed by FPC's model.

I gave a long seminar to the FPC about my findings and recommendation, and then left with my family for Montreal for the beginning of the fall term at McGill University. Not long after that I received an offer from the FPC to lead the effort to develop the type of model I described in my report to the FPC.

I accepted the challenge enthusiastically.

That was the beginning of a mutually rewarding research association that lasted for several years. It opened up a whole new field of research work, which came to be known as Energy Modeling. I feel privileged to be able to count myself among the founders of that field. My research and publications in energy modeling and related fields continued till the end of my professional career.

It was invigorating to be in the vanguard of a nascent field that was hardly of interest to economists or to economic departments in any university before the 1973 oil embargo and the explosion of the world oil prices that followed in its aftermath.

McGILL

My connection with McGill was accidental.

In the fall of 1966, I met Jamil Hillel during *rosh hashana* services held by Jews of Babylonian extractions living in Manhattan. At that time I had just entered my second year at NYU. Jamil was an old classmate from l'Alliance Israelite. He lived in Montreal, and from him I learned that several of our former classmates were living in Montreal. He invited me to come to Montreal for a reunion.

The idea appealed to me. A visit to Montreal would also give me an opportunity to visit the Spanish and Portuguese synagogue in Montreal, a synagogue I had heard a lot about. When the first Jewish settlers arrived in Canada, they wrote to several congregations in the US asking for help in setting up their own congregation. The only congregation that responded was the Spanish and Portuguese synagogue in New York. They sent prayer books and ceremonial objects and also dispatched a cantor to Montreal to help the new congregation. When in 1767 the new congregation officially incorporated in Canada, its members chose to adopt the same name as their mentor congregation in New York, but they added the word Montreal to their name to identify their location, "Shearith Israel –the Spanish and Portuguese Synagogue, Montreal". While in New York my family and I had attended many services in the Spanish and Portuguese synagogue in New York, itself the oldest congregation in the US, dating back to September 1654. I loved the décor and civility and the tunes of the prayers in that synagogue.

Two weeks after meeting Jamil, my family and I took time off during the *sukkoth* holidays, and drove to Montreal to meet with my old classmates and celebrate the holiday with them.

The route to Montreal was straightforward. We did not think we needed a map to get there. When we were at the outskirts of Montreal, Joan took note of the fact that we had crossed "Point Bridge". Knowing that we crossed it on the way into Montreal would make it easy to take the same route out of Montreal. We would just look for Point Bridge and cross back over it. It never crossed my mind that the sign was in both French and English and that the first word was not the bridge's name "Point" but "pont", which was simply French for bridge. On our way back from Montreal we took the first "Pont Bridge" we came across. We found ourselves in the middle of nowhere by the time we had discovered our mistake. I could kick myself. Joan could be excused. She never took French. But I! I was supposed to be the wiz in French. I should have known that 'pont' was French for bridge, any bridge. But the fact was that up until then I had thought of Canada as an extension of the US and assumed everything was labeled in English just as it always was in the US. After living in Canada for quite some time I realized that while the two countries "appeared" to be the same, there were fundamental differences in culture, worldview, political institutions, the role of the church and the role of the government in those two countries. When in 1975, we crossed the Canadian border on our way to Stanford never to return to Canada, I remember Joan remarking with teary eyes,

"When we left New York for McGill I was an ardent critic of the US. After eight years in Canada, I leave as a roaring pro American".

The fact that the signs in Montreal were written sometimes in English, sometimes in French and sometimes in both languages turned out to be a source of great confusion for me, a nightmare. (I believe that to day all signs are required to be in French only). Not being able to recognize instantly the language of the sign or the ad, I had a tendency to read ads and signs as if they were all French. Perhaps I did so because of my school upbringing in French. But it was frustrating for me when I could not make sense of what I had read, and I felt my world was turned upside down when I realized I had misread an English sign in French. I remember one day when my family and I took a stroll on Sherbrooke Street, a main street that bordered McGill's campus. I spotted a big billboard sign "Sales". It was a store advertising their sales. I read it in French as sales, which means dirty. What dirty things were they calling attention to, I wondered? Dirty air, perhaps? Dirty streets? Was it an ad by a store that sold pornographic material? It took me a while before I realized it was an English ad by a store advertising their sales, and it was frustrating to realize how much I had fretted for nothing.

Our first visit to Montreal was enjoyable. I was happy to meet my former classmates. We updated each other on what had transpired in our lives and exchanged addresses and phone numbers.

My family and I got to worship in the Spanish and Portuguese synagogue, as well. The atmosphere in the synagogue was less formal than in New York's Spanish and Portuguese. The most noticeable difference was that only the congregation's officers in Montreal wore cylinder hats, while in New York many in the congregants wore those hats, too. I noticed also that most of the congregants in the Montreal congregation were immigrants from Central and Eastern Europe, while in New York most of the congregants were well established Americans who were descendants of families that were members of the congregation for generations. I was happy to participate in the services and listen to the majestic tunes of the Jews of Spain and Portugal sung in the congregation in Montreal.

The cleanliness of Montreal, its tree-lined streets and its relatively slow pace of life impressed me. It was a thrill to hear French spoken around, although it sounded very different from the French I had learned from our French teachers in l'Alliance. Montreal had a large Jewish community of mostly observant Jews. The area along Victoria Street, a major street in the residential part of Montreal, wore a festive aura during the intermediate days of the *sukkoth* holidays. People with skullcaps wearing festive clothes walked around, carrying their Lulab (a bunch of palm branch and other shoots that form the four species) and Ethrogh (citrus fruit) - all used in Jewish ritual on the Feast of *sukkoth*. Some strolled leisurely as they held hands with their children, others filled the coffee shops on Van Horne Avenue, a wide street that crossed Victoria Street – a main road in Montreal.

During our reunion one of my former classmates

urged me to move to Montreal. He spoke highly of McGill and suggested that perhaps the university might be interested in a person with my background, in which case I would be able to move to Montreal and be close to my former classmates. He urged me to contact the university and inquire about the availability of a position for a person with my interests. I took his suggestion under advisement. We left for New York at the end of the holiday, and I went back to my teaching responsibilities at NYU.

When I saw no tangible change in the environment at NYU and realized I had difficulty adjusting to the way of life in New York, I contacted McGill to inquire if they had an opening for a person with my interest. They did. I met with the Department in Montreal. We agreed that I would teach the advanced graduate seminar and the undergraduate course in econometrics. I moved to McGill in the fall of 1967.

BASTION OF ENGLISH DOMINATION?

I was very happy to be affiliated with McGill. Founded in 1821 by the Scottish philanthropist James McGill, McGill is the oldest university in Canada. It was initially known as the Royal Institution for Higher Learning, and for many in the British aristocracy, McGill was the university of choice in North America. A sense of culture and distinction was woven into the fabric of McGill, and I could feel it even in the way meals were served in the faculty club.

My undergraduate students were as sharp as my students at Cornell, and I was particularly gratified when the 1968 Course Guide reported "The class viewed Khazzoom as exceptional".

A large number of McGill's undergraduates came from the US. At McGill they could acquire an undergraduate education comparable to that of the leading universities in the US, but at a fraction of the tuition fee. The majority did not continue with McGill past their undergraduate degree. Most were lured away by offers of generous financial aid from first-rate graduate schools in the US, with which McGill did not have the resources to compete. The result was that McGill's Graduate School lost most of the best minds among the university's undergraduate student body.

In my office at McGill, March 1973
Behind me hung art work and a framed *kiddush* cup made by Aziza in the fall of 1965, when she was just two

Within the societal milieu surrounding McGill, there were pronounced differences in the culture and life pattern of French and English Canadians. My recollection of English Canadians was that they tended to be competitive, work long hours, take short breaks from work, and often transact business over lunch to save time. In contrast, French Canadians seemed to be less competitive, less enterprising or ambitious, and seemed to prefer a much more leisurely pace of life. It was probably not surprising that English Canadians stood out in the corporate world and tended to hold positions of leadership in business and commerce while the French Canadians tended to gravitate more toward the government sector and family small businesses.

I also noticed through the years that English

Canadians tended to be more open to and more welcoming of new immigrants than the French Canadians. French Canadians vacillated between shunning immigrants for fear that they would dilute the French Canadian culture and way of living, on the one hand, and bemoaning the fact that the vast majority of the immigrants to Quebec chose to be part of English Canada and sent their children to English speaking schools.

Aziza's *kiddush* cup. It hung in my office

Perhaps not unrelated to this is the attitude toward the Jewish community. There was a greater sense of friendship toward the Jewish community among English Canadians than among French Canadians. Almost the whole Jewish community, including even Jewish immigrants from North Africa whose mother tongue was French and who did not speak English, tended to associate with English Canada. There was also greater evidence of anti-Semitism among French Canadians than among English Canadians, which did not surprise me in light of the differing attitudes of these two groups toward the Jewish community.

But most intriguing were the differences I noticed in the attitudes of French and English Canadians toward the

US. Most English Canadians I have met tended to be wary of Americans; some hated Americans and "US domination". The rhetoric of the English press in Montreal was strident in its antipathy toward the US. The editorials and commentaries of the English network of the Canadian Broadcasting Corporation were often in the forefront in anti American rhetoric. And some of the radio broadcasts and talk shows were so denigrating of anything American that they bordered on the nauseating. I remember once remarking to Joan, when we were on one of our extended stays in Washington, DC, how refreshing it was to turn on the radio and not hear derogatory remarks about the US.

I remember also one time when I was invited to be a panel discussant in a conference, which was sponsored jointly by Sir George Williams University and Loyola University, both English universities in Montreal (now merged together as one university). The conference was called to discuss the oil crisis, following the Arab oil embargo in 1973, and explore policy options to deal with its aftermath. Morry Adelman of MIT, another panelist, was snowed in and could not make it for the conference. He was the only panelist from the US who was invited to participate in the panel. The rest of the panelists were faculty members from Canadian universities.

The moderator introduced the panel and as he announced that MIT's Adelman would not be in, he added

"And isn't wonderful that our panel is made up exclusively of Canadians with no Americans".

That made me furious.

When it was my turn to speak I took time first to disassociate myself from the moderator's remarks and to deplore the fact that he chose to inject nationalistic themes in a scholarly conference, of all things. Several participants walked out of the conference room, as I made those remarks. Before proceeding to my prepared remarks, I waited until everyone who wanted to walk out had an opportunity to do so.

Oddly, French Canadians who harbored anti English feelings were generally pro Americans. In fact some of the Quebecois separatists had often talked about leaving Canada and joining the US as the 51st state. Maybe that was their way of spiting English Canada.

Although my early education was in French, I could never get steamed up about whether one spoke English or French. But the whirlpool of the French-English controversy frequently dragged in those who had no interest in being part of the language and cultural battle. In many ways, the problem was similar to the black-white problem in the US, where people sometimes make assumptions about one another based solely on skin color. In Quebec you were frequently pigeonholed as belonging to one bloc or another the moment you opened your mouth and spoke one language or another. Often, that determined the attitude of the other side toward you.

I was caught in those situations many times during the period we lived in Montreal.

One summer evening, I accompanied my eight-year-old daughter Aziza when she went for a bike ride on the campus' main yard across the street from our apartment building. There was no one in the yard when we arrived. Not long after, a man walked in with a big dog. He took the dog off its leash, and the dog immediately charged toward Aziza. Aziza was terrified. She fell off the bicycle and skinned her knee. As I rushed to help her, I asked the dog's owner to put his dog back on its leash. He refused and, in an angry tone, told me in a French-heavy accent,

"If you don't like it, go back to where you came from."

How did he know where I came from? I turned to him.

"Where did I come from?" I asked.

"England, damn you", he responded angrily.

My goodness. I came from England? I never knew that. I spoke to him in English, and that placed me firmly in the camp of the "English Oppressor".

That was not the first time I got dragged into the French-English battle.

When I joined McGill, Marcel Dagenais, a colleague at the University of Montreal, and I planned to meet over lunch on the campus of the University of Montreal – a French university. I got there too early for our meeting, and I took a short walk in the campus' neighborhood. The University of Montreal was located in an exclusively French part of town. It felt as if I was in an entirely different world. In downtown Montreal, and even on McGill's campus one could hear both French and English spoken. But in this neighborhood one could hear only French.

I stopped in a restaurant. When the waiter came, I ordered an English muffin and a cup of coffee. The waiter's demeanor suddenly changed. His face tightened and he seemed to be at a loss for words. Finally, he opened up and in an angry tone told me,

"No English muffins here!"

I was taken aback by his tone.

"Huh. I thought restaurants usually served English muffins," I mused loudly. And then, sheepishly, but perhaps foolishly, I added

"I thought the sign outside said restaurant."

"Well if you can read French, why don't you speak French?" he yelled.

He brought black coffee. I asked if I could have sugar and milk. He ignored me.

When I met with Marcel and told him about my restaurant experience, he laughed.

"You never speak English around here and you never ask for an English muffin in a French restaurant."

That was my first taste of the French-English conflict.

Later I learned one more lesson from that meeting. When Marcel and I sat to have lunch together, I brought up the subject of budgeting for a joint seminar and the fact that some of our speakers would not be bilingual. Marcel did take up those issues. But I noticed that he seemed uncomfortable when he was talking about the subject. Our lunch lasted less than an hour.

It was only a year later when Marcel and his wife came to visit us for dinner that he told Joan that the only time he had ever talked business over lunch was with me during our first meeting on the campus of the University of Montreal. He also told Joan how surprised he was that our lunch was so short. For French Canadians, Marcel explained, lunch was a semi festive occasion, that French Canadians took at least an hour and a half for lunch, and that business discussion over lunch was taboo.

McGill's geographic location in the heart of French-speaking Quebec, coupled with its international reputation as Canada's premier research university, catapulted the university to the center of the French-English controversy about "English Domination". McGill, now labeled the "Bastion of English Domination", became the target of hostility among Quebec's French nationalists. During my first semester at McGill, one bomb was discovered in Leacock building, where my classes met regularly. The provincial government regularly subjected McGill to protracted delays in releasing funds it owed to the university. That hampered the ability of the university to make offers to new faculty in time, and we lost many promising candidates as a result. Instead of building up the French institutions of higher learning to rival McGill, the preferred method of the provincial government appeared to be one of bringing McGill down to the level of the French universities in the province.

At McGill we had to compete in the market for new faculty with other universities in North America. We had to offer competitive salaries in order to attract and keep top faculty. French universities had a much easier time of it. French instructors were captive to the French universities in Quebec. There was nowhere else in North America where they could teach in French, and they had to settle for lower salaries and less favorable working conditions than the faculty at comparable universities in the US and English Canada.

During my last year at McGill, the university dipped into its endowment funds to the tune of six million dollars to finance a gaping deficit it had incurred to maintain its standards in the face of the tactics of the provincial government of Quebec. At the time, McGill's endowment of C$120 million was the largest of any Canadian university. Still, six million dollars was a big chunk of it, and I could see the handwriting on the wall. There was no letup in the provincial government's noose tightening.

It was primarily this antagonistic atmosphere that drove me into leaving that honorable institution.

LUNCHING IN THE "TUMMEL" WITH MY YOUNGER DAUGHTER

Except for a month or so during the summer time when the temperature was warm enough for a swim in an unheated swimming pool, the weather in Montreal was mostly cold. In the depth of the winter months the low temperature dipped to the mid and high twenties below zero Fahrenheit. One time the low stayed in the twenties below for several days. When it finally made it up to minus twelve, the daily Montreal Gazette had a cartoon that showed a man remarking to his friend "Isn't it wonderful to enjoy this warm breeze."

I used to watch the Canadian Broadcasting Corporation (CBC) nightly news and listen wistfully as the weatherman gave his prediction of the weather conditions in British Columbia.

"Vancouver's high to-morrow will be 33 degrees!"

Wouldn't it be nice, I used to think to myself, if we could get those kinds of warm temperatures here in Montreal and have the snow in the streets melt some?

Having grown up in a warm climate, I had difficulty getting used to bundling up every time I went outside. I rarely had to put on an overcoat in Baghdad. In Montreal, I felt so hemmed in between those layers of sweaters, jacket, Inuit snow jacket, earmuffs, fur hat, and tire-like snow boots.

Native Canadians were used to snow, and no one seemed to get too excited when a storm dumped "only" two feet of snow. Montreal was well equipped to clear the streets almost as fast as the snow fell. Aziza and Loolwa loved to play in the snow. I liked to watch the snow coming down, but from the warmth of our living room.

449

Outside I shivered, no matter how much I bundled up. But I did go out to be with my daughters, since they loved so much to play in the snow. We bought a big sled. Aziza and Loolwa loved to have me pull them around in the sled. They joined me enthusiastically for the Friday night trips to the Sephardi synagogue, when we lived in Chomedey, on the outskirts of Montreal. Aziza and Loolwa sat on the sled and I pulled it to the synagogue and back home. They clapped and sang Shabbat songs all the way to the synagogue and back. They loved the ride, and I loved to play the tired horse pulling the sled.

One time, I was scheduled to be in Washington, DC for my regular monthly trip to the Federal Power Commission. The sky was clear that afternoon when I drove home from the university to be with my family before taking the overnight train to Washington. On the way home, I heard the weather forecast – twelve inches of snow expected to fall overnight. That was not terribly much by Montreal's standards. At home I felt too tired to take the trip that night.

"Maybe I should leave to-morrow morning and have a restful sleep at home instead of sleeping on the train," I thought.

Early that night the forecast was revised up to two feet of snow - not comforting, but still not too much of a problem for Montreal. By morning when I got up to look outside, the whole entrance to our house was covered with snow. There were close to three feet of snow on the ground, and it was still snowing.

We were confined in our homes for three days, until Friday of that week when the snow-clearing equipment finally managed to reach our neighborhood. Because of the amount of snow that had fallen, there was not enough equipment to haul the snow away from anywhere except for the main arteries. On side streets such as ours, the snow was cleared from the middle of the street and piled on top of the snow that had already fallen on the sidewalks.

On Friday afternoon Joan and I worked hard to dig a passage out of our house to the middle of the street. Then my two daughters rode the sled as I pulled on our way to the synagogue at the intersection of two side streets, five blocks away from our home. I went a long way past that intersection before I realized I had overshot. When we returned we could barely identify the intersection. The snow was piled so high that the intersection looked like one unbroken wall.

We returned home without attending the services. The children were not a bit perturbed. They got a longer ride than usual that Friday night, and they loved it.

When we lived in the outskirts of Montreal, I drove to campus and parked my car in the garage, a short hundred yards away from my office. The garage was built on a hill. To get to my office I had to walk down the ramp or down the steps outside the garage. Most of the time both ramp and steps were covered with ice, and I invariably found myself sprawled all over the place on my way down to my office. Most of my colleagues were native Canadians and they seemed to enjoy the challenge. When they slid, they slid down with ease and grace. I used to watch and marvel at their skill. Hard as I tried to follow their moves, I was never able to make it.

McGill had an extensive system of heated underground tunnels that connected the university buildings. And I have fond memories of those tunnels. Loolwa, my second daughter -- born in 1969 -- loved the "tummel", as she called it, and Loolwa and I had lunch at the "tummel" every Wednesday afternoon. I loved the occasion and looked forward to my time with my daughter. Loolwa was four when we started this tradition.

Loolwa would get dressed up and ready for me to pick her up from our apartment across the street from campus. "I am going with my daddy to the tummel" Loolwa would announce proudly, when I went to pick her up from our apartment across the street from campus. She carried a little purse with her when we went for our weekly outing. In it she carried neatly folded napkins, which she would spread carefully over the table when we sat together to eat our lunch.

In the tunnel, Loolwa ran, skipped, hopped, danced, and sang happily as we walked on our way for lunch. Then she would run toward me to carry her when she got tired. I loved to watch her unwind. It was wonderful to see her feel free to run around unhindered.

Our apartment building across the street from campus, one of several buildings McGill owned

Mc Gill had a large dining room at the end of the tunnel, with comfortable seats and a score of vending machines. It was a spotless place. Loolwa was in charge, and she chose our menu for the day. She carefully decided on each item, put the money in the slot, picked up the item, and gave it to me to hold until she had finished her selections. I stood behind, amazed at her sense of order. She was so little. Loolwa chose the table on which we had lunch. She took the napkins out of her purse and carefully spread them over the table. She divided up what she had bought between the two of us - half for her and half for me, and we chatted as we ate. I still remember how I relished every bite I took that afternoon. I never kept track of the time, never felt in a hurry to finish lunch on those afternoons.

I wish those moments had lasted forever.

No Church-State Separation

The biggest surprise of our life in Canada was the discovery that in Canada, unlike the US, there is no separation between church and state and that there were no public schools. There were schools that were called public, but they were in fact denominational.

I learned about that when Joan and I were in the process of buying a house in Montreal. We were close to the final stage of closing when Madame Prudhomme, our real estate agent, surprised us with her question.

"To which school system you want your real estate taxes to go - to the Catholic or the Protestant?"

Joan and I were taken aback. Use tax money to fund denominational schools? Could Madame Prudhomme be joking? No she was not. She was dead serious. What if we did not want our taxes to support any denominational school system? That was impossible, if we wanted to own a house. Was there a public school system? Yes, there was but it was "not what you Americans call public". It was the Protestant school system which people call the public school system.

"So there is no non-denominational school system?" I asked.

" No there is not. Canada had no church-state separation."

Our only choice, then, was to dedicate our tax payment to one of the two denominational school systems, otherwise our pending house purchase would not go through.

It did not take us much time to decide we would not go ahead with the transaction. We were against paying for denominational schools with public funds. We lived in rented apartments throughout the rest of our years in Canada.

It was at that time that I began to understand why Montreal had such a thriving system of private Jewish schools. Many Jews did not want to have their children attend Catholic or Protestant schools. The only other choice they had was to send their children to private Jewish schools or private secular schools. Over half of the Jewish children in Montreal attended Jewish schools. Montreal boasted of two modern orthodox Jewish schools, K-12, with large enrolments: the Hebrew Academy and the Talmud Torah. These two schools integrated intensive study of Judaism with the study of secular subjects. Additionally, there were so many other Jewish schools to choose from - the liberal, the cultural, the Yeshiva, the ultra orthodox, the Habbad boys school, the Habbad Beth Rivka school for girls....

The Hebrew Academy of Montreal maintained high academic standards and was very much in demand by modern observant parents. When we arrived in Montreal in the fall of 1967, the enrolment in the Hebrew Academy had already been closed. I searched for an alternative Jewish school of good quality that Aziza could attend. The only candidate was Beth Rivka, Habbad's school for girls. Joan and I had a lot of misgivings about sending our daughter to Habbad, because of their tendency to give priority to boys over girls' education and because of the fact that we suspected their secular curriculum was not up to snuff.

I had a meeting with Beth Rivka's principal. He was an educator with a doctorate in psychology. He assured me that my fears were unfounded, that the school was committed to ensuring that girls received an equally good education as boys and that he intended to make secular teaching an integral part of Beth Rivka's curriculum.

During that meeting, it became apparent to me that the principal was anxious to have Aziza enroll in his school, maybe because it would be a feather in the school's cap to have the daughter of a McGill's professor enrolled in Beth Rivka. I worried a lot about that, and wondered about the extent to which he was committed to doing what he told me he would. But in the final analysis I did not really have much choice. I felt I got as much assurances as I could. I enrolled Aziza in Habbad and had her placed on the waiting list at the Hebrew Academy.

Some two months later, it became clear that Aziza was not being challenged in Beth Rivka. Joan and I had a feeling that things had just been drifting, and Aziza did not seem to be learning much. She talked of being bored. I went to meet the principal and confronted him with my suspicion that, contrary to his earlier assurances, Aziza was not learning much and that girls were given short shrift in that school. His response was revealing.

"But isn't it better than nothing?" he exclaimed

I remember those words, and I remember my response as well.

"Is the alternative for girls really nothing?"

I could not believe that a professional with a doctorate in psychology would hold the view that all little girls could get were the crumbs and that the alternative was just nothing, not even crumbs.

That day I went to the Hebrew Academy and met with the principal. I explained that we could not afford to let a bright Jewish child wither in a school that viewed the education of girls so poorly. I appealed to him to make room for Aziza in the Hebrew Academy during that semester. He agreed. I went to Beth Rivka, picked up my daughter and drove back to the Hebrew Academy.

Aziza at Montreal's Hebrew Academy, April 1968   Aziza ironing Meidi cover for Sabbath

Aziza adjusted beautifully in the Hebrew Academy. It was a thrill to see how she thrived in that environment, how excited she felt about the new things she was learning and the new skills she was acquiring. I appreciated the learning environment in that school.

I went to the Hebrew Academy once every week to join Aziza for lunch and I remember those occasions warmly.

455

Joan and I served on the board of directors of the Hebrew Academy of Montreal during the years we spent in Montreal. It was gratifying to be part of a small community of board members that was so committed to excellence in modern Jewish education.

Joan volunteered to help the school in many ways. Her trademark was her unique design of Kippot, the skullcaps she crocheted for the school. The school sold those skullcaps and the proceeds went to fund the school's operation. In time a growing cadre of Jewish people, young and old, students and parents of students of the Hebrew Academy could be seen in the streets of Montreal wearing Joan's trademark Kippa. Joan developed an elbow inflammation because of the incessant crocheting she did.

Joan's Kippot – Different color combinations, sizes, thread weight
all had in common the design of the six-pointed Star of David

BUILDING BRIDGES

Not long after we arrived in Montreal, I watched an interview Quebec's provincial Minister of Immigration gave on CBC's French network. The minister bemoaned the tendency of the immigrants to Quebec to turn their back on French Canada and associate themselves with English Canada. He dwelt, in particular, on the Jewish arrivals from North Africa.

"Fifteen thousand Jewish immigrants from North Africa now live in Quebec. Their mother language is French. Most of them did not speak a word of English when they came here. Yet practically all of them are now part of English Canada," the minister noted in a grieving tone.

I felt touched by what the minister had said. I thought highly of the French culture and felt sympathy for the plight of the French Canadians, who seemed to have been shunned by the rest of the Canadians, old settlers and recent comers alike. I felt it was abnormal for the English and the French cultures to be living side-by-side, yet staying miles apart from each other. We needed to find a way to build bridges to overcome this divide, I thought. There was much to be gained from breaking down barriers.

I thought particularly of the Jewish community in Montreal, one hundred and twenty thousand strong. It aligned itself almost exclusively with English Canada. Wouldn't it be nice if we could establish closer ties between that community and French Canada? And what better way was there to do that than to start with the French speaking fifteen thousand Jewish immigrants from North Africa? They would be the natural vanguard of any effort to create links between the French and the Jewish communities in Montreal.

I mulled over the idea for a long time, and decided a Jewish school where the language of instruction was French would be the best place to start. I felt such a school would open additional avenues for a rapprochement between the French and the Jewish communities in Montreal.

I discussed the idea with the elders of the immigrants from North Africa. The North African community was headed by a council elected to look after the needs of the community and help in the settlement of new arrivals from North Africa. I was the only council member who was not North African, and my membership on the Council gave me easy access to the elders of the community. The first reaction I received from the leaders of the North African Jews varied from the lukewarm to the icy. I decided to proceed regardless.

In February of 1968, I advertised through the Sephardic Studies Program at Yeshiva University, New York, for a rabbi from North Africa. He needed to be a licensed educator, fluent in French and English, and interested in coming to Montreal to help set up a Jewish day school where the language of instruction would be French. I felt I needed to limit the search to North African Rabbis because that would make it easier for the newcomer to earn the trust of the North African parents. I offered the selected candidate free use of our apartment in Montreal from mid April to mid September.

I knew that was a tall order. During that time, there were hardly any Rabbis from North Africa who lived in the US or Canada. And the added stipulation that the candidate be a licensed educator reduced further the likelihood that anyone out there would fit the bill. It was a shot in the dark, and I knew it. But against all odds and to my utter delight someone did come forth. Rabbi Edery, a native of Tangiers, Morocco, contacted me only days after the publication of the ad. He was a licensed teacher who served on the faculty at the Hebrew Academy in Washington, DC. He was fluent in English, French, Spanish, and Hebrew. He was familiar with the English-French problem in Canada. He was eager to take on the challenge of establishing the first Jewish day school in Canada, with French as the language of instruction.

It was nothing short of a miracle. Never in my wildest dream did I think I would find such a qualified individual, and so soon after publishing my very first ad.

In mid April I left with my family for Washington, DC to spend the next five months working on the first stages of my natural gas model. Rabbi Edery did not waste time. He and his family moved in our apartment the day we left.

Rabbi Edery went to work immediately. He went door to door to meet with North African parents and convince them to enroll their children in the new Sephardi Jewish school, with French as the language of instruction. He arranged to lease classroom space from Beth Rivka, Habbad's school for girls. He traveled to Quebec City to arrange for the issuance of a license for the new school. He got the commitment of former teachers, secular and religious, from among the North African immigrants to teach in the school. Since most North African immigrants could not afford to pay tuition fees for their children, Rabbi Edery traveled to New York, Boston, and Toronto and Ottawa to raise enough funds to offer full scholarship for every child enrolled in the school. And to top it all off he started a new synagogue for immigrants from Spanish Morocco, whose mother tongue was Spanish.

When we returned from Washington in mid September, I could not believe my eyes when I saw how much Rabbi Edery had managed to accomplish during the five months he had been in town. He was all set to start the first semester of the school he had set up. He had managed to enroll over two hundred and fifty students, all children of North African immigrants. The majority of those had attended English (Protestant) schools; a handful had attended French (Catholic) schools. All of the children spoke French.

Rabbi Edery's energy and accomplishment fired up many in the North African community. People were ready to do almost anything to keep the newly founded school going. They had no money to give, but they gave of themselves. They swept the floors; they took the sheet covers off the lunch tables and hand-washed them in their homes; they replaced the burned electric bulbs; they watered the shrubs; they organized car pools to drive children whose parents did not own a car.

I remember, in particular, how Mr. Peres, an immigrant from Morocco in his late fifties, lovingly swept each table in the dining room at the end of the day. He exuded love as he gently spread clean sheets on the table and smoothed out the creases with the palm of his hand, as if to spread his blessing over the children that would eat at the table the next day.

For some in the North African community, it was as if a new ray of light had suddenly come to their life, and they did not want to let go of it. It was heart warming to see how Rabbi Edery's leadership had galvanized members of the community and how they coalesced behind him.

Outside of Montreal, Rabbi Edery attracted support primarily from orthodox Jews. They applauded his untiring effort on behalf of the children of the North African immigrants, and they voted their approval with their pocket books. Within the Jewish community in Montreal, Rabbi Edery attracted support from people with varied background. I remember, in particular, a young mother, a transplant from Baltimore, who was brought up in reform home. But she was so impressed by Rabbi Edery's hard work and commitment that she was ready to do anything to help. She drove him to the airport when he went on fund raising tours, and she picked him up at the airport on his return. She led the search for a professional fundraiser for the school and took notes at meetings we held to work on school matters.

I worked on organizing a board of directors for the school, and dedicated part of my salary to the school. Dictaphones were uncommon at the time. I owned an expensive model that I used for dictating my manuscripts, but I gave it to the school to help lighten Rabbi Edery's workload.

But while the school was receiving contributions from many people, not enough was coming in to meet all school expenses, and the flow of contributions was uneven. It was becoming increasingly evident that the school could not go on without being able to count on a core income, around which we could build a budget. Rabbi Edery was working non-stop to keep the funds coming. But it was clear he could not maintain his hectic pace ad infinitum. The incessant work was beginning to take its toll on his health.

Up to that point, the school, whose language of instruction was French, had received financial help from

Jewish communities in major cities in the US as well as Toronto, Ottawa and Vancouver - all English speaking communities, but not a penny from French Canada, the very group that had so vociferously decried the "Anglicization" of Quebec. Quebec City repeatedly turned down Rabbi Edery whenever he turned to it for help in the maintenance of the school. What happened to the complaint voiced so many times by Quebec's provincial government and French Canadians that new arrivals had shunned French Canada and distanced themselves from the French language? What happened to Quebec's Minister of Immigration who had bemoaned the tendency of the majority of the North African Jewish immigrants to send their children to English schools? Were the Quebecois just crying wolf, or did they really mean what they said, I began to wonder? Were they really interested in those immigrants? They did not seem to want to lift a finger to make it more attractive for newcomers to be part of the French community. And they did not seem to be particularly encouraging to those of us who took the first step to becoming their friends. What was it that they really wanted? The cry of "English Domination" and "Anglicization" of French Canada was beginning to sound hollow. If French Canada acted inhospitably toward newcomers, even when the newcomers reached out to it and extended a hand of friendship, who did it have to blame but itself for being shunned by the newcomers?

The issue came to a head when a school delegation went to Quebec City toward the end of the school's first year and warned that the school would have to shut down for lack of adequate funding. The response of the Ministry was mind-boggling. If the school affixed crosses on the front walls of the classrooms, the Ministry would consider providing financial assistance. The delegation members were stunned. This was a Jewish school, they pointed out. Did the Ministry know that Jews did not wear a cross or affix crosses in their classrooms? Yes it did, but that was the condition for receiving aid from the Ministry. Were the Protestant schools required to hang crosses in their classrooms as a condition for receiving aid from the Ministry? No they were not. So why impose that requirement on a Jewish school? No answer. Take it or leave it.

We chose to leave it.

The school shut down at the end of its first year of operation.

It was a sad day for me and for many others. I felt drained at the end of that year - emotionally, physically and financially. It was a painful experience. From that time on, I saw the lament about the "Anglicization" of Quebec in a different light.

But the spark that the opening of the school had ignited did not die out. Having had once a school of their own, the North African immigrants longed for a revival of the idea. There was talk about reopening a scaled-down version of the school, hopefully with even wider support from the North African community. But I was too disillusioned with Quebec City to take part in any effort to revive the school.

By the time my family and I had left Canada for good in the fall of 1974 no other school was opened to take the place of the one started by Rabbi Edery.

I do not know what transpired exactly during the thirty years since we left Canada. I do know that the North African community in Montreal is thriving and that it has at least one Sephardi day School, with instruction in the French language.

In September 2003, I received a *rosh hashana* greeting card from an old friend, Rabbi Herbert Dobrinsky, Vice President of Yeshiva University, who was instrumental in founding the Sephardi Studies Center at Yeshiva University. I was deeply moved when I read what Rabbi Dobrinsky wrote in his greeting card.

"Daniel, your good work in Montreal still yields results".

That meant a lot to me.

WHEN MAMA PASSED AWAY

Mama suffered a massive cerebral hemorrhage on Saturday night, July 24, 1967 (Ab 7, 5727) and died almost immediately. She was sixty-six years old.

A week after I had learned from my brother that Mama had died, I received a letter from my father.

" My dear Son: I am writing this letter not with ink but with the tears of my eyes to tell you of our tragedy. Dear mamma Looloo is gone."

Baba went on to describe a normal Saturday evening that turned out to be anything but normal and said he had no reason now to go on living.

My mother, father, siblings, and friends sat on the balcony at my parents' apartment on Saturday night and had tea together, as was the custom at the end of the Sabbath day. When Mama said she had a headache and went in to lie down, my father went with her. Suddenly her body began to shake violently, and she lost consciousness. My father called the medics, and they rushed her to Belinson Hospital. The physician in the emergency room declared her dead.

Baba's letter ended with,

"May Mamma's soul in heaven intercede on your behalf and on behalf of your precious family."

I remember that sentence word for word. It tore my heart. It capsulized the finality of Mama's death. Mama was among the dead now. In the Babylonian traditions, only the dead can intercede on behalf of the living.

The suddenness of Mama's death haunted me. Death is hard to take no matter how and when it occurs. But I felt it would have been easier for me to deal with Mama's death if it had been preceded by a long illness. That would have given me time to prepare for the inevitable. Mama was not old. She might not have been in the best of shape, but she was not teetering on the edge either. No one expected her to pass away so soon. It was difficult for me to come to terms with her death.

When I told Abe Abraham, a friend, about my mother's death and the pain I was experiencing because she had died so suddenly, he remarked,

"That is the best way to go, believe me."

I was stunned to hear Abe say that.

"That is crass! How could he be so flippant about it?" I said to myself.

But now that I am nine years older than my mother when she died and have seen how friends and family members have suffered from an incapacitating illness or an incurable disease, I realize I was wrong in my judgment of Abe's remark. I dread being incapacitated, just lying in bed waiting for the day when I can just die. It would be a blessing if I could go as fast as Mama did. Abe might not have worded his remark tactfully. But he certainly had more empathy for the dying than I credited him with.

I did not learn of Mama's death until more than a month after she had passed away. By Jewish law when a person learns of the death of a parent or a sibling within thirty days of the burial date, one is required to rend one's clothes as a sign of grief, stop all manner of work for seven days, and sit Shib'a to honor the memory of the deceased. But if one does not learn of the loss within those thirty days, one does not sit Shib'a.

My family in Israel knew that I was planning to take up a new position at McGill. They worried that it would be disruptive for me if I were to learn of Mama's death and sit Shib'a while I was in transition. They chose to withhold the information until the thirty days had passed.

We were already settled in our new apartment at 4685 Bourret Street in Montreal when Jacob called to tell me of Mama's death. I was devastated. It happened at a point in my life when I could see the day I would be able to travel with my family to Israel and spend time with my parents. Joan was looking forward to meeting my mother and father. My parents thought of her as their daughter, and they waited for the day when they could meet her and Aziza.

From as far back as the time when I joined the Faculty at Cornell, I had wanted to take a trip with my family and visit my parents in Israel. But I had to put off the trip, partly because I did not have the money and partly because I was at the beginning of my academic career. At that stage, the pressure to publish in refereed journals to demonstrate academic prowess was relentless. I felt up to the challenge, once I had time to find my bearings, but it took time to get there. In the interim I was pinned down, day and night, summer and winter. The one time I experienced a sense of relief was during the Sabbath. From Friday sundown to Saturday sundown I shut myself off from the every day rat race and enjoyed my time with my family. Had it not been for the Sabbath break, there would have been no let up. It was a ruthless environment of cutthroat competition. And it was particularly unsettling to find some colleagues publish, but still perish. Unfortunately, by the time I was over that hump, it was too late. Mama did not wait.

Mama and I spoke over the phone for the first time and -- as fate would have it, the only time -- a year before she passed away. It was the first time I could afford the cost of a transatlantic call. We were on the phone for a long time. Mama cried when we spoke. She said she could not believe she was speaking to me. I fought back tears when I heard her say that. That moment brought back memories. I saw an instant replay of our life together in Baghdad. There was my parents' home, and there was my family sitting together around the kerosene heater, drinking hot tea with milk on a cold winter night. There were my bedroom and my desk and there was the big picture of the snow-covered village that adorned the living room in my parents' home. There was the synagogue I had attended, two blocks away from my parents' home. I could see it all, as I listened to my mother.

I turned the phone over to Joan. Mama spoke in Judeo-Arabic and Joan responded in English. They were on the phone for a good while. Joan knew a few words of salutations in Judeo-Arabic, but neither one could speak the language of the other. Somehow they managed to bond together. Joan was tearful as she turned the phone over to Aziza.

Aziza was almost four years old then. She was fascinated to hear my mother speak to her in a language she had never heard before. For a while she listened intently, with her big brown eyes wide open. Then she had a torrent of stories to tell about what she had been learning in the kindergarten, her painting, her dress, and her new pair of shoes. Little Aziza ended the conversation with a Sabbath song " yom hashabbath ane kamohoo …The Sabbath day, there is nothing like it…" That must have delighted my mother.

Aziza's painting, Dec 1966, Yonkers
Done when Aziza was attending the kindergarten at Greystone Jewish Community Center

We were all pumped up at the end of that phone conversation. It was a first for me. And now I knew it would never happen again.

I told Joan the news about Mama's death. She broke into tears. We held hands, sat on the floor, and cried together. Joan called the late Abdullah Hillel -- an old friend of my parents and a scholar in Jewish Law -- and notified him of my mother's death. Joan drove me to the Spanish and Portuguese synagogue in Montreal where I was to meet him.

Mr. Hillel rent my shirt and asked me to repeat after him, "God hath given, and God hath taken away". I could repeat the first half, but could not say, "God hath taken away". I struggled, but the words just would not come out. I just sobbed. It was the hardest thing I ever had to utter. Mama's death was the first death I had to face as an adult.

For months after my mother's death, I was tormented by the thought that my family had left Mama by herself under the ground and went back home. She was left under those smothering piles of sand piled on top of her? And she was left behind with the dead? In the darkness of the night in a cemetery? I could not get it through my head that Mama was dead, like the rest of the dead slumbering in the dust in that cemetery.

I called Jacob back the same day he relayed the sad news to me and asked him how much the burial expenses were, but he would not say. He kept telling me not to worry, that he would take care of things. I knew he could not.

I thought of my parents. They were lovers. They had known each other during my mother's whole life. I thought about their life together and their love for each other. They were never separated from each other, and I felt that death should not be allowed to separate them either. We needed to act quickly before the plot next to my mother's burial site was taken. I talked it over with Joan, and we decided to send my brother the money we had in our contingency funds. That money would be more than enough to purchase the plot next to Mama's burial site and reimburse my brother for my mother's burial expenses.

I shared with Jacob my feeling that we should not let death separate our parents and told him about the funds we would be sending. I asked him to act quickly and buy the plot adjacent to our mother's burial site before it was sold to others. He bought the plot soon after. Joan and I felt relieved.

Few things stand out in one's life as instances in which one is grateful for quick thinking and for having done just the right thing. This was one such instance in my life. I feel fortunate to have thought about the purchase of a plot for my father's burial on a day when I was in shock – the most painful day in my life. And I am so grateful that we were blessed to have the means to do what was right.

BITTERSWEET FAMILY REUNION

In the summer of 1968 when we lived in Washington, I was still observing the one-year mourning period for the death of my mother. My family and I lived in an apartment in the Summit Hill Building, a sprawling Silver Spring apartment complex. We chose that complex primarily because it had a synagogue in the building, which made it easier for me to attend daily services, morning and evening, and recite the Kaddish in Mama's memory.

When the memorial year drew to a close, my family and I left for Israel to be with my father and to attend the closing memorial services at my mother's gravesite. It was late afternoon when Joan, Aziza and I arrived at Tel Aviv's airport. Aziza was almost five years old. This was my first trip back to Israel since I had left for Harvard in 1958.

Both Joan and I felt uncomfortable to be airborne. I had avoided flying during the ten years I had spent in the US since my arrival from Israel. I traveled by bus and train. But often my family and I traveled by car. Joan loved driving and I was happy to sit back "and leave the driving to us," as Greyhound's famous ad goes.

When the plane was buffeted by clear-air turbulence, we felt violent jarring and we shook in our seats. Joan would turn to me and say "flying is not natural for people". I do not know what went on in my mind then, but I was scared. When we approached the airport in Tel Aviv, the pilot opened the wing flaps. The plane made a big rattling noise. I shrunk in my seat. Joan turned to me with a frightened look in her eyes, "What is happening?". Aziza thought it was all fun. She seemed to have the time of her life on her first flight.

A whole crowd of family members and friends awaited us at the airport. There were my father, my brother; my five sisters and their young boys (Jamila, my oldest sister, and her family were still in Iraq); my friend, Albert; my paternal cousin, Abed, and his family; my maternal cousin, Sammy; classmates from l'Alliance; and co-workers from my days in Bank in Bank Leumi. The size of the crowd reminded me of the crowds I had seen in Baghdad, when traveling was rare and family and friends went out en masse to welcome family members when they came for a visit from a far away land.

During Mama's memorial year, I wore a black ribbon sewed to my shirt, as is the tradition among Babylonian Jews

We hugged and kissed and we laughed and we cried. Baba reached for me. We hugged and I cried. Then he stepped back and looked intently at the black tie I was wearing and the black ribbon sewn on the left pocket of my shirt. It was a sign of mourning worn by Babylonian Jews during the year following the death of a loved one. He seemed to be struggling to find the words to express his feelings. Then he reached out and gently ran his hands down the length of my tie, and gave me one more hug as if to express his gratitude that I chose not to walk away from those Babylonian customs of honoring the memory of a loved one.

Baba put his arms around Joan and my brother and sisters crowded around her. They hugged her and kissed her.

Every one tried a few words in English to make her feel at home with the family. Joan was beaming.

But the greatest fuss was over our daughter Aziza. She was the first female child born to our family. All my sisters and cousins had only boys. Everyone longed for a daughter to be born to the family. When Aziza was born, Joan and I received congratulatory letters from everyone in the family. They all told me how Mama could not believe that she now had a granddaughter. My family could not have enough of Aziza. "She is beautiful! Gorgeous! She has dark skin, just like the rest of us! She has black curly hair, just like Mama's! She has big brown eyes! Look at her smile. Isn't she gorgeous!" They hugged her. They kissed her. They carried her. In the US we lived as a nuclear family. Aziza was not used to so much attention from so many people all at once, and she basked in the new attention she was getting. She had a broad smile on her face. And she loved it when they acted as if they were fighting over her to get to carry her. Joan stood watching with a broad smile on her face. She and I were the only ones that used to play the game of fighting over who gets to hold Aziza and declare her to be "only my daughter". Now there were quite a few others playing the same game, fighting over her.

I took Aziza to my father. He picked her up and gave her a big kiss. Aziza put her arms around his neck and rested her head over his shoulder. It was as if they had known each other for some time.

My family did not let us lift a finger – they carried our luggage, took our passport to be stamped, cleared our belongings through customs, called a taxicab. I was touched to see how happy they were to see us.

We drove to my parents' apartment. On the way I noticed how quickly it changed from day to night. The transition from daylight to night was so much shorter than we were accustomed to in the US.

I was glad to be back in the familiar environment of my parents' apartment. But it was a sad time, too. I could feel the void left by Mama's death. While I was gone, I looked forward to the day when I would be back to see her. But now that I was back, she was gone.

Baba told me how Jacob had learned of Mama's death. It was a struggle for him to talk about it and he stopped frequently to swallow deeply before he could get the next word out.

Just four days before Mama's death, Jacob left by boat for Istanbul on his first vacation abroad. He stayed in Istanbul with family members. When Mama passed away, my father was faced with a quandary. Should he or should he not notify Jacob? Jacob would want to attend the funeral and he might be angry if he were not told of Mama's death. On the other hand, this was his first big vacation and Baba was reluctant to do anything that would destroy it. There was also the possibility that, even if he were notified, he might not be able to make it in time for the funeral. By Jewish law the dead had to be buried on the day of death, which did not leave much time for Jacob to make it back for the funeral. In the end, the family decided that the appropriate thing to do was to postpone the funeral by one day and to notify Jacob immediately in the hope that he would be able to make it back in time.

Felix, my brother-in-law, sent Jacob a telegram telling him of Mama's death. As it happened Jacob was away from Istanbul on a one-day excursion. He did not receive the telegram until the following day when he returned to Istanbul. He took a plane and flew back to Israel immediately. But by that time Mama had been buried, and the Shib'a period had begun.

My father and my sisters sat on the floor, as is customary during the seven days of mourning. When Jacob opened the door and saw everyone sitting on the floor he let out a cry of pain and yelled "Mamma". Baba broke down when he described Jacob's anguish at that moment.

"Jacob ran around like a chicken with her head cut off, not knowing what to do with himself. He would not be consoled and he cried incessantly," Baba told me.

I had never seen my father cry before. When I walked toward the vestibule of our home in Baghdad late the night I left for Israel I noticed my father's eyes were red, but I had never seen him cry.

With Baba at our First Friday Night *kiddush* in 1968

A couple of days after our arrival, we celebrated the first Friday night *kiddush* with my father and my siblings. It was a bittersweet occasion. We were happy to be back together. At the same time we all felt the void left by mother's death. It was the last week of my mother's memorial year. In a few days we were to go to the cemetery to recite the Kaddish, a prayer sanctifying God at our mother's grave. Our pain was palpable. We chanted together "The Woman of Valor", as we always did in honor of our mother when we were growing up. This time our mother was not with us. Baba led the chanting. His sad look betrayed the depth of his sense of loss. But he pressed on valiantly. He broke down when he came to the verse "Many daughters have done valiantly, but thou excellest them all". I held his hands and chanted with him as he tearfully continued, "Grace is deceptive, beauty is illusory. But a woman who reveres the Lord she shall be praised. Extol her for the fruit of her hand, and let her own works praise her in the gates"

Baba left for the bedroom. My siblings and I huddled

together on the balcony. Jacob had a recording of Mama's ethical will. Mama had made the recording a while before she died and entrusted it to Jacob. Jacob asked if I wanted to listen to it. I said I did.

The voice sounded real – it was as if Mama was sitting with us and talking to us, as she used to during our years of growing up. Was she really with us? I turned around. There was no trace of her. I broke into tears as I listened to her and felt her love through her voice. Baba walked back into the living room. Hurriedly, Jacob turned off the tape recorder. Baba could not bear to listen to Mama's voice now that she no longer was with us, Jacob explained.

It was agonizing for me too, and I suppose that is why I never pressed Jacob to listen to the rest of Mama's ethical will.

On the first Memorial Day of our mother, my father, my siblings, relatives and friends all traveled to Holon's cemetery where Mama was buried. Joan and I took little Aziza with us. No one else in the family took their children with them to the cemetery. Babylonian Jews have a fetish about not exposing children to the dead or to cemetery. I talked with Joan about it and we both agreed that Aziza should come with us. It was her grandmother after all.

We stood in front of Mama's gravesite. Following the Sephardi traditions, those assembled recited passages from the Mishnah. They started with letters, which taken in sequence, formed Mama's name, Looloo. I could not join in. I just stared at Mama's gravesite. Then came the moment for reciting the Kaddish. Traditionally, it is the responsibility of the deceased's sons to recite the Kaddish. Daughters could join in, however, if they wished. I turned to Jacob. We started. Baba joined in. I broke down midway through. It was true. That was my mother lying down there under all that heap of sand. No illusion. It was not a bad dream. She was dead. It was final. I could not continue. I tried hard, but the words would not come out. I just sobbed. I bent over Mama's grave. Uncle Moshe put his arms around me and tearfully recited the rest of the Kaddish as I struggled to repeat the words after him.

I looked at my father. He looked so much older and run down. Tears were running down his cheeks. I looked at the vacant plot next to my mother's burial plot. It was the one we bought for him. I wondered what went on in his mind when he saw it. He must have noticed it, since all the other plots in the immediate vicinity of my mother's grave had filled up, and the plot next to my mother's was left untouched. It was not customary in the Middle East to buy a plot for a person before that person's death. Some people were offended by the mere mention of the idea, because it was taken as a wish to hasten someone's demise. Could that possibly have been what went through in my father's mind? On the other hand, he was a modern person. Might it be that he was grateful, knowing that his children cared enough to ensure that when the time came, he would lie next to the only woman he loved? Baba and I never talked about it.

As I stared at the empty plot, I thought that one day that plot would have my father underneath it. And that might happen sooner than we might think. We were now motherless. We were destined to be fatherless, too, some day. Perhaps we should make the best of the time while we had our father with us. He might not be with us much longer.

That thought had a lot to do with the affection and closeness I developed with my father following our first Memorial Day at my mother's gravesite on that summer day in 1968.

TURNING A NEW PAGE

Even though the Jewish year of mourning is an artificial creation, it has a perceptible psychological effect. Memorial day, the end of the twelve months of mourning, signaled for us the beginning of a new life. Gloom and grief had begun to lift by the time we had returned from the cemetery. We couldn't forget our mother. The wounds were still fresh, but we understood that it was time to turn a new page. We were now open to the joy of being together. I saw signs of it on the faces of everyone around me - my father, brother, sisters, aunts, and uncles.

My father taught Joan to play *tawlee*—absurdly explaining the rules in Judeo-Arabic, a language she didn't understand. Somehow, she became an accomplished player by the time we left.

Baba teaching Joan to play *tawlee*

Joan and Baba looking at family pictures

My father lavished attention on Aziza, holding her in his lap and telling her stories, again in Judeo-Arabic. She listened intently, seeming to respond to his love, if not his words.

Often Joan took my father and Aziza for a walk in the neighborhood. He seemed to look forward to those occasions. It was wonderful to see how he revived as he dressed up for those walks, how carefully he held Aziza's hands as they crossed the streets.

Helwa dropped in every now and then and delighted us with a mouth-watering dish of okra or crispy brown Ajja-b'jibin (Babylonian cheese omelet) or brown rice fried with roasted almond and raisin. Joan and Aziza went wild over those dishes. It gave me such a pleasure to see the two of them enjoy Helwa's dishes. I often stayed away just so that they could have those dishes all to themselves. Friends and distant family relatives that I had not seen for years came to visit us. Sometimes they stayed until late at night. It was such an enjoyable environment, so different from the nuclear life we had in the US and Canada.

The children in our extended family moved together like a herd--from the backyard to the front yard, from the front yard to the park, and from the park to one my sisters' apartments. My sisters took turns looking after them. They ran, they hopped, they skipped, and they giggled. Aziza, an only child who lived oceans away from her large extended family, delighted in the company of so many newfound cousins.

Jacob took us on a three-day tour of Haifa, Acre and the surrounding area in Northern Israel. Haifa is a beautiful port city, but its most beautiful part is "Upper Haifa", the part built on top of Mount Carmel. It was a gorgeous, heavenly place, with clean streets, beautiful outdoors coffee shops, an impressive view of the Bay, and cool weather. Overnight we stayed in a beautiful hotel to which Jacob led us. The hotel was built high on top of Mount Carmel and it had a breathtaking view of Haifa's Bay.

I noticed Jacob was deep in his thoughts as he led us to the hotel. I can still see in my mind's eye the broken look on my brother's face, his drooping shoulders and his bent head as he led the way to that hotel. Later Jacob told me that hotel was where he and his bride had spent their honeymoon a few years before. The two were no longer married, their marriage having lasted but two years. I wish I had known that before we went to the hotel. I would have insisted on going to another hotel and spared my brother the agony of having to deal with old wounds and relive painful memories.

Top two rows: Aziza savoring the moment on Baba's lap; Third row: Baba, Aziza and Joan holding hands on one of their frequent walks together.

Daniel (left) playing *tawlee* with Uncle Guerji

Joan and Aziza loved to take walks and ride the motorboat along the Yarkon River near my parents' apartment

Aziza playing at the bank of the Yarkon   and admiring its gigantic Eucalyptus trees

Our hotel on Mount Carmel, Upper Haifa

Aziza on the steps of the hotel

Dome, Bahai World Center, as seen from hotel

Below: A view of the Bay of Haifa from our hotel room

479

R to l: Silhouettes of Jacob, Aziza and Daniel sipping tea
at Abu Christo, Acre

Smoking Nargueela (Hookah)   Father and daughter at home's entrance, Acre
at Acre's Shuk entrance

Jacob in Acre's Shuk

CONNECTING WITH LEADERS OF JEWS FROM ARAB LANDS

During the ten years I spent in the US before visiting Israel in 1968, I gave occasional talks and published articles on the history and life experience of Jews from Arab lands who had immigrated to Israel. But until my 1968 trip to Israel, I acted alone. I had no link or contact with any individual or organization in Israel that shared my concerns for or interests in the life of Jews from Arab lands in general or the Jews of Iraq, in particular. All that changed with our 1968 trip to Israel.

The trip gave me my first opportunity to connect face to face with people and organizations with interests similar to mine. It was during that trip that I met and established enduring links with leaders and intellectuals from among the Middle Eastern Jews in Israel. I began to collaborate with them in encouraging and funding the intellectual and educational pursuits of Jews from Arab lands who had been trying to pull themselves up by their own bootstraps. It was gratifying for me to do the little I was able to do to help those individuals and educational organizations in the years since our 1968 trip.

I would like to chronicle my recollections of meeting I had with two of those entities – the late Abraham benYaakov and the Sephardic Council of Jerusalem.

Abraham benYaakov is the scion of an illustrious Babylonian family. He has published extensively on the history, culture, traditions, language, poetry, songs, leading personalities and non-conventional medical practices of the Jews of Iraq. At the time we met he served as a high school principal in Jerusalem, while devoting time to researching and publishing on topics about Babylonian Jewry.

I had learned about benYaakov through a monumental work he had published in 1965 on the history of Babylonian Jewry, a book my father had sent me soon after its publication. I read it and learned a lot from it. I was impressed by the painstaking work that had gone into researching and documenting the sources the book drew on.

Because of our commonality of interest, I sought out Dr. benYaakov at my first opportunity.

BenYaakov and I had a cordial meeting when I visited him at his home in Jerusalem. We talked about areas of mutual interest, particularly research work in Israel on the history and life experience of Babylonian Jewry. He briefed me on the difficulties faced by researchers of topics dealing with the history and culture of Jews from Arab lands. Researchers of Jews from Arab lands had a hard time finding support for their research work and getting it published. He showed me a thick manuscript he had completed about the history of Jewish sacred tombs in Iraq. He told me the manuscript had been sitting on his shelf for some time because he did not have the money to have it typed before circulating it for review and criticism.

I was interested in the subject of Jewish sacred burial sites in Iraq. Some of those sites go back several centuries, some to periods not long after the exile from Judea. I thought it would be timely to have such a book published to preserve what we knew about those places, particularly since the Jewish community had by that time left Iraq, and no one was left in that country to preserve our historical records.

I gave benYaakov a check to cover his estimated cost of getting the manuscript typed up and readied for review and criticisms. I thought there could be no better way to memorialize my mother's dedication to the education of her children than to fund the typing of that manuscript. I very much hoped that my contribution would pave the way for the publication of that book some day.

Five years later I was pleasantly surprised to receive an autographed copy of the book from benYaakov. It had been published under the title "K'vareem K'dosheem beBavel"- Sacred Burial Sites in Babylonia.

BenYaakov and I maintained contact ever since. I visited him and Latifa, his wife, every time I went to Israel. He had since published twenty-two more books about the Jews of Iraq. I have copies of every one of them. Occasionally graduate students at UC Berkeley's Department of Middle Eastern Studies have borrowed some of benYaakov's books from my library to use as a source in their research work. One of them told me that benYaakov's book on Jewish Babylonian amulets was pivotal for the PhD dissertation he had completed.

The Sephardi Council of Jerusalem is an organization headed by well established Israeli Jews of Spanish descent. The late Elyahoo Elyashar, who was a member of Israel's K'neset, chaired its board of directors. The late David Siton, a journalist, served as its president. According to the Council's leaders, the Sephardi Council of Jerusalem had been in existence since 1267, the year when the Spanish Jewish sage, Nahmanides (1194-1270), had founded it.

The Council published a monthly journal called Bama'arakha. For a long time, it was the only organ in Israel that publicized the plight of Jews from Arab lands in Israel and spoke in unvarnished terms about the unfriendly attitudes those Jews faced in Israel. The Israeli press and the Israeli establishment spoke in disparaging terms about the Council. Some labeled its leadership as extremists and agitators. Remarkably, when the pot boiled over in the seventies and the Israeli Black Panthers, following in the footsteps of Robin Hood, drew attention to the plight of Jews from Arab lands, the Israeli establishment changed gear. Now it viewed the Sephardi Council as moderate and no longer referred to it in derogatory terms.

Bama'arakha was the medium that brought the Council to my attention. While on the faculty at NYU, I met, through a mutual friend, an Israeli of North African ancestry who was visiting the US. He gave me the issue of Bama'arakha he had with him. I subscribed to the publication and planned to meet with the Council on our next visit to Israel.

Among the philanthropic enterprises that the Sephardi Council funded and operated was an educational institution called "haMetivtah haG'dola Beit haRashal" in Jerusalem, where school dropouts from among the Middle Eastern and North African children were brought in and taught in their own milieu.

The Council paid a stipend to parents who might otherwise have had to count on the help of those dropouts to support their large families. *Hakham* Obadiah Yosef, who at the time served as Tel Aviv's Sephardic Chief Rabbi and who was later (Oct 16, 1972) elected as Israel's Chief Sephardic Rabbi, served as the educational director of the Metivtah.

Sign of the Metivtah atop the Metivtah stone building

The Council's efforts to rehabilitate the school dropouts yielded astonishing results. Those children, who had dropped out from the European-oriented lily-white schools they had attended, flourished when they were taught in their own milieu. Some of them continued their studies and went on to become Hazzaneem (cantors), Dayyaneem (judges in Jewish law), and Mohaleem (Jewish circumcisers). Some of them went abroad to serve in Sephardic communities in South America and Europe.

I was so impressed with the Metivtah's achievement that I sent all my charitable contributions directly to the Metivtah and encouraged colleagues and friends to do the same.

While in Israel, I traveled to Jerusalem with Joan and Aziza to visit the Council's office. There I met with Elyahoo Elyashar and David Siton. As it turned out, I did not need to introduce myself to the two gentlemen and tell them of my interest. They had read an article of mine ("The Middle Eastern Jew"), which I had published in the December 24, 1965 issue of Reconstructionist, a bi-weekly of the Jewish Reconstructionist Foundation. In that article I addressed the misconceptions surrounding the history, culture and traditions of the Sephardim in general and the Middle Eastern Jews in particular. Messrs. Elyashar and Siton said they were so glad I had taken the initiative in looking for the Council. They were amazed at the similarity between their own views and the views I had expressed in that article.

The two invited me to come back with my family to a reception they would hold in our honor later that week. They also said they wanted to take me and my family on a two-day tour of the Old City of Jerusalem, Judea and Samaria, all of which had been recaptured from the Jordanians the year before. I accepted the invitation enthusiastically.

Early on the day when we were getting ourselves ready to leave Ramat Gan for Jerusalem, my father got all dressed up and said he was going with us. I worried the trip would be tiring for him. But he said he was eager to come with us, regardless how inconvenient that might be for him. I did not appreciate his real motivation at the time, but it was only when my children left for college that I began to understand why my father wanted so much to be with us during our short stay in Israel, as inconvenient as the travel to Jerusalem might have been for him. I missed our children very much when they were gone. When they came home from college for a short stay, I was ready to drop everything just to be with them. Maybe it was the same with my father.

David Siton took us all around. I could not have dreamed of a better guided-tour. David was born and raised in the Old City of Jerusalem. He knew every nook and cranny in Old Jerusalem, both the Jewish and Arab quarters of the city. We got to see things that I doubt any guide knew much about. I took pictures of the places we visited.

David walked us through the winding streets of the old City, and at every little corner he had a story to tell. As we passed by homes in Jerusalem's Jewish quarter -- inhabited by Jews prior to the Jordanian occupation -- I noticed the scars left on the marble doorposts when the Arabs pried out the mezuzahs inset into those doorposts.

We walked through the ruins of the centuries-old five-synagogue compound in Old Jerusalem, known as Yohanan benZakkai, which was being rehabilitated by the Sephardic Council. I was appalled to see the destruction wreaked on that compound during the time when the Old City was under Arab rule.

Signs of past neglect and destruction could still be seen throughout the plaza of the Western Wall, the most sacred Jewish place. The Israeli authorities were still cleaning up the area, but there was still a lot of rubble around.

I had never been to the Western Wall before. When I lived in Israel, I could not go to the Western Wall. The Old City was under Jordanian rule, and Jews were not allowed to be anywhere in the Western Wall Plaza.

I stood still in front the Western Wall. I had heard and read so much about it, and had seen pictures of it from my days of childhood. In the pictures it looked impressive and it carried so much meaning for me. But now that I was standing in front of it, I found the Wall to be a disappointment. I wondered why I was so disappointed. Was it the neglected state of that holy place? Was it because I had heard so much about the Wall that I had formed an unrealistic image of what it really was? Was it because I expected the sight of the Wall to evoke the history, courage, devotion, and martyrdom of the Jewish people, and was disappointed that none of that happened? Was I expecting a halo to surround the Western Wall and was disappointed to see, instead, large growths of weed sticking out from the crevices between those enormous boulders? Where were the smooth stones used to build the Temple, the stones I had learned about in my childhood when I learned about the construction of the Temple? I expected to be awed when I stood in front of the Wall, but I was not. What was wrong with me? I felt guilty for not experiencing the sense of awe that many said they had experienced on first sight of the Wall. But then I wondered if

Entrance to two Jewish homes in the Jewish Quarter of Old Jerusalem
The Mezuzahs were pried out from their inset in the marble doorposts during the Jordanian occupation of Jerusalem in 1948. The slanted scars left after the removal of the Mezuzahs can be seen on the right doorposts. In the lower picture the writings to the right on the front side (the side facing the street) is numerals used in Arabic. The upper number is 938 and the lower is 76.

David Siton walking Joan through what used to be the interior of a five-synagogue compound

Remains of what used to be the Holy Ark that housed the Torah scrolls

David Siton showing Joan the destruction atop the five synagogue compound

A stone mason, part of the crew retained by the Sephardi Council to rehabilitate the compound.

they really all experienced that sense of awe. Was I really the only one who was disappointed on my first visit to the Wall?

I did marvel though at the technical skill that the construction of the Wall required. Those boulders were enormous. Some are almost a flight high. How did they manage to lift them up that high?

Congregants reading from a Sephardi *sefer Torah at the Wall*

Joan at the Wall's Plaza

It took me two or three more visits to the Wall during our subsequent trips to Israel to accept the Wall as it was. It was only then that I began to experience a sense of reverence when I was in the Wall Plaza. For the first time I felt I comfortable joining a group of Yemenite Jews as they recited the evening prayers at the Wall. And it was during those services that tears of joy streamed down my cheeks. I had finally reconnected with my heritage.

The old Sephardi cemetery in Jerusalem, or what was left of it

As I stood at the Sephardi cemetery in Jerusalem, perhaps the oldest cemetery in Jerusalem, I shivered at the scene of destruction I saw. The cemetery looked like a war zone. All the headstones were removed, crushed to pieces and scattered around. There was no way to identify the graves any longer. What kind of pleasure could people have derived from doing that to the memory of the dead? Some of the marble stones in the cemetery were later tracked down by the Israeli authorities. They had been used in the construction of homes in the West Bank during the Jordanian occupation.

My father and I were moved at the sight of Rachel's Tomb. Babylonian Jews venerated Rachel. A simple drawing of that Tomb appeared on the first page of all prayer books that we used in Iraq. Babylonian Jews lovingly referred to Rachel as "Rahel Immainoo" – Our Mother Rachel. I stood in front of that tomb motionless as tears rolled down my cheeks.

David drove us to the Machpela Cave in Hebron, also known as Abraham's Tomb, where according to tradition, the three Patriarchs and three of the Matriarchs were buried. To get to the burial sites, one had to climb up several steps. I noticed my father stood frozen at the bottom of the steps, looking up. I wondered if he was having difficulty climbing up those steps. Yes he did, but it was not that. He told me what it was. Every time he had traveled from Baghdad to Palestine, he went to Hebron to recite the Kaddish at the tomb of the patriarchs and matriarchs. Only once, in the twenties, was he allowed to go up the steps and recite the Kaddish at the gravesites. Then the Arabs banned all Jews from going up the steps to the burial sites. He could only stand at the bottom of the steps. Now, with Israel in charge, he was free to go up to the burial sites. But my father was frozen at the boundary the Arabs had not allowed him to cross.

I took Baba's hands, and together we climbed up the steps. There, in front of the gravesites and in a choked voice, Baba recited the Kaddish and intonated a prayer of thanks to God for giving him one more chance to recite the Kaddish in front of the gravesites of the Patriarchs and Matriarchs. As it turned out, that was also the last chance. He was never able to make it to Hebron again before he died in 1977.

I was so taken over by the emotions generated by the experience at Machpela Cave that I did not take any pictures of the Cave. I did take a picture of the road sign as we made the turn to Hebron. It was not a good picture, but it is all I have. Here it is.

Road sign to "Abraham's Tomb"- the Machpela Cave

We visited the Shuk in the Arab quarter of the Old City of Jerusalem -- a sprawling market with an incredible variety of goods - textile, clothing, groceries, toys, electrical appliances, house wares, fruits, vegetables, and almost any thing imaginable.

Merchants sold mostly out of shops. But some sold their wares from stands, carts and barrows. The market stretched over several winding streets and alleys. Merchants hawked their wares and called passers by to stop by and take advantage of their cut-rate prices.

It was wonderful to be in that lively environment. But there was one thing I remember from childhood that I did not particularly care for in those markets —the endless haggling over price. I spotted in one of the shops a gorgeous all-mosaic *tawlee*. It was workman's *tawlee*, made in Damascus. I very much wanted to buy it, but I dreaded the haggling process I would have to go through. I had seen enough of that in Baghdad and was not in the mood of going back to it. Joan had an idea. "Let us ask the seller how much he wants for it. Then let us look for other stores that have the same *tawlee*, and let us buy it from the one who asks for the lowest price". That made sense. Remarkably, several others had the same *tawlee*. Some had look alike and they tried to pass them as Damascus authentic. But I could tell the difference. I had seen the authentic ones in the old country. But Joan's suggestion saved the day. I got my *tawlee* without haggling. Most likely I overpaid some, but it was a price I was willing to pay to save time and to avoid going through a show I hated.

My father loved my new *tawlee*. He and I played *tawlee* many times using that *tawlee*. I took it back with us to the US. I taught my children how to play the game. I still have it -- it looks as new as on the day when we bought it.

The Council held a reception in our honor. I was asked to say a few words about my interest in the problems facing the Middle Eastern immigrants in Israel, and about what motivated me to speak out and write on the subject. In my talk I paid a special tribute to my father from whom I learned to look beyond my immediate personal needs and devote time to help the weak and the needy. Everyone in the audience turned to my father and applauded enthusiastically. It was touching to watch the expression of gratitude on my father's face at seeing his past work for the welfare of the weak and the downtrodden had not been forgotten, even though he had fallen from his position of power and influence.

Joan and Aziza high atop Jerusalem's YMCA's tower

For many years since our first meeting in Jerusalem, the Council and I collaborated in various ways to help people in need, and sensitize the Jewish communities in Israel, the US and Canada to the plight of Jews from Arab lands and the need to help them pull themselves up by their own bootstraps.

Addressing a conference organized by the Sephardi Council of Jerusalem

492

HEKHAL SHLOMO

During my mother's memorial year, I attended daily services to recite the Kaddish. One day when I was in Jerusalem, I went for services at Hekhal Shlomo - the seat of the Sephardi and Ashkenazi Chief Rabbis of Israel. I remembered reading in a brochure distributed by the Israeli Consulate in Montreal that Hekhal Shlomo was where the two Chief Rabbis worshipped. Since Sephardim and Ashkenazim have different rites, I took that to mean that there were two synagogues at Hekhal Shlomo – one Sephardi and one Ashkenazi.

I entered the first synagogue I came across, but soon realized that it was an Ashkenazi synagogue. I asked the Sexton where the Sephardi synagogue was. He said there was none. That surprised me - the Consulate's brochure stated that the two Chief Rabbis prayed at Hekhal Shlomo. So where did the Sephardi Chief Rabbi pray, I asked? Dismissively, the Sexton replied: "In his home."

Hekhal Shlomo was the seat of the two Chief Rabbis, who were officers of the government of Israel. Yet it accommodated the religious needs of one, the Ashkenazi rabbi, but not the other. I felt I was misled by the Consulate's information. The brochure was probably sanitized before it was published in North America - maybe to avoid offending the sensibilities of the North American public about the double standard built into Hekhal Shlomo's accommodations.

There was a sense of friendship and ease in the home of the Sephardi Chief Rabbi. The worshippers made me feel welcome, and although the services had nearly ended by the time I arrived, I was glad I chose to go to the Sephardi Chief Rabbi's home rather than stay and take my lumps at Hekhal Shlomo.

I had never met *hakham* Yits'hak, the Sephardi Chief Rabbi. He looked more impressive in person than in the pictures I had seen of him. He wore the traditional silk gown over a gray suit, with large olive branches embroidered on both sides of the upper part of the gown. On his head he wore a round black turban laced with white ribbon. He had a long white beard and a warm smile.

The late Yits'hak Nissim – Israel's Sephardi Chief Rabbi

Hakham Yits'hak was known as an erudite biblical scholar and as a person who built bridges between men of religion and science. He had a broad smile on his face when I introduced myself.

"Do you happen to know an attorney from Baghdad by the name of Abraham Khazzoom?" he asked.

"I do. He is my father," I said.

He held my hand tightly and shook it warmly.

"I am so happy to see you, and I want to tell you how grateful I am to your father for his devotion and for the conscientious work he did on my behalf, when he served as my attorney."

Hakham Yits'hak made me promise to bring my father on my next trip to Jerusalem for a visit at the Chief Rabbi's home.

It was a difficult period for my father. He missed my mother terribly. We were two days away from my mother's first memorial day, and he was having a hard time focusing. But he lit up when I told him about the Chief Rabbi's invitation.

A week later, my father and I went to visit *hakham* Yits'hak. The two had not seen each other for years, and they had a cordial reunion. *Hakham* Yits'hak was jovial; my father was more restrained. I could see his pain. Had my mother been alive, she would have accompanied him to that historical reunion. No doubt he was feeling the void.

The two reminisced about the case that my father had handled for *hakham* Yits'hak, about their mutual friends, about the Sephardim in Israel, and about the future of the Sephardim in Montreal. They seemed happy to renew their friendship. I, too, was happy to have been the medium that brought those two old friends back together.

That was in 1968. It was the first and last time I went to worship at Hekhal Shlomo.

A GOLDMINE: MY FATHER'S MEMOIRS

We had a wonderful time with family and friends. But it was getting to be time to return, and it was hard to accept that pretty soon we would be back to the small nuclear family in the US, away from family and friends I grew up with. No longer would I be able to just walk a short block to one of my sisters' apartment and enjoy a cup of tea with her and her family; no longer would I be able to sit late at night with my father and listen to him reminisce about his earlier days when he was growing up as a fatherless schoolboy or as he was serving as an elected member of the Jewish Governing Council in Iraq. No longer would Helwa drop in with her wonderful dishes that she prepared especially for us.

But there were also some positives to going back. I was looking forward to going back to Washington and resuming my research on modeling natural gas supply in the US. That was a hard nut to crack. But just the same that made it a challenge. When we returned I would be able to spend more time with my wife and daughter and I would be able to return to the peaceful moments I spent with my daughter when I sang to her at bedtime.

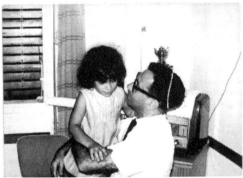

With little Aziza in my parents' apartment

But as the day of our departure neared, I worried more and more about my father. What would maintain his interest in life? My siblings were inclined to keep him more or less confined to the apartment. Baba didn't like that a bit, but he no longer had the stamina to stand up to his grown children.

Our father was artistic. He drew beautifully, and was an accomplished *ood* player. Joan and I wondered whether he should take a class in music or art, weaving, or anything that would rekindle his artistic talents and stimulate his imagination. But my siblings would hear none of it. He was too old, too fragile to travel, too weak to take the stress of a regular program – all the pat excuses.

Then I thought of the memoirs Baba had read to us children so long ago, about his early life. They had been left behind when my parents fled Baghdad. Wouldn't it be nice, I thought, if he could rewrite his memoirs, or whatever he still remembered of them? It would be a treasure for our children, and might also boost his spirits to realize that our mother's death had not rendered him obsolete.

I broached the subject with my father. To my great

pleasure his eyes lit up.

"My son, I promise I will write as much as I can remember."

I was ecstatic. I could sense his pleasure as well.

Page one of Baba's memoirs.

Baba worked full time on his memoirs. He mailed me the original, written in Arabic, a year later. His introduction began: "Today is *purim* day, [known in Judeo-Arabic as] *m'djalla* holiday, the 14th of Adar in the year 5729 of the Hebrew calendar, which corresponds to the 14th of March

1969 of the common era. I, attorney Abraham, son of Abboudi Khazzoom, came on this blessed day to reveal the story of my past life according to the request and wish of my dear children and especially my younger son, named Joseph Daniel, may God keep them. I will write in as much detail as my memory allows me."

It touched me that his memoirs were written in the style of a legal brief. But that was who my father was – exact, detailed, meticulous.

PAIN OF SEPARATION

I could see Baba's anguish on our last Friday night in Israel, as we got ready for the *kiddush* ceremony. He looked downcast, his shoulders drooped, and his voice was barely audible. I put my arm around him as we chanted the "*shalom aleikhem*." He revived some when we sang the traditional Sabbath *sh'bahoth* after dinner, but his sadness never lifted. Was he anticipating the void we would leave behind when we returned to the U.S.? Was he worried I would never return to Israel? Was he thinking he would no longer be around when we returned?

Baba, Daniel, and Joan at our last Friday Night *kiddush*
before we returned to Washington

On Monday, our last day in Israel, Baba sat in the

living room, opened a small box that contained Mama's jewelry, and tenderly stared at it. Then he turned to me and asked me to take what I wanted of the jewelry. I said I could not do that. My father pleaded.

"Please take some as a souvenir," and then broke into tears.

I complied. I took Mama's engagement ring and another gold ornamental ring, which she wore occasionally. I have the two rings in my bank safe.

In the afternoon of that day, Baba, Jacob and I went for a last visit to my mother's gravesite. There we recited the Kaddish. At the end of the Kaddish, Baba looked intently at Mama's grave and tearfully talked to her. He was talking to an old friend that he missed very much. Jacob had been divorced not long before Mama's death. I can still see my father taking the handkerchief from his pocket to wipe his tears as he haltingly asked Mama to intercede on Jacob's behalf to bring to an end Jacob's sufferings. He prayed that Jacob be granted the privilege of meeting a loving spouse and having children. Jacob stood still throughout Baba's supplication.

It was a hot afternoon, and there was utter silence. Not a soul could be seen anywhere in the cemetery -- just the three of us standing together in front of Mama's grave. We chanted the Woman of Valor. It was a painful good bye to Mama. I missed mother. It was somewhat of a relief to be able to take the short ride to the cemetery to visit her grave. But in a day my family and I would be oceans away from our extended family and my mother's gravesite. What would I do when I missed her? I chanted on, but when we came to the verse "Many women have done valiantly, but thou excellest them all," it was I, this time, who broke down.

Jacob did get married not long after. He was excited when he wrote to tell me that Balforia was pregnant. Unfortunately the baby was stillborn. One more time, among many others, I was too insensitive to fathom a tragedy. I did not come to Jacob and Balforia with words of loving comfort. Callously I thought they would have another chance. They never did.

We stayed up almost the whole night before our departure to the US. My parents had brought with them a handmade Persian rug that I remembered from childhood. My father said he wanted to give it to me to take with us to the US. He and Jacob, with a good deal of help from little Aziza set out to roll the rug tightly and tie it meticulously. They worked on the project for over an hour. Baba ran several loops around the rug, tied each loop individually and then tied all the loops lengthwise. In his painstaking way, he wanted to make sure the rug would not unroll unless every separate loop was cut. It was workman's job. The rug was so tightly rolled that it felt as it were one rigid piece. It could stand straight without support. Then it was the turn of every one in the family to inspect the work and comment on how well the tying was done.

Baba took a long look at the rug, put his right hand on his hip and went into a deep pensive mood. What was he thinking about? Was he thinking of the day when he had bought that little rug? The memories that rug brought back? Was he thinking perhaps about how he furnished every room in our home in Baghdad with those large, beautifully designed Persian rugs and then had to leave them all behind? I remember one time when Baba won a major case in court. It was a lucrative case. That day he had an enormous, incredibly thick Persian rug delivered to our home. The porters unrolled it in the living room. I believe I was then five years old. I remember when Baba came home that night. We all sat in the living room and admired that rug. I was impressed with its thickness and the beauty of its design. For my father it was a milestone. He often commented on the beauty of that rug. That rug was part of his history. As I watched him with his hand on his hip, sunk in his thoughts, I wondered if he was thinking of that memento. I waited to hear what he had to say after that long pensive pause. He did not say anything. He pulled out from his dream world and quietly headed for his bedroom.

Joan was happy for us to have the rug that my parents had brought with them from Baghdad. She was eager to preserve this and other mementos from my parents as a living testimony to the history and traditions in which I grew up.

Baba tying the rug as Aziza and Jacob (partially hidden) look on

Jacob, Aziza and my father
checking that the tightly tied rug was stiff enough to stand straight without support

She wanted to have those mementos passed on to our children and our children's children. She had proudly hung in our living room Mama's silk Abayi and Baba's Arab cloak made of camel skin, which my parents had sent us when we got married.

I too was happy to have the small rug. It was part of my life and part of my parents' life. But my enthusiasm for the rug faded when I read a report that the Iranians used child labor to make those handmade Persian rugs, that some

501

of those children were as young as five years old and that they worked long hours under dismal conditions. As much as I cherished my memories of that small rug, I could no longer relate to it. I rolled it up and put it up on a shelf out of my sight. Joan understood my aversion to the idea of using that rug and went along.

When Aziza was at Wellesley College, there was a period when I had difficulty putting enough cash together to pay the quarterly installment I owed on Aziza's tuition fee. I thought of that rug. I had no use for it. It was just sitting on the shelf. I was no longer happy to own it and I wanted to get rid of it. What better way to get rid of it than to sell it and use its proceeds to pay for a good cause, the education of my child? I shared with Joan my thought, but she would not hear of it. She agreed that it was inhumane to use child labor to make those rugs. It was a blot in our history that we had, knowingly or unknowingly, encouraged child labor. But it was our history nonetheless. Selling the rug or getting rid of it would not change my history or remove the blot from it.

I managed to get a loan from the Hebrew Free Loan Society and paid Wellesley.

On August 21, 1968 we headed with friends and family for the airport. One of my sisters stayed behind. She held a big bucket of water ready to spill behind our taxicab, once we got underway. In our tradition, water spilled behind a traveler was an omen of safety and peace.

At the airport we gathered together, eagerly talking to each other, not wanting to miss a fraction of the precious few minutes left before my family and I boarded our plane. Then Joan turned to me and said, " Look at him. Look at him" and broke into tears. I turned around to look. It was my father. He was sitting on a chair in a corner all by himself. Everyone seemed to have forgotten about him. He had a lonely look on his face. And indeed he was now truly alone. While no one was saying it, actions spoke louder than words. He was now of the generation whose time had come and gone. His days of glory were gone. His position in the community was gone. Had Mama, his lifelong companion, been alive she would have been sitting next to him. But now she was gone.

My father at the airport, minutes before we left.

Joan and I joined him. I didn't say much. I couldn't. My thoughts were crowded with memories of my childhood with my parents in Baghdad. Then we were called to board our flight.

I hugged Baba. He hugged me tight for a long time. Then he placed his hands on my head and intoned the priestly blessing, "Yebarekhekha Adonai Wayishmeraikha," May God bless you and keep you.

I embraced my brother and sisters. There were so many tears. I took Aziza and Joan's hands and headed for the plane. I couldn't bear to look back.

WASHINGTON, DC

GUARDING AGAINST THE RAVAGES OF POLITICS

Soon after our arrival in the US, I resumed the work on my model of natural gas supply.

From the very start, I was aware that political overtones underlay much of the debate about the adequacy of natural gas supply in the US. But I was determined to stay clear of the crossfire between interest groups. I had no ax to grind. I was a scholar, and I wanted my model to be a first-rate scholarly work. I felt the best way to accomplish that was to open my work to all groups, in a scholarly spirit, and subject it to the criticisms of the oil and gas industry, consumer advocates, environmental groups, and government agencies. I wanted to listen to all criticisms, learn from them, and incorporate any insight I gained in the formulation and estimation of my model.

I contacted members of the oil and gas industry. The industry had fought strenuously FPC's pioneering effort at modeling the natural gas industry. I offered to meet with them and show them what I was doing. I invited their criticisms and suggestions.

The industry's response was not encouraging. They did not feel that I could possibly be interested in their input, since the sponsor of my research work, the FPC, was the very agency that regulated the wellhead price of natural gas, and the industry was opposed to regulation. It was evident that suspicion and antagonism lingered from past adversarial proceedings. I persevered. They finally agreed to meet. I sent them a synopsis of what I was doing.

When we met they had several criticisms and plenty of reservations about the feasibility of modeling the supply of natural gas in the US. I listened to them. I had my own worries about model development and shared those with them. I felt several criticisms the industry had made were valid, and I told them so. I expressed my gratitude to them for criticizing my work. They were taken aback.

From that point on, I noticed a growing sense of appreciation within of the industry of my commitment to developing a model free of predilections. Several members of the industry became frequent visitors to my office at the FPC. They stopped by whenever they came to Washington to transact industry affairs. Some went out of their way to help. The realization that I welcomed their criticisms seemed to have given some in the industry a stake in my modeling effort. Some, who had vehemently opposed the idea of mathematical modeling of gas supply, grudgingly began to see the potential contribution a model, such as the one I was developing, could make in decision making. One member of the industry provided me with confidential data to help with my work on directional drilling for gas - an aspect I was working on as part of my model development. I published that part of my work as an article in the December 69 issue of Public Utilities Fortnightly.

Still I am not sure that I ever gained the full trust of those within the industry who appreciated my willingness to listen to criticism. I remember when I gave a paper on my model at the Annual Conference of the Econometric Society in December 1968, members of the industry descended in force and huddled together in the back rows, listening to my presentation. They seemed to want to distance themselves from me in public. They did not even wave a greeting when they walked in. It was as if we were total strangers. They came in, they listened, and they left. I wondered why they showed up. Could they have been expecting to hear criticisms from the conference participants, which could serve as ammunition in any future regulatory proceedings?

I followed the same tack of openness with other groups with interest in the subject. All responded positively, and without reservations, to my overtures.

On January 20, 1969 Richard Nixon was inaugurated as President. President Nixon appointed a new FPC chairman to replace Lee C. White, an appointee of the Johnson Administration. There was talk that the new chairman was pro-industry and that he was hostile to the idea of FPC sponsoring university research work on energy modeling. I worried that my research work would become a political casualty and felt I should do what was necessary to protect it from the ravages of politics. Friends at the FPC advised me to take a leave of absence from McGill and spend full time in Washington until I had completed my work on the model.

In April 1969 I joined the civil service as Chief Econometrician of the Federal Power Commission. I completed the work on my model in mid September 1970 and returned to McGill for the beginning of the 1970-1971 academic year.

Sign affixed to my office door:
J. Daniel Khazzoom
Chief Econometrician

During the time I worked on my model, I gave free reign to my originality, and my creativity came to full blossom. That was the time when I came into my own and surged fully ahead.

It was also the time when new sunshine came to our life: Our second daughter was born.

BIRTH OF LOOLWA

On Friday afternoon, August 1, 1969, our second daughter, Loolwa, was born. When Joan's gynecologist announced it was a girl, Joan clapped her hands and joyfully called,

"It is Loolwa!"

I remember that moment vividly. I can still hear Joan's voice. Joan was elated. She radiated joy and happiness.

"O my dove in the rocky clefts,
In the covert of terrace high,
Let me see thy countenance,
Let me hear thy voice,
For sweet is thy voice
And thy countenance comely."
(Song of Songs)

יונתי בחגוי הסלע בסתר המדרנה.
הראיני את מראיך. השמיעיני את
קולך. כי-קולך ערב. ומראיך נאוה.
(שיר השירים)

Professor and Mrs. J. Daniel Khazzoom

announce the birth of their daughter

Loolwa

Ab 17, 5729 - August 1, 1969

Announcement of the birth of Loolwa,
with a quote from Song of Songs - part of the "celebration of the gift of a daughter"
known as Leilt elSittee that Babylonian Jews held on the sixth night of the birth of a
baby girl.

Joan became pregnant with Loolwa a little over a year after Mama's death, and we both pledged that if our prayer was answered and the newborn was a girl we would name her Loolwa, Judeo-Arabic for "Pearl in a million". This was the diminutive Baba had coined for Mama's name, Looloo.

I was exhilarated when I laid eyes on little Loolwa. I felt sunshine and light all around us. I felt little Loolwa brought with her goodness, the same goodness that Mama had in her. And that was how I saw her later throughout the years she was growing up – a tender, thoughtful human being who radiated goodness.

Joan exuded love when the nurse brought little Loolwa to her. She pressed Loolwa to her chest and kissed her. Loolwa looked as if she was wondering, "Where am I?"

I held Loolwa's little arm and recited a blessing for her safety and happiness.

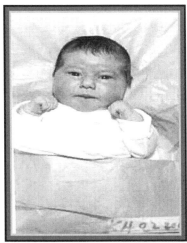

Loolwa – Minutes after birth
Below: Loolwa, three-day old, in mommy's arms, in hospital

When I took Joan early that morning to the hospital, I left Aziza with Sue and Gary Dekelmann, our neighbors across the hall. The Dekelmanns' four daughters - Katie, Coley, Cara and Carmel – were about one about year apart from each other, with the youngest about Aziza's age. Aziza and the Dekelmanns' daughters played beautifully together, and Aziza was happy to stay with them.

508

I called Aziza to share with her the good tidings. She was excited to hear that she now had a little sister with whom she could play. She asked me to describe how Loolwa looked, how big she was, what her skin color was. I provided the information she wanted. I also told Aziza that both her mommy and daddy loved her just as much as they did before the birth of her sister. She seemed to be pleased to hear that. I returned home to celebrate the *kiddush* with Aziza and give thanks to God for the birth of Loolwa.

Joan was five days in the hospital before she came home. I took off from work and spent those days with Aziza. Except for the short times when we went to visit Joan and Loolwa in the hospital, I gave Aziza my full attention. That was a most rewarding period for me. I discovered traits of Aziza that I had never known or seen before. I discovered that my six-year old was a courtly, well-mannered, gracious little girl. Throughout that whole period she conducted herself magnificently. She was also very helpful around the house. She helped me cook the meals; she set the plates on the table; she folded the napkins and put the silverware next to the plates; and she helped me wash the dishes. Her table manners were impressive. At mealtime we talked about a lot of things – birth, life, the sky, Judaism, the Jewish holidays and the times when they occur. And here, too, she amazed me with her grace and manner of speech. She listened attentively and talked slowly and deliberately.

During that period she dressed herself without any help. She chose the clothing she wanted to wear and dressed beautifully.

It blew me away. Where was all that hidden? Was it there all the time and I had been blind to it? Had it been latent, coming now to full blossom because she had my undivided attention? Was it the knowledge that she was now the big sister, which brought out the adult in her? Whatever it was, it was, for me, an amazing discovery. I felt so proud of my gracious little girl, and I felt blessed to have her as my daughter.

It was wonderful to spend those few days in Aziza's company. I wished I could have spent all my time with her and just watch her grow. Deep down I hated the rat race. I wished I did not have to be the breadwinner and could just be a nurturing stay-at-home parent. That feeling stayed with me since then, as I watched my two daughters grow up. I wished I could just be with them and never have to worry about earning a living for us.

CELEBRATING LOOLWA'S BIRTH

We held a joyous party in our home the sixth night following Loolwa's birth to celebrate the birth our daughter and to announce her name. We invited friends and neighbors and we celebrated the occasion in accordance with the Babylonian traditions.

Over the years, my return to my Babylonian roots was a long and gradual process. When Aziza was born, I was not yet as far along in the process as I was when Loolwa was born. At that time, I followed the local practice of simply naming Aziza in a synagogue when I was called to the Torah for the occasion, as is the custom among Ashkenazi Jewry. I wish I had been as aware then as I was when Loolwa was born, and had welcomed Aziza's birth in my own ancestral traditions.

For our neighbors, both Jews and non-Jews, a religious ceremony celebrating the birth of a daughter was a novelty, and they looked forward to being part of the ritual. They were pleased that Joan and I had chosen to depart from the prevailing practice within the Jewish community of giving the short shrift to the birth of a female baby and were delighted that we had chosen to celebrate Loolwa's birth as a major event in our life and in the life of the community.

I remember gratefully how our neighbors pitched in to help me prepare for the celebration. And I still remember how one of my neighbors came to my rescue when we had a glitch with the coffee maker.

I felt celebrating the birth of our daughter was a very special occasion, and I did not want to serve our guests just instant coffee. I wanted to treat them to freshly brewed coffee. We had a gorgeous big pot for brewing coffee. I put the ground coffee in, turned on the electricity, and left. But when I opened the spigot to serve our guests, all I got was hot water. My gorgeous coffee pot had broken down. I was at my wits' end.

"What do I do now?" I asked one of my neighbors who stood by my side.

"Calm down, Daniel" she said. " Do you have instant coffee?"

"Yes I do. But it won't taste as good as brewed coffee," I said.

"Don't worry. No one will notice the difference. Give me the instant?"

She opened the jar of instant coffee, poured some in the pot and stirred. Then she announced to our guests the freshly brewed coffee was ready for any one who wanted to have coffee.

Several of our guests commented how much they loved the taste of the brewed coffee. My neighbor winked at me and she had a wicked smile on her face. I kept my mouth shut.

It was time to start the religious part of the ceremony – the naming ritual. Joan came out of the bedroom with the baby in her arms and little Aziza holding on to her mommy's arm. Joan looked weak, but she radiated peace and happiness.

I began with the traditional reading of the beautiful poem from the Song of Songs, which I had included also in Loolwa's birth announcement. I read it both in Hebrew and English, so that everyone could understand and feel part of the ritual. Then I announced, slowly and deliberately,

"This newly-born babe shall be known in the House of Israel as Loolwa daughter of Joan", as is the custom of the Babylonian Jews, who named their children by their mother.

I recited a blessing for little Loolwa's well being and concluded with my personal prayer for mother and daughter.

Loolwa Coming Home

Joan being wheeled out of hospital with Loolwa in arm

Aziza taking her first peak at sister on arrival

Proud to hold Loolwa as mommy
comes out of car

Cuddling little sister

Amazed at the little newborn

Several of our friends said they loved the simplicity of the ritual.

That evening is one I will always remember.

WHEN HELL BROKE LOOSE

Much of our attention during the first few days after Joan's return from the hospital was focused on Joan and our newly born. We began, however, to notice a disturbing change in Aziza's behavior. Aziza closed in on herself and became increasingly irritable; she cried for the slightest reason and would not be comforted; she did not like what we ate, and she did not like her clothing. Her room was in disarray, and she seemed to have lost much of her ability to focus; she switched from one game to another, and she threw her toys. She looked restless and was in constant, aimless motion. No longer did she seem to know what she wanted.

It felt as if all hell had broken loose, and I was terrified to see what was happening to our little girl, all within just one week, since Joan and Loolwa had come home. Aziza was now so different from the gracious little girl I had known. Something terrible had been happening. We needed help.

I did not wait.

I called my psychiatrist and scheduled an appointment for the following day.

The psychiatrist diagnosed Aziza as hyperactive. He assured us she would outgrow her hyperactivity without any residual effect, as long as we continued to show her love and worked to help her with her daily tasks. He explained that we did not notice Aziza's hyperactivity until Loolwa's birth, probably because, until then, Aziza was the only child. She got all the attention and all the help she needed, until Loolwa's arrival when Aziza received only part of the support she was used to getting.

My mind flashed back to the time Aziza was attending nursery school in Yonkers when, one day, I went to pick her up from school. To my surprise, her teacher complained Aziza was undisciplined, that she did not pay attention, and would not sit still. The child the teacher had described was not the Aziza I knew. I asked what the teacher thought we should do.

"Give her a good spanking. That will catch her attention".

I was appalled to hear a teacher recommend spanking. I took Aziza out of the nursery school that same day.

We enrolled Aziza in a kindergarten at Greystone Jewish Community Center, where she received individual attention. She blossomed. We never had any complaint about fidgeting or inattentiveness.

As I juxtaposed our experience at the Greystone Jewish Community Center and what the psychiatrist told us, things began to fall into place in my own mind.

The psychiatrist prescribed Ritalin. There was little experience with Ritalin at the time, and its long-term effects were unknown. Joan and I thought it over and decided to take our chances.

We saw immediate improvement when we started the Ritalin treatment. Aziza became calmer, focused and settled.

Joan deserves credit for taking the lead in making lists that broke Aziza's daily chores into smaller, manageable tasks. For the mornings, Joan placed a list in the bathroom that detailed in chronological order what needed to be done: -

1. Wash your hands
2. Wash your face
3. Brush your teeth
4. Recite the prayer of thanks for being alive
5.
    .

Every time Aziza finished a task, she would cross it out and move to the next one. Joan made similar lists for after-school and bedtime tasks. I was touched as I watched how our little girl worked diligently through those tasks, one by one, and crossed out each task as she finished it.

Joan and I joined a group of parents with hyperactive children and enrolled in classes about hyperactivity. We were saddened to read the stories of hyperactive children whose adult lives were ruined because their hyperactivity was not treated for what it was – an illness.

Aziza's perseverance is legendary. She did amazingly

well in school. I marveled at her accomplishments in spite of her handicap. In time she no longer needed the Ritalin.

As a parent, I can think of many times when I was too slow in recognizing the import of what was happening around me. But this is one time when I look back with gratitude at my decision not to wait one more hour before seeking professional help. Discovering that Aziza was hyperactive and learning how to deal with a hyperactive child made a difference in our child's life and in our life as a family. And I am ever so grateful for that.

To day Aziza is a Faculty member at the Hebrew University, Jerusalem.

A LOOK BACK ON MY LIFE IN WASHINGTON

During the year and a half we spent in Washington, we lived in a garden apartment at 2415 Ross Road, Silver Spring, Maryland - a beautiful complex with a bucolic feel, surrounded by tall and regal Maryland trees, and bordering a lush park with lots of trees, a playground, and a large community hall. The complex had also a large swimming pool where my family and I loved to go swimming together. I never managed to do the flip as well as I did from the springy diving board there.

We became friendly with many of our neighbors in the complex. I found it much easier to make friends in Washington than anywhere else. Perhaps that was because many residents of Washington and its outskirts were transients like us who planned to stay in the area for a limited duration. And unlike the population in Montreal where the majority traced their families for generations in the area, most of the people we met in Washington were first generation Washingtonians, who had very few, or no, relatives in the Washington area.

There were two synagogues within walking distance of our apartment, one Reform and one Conservative. I wished there was a Sephardi synagogue in the Washington area. I could never get myself to identify exclusively with any one of the four major Jewish denominations. Sephardim do not have denominations. We pray together without regard to the religious conviction or the level of observance of our fellow Jews.

Instead of devoting most of the time to prayers and sermons, as was done in congregations on the Sabbath, I preferred to devote most of the time to discussing the Torah and striving to gain insights from the weekly portion of the Torah. Fortunately, there were a dozen or so among the residents in our complex who felt the same way. We got the Conservative synagogue to set aside a room for us in the building where we met every Sabbath and spent most of our time discussing the Torah portion of the week. I learned a lot from our discussions and was inspired by the insights I gained from them.

Every Sabbath, at the end of our gathering, we met for a potluck lunch in the apartment of an older couple who were members of the group. Joan walked into the apartment with a big bowl of salad, glowing with its colorful ingredients. Everyone admired those big bowls of salad.

We ate, chattered, and sang. This was our extended family during the period we spent in Washington. There were times when there was tension, but, on the whole, I remember the time we spent together on the Sabbath as a wonderful period.

I never had a similar experience in any other community we lived in.

Aziza attended the kindergarten at the Hebrew Academy of Washington during the first two months of our stay in Washington. The Kindergarten held a big graduation ceremony in June 1969. We were proud to see little Aziza march in the graduation ceremony that day.

We enrolled Aziza in the Solomon Schechter School, which was housed in the building of the Conservative synagogue. It was a much smaller school than the Hebrew Academy and Aziza blossomed there. She had a Hebrew teacher who loved her and was thrilled to have a student who could pronounce the Hebrew consonants in the way of Middle Eastern Jews. Aziza loved Hebrew and most of the time she accompanied me to the synagogue on the Sabbath.

One Sabbath in June 1969, a few months before Loolwa was born, Aziza wore a beautiful pair of tights I had just purchased for her. We strolled together on our way back home from the synagogue. Aziza stumbled and, as she fell, her tights got caught in the bushes and tore. I picked her up. Aziza was crying. I worried that she might have been hurt.

Aziza marching in the kindergarten graduation procession

I checked to see if she had skinned her leg or suffered any injury. I was glad to see she was not hurt and did not really pay attention to the tear in her tights. We resumed our walk home. Aziza looked very sad but did not say anything. But then she suddenly burst into tears.

"The new tights that you bought me and I liked so much are torn. They will never be the same again."

I wiped little Aziza's tears and was so moved by what she said. Aziza rarely, if ever, had verbalized her interest in her clothes, and I was under the impression she did not particularly care. But she did.

It was also the first time I realized it meant something to her that I bought those tights for her. I comforted her and told her how sorry I was that her new tights were torn, but that it was more important that she was not hurt than the fact that her tights were torn.

We held hands and walked back home together.

Aziza – June 1969

It was one of those occasions when I got to know one aspect of my daughter, which I had not known before. Aziza did not talk much about what she cared for. It was up to me to try harder to find out what went on in the mind of my child.

As I look back, I think of the time that I spent in Washington as the golden period of my life. There were some clouds that occasionally covered the sun, but a strong wind always blew the clouds away and I was, once again, left standing in the sun. I think it was the happiest time of my life.

My career was taking off. I was doing work that I loved. My family was growing. My younger daughter, my pearl in a million, had graced our lives with her presence. She bore my mother's name and I felt the continuity of the generations. It was almost as if my mother were with me again, filling my life with her love.

When Aziza was born my career was just beginning and life seemed so uncertain. Now I was standing on firmer ground. I could catch my breath and enjoy life, enjoy being with my family. We went camping on the weekends of the summer and the fall. On the campgrounds we celebrated the Sabbath together, communing with nature and with each other. We combined praying and playing in the most delightful way. We frolicked in the pool and we sang Sabbath songs, feeling that our voices were lifted beyond the topmost branches of the trees up to the heavens. It was the best of times and I gloried in them.

We visited my father-in-law in McHenry Shores, Illinois a few weeks after Loolwa's birth. He was thrilled to see his new grand daughter. It must have given him a big boost to have a new addition to the family, having lost his wife not long before Loolwa's birth. My father-in-law lived on the bank of the Fox River. He loved boating, and he took us for long rides on the Fox River.

Camping

Packing the car rack for camping

Joan, Aziza and Loolwa
at Crow's Nest Lodge, Thurmont, Maryland

In Delaware camp: Joan playing the recorder ... and Loolwa in playpen enjoying
her bottle

On Acetique Island, MD, where wild ponies roam free (June 9-15,'70)

Aziza in grandpa Hicks' boat, Fox River
Below: On Grandpa Hicks' porch, McHenry Shores

Knowing how much I loved ballet, Joan bought us season tickets to the ballet and, though we felt a little guilty about leaving the children with a baby sitter, we attended every performance and thoroughly enjoyed them. It was so much easier to be focused only on research work and not be dividing my attention between research work and teaching and never having enough time to spend on either.

Ballerinas - picture of graceful movements. Joan bought this picture for me when she bought season's tickets for the Washington Ballet. I loved this picture. It hung in my office until my retirement in June 2000.

In the office I explored not only my work, but also my growing friendship with Sy Wenner. I have never before, or ever since, had such a close friendship. Since he worked in the same building, we often had lunch together and took walks after lunch around the building. Our talks covered everything from Torah to the mundane. Sy and I were on the same wavelength. Our superficial differences faded into the warm glow of our friendship. It was a wonderful period in which everything fell so perfectly into place.

In the beginning of my work on the model there were

times when I felt I would never get it to work. Even at those times I persevered doggedly and took pleasure in my perseverance. Sometimes I sat before the computer with my assistant for twelve hours at a time. It was grueling work, but the reward that could come in the end from the knowledge that I had created a model that actually worked and did what it was designed to do, spurred me on.

Several before me had tried to develop a reliable gas supply model. There were missing pieces of the puzzle and it was up to me to find them. Find them I did. I worked long hours, trying one solution only to discard it and try another.

Joy in my work blended with family happiness. Every day I went home for dinner, ate with my family and sang to my children when I put them to bed. Aziza was a gorgeous little girl. Loolwa shone as only a priceless pearl can. Joan and I treasured our children. The luster of contentment filled my days. During the long nights, while the rest of the family slept, I worked on my model and listened to the sweet strains of The Magic Flute. Its throbbing notes spoke to me of the pleasure that one takes in the quest and the glory that fills mind and heart when the goal is within reach and the golden grail is in one's possession. So it was with me. But it was even more than that. My two little girls were asleep in the room next to the one in which I worked. It was they who really made my world complete. There was the music of The Magic Flute inextricably mingled with the song that my children brought to my heart.

In April of 2004 I went to a performance of the Magic Flute at California State University, Sacramento. Tears rolled down my cheeks as I listened to the orchestra and remembered those long nights I spent in my study at Rock Creek Forest Apartments in Silver Spring next to the room in which my daughters slept. I remembered also the joy of being absorbed in the development of my model.

Watching our children grow

Celebrating Aziza's birthday, Sep. 13, 69   Loolwa, Nov 69

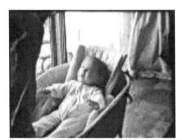

Loolwa listening as I talk to her, Dec 69   Aziza practicing Babylonian finger clicks, winter, 70

Entertaining each other, spring 70   Loolwa loved "Cosheez" , spring70

Aziza cutting out her dress, spring 70   Helping sister take her first steps, spring 70

The two sisters – July 1970

There were the long hours of hard work and the magic of discovery. By testing, by sharing test results, by listening to everybody who knew something about gas exploration, I found the missing pieces. I talked to geologists and drew on their expertise. The knowledge I gleaned from them helped me see my work in a **clearer, better defined light. Even casual conversations with members of the industry yielded nuggets of information. I**

525

learned that in some natural fields liquid gas price is a major driving factor for gas discovery. It was the last piece that marked the completion of the puzzle. Everything was in place. Or so it seemed. I tested the accuracy of my model's prediction of gas supply by running it using data from past years and checking my predictions against the following year's discoveries. It ran like a dream. I was pleased and was ready to declare the work finished, when I ran into a snag. For the last year for which data had just become available, my predicted results were far out of line. I couldn't understand it. What had happened? What was it I hadn't taken into account?

STANDING UP TO THE BULLY

I was ready to tear my hair out when I discovered that the year before the most recent data became available, a clerical error had resulted in the available gas supply data being overstated by billions of British thermal units. Instead of correcting the error in the year for which it was reported, the industry compensated for the error by subtracting the error from the supply of gas in the following year. Not alone that, but news began circulating that the supply of gas had dropped in that particular year due to the government's regulation of the price of natural gas. Price regulation was blamed for the drop in the supply of natural gas.

When I uncovered this finagling I was appalled and wrote a memo to that effect. I circulated the memo within the FPC. It was within my province to do that since I had made autonomy a condition of my serving as a civil servant while on leave of absence from McGill. Regular government employees had to clear all memos with their immediate supervisor. I didn't.

My memo incensed FPC's chairman, John Nassikas. He sent for my colleague Haskell Wald.

"The chairman is furious. He wants to see you" Haskell told me, as he came out of his meeting with FPC's chairman.

That night Joan and I went over our finances and determined we could manage if I were fired. I could lose my job, but I couldn't compromise my principles. Joan understood that.

Next morning John Nassikas' office asked me to stop by to meet with the chairman. My colleagues knew of the summons and their worried looks followed me all the way to the door.

I sat opposite the chairman on the other side of his desk. He had a copy of my memo in his hand.

"What is this?" he barked, and tossed the memo toward me.

I picked up the memo and tossed it back to him.

"Don't ever throw things at me," I said calmly and looked him straight in the eye.

His face turned the color of a beetroot, his jaw dropped and his eyes opened wide in astonishment. He was speechless.

I took advantage of the moment to open the discussion.

"What is the problem here?" I asked.

The story unfolded and to my amazement I discovered that Nassikas thought I was in cahoots with Senator Ted Kennedy. It turned out that Senator Kennedy had made a speech in the Senate accusing the oil and gas industry of trying to mislead the government and the public. Nassikas thought I had given the senator ammunition for his attack by sending him a copy of my memo.

Now it was time for my jaw to drop, though I couldn't help but see the irony in the situation. I had never spoken with Senator Kennedy, and I had never wanted my work to be tangled up in any political maneuvering. Throughout the period I worked on my model I stayed as far away from politicians and political influence as I could. I was a scholar and I did not want my research work to be compromised for anything.

Once the chairman and I got that straight, our conversation was positively cordial and he took the occasion to praise some other work I had published. He went to great lengths to tell me how much he had learned in particular from an article on gas directionality that I had published in the December 1969 issue of Public Utilities Fortnightly.

From that time on, to the surprise of my coworkers, John Nassikas' attitude toward me was deferential and respectful.

TIME TO LEAVE

As the end of my leave of absence drew near and as the work on my model approached its conclusion, I became increasingly conflicted about leaving Washington and returning to Montreal.

I could have stayed in Washington. The FPC wanted me to stay and wooed me with a tempting offer. I felt, however, that if I stayed in Washington, I would be saddled with administrative responsibilities, organizational meetings and committee work that would take me away from my research work. I wanted to stay focused, and I had managed to do so because when I had come to Washington I was committed to achieve one well defined goal – the development of a model of natural gas supply in the US. That would not be the case if I stayed.

My project had been a potentially politically explosive one, but I had managed not to become politically involved. Would I be able to continue to do that if I stayed in Washington? It didn't seem likely.

Returning to Montreal had its plus, but it had also a lot of minuses.

I liked McGill, and how I wished McGill University were located in Washington! I hated the weather in Montreal. The winters were cold and long and we had to bundle up every time we stepped outside the door. Dealing with the bureaucracy in Quebec was a nightmare, and I was constantly being dragged into the French-English conflict. I was also very uncomfortable with the anti Americanism that surrounded me in Canada. America was the country in which I had chosen to live. It was a free and open society and there I was not continually dragged into bureaucratic entanglements.

When we were in Washington, Baba had often sent me big packages from Israel. I never had any trouble receiving them. In Canada I received LP records monthly from the Musical Heritage Society in the US. If my memory serves me correctly, these records cost a dollar and a half for the Society's members. Every time I received a record I had to go to the customs office, fill out forms, pay a dollar duty and wait for the paper work to clear before I received my record. Sometimes that took a month. In disgust, I canceled my subscription to the Musical Heritage Society.

In Washington I was thrust into the center of activity. I was in the heart of the nation. I loved being there. The hustle and bustle around me energized me. My good friend Seymour Winner, who added so much grace, beauty and intellectual stimulation to my life, lived in Washington. I loved the Jewish community in Silver Spring, Maryland, and its easy-going attitude. I loved our neighbors in the complex, our friendly get-togethers, our Torah study group and our Sabbath lunches. I loved the weather in the Washington area, and I loved the outdoors life in Washington. I really didn't want to go.

My daughter Aziza didn't want to leave either. She liked to play with her sister, but Loolwa was six years younger than she. The Dekelmann children next-door were ideal playmates for Aziza and they included her easily in their play. She loved being with them.

Joan and I agonized over what to do. In the end we decided that it would be best to go back to McGill. I talked with little Aziza about it. I notified the FPC of our decision. With heavy hearts we began packing.

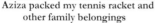

Aziza packed my tennis racket and   Loolwa, too, helped with the packing
other family belongings

Two days before we left I went to my office for the last time. Joan came to visit me and bid goodbye to my coworkers. At the end of the day when everyone was gone, we took pictures of the "Chief Econometrician" sign on my door and the "Please Do Not Disturb" sign that hung on my door during those many hours when I worked on writing the manuscript. In some ways it reminded me of my leaving my office in the military, but my sadness at leaving Washington was much more profound.

I took a picture of my blackboard where the last diagram and equation I had worked on with my assistant, Alan Gruchy, were still recorded. He and I worked and worked on the blackboard until my ideas crystallized and I could commit them to paper. The blackboard and I had been through so much and now it was over. As I erased the blackboard, I felt as if I were in mourning. I would come back to Washington, but it would never be the same.

The night before we left, Sy and Naomi Wenner came to visit us. It was hard to say good-bye.

530

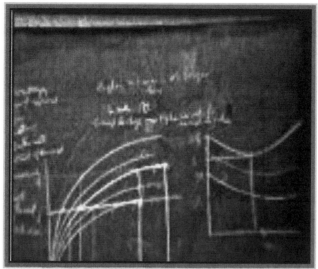

My office blackboard – the last problem we worked on

Aziza wrote a letter to the Dekelmann daughters before she left. It broke my heart when she showed it to me. "Wen I em older" Aziza wrote, " I will feal so bad that I lost you wen we war yung".

I asked Aziza if it was OK for me to make a copy of her letter. She said it was. I made a copy and kept it in our family scrapbook.

The day we left Silver Spring Aziza was heart broken. She sobbed and sobbed. The Dekelmann children, who still had each other, did not feel the same grief. Aziza hugged them; they hugged her back and resumed their play without her soon after. I know Aziza felt desolate. I am sure she missed her school too. She had blossomed there.

I held little Aziza's hands and together we walked to our car for the drive back to Montreal.

Aziza's letter to the Dekelmann daughters
When I made the copy I added the inscription in the upper right corner
"A letter from little Aziza to the Dekelmann children as we left Silver Spring in Sep
1970"

TESTIMONY, INTRIGUES

I returned to McGill for the academic year in mid September 1970, but the work on my model did not end with my return to Montreal. The model needed to be subjected to a litigatory process before the Federal Power Commission could utilize it in regulating the price of natural gas. The oil and gas industry would try to disprove the reliability of the model in arriving at a reasonable price for natural gas; I would appear as the FPC's witness to respond to the issues raised by the industry. As part of the process each side would cross-examine the other side's witnesses. An Administrative Law Judge would preside over the hearings and he was the one who would render a decision that could, of course, be appealed to a higher court.

In point of fact, hearings on the FPC's earlier model of natural gas went all he way to the US Supreme Court where it was finally turned down. For those hearings the oil and gas industry had retained the late Paul Cootner, an MIT economist, as its star witness to rebut the FPC's model. This time, too, the industry turned to top universities to recruit witnesses to rebut my model. But this time the industry had no takers. I was pleased to learn that two colleagues, in particular, at Harvard and Columbia's Departments of Economics refused to serve as witnesses for the industry saying they felt the model was credible work, that they were unwilling to engage in nit picking. Willy-nilly the industry settled on a Washington consulting firm to rebut my model.

THE MYSTERIOUS PHONE CALL

Shortly before the hearings I received a call from someone who introduced himself as a member of an institution whose name included the word "Research" and asked if he could ask me a few questions about my model. I did not get the full name of the caller or the institution with which he was affiliated, but the word "research" in the institution's name led me to believe this was a bona fide research organization. During the period since my return to McGill, I had received similar calls from universities and research organizations interested in learning about my model and exchanging information on the subject.

The caller first asked me some innocuous questions and then asked if I would list what I considered to be the limitations of my model. I was open with him, as I was with others before, and readily told him about limitations of which I was aware. In the course of listing these limitations, I told him about some incorrect data I had used in one sector of my model. Later when the FPC staff double-checked my data, they found out that I actually used the correct data. I would have gotten in touch with my caller to say I had inadvertently misled him, that it turned out that I had used the correct data, but I had neither his name nor his number. I shrugged and let it go. If the caller checked on what I had told him, he would discover my mistake for himself. I had other things to think about. I had to prepare myself for the hearings.

During the course of the hearings the main witness for the industry took the stand. To my surprise he listed verbatim all of the model's weaknesses I had outlined on the phone to my unidentified caller. Unfortunately for him, he included in his list the data, which I had erroneously included in my list of model limitations. Under cross-examination, he fell apart. He could not explain why the data was erroneous and had to confess he had extracted the information from me by questionable means. I was flabbergasted. Until that moment I was unaware that my mysterious caller worked for the consulting firm retained by the industry. I had not been on my guard. I was an innocent party to what happened, completely unaware that such underhanded methods were commonly employed.

MORE SHENANIGANS

I remember another incidence of unsavory practice.

In the course of one of my visits to Washington a year or so later, I went to visit my friend Joe Lerner who served as Chief Economist of the Federal Emergency Preparedness. He showed me projections of natural gas supply that his agency had purchased from a consulting firm in Washington, DC. As I skimmed through the predictions I was pleased to see that the forecasts seemed to be in line with the predictions from my model. But as I read further, I became suspicious.

"Joe, these forecasts look awfully close to the forecasts from my model," I exclaimed. "Do you know how they arrived at those predictions? Could they have come from my model?"

My model was free and open to the public. I had published it with all of its parameters in the spring 1971 issue of the Bell Journal of Economics and Management Science. Joe was bewildered.

"We paid for this!" he exclaimed.

Further investigation revealed that that consulting firm was actually running my model and charging its clients for the model's output.

AN OFFER OF A DEAL I TURNED DOWN

Weeks before the start of the hearings on my model, the legal team of the oil and gas industry offered a deal to the FPC:

"We will forego cross-examining Professor Khazzoom if he foregoes cross-examining our main witness".

My response was short.

"Not on your life".

My reasons were simple. I approached the hearings as a scholar. I did not see them as a battle between two opponents, even though they were held in a litigatory setting. Rather, I felt the hearings provided a valuable opportunity for me to learn more about infirmities my model might have so that I could use the knowledge gained to improve my work.

The FPC forwarded my response to the industry. Interestingly, the industry still chose to unilaterally refrain from cross examining me or challenging my cross-examination of its own witnesses.

The hearings had, at least for me, some light moments. The cross examination of the industry's witness often dealt with econometric technicalities, and I could see the look of discomfort on the judge's face as he struggled to understand. I sympathized with him. Econometrics deals with measurements in economics and draws extensively on mathematical statistics, a subject with which people not versed in the field often have difficulty. This judge was no exception, but the FPC's lawyer was not focused on the judge's discomfort. He continued in his cross examination of the industry's witness pressing him to admit that he had had incorrectly used a particular statistical test

"It will clarify things for the court, if you would explain the relationship between the F distribution and the Chi-square distribution," the lawyer declared.

On hearing this, the Judge's eyes rolled, his head dropped, and his shoulders slumped as he muttered in disgusted tones,

"I am sure that will clarify things for the court."

RULING FAIRLY ON TECHNICAL TESTIMONIES

That was an amusing moment for me, but it had serious overtones and raised a legitimate question. How does a judge rule fairly and justly on issues that involve highly technical testimonies? When the FPC's earlier model of natural gas was submitted to hearings before an Administrative Law Judge, the industry's witnesses took advantage of the fact that the judge was not knowledgeable in the subject and took pot shots at the model. They sensationalized minor infirmities and used technical terms to blow up the infirmities out of proportion to reality. It was nothing more than nit picking, made to sound like weighty allegations. The judge who was not familiar with the technicalities of the subject could not separate the wheat from the chaff, and was swayed by the sensationalism of the industry's witnesses. The FPC staff present at those hearings told me that, distressed by the way those hearings went, the FPC's lead staff member who worked on that model became depressed. His hands trembled and he lost weight. His health deteriorated so badly that he died not long after the end of the hearings on that model.

Another such case where the judge's ignorance of technical subjects was exploited to pull the wool over the judge's eyes occurred once when I was present at administrative hearings before the California Public Utilities Commission, in my capacity as an observer on behalf of Pacific Gas and Electric Co. (PGE). PGE was contesting a model the California Energy Commission had submitted. The fact that the model was an awful model is not the issue here. What is at issue is the method employed to discredit it.

The author of that model used a method that yielded what econometricians term "biased" results. This is a term used in econometrics, but it does not mean what "biased" means in ordinary, everyday language. In fact, "biased" estimators are sometimes preferable to "unbiased" estimators. The judge, of course, was not familiar with those subtleties, and PGE's lawyer capitalized on that fact.

When the author of the model was called to the stand, PGE's attorney, on cross-examination, asked him if the estimate he got was biased. The author admitted that it was. Then PGE's lawyer raised his voice.

"You have knowingly submitted a model with biased results and you want the Commission to rule in favor of biased results?"

On hearing that the judge's eyes bulged. He probably thought that "biased results" was tantamount to "rigged results".

PGE won that case.

At the time when I developed my model of natural gas, econometrics was still at a relatively new, albeit a very useful science, but the government was not able to take full advantage of its capabilities. Lawyers used its technical terms in ways that were misleading. The end result was that judgments rendered were not based on a true and full picture of the facts and society was being deprived of the benefit that this science could have made. I wanted to find a way to remedy the situation.

On this endeavor I worked with Haskell Wald of FPC and Bill Capron of the Brookings Institution. The three of us thought of organizing a conference that would deal with this issue. Our objective was to find ways that make it possible to present a highly technical testimony at regulatory proceedings in such a manner that it would be understood and not subjected to inflammatory and misleading examination. We worked long and hard on drafting the proposal for the project and were, we felt, lucky that Bill Capron had a grant that could provide us with funding.

Our efforts came to naught when Capron left the Brookings and his replacement had no interest in the subject.

My Family In The Early Seventies

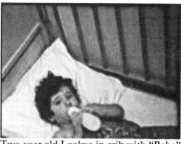

Aziza riding her new bicycle in front of
Our apartment house, Chomedey, Quebec
August 71.

Two-year old Loolwa in crib with "Baba"
as she called the bottle. Chomedey.

Aziza (back to camera), a neighbor, Loolwa,
Daniel in backyard swing, Chomedey, Aug 71

Loolwa riding her new tricycle in
camp, Labor Day 1971

Mommy playing with Aziza and Loolwa

Loolwa dressing up, Aug 71

Every day before it was time to drive Aziza
to the Hebrew Academy in Montreal, Loolwa
sat on Aziza's lap and the two watched intensely
the half-hour wonderful show "Rupert the Bear"

Performance by Aziza and Loolwa

Aziza on her eighth birthday celebration

Mommy serving the guests on
Aziza's 8th birthday

Teaching Loolwa to swim, August 71

At Writers' Manor, Denver. CO, Aug 71

540

Mommy and Loolwa

Aziza, Loolwa and Khalu (uncle) Guerji at the Royal Victoria Swimming Pool,
during Khalu Guerji's visit in July 1973

Khalu Guerji at Royal Victoria Swimming
pool

Aziza's appearance on CTV's
program "What Say You", Aug 1973

ACADEMIC INTEGRITY

My colleague at McGill's department of Economics, Tom Asimakopoulus, served as the editor of the Canadian Journal of Economics (CJE), a quarterly journal published by the Canadian Economic Association. After stripping the submission of anything that revealed the identity of the author, Tom sent every submission he received to two, sometimes three referees for review and evaluation. The referees' report served as the basis for the editor's decision on whether the submission merited publication. When the submission entailed the use of econometric methods, I was often one of the referees.

I took my responsibility as a referee very seriously. I knew the buck stopped with me, and I always wanted to make sure the data used in the submission were defensible and the empirical results replicable. I was very cognizant of the fact that faculty members in research universities were under tremendous pressure to publish. A dictum that echoed through the academic halls is the familiar "publish or perish." Additionally, anyone who made a significant breakthrough in her field rose above her fellow researchers in that field. For young faculty members that was also the sine qua non for promotion and tenure. As a result, the temptation to claim a breakthrough was great. I always worried that the drive to claim a breakthrough might be great enough to lead some to falsify empirical results in order to support the claim of a breakthrough.

I remember one incident that happened when I refereed one econometric paper for CJE.

The author reported empirical results that seemed to fly in the face of anything we knew from a priori knowledge. I felt that, if those results were indeed accurate, they would demand a fundamental change in Canadian government policy. One cannot rule out results just because they depart from a priori expectations. Pushing the frontiers of knowledge often involves just such radical departures from existing knowledge. But, in this case, the findings had such drastic policy implications I felt I needed to leave no stone unturned in checking every detail the author had reported.

As a first step, I decided to re-estimate the author's model myself to see if the results the author had reported were replicable. I asked Tom to have the author send him all the data he used as well as the printouts of his estimation results.

Oddly, the author wrote back that he had decided to withdraw his paper.

A year or so later, the author resubmitted his article to CJE, only this time the results were not so spectacular. By now I was suspicious. Again I asked Tom to have the author send his printouts and the data he used in estimating his model. This time I received a blistering letter from the author blasting me for making such demands.

At this point, Tom notified the author of CJE's decision to reject his submission.

The incident took me aback. It brought to mind a similarly intense encounter I had earlier in my career, one that involved teaching rather than refereeing.

In my capacity as a Teaching Fellow at Harvard, I assisted Seymour Harris, my thesis advisor, in teaching Harvard's Freshman Seminar, a small seminar, set up on an experimental basis, for a group of about fifteen freshmen who came to Harvard with exceptional academic backgrounds. One member of the seminar, a tall, overweight, blonde young man, stood out for his active participation in seminar discussions. Often he contributed bright ideas, but he seemed to be driven by an intense need to outdo his classmates and to shine above all the rest. He was the scion of a publicly active family and the son of the CEO of a major oil company.

At the end of the semester, he submitted a very good term paper, which did not surprise me, except that the analysis was so systematic that it raised my suspicions. Where did a freshman acquire this level of maturity? Before deciding on a final grade, I invited the student to come to my office, told him how much I appreciated his paper and asked him if he would elaborate on some of the thinking he had expressed in that paper. Unexpectedly, he bristled at my request, his face reddened, his eyes bulged and he refused to cooperate. He argued that I should grade his paper without interrogation. I was surprised by his reaction and tried to calm him down, but, inexplicably, he grew even more agitated. When I told him I was ending the meeting he became nastier, called me names and slammed the door behind him as he left. I was stunned.

I reported the incident to Professor Harris. He was no less surprised. He suspected plagiarism. Together with another Teaching Fellow, I worked on tracing the sources. It did not take long to discover that substantial parts of that paper were plagiarized from various articles. I knew very little about the specifics that surrounded the life of that young man. But I remember wondering - that student was bright enough to write a good paper all on his own. Why did he feel that would not be enough? What drove him to try so hard to beat everyone else?

Harvard expelled him, with no possibility of readmission as far as I remember.

SCHOLARSHIP AND CONFIDENTIALITY DO NOT MIX

I have always believed that the truth should not be perverted for political ends, no matter how worthy that end may be. At one point in my career, adhering to this principle almost succeeded in pulling the rug out from under my research work and, in the process, my career.

Energy usage has been a focus of my scholarship for a long time. After I developed the Natural Gas Supply Model for the US, I began work on a comprehensive model to estimate the demand for all sources of energy in Canada. It was an ambitious undertaking and, in time, the model I developed played a major role in the energy landscape in Canada. McGill provided a seeding grant to support the initial stages of the research, but we needed data in order for the research to progress. Canada's Ministry of Energy Mines and Resources (EMR) had the data in their archives, but it was, unfortunately, in an unusable format and needed extensive work. Fortunately, EMR had an interest in the model I was developing and offered to provide financial support to construct the required data from their archives.

In mid April 1972, I moved to Ottawa with about fifteen of my graduate students to begin work on the data.

But no sooner had we arrived than we encountered a potentially fatal hitch, one I had not anticipated. EMR told us that, for reasons of trade secrets, the data we came to compile had to be kept confidential.

I told EMR I did not engage in any confidential work, that my commitment to scholarship required my work be open to the public. That meant any data I used in the estimation of my model, including the data we would be compiling from the Ministry's archives, had to be made available to anyone who wanted to check my model's results or make any other use of the data.

For a while it looked as if my students and I had traveled to Ottawa in vain. But as I was getting ready to return to Montreal, EMR changed its mind and agreed to make the data public. I breathed a sigh of relief. My students and I started our work in earnest. My family came to join me for the summer.

I worked long hours during the day, but the evenings and weekends I spent with my family. During the week we stayed at campgrounds near Ottawa; on the weekends we returned to our apartment in Montreal.

Everything seemed to be going so well. I worked and played hard and felt I was on top of the world. My family, too, was enjoying the summer. Loolwa fell in love with Nelly, one of the ponies at the camp, and kept her supplied with sugar cubes. In the evenings we ate dinner together under the clear starry sky. A skunk invariably came to our campsite to rummage for food once we had gone into our camper to sleep. We called it "our resident skunk" and its smell always gave its presence away. Every night Joan left our dinner leftovers on a paper plate outside our campsite. Unfailingly, our resident skunk showed up, ate its dinner and left an empty plate before moving on.

It was an idyllic summer. By the end of July 1972 my students and I had compiled most of the data we needed. It was then that the blow fell.

The EMR's Assistant Deputy Minister (ADM), the equivalent of Assistant Secretary in the US, was in the process of drafting a major plan dealing with Canada's Energy Policy. He wanted to have EMR run my model and incorporate its forecast of energy demand into the plan. I was delighted, but as our talks with progressed, I became increasingly uneasy. It seemed EMR would be selective in choosing only the forecasts that fit what the government had already been promoting about the energy landscape in Canada, while giving an impression of objectivity by stating the model it was using was developed at McGill. I did the only thing I could do under the circumstances. I told the ADM I would be happy to provide the requested forecasts on condition EMR would give me assurance that it would not suppress results that did not support the government's point-of-view.

The ADM would not accept my condition. I told him I could not be a party to scholarly work being perverted for political ends. EMR terminated its support for the completion of the rest of the work.

My family bade a tearful farewell to the ponies and to the resident skunk. My students and I packed up and we returned to McGill

WAS IT WORTH TAKING A STAND?

I applied to the Canada Council for a grant to continue work on my model. Canada Council is Canada's main organization that promotes research in science and technology. It is a crown corporation owned by, but managed independently of the Canadian Federal government.

Canada Council usually took a few weeks to respond to a grant application. This time they took months. Those months were an excruciating period in my life. Often I could not sleep, and I could not concentrate. I ate erratically. Sometimes I did not eat for a whole day. It was a period in which I had grave doubts about myself and what I stood for. Was I too bogged down in insisting on the integrity of scholarship? What good was taking a stand when I had nothing to show for it? Should I have been more accommodating? Had I been willing to compromise, I could have the model finished by now. Was it better to have high standards and no model or to have a model with the attendant risk of its being used for political ends? In my heart I knew I had done the right thing. Still my pain was hard to bear.

A little over three months after I had submitted my Canada Council grant application, I received a call from the Council. The caller said the Council took the unusual step of calling me because my application presented a puzzling problem. The Council had sent my application for evaluation to four referees. Three of them praised my work highly and recommended the grant application be approved; the fourth referee wrote a scathing report characterizing my work as worthless and strongly recommended against my application. The caller explained that the Council was in a quandary. On the one hand, there were favorable recommendations from three scholars. On the other hand, there was that negative report by a very important and influential referee. He asked what my reaction was.

I told him that unless he gave me the fourth referee's report to read and comment on it, my view was that the Council should approve my application, since the majority of the referees voted in favor. He said he was not at liberty to divulge the referee's report. I asked if he would divulge his or her name, in the hope that it might help me shed some light on the problem. He promised to consult with his colleagues and be back in touch.

A few days later, he called back to disclose the name of the fourth important referee. It was none other than the ADM I had dealings with at EMR! I was stunned.

I told the official everything that had transpired between that ADM and me. But at the end of our call I felt I was up against an insurmountable obstacle, and that I should not count on the Council coming through for me.

I called friends in Washington and made plans to fly to Washington hoping to garner support from the US Federal Government to finish the work on my model. It was a move of desperation. There was only a thin sliver of hope, if any, that the US government might be interested in funding research for a model developed for Canada. Nonetheless, I thought I should leave no stone unturned.

Three days before my scheduled flight to Washington, I sat in my office at McGill working on my lecture notes. The telephone rang. It was the University's Office of Sponsored Research.

"Congratulations, Professor Khazzoom," the man exclaimed at the other end. "We just received a check from the Canada Council for the full amount your grant application."

I was speechless. But my tears said it all. I felt vindicated.

TO THE RESCUE OF THE CREE AND INUIT

JAMES BAY

My work on energy modeling drew me into another controversy while at McGill. This time it involved the threatened uprooting of some of Canada's native people, a cause that resonated deeply with my own history. I did not want to see the natives being uprooted as I once was.

In 1971 the Provincial government of Quebec announced its plan for the construction of a C$13 billion hydroelectric power project in Northern Quebec. The project, which came to be known as the James Bay Project, was massive, and it involved the construction of extensive dams on several rivers that flow from Northern Quebec into the James Bay. It was to be administered by Hydro Quebec, a crown corporation that served as Quebec's electric utility.

The indigenous Indians of Northern Quebec, mostly Cree and Inuit, opposed the project. By flooding their hunting and fishing grounds, the Indians argued, the project would destroy their livelihood and way of life. Quebec offered the Indians C$100 million in compensation. The Indians rejected the offer – they had little use for the money, they said; they only wanted to preserve their livelihood and their way of living. Quebec refused to negotiate with the Indians. With funding from the Canadian Bureau of Indian Affairs, the Indians took Quebec to court.

The controversy pretty soon took on the tone of French versus English Canada. French Quebecois almost universally sided with the provincial government; English Canadians almost universally sided with the Indians.

The court battle figured prominently in daily papers, radio talk shows, and television programs. But it was clear that the Indians were no match for Quebec's government. Hydro Quebec had several teams of lawyers that managed its court case. The Indians had a team of two lawyers from two small law firms in Montreal. The financial support that the Indians received from the Federal government was peanuts compared to the resources that Quebec's provincial government poured in the court battle.

When in the spring of 1973 Max Bernard, one of the two lawyers on the Indians' legal team walked into my office to explore with me the possibility of helping the Indians in their court case, I was probably the only one in my department at McGill that had not spoken in public about the ongoing court battle. The Indians' legal team was referred to me by one of my colleagues in the department, George Grantham, who had volunteered to help the Indians and who was aware of my energy demand model and its capabilities.

Hydro Quebec had forecasted the demand for electricity in Quebec to grow at an annual rate of 7.5 percent, and used its forecast as its cornerstone to argue for the urgency of going ahead with the James Bay Project to avoid electricity shortages and unemployment in Quebec.

Max Bernard asked me if there was anything my model could do to address Hydro Quebec's fundamental argument of 7.5 per cent annual growth. I told him that my model had the capability of generating forecasts of electricity demand in Quebec but that it would require time to focus the model on Quebec and compile the data required to generate those forecasts. I also made it clear that if I did generate those forecasts, I would report in court whatever results I got, regardless of whether they favored or disfavored the Indians' court case. Max said he would consult with the Indians and be back. To the credit of the Indians, they agreed to those terms.

I assembled a group of six of my brightest graduate students in econometrics and we worked day and night for two weeks to focus the model on the Quebec economy, assemble the data we needed and prepare my testimony.

In fairness my heart was with the Indians. I felt they had been given a raw deal, and their treatment was downright humiliating. The fact that the provincial government would not even sit to discuss with them their gripes infuriated me.

Additionally, Quebec's prediction of electricity demand struck me as awfully unrealistic. To put that prediction in perspective, I decided to follow a strategy that gave the Quebec government the maximal benefit of the doubt. My model estimated the demand for electricity as a function of key variables known to drive that demand. The demand for electricity grows more rapidly when population grows faster, when personal income grows faster and when industrial production and commerce grow faster. It also grows faster when the price of competing fuels (natural gas, oil, etc) goes up faster, because that makes electricity cheaper by comparison and encourages the switch to electricity.

In generating my prediction of the future demand for electricity in Quebec I deliberately exaggerated the effect of those factors that would cause an increase in the future demand for electricity and minimized the effect of those that would dampen the demand for electricity. I pretended that in the future personal income would grow at twice the rate Quebec had experienced during the previous decade and that the population would grow three times as fast as it did historically. I made those highly implausible assumptions to see what the maximal growth in electricity demand could possibly be, given the most far-fetched assumptions we could make in favor of the growth of electricity demand in Quebec. In effect I rigged my model's predictions in favor of Quebec's case to see if there was any way their prediction of 7.5 per cent annual growth in electricity could ever be achieved.

Armed with my figures, I went to court.

SWEARING ON THE GOSPEL?

The first hitch occurred when I took the stand. A copy of the bible containing both the Jewish and the Christian testament was produced, and I was asked to swear on it that I would tell the truth.

"I could not swear on the Christian testament," I declared.

The presiding judge, Albert Malouf, smiled but I could feel the consternation my declaration produced in the courtroom. Where could one find a book that contained only the Jewish Bible? Was there such a book? Court assistants scurried off to find a Jewish Bible, while I stood and waited for close to half an hour.

I cast my eyes around the courtroom. I could see the lawyers for the opposing side fidgeting impatiently. It was the demeanor of the Indians that tore at my heart. They sat together clustered around their chief, an imposing, but gentle looking, tall man with a long ponytail. He looked subdued, but the members of his party already looked beaten. They had not been listened to by the giant corporation, and this was their last effort to obtain justice. I could see they didn't really expect it to work.

"We'll see about that," I said to myself.

Just as my Bible arrived, a two-tier cart stacked with printouts was wheeled into the courtroom.

"The printouts of our findings, your honor. Supporting evidence," the opposing lawyers explained to the judge.

I looked disdainfully at the over-heaped cart.

"Paper instead of wool to pull over people's eyes," I thought, as I repeated to myself, "We'll see about that."

I was sure of my ground. I knew my facts, and I knew my model inside out.

A WINNING STRATEGY

The words of my friend Sy Wenner rang in my head. "When you testify as an expert witness," Sy told me once "you must remember one thing. You are the expert. There is nothing in the world any one can do to coerce you into conceding anything that conflicts with your expertise."

But the best thing of all was the fact that my strategy of inflating the numbers in favor of Quebec's case turned out to be a most effective strategy for refuting Quebec's rationale for the construction of the James Bay hydro project.

My model showed that, even under the most ridiculously rosy conditions tilted in favor of the growth of electricity demand in Quebec, electricity demand would grow maximally at an annual rate of 4.5 per cent, nothing even close to the 7.5 per cent predicted by Quebec. When the judge realized that my prediction of a maximum rate of 4.5 per cent was predicated on a ridiculously optimistic combination of assumptions about the growth of income, population, manufacturing production etc., he mumbled out loud,

"How can that 4.5 per cent ever be achieved when it depends on a combination of rosy events that are so unlikely to happen?"

Thank goodness! That was the point of my exercise. The judge got it! "We are home safe," I said to myself. The 4.5 per cent growth in electricity demand was unrealistically high. Quebec's projection of 7.5 per cent was even more so. It was out of the question.

In fact while I was still on the witness stand, Statistics Canada, Canada's data- collecting agency, released preliminary figures of the most recent growth of electricity demand in Quebec. They showed a meager 0.4 per cent year-over-year growth. One of my students brought Statistics Canada's table to me while I was on the stand. I told the judge that I would like to report to the court the most recent figures on the growth of electricity demand, which had just been released by Statistics Canada. Quebec's legal team objected on a technicality. I did not get to divulge the figures. But the judge appeared to have gotten the message just the same.

The other side was devastated, but they weren't giving up yet. I was cross-examined for hours, the same questions repeated to see if I would answer differently the second, third, or fourth time around. I held my ground, and the growing relaxed attitude and the wide smiles on the faces of the Indians was reward enough for me. I answered each question patiently and clearly. They were questioning my numbers; they tried to lead me to refute my own results. I knew where they were going and I knew they would be disappointed when they got there. Finally they delivered what was expected to be the coup de grace.

"And isn't that a statistically insignificant number?" the lawyer thundered.

I stopped for a minute, leaned forward and, looking him straight in the eye, I calmly responded,

"No, it is not".

On May 22 and 23, 1973, Dr. J. Daniel Khazzoom blazed and flashed like a beacon of intellect from the witness stand in the Superior Court of Quebec. He was the last in a six-month parade of witnesses presented by the James Bay Task Force before Judge Albert Malouf and he was, in the words of task force organizer Dr. John Spence, "the most arrogant, testy, splendid and irrefutable witness" the judge had heard. For two days he turned the courtroom into an intellectual fireworks display and, when it was over, Hydro-Quebec's rationale for the James Bay project had been ripped to shreds.

Dr. Khazzoom was a forty-one-year-old economics professor at McGill, a scholar of international brilliance, and former chief econometrician for the Federal Power Commission of the United States. His speciality was to set up econometric models, the purpose of which he defined as "to quantify what the economist talks about in general qualitative terms." He had submitted Hydro-Quebec's projections for electricity consumption in the province up to 1985 to the test of an econometric model and he delivered his verdict at the start of his testimony.

"What," he was asked, "is your opinion of those projections?"

"I think they are exaggerated. I think they are out of line with anything that could be realistically expected.".

For two days on the stand, Dr. Khazzoom displayed a vast erudition about all forms of electricity usage, the economics of power utilities and the mathematical structures of his science. Though he was exhaustively and sometimes repetitively cross-examined, he never flinched from his judgement that Hydro's projections were quite unreal.

Philip Sykes, Sellout, Huntig Publishing (Edmonton: 1973), p. 194

My answer was not expected to be in the negative and it threw Quebec's team of lawyers into disarray. They consulted with their experts at the table.

"Why isn't it insignificant?" Quebec's lawyer asked in a much more timid tone.

"Because it is not important within its context," I answered and went on to explain and to demolish the opposition.

The Indians were smiling even more broadly now. They had been so beaten down. It felt so good to be able to come to their defense and help them win their case. Their whole way of life was at stake. I knew what it was like to be uprooted from my home. I could not have done anything to prevent it from happening to me, but it was good to feel that my model was able to play a part in preventing the uprooting of these people.

The verdict came down a few weeks later. The judge ruled in favor of the Indians.

I felt honored when the Inuit declared me an honorary member of their tribe.

IN OSLO WITH THE ECONOMETRIC SOCIETY

In the summer of 1973, when the Econometric Society held its meetings in Oslo I was scheduled to give a paper on the theoretical underpinnings of my model of energy demand in Canada, which rested on an innovative distinction between captive and free demand for energy. The Canada Council provided me with a generous travel allowance to attend the meetings.

My family and I almost always traveled together. Aside from the fact that we valued being together, Joan and I felt that it was educational for our children to be exposed to different cultures, different ideas and different parts of the world. Since we would be in Oslo anyway, I thought it would be a good idea to take advantage of our proximity to Israel and fly from Norway to visit my father in Ramat Gan. The timing was perfect. , *rosh hashana* fell in early September that year, just before the start of the fall term at McGill. That gave us a special opportunity to celebrate *rosh hashana* with my father in Israel, something we might not be able to do again during my father's lifetime.

Our travel agent in Montreal knew his business inside out. He scrapped my original plan to fly directly from Montreal to Oslo and rearranged our flight schedule so that my airfare to Oslo was enough to cover my airfare to Tel Aviv, too. The additional cost of flying my family with me on a family plan was minimal. His travel acrobatics were mind-boggling. Instead of flying us directly from Montreal to Oslo, he had us fly first to Copenhagen, from Copenhagen to London and from London to Oslo – all to take advantage of special deals that I could never have dreamed of. Our flight from Oslo to Israel followed a similarly incredible zigzag route.

Copenhagen's airport was a treat for my children. It had two-wheel scooters that people used to travel the length of the sprawling corridors of the airport to reach their flight gates. Aziza and Loolwa went wild over those scooters. They giggled and waved to passers by as they roared through the length and the width of the airport where we had a two-hour layover. I thought they would get tired of running with the scooters long before it was time to board our plane. They didn't. It was delightful to watch how much fun they had and how much they enjoyed themselves.

In Oslo, we stayed in a three-story-hotel which must have been a noble family's mansion sometime in the past. It was an impressive building, surrounded by a gorgeous garden with an incredible assortment of fragrant roses. Modernity had not touched the hotel, but that did not matter. It had a charm and grace that only mansions of olden days possessed.

Aziza and Loolwa in airport scooters, Copenhagen, August 1973

When we went down to the hotel's dining room to have our breakfast I noticed the incredibly large assortment of cheeses. My goodness! How did they manage to create so many varieties? In Iraq there was only one kind of cheese – Feta cheese. I had seen many kinds of cheeses as I traveled the length and width of North America. But to see so many kinds all in one dining room was a first for me. I was amazed.

While I gave my paper at the meetings, Joan and the children went sightseeing. I was glad that I had the opportunity to present my model in those meetings. I valued the views of my colleagues in econometrics and I was very encouraged by the reception the model's construct received.

I attended several sessions at the meeting, but by midday of the second day, I felt I had enough.

MEMORABLE NIGHTS IN BABA'S COMPANY

The flight from Oslo to Israel was uneventful. I sat in the plane and kept thinking that my father was going to meet Loolwa, my mother's namesake, for the first time. Loolwa, unaware of the importance of the occasion, just held on to her toy cow, her moocow, as she called it. She never liked to be separated from that particular cow. Would my father hug her while she was holding on to the cow? Would she be shy and wriggle out of her grandfather's arms? Aziza had already met him, but this was Loolwa's first time.

I will never forget the look on my father's face when he opened the door. He stood in the doorway staring at me, almost as if he could not believe I was there. I, too, looked into his eyes. I was so happy to see him again and to have brought my mother's namesake to him. But in those first few moments, my father saw only me. In that short space of time, my wife and children did not exist for him. I was the one he wanted to welcome. I was his child, the one who lived so far away, the one he could never count on seeing again when I had returned to the United States five years before.

I bowed my head as my father covered it with his hand and recited with a loud, but trembling voice, the Shehehiyyanu blessing, "Blessed art Thou, our Lord, Ruler of the Universe that hast given us life and sustenance, and brought us to this happy occasion." I hugged my father, but I did not fully appreciate what he was doing or what he was feeling. Now, that my own children are so far from me, I understand what was in my father's heart and, in reliving that moment, my own heart swells and tears prick at my eyelids.

My father seemed to have a special warm spot in his heart for Loolwa. At first, when he and I corresponded following Loolwa's birth, he referred to her as Lailwa, instead of her real name Loolwa, as if no one were to share in the diminutive he had coined for my mother. But by the time we arrived in Israel he was already using her real name, Loolwa, in the letters he had sent to me. When he finished blessing me he turned to Loolwa, lifted her up and gave her a big hug. Even though he did not speak English, he listened to her attentively as she told him about her little cow and demonstrated how opening and closing the door to the barn miraculously made the cow moo. He hugged Aziza and Joan warmly. By now those two were old friends. He had always mentioned them affectionately in his letters to me.

That was my last *rosh hashana* with my father and it almost did not happen. Joan suffered from a severe attack of asthma a few days before the festival. "That's it!" she declared. "We're leaving."

My heart sank, but what could I do? I brought her to the doctor at the same time as I prepared to leave, although my heart was torn at having to turn my back on my father at such a time, particularly when I might never see him again.

Fortunately, the doctor was able to help Joan in more ways than one. The injection he gave her helped her breathing. He pointed out that her condition was not life threatening and asked her if she really appreciated the disruption it would cause my family and me if we were to leave just before the High Holiday.

"Do you know how important it is to both father and son to spend *rosh hashana* together?" he asked her.

Joan decided she was well enough to stay and we celebrated the holiday with my father.

This time again the Sephardic Council of Jerusalem took us on an extended tour of sites and shrines in Judea and Samaria. Much had been revamped since our last tour with the Council five years before.

Aziza and Loolwa had a wonderful time with their cousins. I enjoyed my times with my siblings and with our relatives. But some encounters reminded me that, as close as we were on some matters, we were worlds apart on most others. When Muzli's husband, Naim, asked me what I did in Montreal, I told him I was a faculty member at McGill University. Naim shook his head.

"You were doing so well here. Had you stayed in Bank Leumi you could have become a branch manager by now!"

Later, I recalled Naim's comment when I read about Richard A. Grasso, the first president of the New York Sock

Exchange who worked his way up through the ranks. When Grasso became an officer of the Exchange he called his mother to share the good tidings. She chided him saying if he had listened to her and joined the police department, he would have been a sergeant by then.

During my visit to Israel, my father and I stayed up late, sometimes almost till dawn. Those nights together, after everyone else had gone to bed, were the best times I ever spent with my father. I listened to him as he recollected events in his life. His fights on behalf of the downtrodden and the poor were very much on his mind.

"I was fatherless. I knew what it was to be poor and I knew the difficulties of attending school without having enough space in which to prepare my homework. When I was elected to the Jewish Governing Council, I devoted my energies to helping the needy get an education, so they could pull themselves out of their poverty, just as I did."

Baba spoke of his dream of one day taking possession of the lot he had purchased on Mount Scopus in East Jerusalem. He and other Babylonian Jews had invested in this area at the urging of Jewish emissaries from Palestine back in 1920, and they had held onto the land in times when any association with Palestine was grounds for imprisonment in Iraq.

By the time my parents arrived in Israel in 1958, East Jerusalem was occupied by Jordan, and the Jordanians had declared my father and the other investors absentee landlords, according to Jordanian law.

"When Israel captured East Jerusalem in 1967," Baba told me, "I went to claim my land. I had managed to smuggle the deed out of Iraq at great risk. The Bureau of Land Management confirmed my ownership, but told me I could not have the land, since Israel had decided to expropriate the lots on Mount Scopus."

"Do you still have the deed, Baba?"

"Yes, I do. But what I want is possession of the land. Can you imagine," Baba continued, " I have shouldered all those many years in Iraq the risk of being discovered and penalized for holding title to a piece of land in Palestine. Now

Israel, August - September 1973

Aziza enjoying a hearty laugh watching Jacob swing Loolwa. Joan in background

Aziza with cousins Shlomo (l) and Erez in Naim and Muzli's backyard

Loolwa with cousins climbing over the balcony's rail in my parents' apartment

Ronny, my nephew, and Jacob

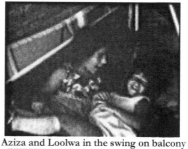

Baba in his regular seat on the balcony

Aziza and Loolwa in the swing on balcony

Loolwa and Baba

561

Aziza with David Siton of the Sephardi Council at the steps to the Machpela Cave, Hebron

Entrance and famous Dome of Mother Rachel's Tomb

Joan and Aziza at Caro's Synagogue, Safed

that I am finally here, they want to take my lot away. I had dreamed of building our home in Jerusalem, on Mount Scopus. It is not fair that I, and the rest of the Babylonian Jews who answered the call to buy land in Jerusalem, should be stripped of what we have risked our lives for, precisely when everything is ripe for us to benefit from the risk we took. Perhaps Babylonian Jews don't count in Israel."

"Is there anything you can do, Baba?"

"I and other Babylonian landowners have appealed the government decision but the appeal continues to wind through the courts. Who knows how it'll end. I am clinging to the hope that one day I will be able to reclaim my land on Mount Scopus."

Baba did not live long enough to hear the court's decision. The appeal was denied. The government expropriated the land on Mount Scopus, compensating owners - at pennies on the dollar - as absentee landlords, even though they were all residents of Israel by then.

I often thought about that discussion with my father and reflected on the government's action. It was legal, I guess. At least that was what the court had decided. But was it fair?

As Baba and I talked late into the night in 1973, I could see that his physical strength was waning, even as his memories of his former days of glory were still fresh. It was characteristic of him to dwell on milestones in his life, without expressing deep emotion or affection. Verbalizing feelings is customarily avoided in the Middle East; it is virtually taboo. I can't recall whether I ever heard my mother say she loved me; I know my father never said it. Instead, we would read one another's expressions and gestures to understand what was felt.

This time my father didn't feel up to joining us on our tour of the country. But he did join us on one bus trip to Jerusalem. Joan sat on the front-row seat and Loolwa sat on her lap. My father sat next to Joan. Throughout the trip that lasted more than an hour, he held up his big handkerchief above Loolwa's head to shield her from the sun as she slept in Joan's arms.

SAD ENCOUNTER

There was also one sad encounter about my parents' apartment.

My mother must have had a presentiment of her impending death. A few months before she died she was scheduled to be hospitalized for observations. Before entering the hospital she asked that her name be removed from the deed to the apartment in Ramat Gan and that it be recorded in my father's name only. After she died two of my brothers-in-law demanded money for the share of the apartment their wives had inherited. Due to my mother's foresight there was no inheritance, and my father could remain peacefully in his apartment. But my father knew he would not live forever and he wanted to put his affairs in order. He decided to leave the apartment to my brother and me jointly.

The first I heard of the decision was when my sister Latifa wrote to me and suggested I tell my father he should leave the apartment entirely to Jacob since I was settled in the United States with my family and financially comfortable. I concurred with Latifa and wrote to tell my father so. At that point my father willed the apartment to Jacob. However, the only constant in life is change and several changes took place at once.

Latifa had a falling out with Jacob and told my father I should be given my share of the apartment in my father's will. Baba might or might not have listened to Latifa. However, something else transpired that made my father think he should change his will.

Jacob and Balforia, his wife, were living with my father. When, in 1972, they decided to move out, they prepared themselves to leave early one morning, removing several objects, my father felt belonged to him, from the apartment. When my father woke up he insisted the objects be put back. At that point, according to my father, Balforia angrily exclaimed that my father wanted Daniel to have everything and that Jacob would be left with nothing.

All this my father wrote to me when he wrote to tell me he had decided to leave the apartment to me. It was the place in which my mother lived and he wanted it to stay in the family and be passed down to the next generation.

"I know I can count on you to do that," he told me.

He asked me to pay Jacob half of the apartment's worth whenever I had the money in hand. I was upset by what was happening. Material possessions should never divide a family. My father was adamant. But the matter was to be talked about during my visit to Israel and settled amicably, my father hoped. He wanted Jacob to understand and accept the fact that he would inherit half of the apartment and that I would buy out his half when I had the money to pay him off. Jacob refused to talk the matter over. He would have none of it.

On the last day of our visit, my father awoke and sat on the edge of his bed. His face reflected a quiet despair.

"What did we accomplish after you came all this way?" he asked sadly. "I wanted Jacob to understand why I had willed the apartment to you. I wanted us all to be at peace with each other."

Jacob was angry and his mind was far from wanting peace.

"All you want to do is punish me," he yelled at my father.

Then he turned to me and held out his hand.

"Pay me! Pay me!" Jacob demanded.

"I don't have the money," I told him.

"You have the house," he snarled.

I didn't point out to Jacob that, by this kind of reckoning, he had the house just a short while before. Nor did I say that my father, and not I, had the house. If I had the money I would have given it to my brother. Nothing was worth this. I recoiled from the angry flames that were darting from my brother's eyes. I felt that my father and I could be consumed in their heat.

It was a sad last day. The only comfort I had was that Joan's asthma had subsided, but nothing could lighten the load in my own soul. I loved my father. I loved my brother. Why did it have to be like this? Why can't families just love and let be? Isn't love more important than anything? Why couldn't we just accept one another and honor our father's wishes?

Now 83, my father was too feeble to come to the airport with us. He waved goodbye from the doorway. I looked back to see a lonely, broken and sorrowful old man. He was my father and I was again leaving him behind to face his own fate.

When we reached our apartment in Montreal I just wanted to be alone for a while. I retreated to the room at the far end of the apartment and gave way to my grief.

In 1991 I paid Jacob for half of the original value of the apartment plus the interest that had accumulated from the time of my father's death in December 1977 until then.

AOPEC STRIKES

Two days after our return from Israel in 1973, the *yom kippoor*'s War broke out. Days after, the Arab Organization of Petroleum Exporting Countries (AOPEC) imposed an embargo on oil exports to countries friendly to Israel and caused devastation to the economies of several Western countries.

I felt those of us who did our research work in the energy field and saw the handwriting on the wall did a disservice to the community by confining our writing to professional journals, which were not accessible to the public, instead of speaking out about the subject and alerting the public to the gathering storm.

I decided to take action even at that late stage. I published articles and letters to the editor in financial and local newspapers on the subject. I accepted invitations to appear on daytime and nighttime TV and radio programs. I also helped the Canadian Broadcasting Corporation in Montreal put together a major documentary on the problem of oil supply and its economic and security implications.

It was not an easy time. I remember watching myself on one early TV program and being taken aback by my emaciated appearance: pale face, and eyes deep in their sockets. But the work I was doing was worth the toll it took. I was not in Iraq any longer. I was living in the free world, free to be me, free to express my opinions. I could make a difference.

When AOPEC declared its embargo, the Jewish Community Center (JCC) in Montreal held a big rally, which several thousands attended, to address the issue. I was invited to be one of the speakers.

I outlined what I thought we could do to conserve energy and use the available resources more efficiently. The issue, I pointed out, was particularly serious in Canada, where the climate is harsh. People, when they have no oil to heat their homes, could, I told the crowd, die from the cold. I was open about my anger with AOPEC for the punishment they decided to inflict on the west. I felt that, in addition to

567

doing what we could to save on the available energy resources, we should fight fire with fire.

"We seem powerless in the situation, but we aren't" I told the crowd. "AOPEC holds vast assets in the US and Canada. We can freeze those assets. Freeze those assets", I said "and you will be surprised how quickly AOPEC will come to its senses."

As I spoke I remembered how the Iraqi government had frozen Jewish assets, reducing millionaires to paupers. Such tactics could work both ways, I felt.

My remark brought the crowd to its feet. They gave me a standing ovation.

That evening, my speech was carried on two TV stations and next day, by Montreal's English papers.

The standing ovation I received at the JCC rally was not the only consequence of my talk. Within a few days I received several nasty notes, two of them threatening my life. I reported the threats to the police. While I was upset to receive those threats, I was not frightened for myself. What terrified me was the possibility somebody might try to kidnap or harm my children.

Not long after the rally I took a trip to Winnipeg, where I served as energy advisor to Manitoba's Minister of Industry and Commerce. My family accompanied me. We went by train and enjoyed the ride.

While on the train, both my wife and I noticed a man who looked like an Arab, and he seemed to be paying particular attention to our little group. He sometimes changed seats and train cars, but we were always in his sight. Our suspicions were heightened when we left the train. He followed behind us in the train station and, when we walked into our hotel, he suddenly appeared in the lobby where he seemed to be just hanging about.

I called the Royal Canadian Mounted Police (RCMP), which is Canada's national law enforcement agency. I told them about the death threats I had received in Montreal and about the man whom we suspected was stalking us. RCMP immediately sent us an around the clock bodyguard. RCMP guards stayed close to us during our entire stay in Winnipeg.

Miraculously, our stalker was nowhere to be seen during the rest of our stay.

I took several trips to Winnipeg during the following two years, but in spite of our stalking encounter, I have the warmest memories of that first trip my family and I took in late 1973. I had thought Montreal weather was cold. There, we had three electrical connections plugged in to our car every night: one to the engine block, one to the oil, and one to the car's interior. In Winnipeg, I discovered, people had to plug their cars to electric heaters, not only at night, but also during the day. Winnipeg's parking meters were all equipped with electrical outlets to which cars could be connected to avoid engine freeze. The temperature was minus 40 degrees on our first day in Winnipeg. I was told that, if one was not careful, one could die of exposure to the cold. Because of this, I was scared to venture outside and tried to find a taxicab. But none was available. I weighed my options. I didn't want to die, but I didn't want to be late for my meeting either. I decided to take my chances and, accompanied by one of our RCMP guards, walked to the Parliament Building, where the office of the Minister of Industry and Commerce was located. It was cold, but it was dry and calm. I was surprised to find it invigorating rather than bone chilling to walk the six blocks from our hotel to the Parliament Building. So much for minus 40 degrees, I thought.

Winnipeg was cold, but the community was warm and welcoming. People were extremely friendly and the bus would stop midway between stops to pick up passengers and get them into the warmth of the bus out of the cold, cold streets. The Jewish community, too, made us feel at home. Additionally, I remember Winnipeg, as having the most elegant *kasher* restaurant of my experience. It was a treat to go there on Saturday night. Unlike most other *kasher* restaurants where the emphasis is on food and little or no attention is paid to the ambiance, that Winnipeg restaurant was outstanding not only for the quality of the food it served, but for its ambiance and its very pleasing decor.

STANFORD

During my **74-75** sabbatical year, I was a visiting professor of Statistics at Stanford.

Stanford was not my first choice. At the time I was working on the generalized inverse of matrices and had just finished writing a paper on the subject, which subsequently appeared in the July **1976** issue of Econometrica ("An Indirect Least-Squares Estimator for Over-Identified Equations.") My first choice was to spend the summer of '74 with the Indian Statistical Institute in New Delhi working with C.R. Rao, who had done work on the cutting edge of generalized inverse of matrices, and spend the 74-75 academic year with the University of Indiana, Bloomingdale. There a group of C.R. Rao's former associates was doing work on the frontiers of generalized inverse of matrices.

Unfortunately, cholera broke out in several countries in the Middle East in late spring 1974. I worried that our daughter, Loolwa, who was not yet five, might not be able to tolerate an anti-cholera inoculation. I canceled my plans with the Indian Statistical Institute. I abandoned my plan with the university of Indiana, as well when I discovered there were no Jewish schools in Bloomingdale.

San Francisco had one Jewish school, the Hebrew Academy, and, because of San Francisco's proximity to Stanford, I chose Stanford.

A WALLOP FROM RELIGIOUS INTOLERANCE

It was all arranged. We enrolled our children in San Francisco's Hebrew Academy. We would live in San Francisco to be close to the Hebrew Academy, and I would commute to Stanford. I mailed my books to Stanford.

It was early Friday afternoon. Our belongings were all packed in a U-Haul trailer outside our apartment, and our apartment was practically empty, except for the essentials we needed for the Sabbath day. We were ready to leave early Sunday morning on our way to San Francisco. The telephone rang. It was Rabbi Lipner, the principal of the Hebrew Academy in San Francisco. He rescinded the enrollment of our children in the Hebrew Academy, because a Conservative rabbi had converted Joan to Judaism. For this reason, Rabbi Lipner did not consider Joan and our two daughters to be Jewish.

It was an awful blow. Joan was devastated, and I was angry and upset for her sake. Throughout our married life, Joan was unequivocally committed to Judaism. She had devoted her life to bringing up committed Jewish children, and had worked for the welfare of the Jewish community. She devoted much time and effort to helping the Jewish schools in

Yonkers, Washington, and Montreal. I was furious at Lipner for his claim she was not Jewish.

"Ignore him," I told Joan. "Who needs him? Why would we want to send our children to a school run by closed-minded people?"

I had let my professional needs take a back seat to the Jewish education of our children. But now that I had a taste of Lipner's thinking, I did not want to touch San Francisco's Hebrew Academy with a ten-foot pole.

There was no other Jewish school in the Bay Area. We would have to send our children to a public school. It was ironic that I had given up on a unique opportunity to do the work I wanted to do because there was no Jewish school in Bloomingdale. Now, when it was too late to change course, I found that my sacrifice was in vain. I would be leaving for another city that had no Jewish school for our children. But so be it, I thought. I felt I did not want to have anything to do with bigotry, Jewish or not. I would much rather have our children attend a good public school than study in an intolerant Jewish environment.

But devastated as she felt, Joan was not ready to give up. She called the director of the Hebrew Academy in Montreal, where our two daughters were enrolled. The director, who himself was an orthodox rabbi, was flabbergasted when Joan shared with him what had happened with Lipner. He immediately called Lipner in San Francisco. He called back shortly after to say that our children would be able to attend San Francisco's Hebrew Academy, but that Lipner made it a condition that Joan convert to Orthodox Judaism within three months. I told Joan I did not want the children to attend a school headed by someone intolerant of Jews who did not have the same definition of 'Who is a Jew?' as he did. But Joan smoothed my ruffled feathers and we accepted the condition.

On Sunday morning we hitched our trailer to our car and left for San Francisco. When we crossed the border into the US, tears streamed down Joan's cheeks.

"I never knew I was such a patriot," she told me.

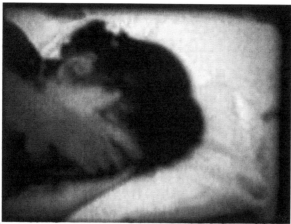

Loolwa reciting the Sh'ma, Hear O Israel, the night before we left Montreal

U-Haul hitched to our car
in background Joan, Aziza

Stopping at a lake on the way to California

At Camp KOA, Omaha City: Loolwa enjoying a slice of watermelon, Aziza opening a
can of coke

It was indeed wonderful to be back on US soil. In the
back seat Aziza sang "Home on the range where the deer and
the antelope play, where seldom is heard a discouraging word

and the skies are not cloudy all day". There was an inspiring feel to the air. I felt I was breathing freedom as we drove on the long stretches of US highways. I looked forward to spending an extended period in our favorite country. I wondered as we drove along: did I really want to go back to the French-English constant battle, the Quebec smothering bureaucracy, the hostile, anti-American attitudes, the hostility I encountered for doing research on US topics, the freezing inclement weather of Montreal?

I loved the Moorish architecture of Stanford's campus - the arches, heavy columns, and wide walkways, which reminded me of the architecture of the girls' Alliance school I attended during my kindergarten years.

I remember the first day in mid September '74. I went to Stanford after we had settled in San Francisco. It was foggy and cold in San Francisco, and I had dressed accordingly. But when I reached Stanford, I realized there was no need for warm clothes. There the sky was cloudless and the sun shone brightly. It was hot, and I loved it. This was more like the California weather I had heard about. How come the weather in San Francisco was so awful, so depressing? What was I doing living in San Francisco?

At Stanford, I continued my work on the generalized inverse of matrices, but it was more dabbling than deep work. I had no interaction with faculty members on the generalized inverse of matrices. Neither the Math nor the Stat department was a hotbed for research on the subject.

I sat in seminars in the mathematics department, and enjoyed them immensely. It was wonderful to be totally immersed in the world of math. I felt as if I was freed from the shackles that had kept me tied to a field I did not have my whole heart in. Math was my love. I began to think seriously about working on a PhD in mathematics and switching fields. That would free me to forge ahead. I sat in math courses and seminars regularly since I began my teaching career at Cornell. But doing it piecemeal did not cut it. I needed to do it fulltime. But how would I go about doing that? It would require a good deal of money for the three years or so I would have to spend working for the PhD. In the meantime who would support my family? It was one thing to do graduate work when I was single. It was another when a spouse and children were involved. But that did not stop me from dreaming about changing fields.

We were coming to the middle of the first semester when, one day, I came face to face with a member of the Energy Institute at Stanford. He had read my article in the 1971 Bell Journal of Economics, and he invited me to join the Institute's members for their weekly lunch and give a talk about the work I had done in energy modeling.

I had mixed feelings. It was nice to be recognized for the work I had done in energy modeling. At the same time I hesitated to set in motion a process that could take me away from math. But in the end I decided that meeting other people in the same field and discussing areas of common interest was part of what a sabbatical was for. I accepted the invitation.

It was exciting to see how many people were interested in the work I had done. Not long after that meeting, the Institute broached the subject of my staying on at Stanford and offering a graduate seminar in energy modeling. The Institute's chairman mentioned that he had a discussion with the Vice President of one of the large oil companies -- I believe it was Exxon -- to fund a three-year chair for a visiting professorship in the Institute, which could become a permanent position.

The temptation was big. I knew if I accepted the offer it would foreclose any chance I would ever be fully engaged in mathematics. At the same time, it was exciting to continue work in the forefront of energy modeling, a field I had a hand in founding. I thought also of the environment in Montreal – the French-English hostility, Quebec's monstrous bureaucracy, the pervasive anti-Americanism, and the harsh weather conditions. Now that I was back in the land of the free, I was not sure I wanted to face that environment in Canada again. Maybe accepting the offer would be a way out. At McGill I was tenured. A visiting professorship appointment was not. But even if the permanent appointment would not eventually materialize, I would still have enough time in a three-year breather to find an alternative position.

I decided to accept the offer and take my chances.

I wrote to McGill to notify the University of my decision to resign my position.

I regret never being able to go back to Montreal for the children's memorabilia packed in the basement of the apartment building to which we had been scheduled to return, or for my office library, which I had to let go.

What happened after I had accepted Stanford's offer to stay on was what I suspected would happen. I gradually let my work in math slip and focused on energy modeling. By the middle of the second semester my math work had slowed to a trickle and my research in energy modeling had filled the space. By the end of my sabbatical year, I transferred to the department of Operations Research, where my graduate seminar was listed and where I had my office.

```
OR 285 B  Energy Modelling
      Khazzoom
              8


"very fine professor--has good, deep interest in students!"
"very understanding of students' needs; quite good at giving motivations and
     stimuli"
"enthusiasm and clarity of explanations"
"covers a broad range of energy models"
"He is extremely knowledgeable in this field."
"Went out of his way to invite and bring to class quite a few very distinguished
     speakers to speak on the topic of energy modelling"
```

Course Evaluation of my Energy Modeling Seminar at Stanford

Unfortunately, the Vice President of the oil company, who was interested in funding my appointment, suffered a heart attack, and the expected funding from the oil company fell through. The Energy Institute stepped in and used its own funds to finance my visiting appointment.

At Stanford, we were the first university in the US to offer a seminar in the fledgling field of energy modeling. I had top graduate students, and their response to the class was gratifying.

Each student worked with me on one sector of a model I was developing. Using engineering information on a large array of energy technologies, my model introduced an innovative approach to forecasting the supply of energy from technologies that were not yet commercialized.

The model did extremely well in predicting future energy supplies. I published the model's results as a chapter titled "The Incorporation of New Technologies in the Estimation of Energy Supply," in W. Ziemba (ed.) Energy Policy Modeling, United States and Canadian Experiences, Vol. I. Hingham, MA: Martinus Nijhoff Publishing, 1980.

During the same period, the debate raged among policy makers, academics and industry specialists about the extent to which energy was a unique commodity, unlike any other, and the role oil shortages had played in the US recession. I received a large grant from the Electric Power Research Institute (EPRI) to research the subject and organize a conference on this question. Nobel Laureates, policy makers, academics, and industry leaders attended the conference. I published the results in Proceedings of the Workshop on Modeling the Interrelationships between the Energy Sector and the General Economy, EPRI, 1976. That compendium was the first attempt at an in-depth investigation of the subject. It was used as a major reference for many years after its publication.

JACOB'S SURPRISE VISIT

A short while after I had began my sabbatical in Stanford, when I was not fully settled in, I arrived one morning at my office to receive a message that my brother and his wife had arrived in New York and were taking a flight to San Francisco. I was supposed to meet them at the airport that evening.

I would be very happy to see my brother, but I wished he had given me advance notice of his coming, that I might be more settled in, better prepared. I did not have enough time to familiarize myself with my surroundings in San Francisco. I was not even sure of my way to the airport. I called Joan and, at the appointed time, we went to the airport to pick up my brother and his wife and bring them back to our home in San Francisco.

Jacob, it turned out, had big plans. He had retired from his job as Inspector of Pharmacies in the West Bank, and was the proud possessor $14,000 in retirement money. The United States was the land of golden opportunity and Jacob had decided to come here and make it big. He had enough money to live on until he struck gold, though, in point of fact, my brother thought all he had to do to become rich was set foot on United States soil. He didn't give a thought to visa or work permit or such mundane stuff. It was all going to happen for him. I was the one who made plans and made sure those plans were in place before taking action. Jacob would seize the moment and follow his dream, never thinking that it might turn out to be a will o' the wisp.

What could I do? He was here. I made him welcome, but I also told him I had no connections in the world of pharmacy or pharmaceutical chemistry. Jacob didn't care. He was going to be rich and famous.

My daughter Aziza connected with my brother and supported him in her own way.

"Ammu (uncle) Yaacoob, you are going to be rich and famous!"

My brother would smile. It was plain there was a connection between him and Aziza. I was glad to see it. It was wonderful for my children to have family in this country.

Nothing worked out and in too short a time Jacob prepared to leave again.

"You're going to be rich and famous, Ammu Yaacoob," Aziza piped up, continuing her game.

"Not now, Aziza," Joan said.

Aziza lapsed into silence.

We drove Jacob and Balforia to the airport. A friend of Joan's came along for the ride. She sat in the front seat with Joan and I sat in the back with my brother and sister-in-law and the children.

It was a sad trip, but not for Joan's friend. She babbled on happily about trivialities, unaware of the sadness that hug like a pall over the back seat, the shattered dreams that covered the roadway behind us. I wished I could have helped my brother, but there was nothing I could do. I felt that I had failed him in more ways than one.

A few times during his visit with us my brother had sought me out. I knew he wanted to talk to me about personal problems he was having. I had made it a rule not to get involved in other people's personal problems or share mine with them. Personal problems are best brought to a professional to my way of thinking. Looking back on those moments, I wish I had been more sympathetic. Jacob wanted to talk to me and I should have listened. But I didn't. Several months later he shared with me his joy when Balforia conceived. When her baby was stillborn, I was still unable to reach out and really talk to my brother. We never did communicate very well.

Just before he got on the plane Aziza reached out to Jacob. It was plain she was sad he was leaving, but she found it difficult to articulate that sadness. Just before he left us she handed a small square of cardboard she had prepared for her uncle. On it was printed just one small word in big capital letters: BYE. It was so sad! It rends my heart every time I remember it.

When he left San Francisco, Jacob did not return to Israel immediately. He felt there was no hope in the United States, but there might be some in Canada. He went to Toronto at the behest of a former college classmate of his. This friend would give Jacob work in his pharmacy for six months, and pay him $400 a month. That would fulfill the prerequisite for working as a licensed pharmacist in Canada. Jacob felt it might be the beginning of something good.

That opportunity dwindled into nothing, too. The friend paid Jacob less than half of what he had promised. Jacob felt the pharmacy was on shaky ground and his wisest course would be to leave before he got into debt. He paid the penalty for breaking the lease on his apartment and left with very little of his original $14,000.

"Don't go, Jacob," I pleaded. "I'll send you $200 a month. If you stay out the six months, you will be qualified to work in Canada."

Jacob was not willing to try any longer. He and Balforia returned to Israel. This time there was no family member to drive them to the airport, no Aziza to write BYE on a square of cardboard. Even now I wish he had stayed. I wanted my brother living close to us and not eight thousand miles away.

AZIZA AND LOOLWA 1974-1975

Aziza, age 11

Loolwa, age 5

Playing horsy in our home at 2182 35th Ave, SF   In *purim* costumes

Reciting the blessing on Mezuzah before leaving for the synagogue for *purim* celebration

Celebrating *purim* in accordance with Sephardi traditions -- with card games…and checkers

Keeping the yard trim at 2182 35th Ave, San Francisco

582

Riding bicycle in camp in Manteca ...   our camper with camp's beautiful lake in
background

On my forty-third birthday, thanking Aziza and Loolwa for the crown and necklace
they made for me

Below - Visit to Disneyland September 4, 1975

RETURNING TO ISRAEL? THE TECHNION

In the spring of 1978, I had a meeting at Stanford with a Faculty member from the Technion, Israel's Institute of Technology in Haifa. I had written to the Technion to explore the possibility of visiting with the school for one year. The Faculty member who came to meet with me was an American Israeli; he was asked by his department chairman to meet with me while on a trip to visit his family in the US.

We had a cordial conversation. My visitor told me that his colleagues were impressed with my credentials, and were interested in meeting with me. He indicated that there might be an interest in my coming on a permanent appointment, and asked me to have copies of my publications mailed out to the Technion.

I had a mixed feeling about that, even though I was the one who initiated the idea of spending a year in the Technion. I had difficulty with the way Jews from Arab lands were treated in Israel and made no bones about it. Judging by the reaction in Israel to my writings, I knew that my views were not welcome in Israel. Although I felt people in academe tended to be more open to new ideas and were less threatened by change, I suspected this might not be true in every institution of higher learning.

I shared my concern with my visitor and explained that I wanted his colleagues to know about me first as a person, to be aware of my views on social issues before we turned to a discussion of my professional publications. I did not want my future colleagues to be caught by surprise later on when they discover where I stood on the social issues confronting Israeli society.

My visitor understood my concern. He suggested that I send his chairman one or two articles of my writings on the problem of Jews from lands to acquaint the Faculty with my views on the subject.

I sent a copy of "Toward Political Action for Israeli Sephardim" – an article I had published in the January 1974 issue of the Reconstructionist. In that article I expressed the view that "the best bet of the Middle Easterners in Israel for gaining their fair share of the national pie lies through the organization of pressure groups, preferably a political party." I explained, "Pressure groups are legitimate entities in a democracy. Indeed the present situation in Israel where a few dominate the rest is the product of a few well-organized pressure groups which are not countervailed by any other group that represents the legitimate needs of the Middle Easterners."

I called the chairman of the department in the Technion and alerted him to what I had sent. He agreed that we should talk after he had had a chance to make copies of the article and circulate it among the Faculty.

Two months after I had mailed my article to the Technion, the chairman and I spoke again. He did circulate my article among the Faculty

" There is no point of pursuing the subject any further. Now I can't get any of my colleagues even to agree to meet with you."

GIVE UP THE ONLY SEPHARDI SYNAGOGUE IN NORTHERN CALIFORNIA?

Magain David, a Sephardi synagogue in San Francisco, was founded in the 1930's by Jews of Babylonian ancestry, who came from Calcutta and Shanghai. The founders did not want to come to San Francisco before they knew they had a synagogue that followed their traditions. They joined hands and paid fully for the synagogue before they came to this country. For a long time, Magain David was the only synagogue in town fully paid for.

When in the early seventies the congregation needed to hire a new rabbi, the board of governors did not insist the new rabbi be Sephardi. They hired a young rabbi from an Ashkenazi background. But the new rabbi chose not to uphold the Sephardi traditions and, instead, moved the synagogue to the Ashkenazi camp. He conducted the services in the Ashkenazi rite, read the Torah in the Ashkenazi trope, and taught the children Ashkenazi practices and songs. But the synagogue still advertised itself as Sephardi

I did not know of the existence of Magain David when we came to California, and was thrilled when I learned in our first week in San Francisco there was a Sephardi synagogue in the city. My family and I made a point of attending the synagogue every time the synagogue's doors were open. The rabbi was welcoming, but I was disturbed by remarks he tucked in occasionally in the course of our conversations, such as "You are not like them!" What did he mean, "You are not like them?" That sounded like a cloaked derogatory remark directed at the Sephardim. I did not need those "compliments". When the remarks kept coming, I told the rabbi I did not appreciate such statements and wanted them stopped. He was taken aback but he stopped.

When *rosh hashana* came, I was looking forward to hearing the tunes and melodies I was accustomed to from my days of childhood. Instead I witnessed a subterranean tug of war between the rabbi and his followers on the one hand, and descendants of the synagogue's founders and their followers, on the other, about the tunes and practices to follow. Mostly the rabbi and his followers prevailed.

I spoke with Mr. Harrar, a businessman born in Morocco, who served as the chairman of the board, and told him I did not think it right that a Sephardi synagogue, founded by immigrants committed to the Babylonian traditions, should be put through such a struggle to maintain its Sephardi character. Surprisingly, the chairman was delighted to hear my critical observations on the state of affairs in the synagogue. He was pumped up as he told me what I said was music to his ears, that he was so pleased someone who was new to the synagogue noticed what was happening and was willing to speak up for the synagogue's Sephardi character. He sounded as if he and some others on the board felt they had made a mistake, but did not know how to rectify it.

Mr. Harrar and I had a short conversation about the similarity between the conditions in Magain David and the conditions of the Sephardim in Israel who were relegated to a secondary place in Israeli society. Mr. Harrar invited me to speak about the condition of the Sephardim in Israel during the services on *yom kippoor*.

It is customary in the Ashkenazi rite to recite public memorial services, called *yizkor* on four Jewish holidays. Two of those occasions are *yom kippoor* and the eighth day of *sukkoth*. The *yizkor*, a sad occasion, is not practiced in the Sephardi rite - Sephardim avoid sad practices on Jewish holidays. Following the customs introduced by the young rabbi, the *yizkor* services were recited on *yom kippoor* at Magain David. I noticed every member of the congregation participated in them. My family and I did not.

I gave my talk. I urged the congregants to stand up for the Sephardi heritage. I implored them to send direct help to the Sephardim in Israel who were struggling to pull themselves up by their bootstraps. Several people came to me after my talk and asked what they could do specifically to help. At the same time, my talk seemed to have agitated some of the rabbi's followers.

But most interesting was the different reaction of the congregants to the recitation of the *yizkor* in the synagogue some twelve days later, on the eighth day of *sukkoth*. The chairman of the board just sat, as I did, and did not participate in the *yizkor* services. Several other Sephardi congregants did the same. Was a new spirit of asserting the rights of the Sephardim to their heritage blowing in the synagogue following my talk on *yom kippoor?* Would we be able to marshal the Sephardi members of the synagogue to assert themselves and insist the synagogue follow Sephardi practices? The rabbi looked askance. The rabbi's father-in-law was foaming mad.

The break came at night, when the *Simhat Torah* celebration began. The rabbi took the children with him and they sang songs that were all Ashkenazi; yet most of those children were descendants of Asiatic parents. Joan and my children began to sing responsive Babylonian songs of *Simhat Torah*. The rabbi objected. His father-in-law hollered.

"We are struggling to bring up Jewish children, to teach them Jewish songs," he said.

Joan was furious.

"What do you mean? Do you mean that we and songs from our heritage are not Jewish?"

We left that evening in disgust, wondering if we wanted to remain as members of the synagogue.

As it turned, out the decision was made for us. The president of the congregation, Mr. Nissim, a native of Shanghai announced he would not support any changes in the practices the rabbi had introduced since his installation in the synagogue.

We resigned from Magain David. I decided to sit it out and wait for more auspicious times to get Magain David back to the Sephardi fold.

In the meantime, leaving Magain David forced me to take an active role in imparting knowledge of my heritage and traditions to the children, Joan and myself. Every Shabbat we studied together in the Ben Ish Hai, a book of Jewish code written by the Baghdadian luminary the late *hakham* Yosef Hayeem. This was a good experience for me, as well as for my family, and I felt it drew our family closer together.

Two years after we had left Magain David, members of the congregation, who hailed from Calcutta, approached me.

"Help us take back our synagogue," they said.

I shared my ideas with the group. One of our friends, Marvin Kussoy, a businessman of East European ancestry, sympathetic to our aspirations to return the synagogue to its Sephardi fold, cautioned that the synagogue would be in disarray if the Sephardim took over. His point was that in North America there were only Ashkenazi Yeshiboth, and they trained only Ashkenazi rabbis. His concern was that there would be no trained Sephardi rabbis to take over Magain David from its present rabbi. And then our taking over the synagogue would be a Pyrrhic victory. I did have a rabbi in mind that would fit the bill, but did not press my point at that stage.

Our first move was to ensure a majority of the members committed to returning the synagogue to its

Sephardi heritage was elected to the board. With a lot of lobbying work we achieved that goal.

It was Wednesday evening when the results were tallied. I went home that evening and called Rabbi Shalom Ezran in Los Angeles. Rabbi Ezran was a rare breed in North America. He was ordained as a rabbi in Jerusalem, and he spoke good English. He is the scion of an old Sephardi family of rabbis who had lived in Jerusalem for generations. I had met Rabbi Ezran at Kahal Joseph in Los Angeles. He and I talked several times about the conditions at Magain David in San Francisco. We shared common views about the conditions of the Sephardim in Israel.

"Shalom, We've won the elections tonight. You've got to come and lead us in the services this Saturday," I told him.

"I don't know that I can just leave on the spur of the moment. I have several urgent things to do before Shabbat," he responded.

"We can't wait. We've got to hit the iron while it is hot. People think we will fall apart, that there are no Sephardi rabbis to take over. We've got to show them they are wrong. Now is the time. You must come."

"How do I get there? I do not know the place. Where do I stay?"

"Don't worry. I will take care of that. Come to-morrow night, Thursday night. I will pick you up at the airport. You stay with us. On Saturday morning we will walk to Magain David. We live within four miles from the synagogue".

I picked up Rabbi Ezran at San Francisco airport and took him to our home. On Friday morning, Rabbi Ezran went to Magain David to check on the weekly portion in the *sefer Torah*, but the rabbi in the synagogue refused to give him access. Rabbi Ezran told me about that incident. I assured him he would have full access on Saturday when we went to the synagogue.

On Friday night Rabbi Ezran and I walked together in our neighborhood. It was one of those beautiful days in San Francisco when the sun shone brightly and the sky was cloudless. As we walked leisurely down the hill, with the gorgeous view of the ocean right in front of us, I remember Rabbi Ezran remarking with pleasure how clean the air was and how much fresher everything smelled in San Francisco compared to Los Angeles. I thought maybe that was a good beginning. Maybe Rabbi Ezran would like to move from LA and join us in San Francisco permanently.

On Saturday morning, Rabbi Ezran and my family walked early to Magain David.

Rabbi Ezran did a beautiful job of conducting the services. He had a beautiful voice, and he chanted from the heart. But his greatest hit was his Jerusalem trope. People were spellbound listening to him read the Torah. Nobody said a word; everybody listened attentively. Marvin Kussoy walked in as Rabbi Ezran was reading the Torah. He sat entranced as he listened to the Torah reading. At the break, he walked to my seat and warmly shook hands with me.

"This is fabulous. I always wanted to be in real Sephardi services. And this is so beautiful. Where did you find him? He is great!"

We had the traditional sumptuous Sabbath meal that Magain David was famous for right after the morning services. The late Meyer Nissim, a native of Calcutta, lovingly prepared that Sabbath's meal, as he did   on every other Sabbath.

The board paid our rabbi for the remaining period of his contract; he left and Rabbi Ezran took over.

Rabbi Ezran's wife, Ora, ran a very successful school in Los Angeles and needed to stay there. For several months I picked up Rabbi Ezran at the airport on Thursday night and drove him to our home to stay with us. On Sunday evenings I drove him to the airport for the trip back to LA.

Rabbi Ezran's presence gave a big boost to the morale of the community and to its sense of pride in its Sephardic heritage. He put a lot of steam behind activities never undertaken before in that community.

Children's choir Rabbi Ezran organized, practicing on a weekday, Sep 77
Loolwa third from right

Aziza and Loolwa singing Sephardi songs
for Magain David Congregation, Sep 77

Every Saturday morning, my children put on their Sabbath dresses and their golden Shaddai necklaces that my father had bought for them, and then we took off for our weekly walk to Magain David through the Golden Gate Park. It was a long but pleasant walk. We sang and listened to the birds sing in the park. We stopped to watch the ducks in Golden Gate's ponds and enjoyed the greenness of the grass and the trees.

FREEING OUR CHILDREN FROM THE TYRANNY OF RELIGIOUS INTOLERANCE.

Joan threw herself into the life of the Hebrew Academy of San Francisco, helping in any way she could. She organized car pools. She crocheted skullcaps and donated them to the school. The school sold them to raise money.

Several months went by, and Rabbi Lipner seemed to have forgotten about his condition that Joan should convert to orthodoxy within three months. He seemed to be happy to have her help, no questions asked. I wondered whether he still held that those who were converted to Judaism by a conservative rabbi were not Jewish.

But while the conversion issue remained dormant, little by little, we began to get disturbing feedback from our children on other matters. Aziza told us that one of her teachers had been telling them that Jews who did not keep *kashruth* were beasts. That included many of the students' parents. I spoke with the principal and noted it would be more in keeping with Jewish law to tell the children how grateful they should be to their parents for providing them with a Jewish education, particularly since the parents themselves had not attended Jewish schools. I also noted it was a violation of Jewish law to turn children against their parents. My reminder to the principal that one of the Ten Commandments is to honor, not to despise, parents did not seem to produce results. The occasional derogatory references to Jews who did not keep *kashruth* did not stop.

I tried to be positive when making suggestions, but it was hard to keep my cool when my children reported that teachers' unabashedly referred to the "Conservative Goyim". I did not want our children to be taught bigotry. It was also difficult to deal with the fact that my children might be indoctrinated with ideas which could lead them to believe that all Christians were anti Semites.

"Many members of Congress and many people who are in high places are Christians and they are friends of the Jews," I said. "It is time to realize we are not living in the ghettoes of East Europe. We do not want our children our children to grow up fearing Christians."

My appeals fell on deaf ears.

In the eyes of the school principal, Sephardim did not appear to be Jewish either.

"I am pleased that the teachers read Jewish stories to the children," I said. "Here are some books with stories from the life and history of Sephardim they might want to include."

"We are desperately trying to teach Yiddishkeit here; we cannot stray from that," the principal told me.

Yiddishkeit is a Yiddish word for Jewish or Judaism. Evidently, in the eyes of the principal, Sephardic was not Jewish.

"Rabbi Langer said today that Yiddish is a universal language," Aziza announced one afternoon when she came back from school. "He said if he went to Egypt and spoke Yiddish, all the Jews there would understand him."

"What did you say to that?" her mother asked.

"I told him my father would not understand him, that my father spoke a different Jewish language, Judeo-Arabic. But Rabbi Langer said there was no such a thing as Judeo-Arabic. He said Yiddish was the only Jewish language. I did not let him get away with it. I argued with him, but he shut me up", Aziza added.

Joan and I were distressed. Our children were being taught intolerance and inaccuracies, and their heritage was being belittled. When Aziza asked her teacher if some of our customs could be included in a *purim* celebration, the teacher did not support her. Instead she referred her to one of her classmates to ask the classmate's permission. The classmate, who was in charge of the festivities, turned Aziza down in no uncertain terms.

The crowning blow came in Loolwa's class.

Prayers were said daily in the school and my children carried the Sephardi prayer books with them and prayed from them. Aziza stood firm and hung on to her prayer book, despite efforts to get her to pray from the school's Ashkenazi prayer book.

Little Loolwa also stood firm, in spite of Rabbi Langer's constant badgering that she should use the Ashkenazi prayer book. Loolwa, our little five-year old, kept telling him that her father had given her the Babylonian prayer book to use in her daily prayers in school.

One day when Rabbi Langer was teaching Torah in Loolwa's class and explaining the contents, he turned to the class and declared,

"And what this means is that it is a sin to pray from a Sephardi prayer book".

Rabbi Langer made it sound as if his declaration followed from the biblical text. Every child in the class, but one, turned to Loolwa and pointed to her with their finger "Shame! Shame! Shame!" Loolwa was devastated. She was pale and terrified when she told us what had transpired.

We immediately removed both children from the Hebrew Academy. When other parents asked the school where our children were, they were told our children had been expelled.

Later, when the Sephardi congregation Magain David planned to found a Sephardi school under the direction of Rabbi Ezran and applied to the Jewish Federation for financial assistance, Rabbi Lipner went to testify against opening a Sephardi Jewish school in San Francisco

"There is no need for more than one Jewish school in the city," he is reputed to have said.

Oddly, not long after that Rabbi Lipner led a small group of followers out of the orthodox synagogue Adath

Israel Congregation on Noriega Street and formed another orthodox synagogue on Noriega Street, literally twenty feet across the street from Adath Israel. Following the logic of Rabbi Lipner's argument against having two Jewish schools in one city, I wondered whether one orthodox synagogue in the same street was not enough. Why start another Orthodox synagogue of his own when one was already in existence? One wonders if the good rabbi was into total control.

Throughout my life I was committed to having our children attend Jewish schools, and I did not let anything stand in the way of that. I let go of my professional needs, turned down tempting academic offers, and lived in towns I did not want to live in to ensure the children's Jewish education. Joan shared fully in my commitment. I never thought anything could dissuade either one of us from sticking to our commitment. But the bigotry and religious intolerance we encountered in our dealings with the Hebrew Academy proved me wrong.

TROUBLE COMES IN THREES

Joan complained of stomach pains. The physician diagnosed stomach flu, gave her some medicine and sent her home. During the next two weeks I took her back to that physician twice. He continued to diagnose stomach flu and counseled patience. Finally Joan's condition worsened. Her pain was unbearable and she was bleeding. I took her to Mount Zion's emergency room. It turned out she had appendicitis, which, when left untreated, caused her appendix to rupture. She was operated on immediately.

Joan was in the hospital for about two weeks. I was so glad when she regained consciousness after the operation. We were both happy that the operation was behind us. But Joan had a disturbing story to tell.

As she was being wheeled to the operating room, the nurse who was wheeling her kept urging her to accept Jesus as her savior before it was too late. Joan lacked the physical and emotional strength to rebuff the nurse, and the nurse kept trying to convert her to Jesus, until the surgeon and his assistants showed up. Joan was so shook up by what had happened that it was the first thing she told me about when she was able to talk coherently.

I was shocked and immediately sent a letter to the Hospital's Board of Directors expressing my outrage. I asked that the matter be investigated to ensure the offense would not be repeated. The Board said it was no less outraged by what had happened. It promised to investigate the matter and take corrective action.

I remember the two-week period Joan was in the hospital as one of bitter sweetness. I was worried about her, but I gloried in caring for the children. Aziza was thirteen and Loolwa was seven. Every morning I prepared breakfast for my two daughters, made their sandwiches, drove them to school and then drove to Stanford for my seminar and research work. I returned home in the early afternoon to prepare the meals before going to pick up the children from school. I did not eat much when Aziza and Loolwa sat to eat their dinner, but I enjoyed sitting and watching them eat what I had prepared for them, and I loved listening to them tell me about their school day. I cleaned the kitchen while they did their homework, and helped with the homework when they needed help.

Every evening after finishing their homework, Aziza and Loolwa took the trip with me to Mount Zion Hospital to visit Joan. Sometimes we stopped on the way at the supermarket to do some shopping. In the supermarket I loved to see my two daughters roaming around picking up the groceries they liked, and I delighted in buying them anything their hearts desired – a candy bar here, a stick of gum there.

When we got to the hospital, I collapsed on a chair next to Joan's bed and went to sleep during the hour or so the children spent with Joan, talking or watching television. That was the only time I felt I could let go and enjoy deep sleep.

Back at home I sat in my study, after the children had gone to sleep, to do my class work and plan for my meeting with my research assistants the following day.

It was an exhausting and at the same time an exhilarating period. I wished I did not have to be the breadwinner. I wished I could stay home with the children for all of their growing up.

I was glad when Joan recovered and returned home. I thought the worry of illness had been lifted from our family. But trouble, they say, comes in threes. It was just like that for us.

Three days after Joan came home from the hospital, Aziza complained of severe stomach pains. This time I went directly to Mount Zion's emergency room. She was diagnosed with appendicitis and was operated on. I could not believe it. Just two weeks ago Joan was operated on for appendicitis. Was appendicitis contagious? No it was not known to be, I was told. Could it have been triggered in both cases by a particular food intake? No one could tell. But it was an amazing coincidence.

Aziza was operated on the following day. She was in the hospital for a week. Some nights I slept in the hospital on an armchair next to her bed, while Joan slept at home with Loolwa. Other nights Joan stayed with Aziza in the hospital while I stayed at home with Loolwa.

I breathed a sigh of relief when Aziza was out of the woods and home again. My relief was short lived.

A few days after Aziza's return from hospital, I came back to my office at Stanford after giving a lecture to find my assistant had taken a message from Joan. Loolwa, taking a playmate's dare, had ridden in circles on her bicycle until she became dizzy and took a tumble. She suffered a serious concussion.

I rushed to Mount Zion, which by this time felt like my second place of residence, and joined Joan as we watched Loolwa being wheeled away on a gurney.

With tears in her eyes, Joan turned to me and said, "Look at her" as she pointed to Loolwa. I was indeed looking at Loolwa, and I was seeing the same horrifying thing Joan was seeing! Loolwa looked lifeless. She lay motionless on the gurney, eyes closed, her body limp. What a frightening contrast with her liveliness and vivaciousness. My heart was in my mouth.

Loolwa was hospitalized for two weeks. It was a frightening period for all of us. I was thrilled when Loolwa regained her strength, opened her eyes and smiled. I felt as if I got a new lease on life.

It was a dreadful time and the awfulness of it all hit me afresh when I went to the synagogue for the first time after this string of misfortunes had struck. When I was called to the Tebah during the services to recite the *birkath hagomel*, a special prayer of thanks for coming through danger, I couldn't get the words out. In front of the whole congregation, I broke down and wept.

We were doubly careful with Loolwa after her concussion. We relived our horror of the initial accident when, six years later, Loolwa suffered another concussion after she was pushed to the ground while playing basketball in junior high. The team was playing unsupervised by their gym teacher. It was a scary time for us. Fortunately Loolwa recovered from her injury.

I wrote to Loolwa's school and asked them to make sure the children were supervised while playing out on the field. The school instead chose to cancel those unsupervised activities. Unfortunately, the students took it on Loolwa, and she suffered a lot as a result.

A REWARDING SERVICE TO THE COMMUNITY

During the mid seventies I joined the Commonwealth Club of California and became chairman of the Club's Energy and Environment Study Section. The Commonwealth Club is one of the nation's oldest, non-profit, public affairs forums, which was founded in 1903. My decision to join the Commonwealth Club was part of my efforts to make amends for the past mistake that those of us who did our research work in the field of energy had made. We had kept our cards close to our chest instead of sharing what we knew with the public at large to alert them to the gathering clouds that culminated in the oil crisis of the early seventies. I, for myself, was determined never to do that again.

When I took over, the section was pretty inactive, and I devoted much of my energies to infusing life into it. I focused on getting top speakers in the fields of energy and environment. They came from as close as San Francisco to as far away as Vienna and the Middle East, all at no cost to the Club. A week or so prior to many sessions I distributed to the members of my section reading material on the following week's topic as well as background information on the speaker. I did my best to encourage focused discussions and the exchange of ideas between the speaker and the audience, on the one hand, and among members of the audience, on the other. I also encouraged members of the audience to join me together in the preparation of section reports on topics we discussed. They responded favorably, in spite of the demanding work involved. They delved in enthusiastically. It was a pleasure to see the thrill of discovery on their faces and watch their pleasure at the depth of the discussion. The attendance grew consistently. We held sessions almost every week.

Although the sessions were officially intended to last for about an hour or so during lunchtime, they often lasted twice as long, and the discussion among the participants often continued more than an hour after the speaker had left. It was obvious that most members of the audience came well prepared and had done their reading on the topic before attending the session. The dynamic quality of the interaction on those afternoons was gratifying. It was gratifying, too, to notice that people who were actively engaged in the field of energy and environment were drawn to those sessions, which proved to be a source of enrichment for all of us.

Our largest attendance was when one of OPEC's top officials, Mr. Chalabi (whose first name I regrettably no longer remember) talked to us. We held that meeting in the evening in a large hall in one of the local hotels and still, as it turned out, there was standing room only. I worked doggedly to get a top official from OPEC to speak to my group. The world was still smarting from the shock waves of the oil crisis, and I felt it was important to have a member of OPEC come and address us since, to many people, OPEC was an unknown quantity, an enigma. I wanted people to understand what OPEC was and what it meant.

Mr. Chalabi was from Iraq, a member of a wealthy and a very dominant clan in Iraqi politics. When I introduced him to the audience, I joked that I was the only other person in the room who knew how to pronounce his name correctly. I think our evening with OPEC was the liveliest evening of all. Questions came flying fast and furious at our speaker. It was over an hour past our allotted time when I finally called a halt to the proceedings.

I stayed with the Commonwealth Club for several years until my daughter Aziza planned on attending Wellesley, and we made an abortive move to settle in New York.

Commonwealth Club of California

661 Market Street, San Francisco, California 94105 · (415) 362-4903

25 May 1981

J. Daniel Khazzoom
380 Kensington Way
San Francisco, Ca. 94127

Dear Dan:

I regretfully acknowledge your resignation as Chairman of the Commonwealth Clubs' Section on Environment and Energy. I hope you found your term to be a stimulating and challenging assignment. From our perspective, your leadership was an invaluable and significant factor in the remarkable achievements of the section over the past year.

As you are aware, the Section on Environment and Energy has had more meetings, larger accumulated attendance, and more finalized reports than any other section. It has clearly established a new plateau for section activity, member interest, and program achievements. The Section stands as a tribute to your dedication and personal efforts.

The Board of Governors join me in thanking you and hoping you the best in your new endeavors on the East Coast. If I can ever be of service, please don't hesitate to call.

Cordially,

Eugene M. Herson
President

cc. Orrin Harder

THE CONTROVERSIAL KHAZZOOM EFFECT

Concerned about the disruptive effects of the multitude of problems that surfaced during the Arab oil embargo, the California state legislature passed a law in 1974, which created a new state agency, the California Energy Commission (CEC). The law invested the agency with the responsibility of addressing all energy facets in California.

I testified many times before CEC.

It did not take me long to realize that the commission had an engineer's view of the world, a world that it saw a collection of systems - fix the system and you fix the problem. The commission had little understanding that the economic system is radically different from the engineering system and that people's response to policy measures should be paramount in assessing the desirability and the wisdom of policy initiatives. I often bucked heads with members of the commission

The commission touted energy conservation as the appropriate response to the energy crisis confronting California, but was practically oblivious to the price implications of the energy conservation measures it trumpeted. While I appreciated the role of energy conservation and supported the use of conservation measures as one means of dealing with the energy problem, I was very concerned with the overly optimistic scenarios CEC depicted regarding what could be achieved by conservation measures, without regard for their economic implications. What would happen when those measures did not yield the energy savings the commission expected? There would be more shortages than we had hither to experienced. Where would we be then? I worried that CEC's lack of realism risked placing us directly and squarely under OPEC's thumb.

No more was this evident than in the commission's promotion of mandated energy efficient standards, without regard for their implicit price effect. CEC's calculations of energy savings achieved by those standards were mechanical. Double the efficiency of the air conditioners and you would save half of the electricity used for air conditioning. Triple their energy efficiency, and you would cut the electricity used for air conditioning to a third of what it used to be. And so on. I thought it would be disastrous if policy decisions were based on those dream world mechanical calculations.

I tried to illustrate my concerns in one of my testimonies before CEC by using the automobile as an example. Consider the case, I said, where you had an automobile that got twenty miles per gallon. "What happens," I asked "when you replace this automobile by one that gets forty miles per gallon?" You could now drive two miles for the price of one. This is equivalent to a cut in the price of gasoline to half of what it used to be. "And what do people do when the price of gasoline drops," I asked? "They drive more." The same is true of any appliance, I argued. Increasing appliance energy efficiency is equivalent to lowering the price of energy, which in turn stimulates greater demand for energy. How much more energy would be used as a result, would depend on the sensitivity (what economists call price elasticity of demand) of the end use to which that appliance is put. For some the sensitivity might be so high that doubling the efficiency of the appliance would result actually in an increase rather than a decrease of the energy consumed by that end use. For some others, the sensitivity might be low, and doubling the energy efficiency might result in close to halving of the energy consumption.

But my ideas did not make much headway with the commission.

In fairness CEC's mechanical worldview was not unique to CEC and its staff members. It was the dominant view within the Carter Administration and its policy makers.

My experience with CEC prompted me to study the matter in great detail. I spent four years working on the subject and eventually published a paper, which appeared in the October 1980 issue of The Energy Journal, "Economic Implications of Mandated Efficiency Standards for Household Appliances". In that paper I derived mathematically the relationship between energy efficiency and the sensitivity of energy demand. My paper showed that not only is the savings achieved by increased energy efficiency standards always smaller than the mechanical calculations would indicate, but that in several instances there may be actually a net increase in energy usage, contrary to the view that dominated policy makers' thinking at the time.

The paper flew (at the time) in the face of accepted wisdom among the majority of energy specialists and policy makers under the Carter Administration. They roundly denounced it and referred to it derogatorily as the "Khazzoom Effect". That name stuck.

Interestingly, the Reagan election team, with which I had absolutely no contact, used the article as added ammunition and as an economic basis to support its less sympathetic view of what conservation measures can accomplish. When Reagan won the elections in November 1980, the new administration rescinded several institutional contracts for work in energy conservation, which the Department of Energy had issued under the Carter Administration. I incurred the wrath of friends in one institution, who blamed my article for the cancellation of a sizable conservation contract they had signed not long before the change in administration.

For a long time I was an outcast. Some colleagues in the energy field would not return my calls. People I knew at Lawrence Berkeley Labs (LBL) said that I should write an article to retract what I had written and apologize for publishing it. LBL was among other institutions that lost a conservation contract. I was ostracized, vilified, and treated with scorn. It was a hard time for me, but, against all odds, I stood by my ideas.

Over time, the "Khazzoom Effect" lost its derogatory aura and came to be accepted as its results gained greater recognition among regulatory agencies and energy policy makers at the Federal and state level. In time, the Khazzoom Effect came to be viewed as a breakthrough.

I continued work in this field. My book on the subject, "An Econometric Model Integrating Conservation Measures in the Estimation of the Residential Demand for

Electricity", appeared in 1986. It innovated in the methodology for deriving realistic measurements of the contribution different energy conservation measures can achieve. By the mid nineties it had gone through three printings.

STANDING UP FOR WOMEN

ROTARY CLUB

The mid to late seventies was a time of intense anxiety about energy. People wondered if there would be enough energy to meet our needs, if the cost would skyrocket and what effect energy consumption was having on the environment. Because I was one of those who had published in the field, I was in demand as a speaker. On my part I was eager to share my knowledge with the public and I spent a great deal of time preparing each speech.

There was only one occasion on which I felt the need to share information about energy had to take second place to a higher ideal. This happened when I was invited to speak at the Rotary Club in San Francisco. My contact at Rotary assured me that my talk would be well publicized and that a large turnout was expected.

I spent a great deal of time researching the material for my speech. I knew very little about the inner workings and policies of the Rotary Club, and I did not spend time researching the Rotary Club. It was, as far as I knew, a highly respected institution that did a great deal of philanthropic work. It was interested in promulgating information about the energy crisis. I was sure that was enough for me, but as it turned out I was wrong.

Two days before I was scheduled to give my speech I was finalizing arrangements with my contact at the club.

"I will, of course, be accompanied by my wife," I remarked casually.

For a few seconds there was silence at the other end of the phone. Then the silence was broken.

"The Rotary Club's membership is restricted to males."

Pictures of the important women in my life flashed into my mind. There were my six sisters. I grew up with them. I had seen from close their suffering and felt in my guts their pain at being treated by society at large as second class human beings, deprived of the dignity and opportunity accorded to men. There was my mother, my wife, my two daughters, several colleagues and many friends. The Rotary Club would exclude all of them. In that case, they would have to exclude me, too, I decided.

"I am canceling my appearance," I said firmly. " I cannot speak in a place that excludes women."

The Rotary Club was not pleased. In fact, it was downright upset. The Club felt my cancellation would disrupt their program. But I stood my ground.

That evening I told my family of what had transpired that day. Although I had always told my daughters that they were human beings equal in every respect to men, that they had every right to aim as high as they wished and that they should never tolerate being put in a second place because of their gender, I never expected the enthusiasm with which they greeted my decision to cancel with Rotary. They were ecstatic. Joan cheered my decision.

My stand had no effect on Rotary's policy toward women. It wasn't until 1989 that they finally opened membership to women, and then only at the order of the US Supreme Court.

Should it Be He or She? An Insight I Gained from Loolwa

I believe Loolwa was in high school, although she might have been in her first year in college, when she read a book, which used "she" in place of the common reference to "he".

"Daddy, for the first time I read something that I felt was talking to me," Loolwa told me.

Loolwa's remark opened my eyes to something I did not think about before. It became clear to me for the first time that the common practice of referring to "he" was no less discriminatory than excluding women from joining the Rotary Club. I felt I needed to do my share to correct that wrong.

Not long after, I submitted an article to a professional journal for publication. In that article I used "she" wherever I would normally have used "he". The article came back to me with the referees' comments and suggestions. Most of the comments were helpful, and I had no problem revising my article to take advantage of them. But one of the referees commented caustically about my use of "she" instead of "he". The referee was particularly incensed by the fact that I used "she" when I was referring to the chief executive of the auto company. The referee questioned where I had encountered a female chief executive of an auto company to justify my use of "she" in referring to the chief executive. The referee recommended to the editor that I be asked to change my references from "she" to "he". In revising my article, I chose to stand my ground and ignore the referee's recommendation. My revised article was published with every "she" in place, including the "she" that referred to the chief executive of the auto company.

SYNAGOGUE

My two daughters can conduct services in the synagogue as well as any male educated in Jewish practices. At one point Loolwa considered becoming a rabbi. During her first year in college, Loolwa enrolled in a joint program that Columbia had with The Jewish Theological Seminary (JTS), but had to drop the JTS in her second year, because of the excessive burden of carrying two full programs simultaneously. Before she reached the age of twelve, Loolwa often led certain prayers that were not part of the main liturgy in San Francisco's Sephardic synagogue, Magain David, and did it well. The late Rabbi Elias Levy of the Babylonian synagogue, Kahal Joseph, in Los Angeles encouraged her, and Loolwa delighted in taking a leading role in the services. But it was often distressing for me to watch how some members of our Magain David congregation reacted negatively to the fact that a young girl, occupied center stage.

They would fall all over themselves to promote young men who could not even read two sentences correctly and who were no match Loolwa's command of the services and the Sephardi traditions, just to have a male, any male, replace the female at the stage.

When Rabbi Cassorla came to Magain David in San Francisco, Loolwa met with further opposition from him.

"You may not take part in leading prayers here, even when they are not part of the main liturgy," he told her.

"But Rabbi Levy allows it," Loolwa protested.

"I am the rabbi here," was Cassorla's reply.

Loolwa did not lead the prayers in Magain David, but she continued to sing during services with great fervor and enthusiasm.

"Restrain her," Rabbi Cassorla told me. "Men are objecting to her singing."

"From here on, my singing will not be heard here either," I decided.

For as long as Rabbi Cassorla remained at Magain David I did not darken its doors. Magain David synagogue meant (and means) a great deal to me. I put a lot of myself into that synagogue. I contributed time, money, and an enormous amount of prayer books for all occasions to the synagogue and took a leading role in reestablishing its Sephardi identity when that was in danger of being lost. It was hard to leave, but I could not stay there and let anyone treat my daughter as a second rate citizen because of her gender.

The place of women within Orthodox Judaism has always been a troubling matter for me. The clearest way Orthodox Judaism can openly display its orthodoxy is by its treatment of women.

Observant Jews are not supposed to drive their cars on the Sabbath, but many do and park their cars a few blocks away from the synagogue building and then walk to Sabbath services. Nor should observant Jews work on the Sabbath, but, if they do so within the confines of their homes, who will know about it?

The separation of women from men during prayer is another matter. It is easily done, clearly visible and leaves no doubt in the minds of anyone who looks into a synagogue and sees a Mehitsa (the opaque partition that separates men's seats from women's in the synagogue) that the synagogue one is viewing is an orthodox one. I suspect that, because of this visibility, the separation of men from women and depriving women of privileges to which they are entitled by Jewish Law have become almost synonymous with Orthodox Judaism.

This is something that often makes me uneasy within an Orthodox setting, but there are other things that make me uncomfortable within a Conservative or Reform Jewish setting. The whole matter is a dilemma for me and often creates a stumbling block in my relationship with Jewish orthodoxy.

In the year 2002 my oldest sister Jamila died and I was at her son Emil's house when the family was sitting Shib'a. Until it was time for prayers men and women sat together.

"The women must move to the far corner of the room. It is time for prayers," Emil, Jamila's son, announced.

"My sisters are mourning their sister just as much as the men are mourning," I said. "I don't see the need for separation."

'They must leave," Emil insisted.

I got up and left with my sisters and sat with them in the far corner of the room. "Come and join the men so that we will have a quorum for the services," Emil told

me.

"I am staying here with my sisters and the rest of the women." I responded.

I held the prayer book and recited the prayers together with my sisters Helwa and Latifa who sat next to me.

BABA TOO IS GONE

In December 1977 we moved into our new house in Forest Hill, San Francisco. It was a gorgeous big house, and we loved it. We invited our friends to join us on Sunday, December 17, for celebration, and our friend Rabbi Elias Levy, spiritual leader of the Babylonian congregation Kahal Joseph in Los Angeles, graciously agreed to lead us in the Home Dedication ceremony.

It was a proud moment when Rabbi Levy affixed the mezuzah to our doorpost. We prayed that our life in our new home would be happy and that the light of hospitality would spill out from our home into the community.

I was scheduled to travel to Sacramento Municipal Utility District (SMUD) on the day following the celebration, and I was looking forward to going. I was overseeing the development of an energy model at SMUD, and I enjoyed the innovative nature of the work we were doing.

I was getting ready to leave for Sacramento when the telephone rang. It was my brother Jacob calling from Ghana.

"Can you go to Israel?"

Jacob's question came out of the blue. What did he mean, "Can you go to Israel?" Did he think I could take up and leave, just like that? Why would I want to do that? What was he talking about? What prompted his question?

Even as my annoyance with my brother grew, ice formed around my heart. My palms began to sweat. I could feel the telephone receiver slip from between my fingers as I made desperate efforts to hold on to it. Something was wrong. There was a tone in Jacob's voice conveying news he didn't want to tell me and I didn't want to hear.

I could hear the hoarseness, the anxiety in my voice as I asked:

"How is Baba?"

The answer came quickly. It was almost too pat.

"Fine."

Fine? What did he mean by fine? What was going on? The answer was knocking at my mind trying to gain entrance, but I wouldn't let it in, couldn't let it in. It was too

THE JOURNEY OF A JEW FROM BAGHDAD

awful. The next time I went to Israel my father would be there to greet me. He had to be there. He just had to be.

Even though I didn't want to hear the words floating in the air between my brother and me, I pressed him to tell me.

"Jacob, what has happened?"

"Nothing has happened. Really."

It was ridiculous, but I accepted his answer. My brother never called me. Telephone calls were very expensive at the time, and we never made contact by phone during the months he and his wife, Balforia, lived in Ghana.

My brother's voice faded into silence. He couldn't find the words to tell me what he needed to say and I couldn't ask the direct question: Has our father died?

I said goodbye to my brother, thanked him for calling and left for Sacramento.

My mind flashed back to a few years previously when my mother had died and nobody in my family had told me until a month after she was buried. Why did my family feel I couldn't handle bad news? Why could nobody in my family just tell me something straight out? They always beat about the bush. It didn't help that I knew it was part of the culture in which I grew up. Everything was handled in a very round about way. Nothing was ever said in a straightforward way. When my brother S'haq died, nobody mentioned it either. I was a child then and I knew something terrible had happened. Sadness hung over our house like a pall, but nobody told me what had happened. Maybe it was imprinted on my brain at that time that death was too terrible to talk about.

It was a strange day. I could not concentrate on my work at SMUD. Deep down I felt something terrible had happened. It must be that Baba had passed away. Otherwise, why would Jacob, who had never called from Ghana, call me that morning to ask, out of the blue, if I could go to Israel? He must have called to ask if I could go to attend my father's funeral or perhaps to sit Shib'a with my sisters, but could not get himself to say so.

I told my friends at SMUD about the ominous call I had received that morning and my fear that my father might have passed away. I remember also listening to Val Engel, a good friend in the office, telling me about her father's death in Germany while she and her husband were in the US. I pressed her hand in sympathy as the tears rolled down her cheeks. Losing a father to death was a terrible thing. It left a great big black hole in one's life, a hole that could never be filled.

I have very blurred recollection of anything that might have transpired that day.

I left SMUD early and found that Joan had arranged for some twenty people or so to attend memorial services in our home that night in memory of my father. She might have spoken that day with members of my family in Israel and learned that my father had passed away and had been buried already. I never asked her how she found out that my father had passed away. Joan had also called Rabbi Levy during the day and arranged with him to come that night to conduct the memorial services in our new home. The night before he had officiated at a warm and wonderful ceremony, tonight he was going to mourn with us and memorialize my father.

I told Joan she was a woman of valor. I felt so grateful to her for having gone through the trouble of calling all those people and making sure all the necessary preparations for conducting the memorial services according to the Babylonian traditions were in place.

SITTING SHIB'A

For the days of mourning, we held services in the morning before people went to work and at night when they returned. I appreciated the support and the outpouring of sympathy. I was grateful to Rabbi Levy for the eulogy he delivered. I was grateful to Joan for supplying him with the information about my father, which made it possible for the rabbi to write the eulogy.

Gradually the reality about the loss of my father began to sink in, and increasingly I began to feel the void he had left. It was on the third day of Shib'a, after the morning services, when I sat with Aziza on the steps to the third floor of our home. Aziza had spent the summer in Israel with my father and had bonded with him. When she returned, she and I had gone to Marine World, a place we both enjoyed. There, I remember her telling me about her time with my father. I was so grateful to Aziza for bringing my father into my life in a new way.

Baba in his last years
Last picture I have of my father before his death. Taken on Dec 30, 74

Now she sat with me on the steps, with tears running down her cheeks. Suddenly she remembered a cap my father wore during the summer.

"It was too big for him," she chortled. "It fell down over his eyes and he kept on walking though he really couldn't see where he was going."

Her laughter dissolved into weeping, as she realized afresh that she would never see her grandfather again.

When Aziza was in Israel during the summer, my

sister Reyna insisted Aziza call me.

"You have to come, Abba. You have to come to Israel. Amma Reyna says you have to come."

Reyna took the phone from my daughter.

"Get on a plane and get over here. You have to come."

Didn't she know that I couldn't afford to fly to Israel and leave everything behind? I had done the best I could by sending Aziza. But the push and pull on my soul was unbearable. Was I doing the wrong thing by not borrowing the money to fly to Israel to see my father one more time? Were my priorities wrong? Reyna will never know how much torment her call caused me. Was I always to be pushed and pulled between one demand and another? Why was it necessary to make choices that were both right and wrong at the same time? Why couldn't something be clearly and easily the right thing to do?

As Aziza and I sat on the steps to the third floor of our home talking about my father, our conversation turned to the letters I had received from my father over the years. No more letters would be coming. I wanted to organize those letters in a scrapbook, but knew I couldn't bear to look at them, now that Baba was gone. Aziza felt she might be able to organize them in a scrapbook. But every time she turned to them, she felt overwhelmed with sadness. In the end, neither one of us could gather the strength to do it. Two years ago, I tried my hand again at organizing Baba's letters, but still could not do it. I felt as if I would be disturbing my father in his resting place. To day the letters are still sitting in the same pile that I had left them before I learned of my father's death. With them is a strange picture.

Sometimes, I am told, people see others walking on the street who remind them of a loved one who has passed away. That never happened to me, but I did see what I thought was my father's picture in the San Francisco Chronicle three years after his death. At first I could not believe my eyes. Upon examination, I saw it was the picture of an old Serbian soldier giving a last salute to President Tito at the president's funeral. The picture was connected with death and I cut it out with a heavy heart and put it with the letters I will never organize. It reminds me of my father. It reminds me of the sadness I felt at his passing.

Baba's look-alike, SF Chronicle, May 8, 80

Rabbi Ezran came the second night of the Shib'a. I was sitting on the floor wearing my shoes.

"Take off your shoes," he told me.

I looked at my shoe-clad feet. Was one supposed to remove one's shoes when sitting Shib'a? I had forgotten. What else had I forgotten? At least taking off one's shoes was a clear-cut and easy decision. I was grateful for one choice that was easy to make.

During the first month after a parent's death a man is supposed to let his beard grow. I had to meet the public in the course of my work, and I looked terrible with a beard. I had not grown a beard after my mother died, since I hadn't known of her death until she was dead for a month. There was no other parent left. My father was the last one to die. The choice was clear. I did not shave for a month. Even now I remember the difficulty I had in shaving when the month was over.

During the year that followed my father's death I went to the synagogue, sometimes twice a day to recite Kaddish in his memory. That is the duty of a son. I was honoring my father's memory. I went to the Sephardic synagogue in San Francisco and stayed there for services even when I was unable to recite the Kaddish because there was no minyan (quorum) present. I felt that was what my father would have wanted and the important thing to me was the honoring of his memory.

My parents' Gravesites at Holon's cemetery

I was not present at the funeral of either of my parents. I was the child who lived eight thousand miles away from them. I was the youngest son, the second youngest child, but I was the one who had left the fold, first to go to Israel and then to the United States. Sometimes we make choices not knowing all of the consequences. It saddens me not to have been with my parents during their last moments, not to have followed their bodies to their last resting places.

I thought about them lying side by side in their graves in Holon and wished I could have followed the Middle

Eastern custom of visiting the grave of a loved one every Friday during the first year following the death.   I lived thousands of miles away from them, but even from thousands of miles away I had managed to do one thing for them. I had bought the graves, one next to the other, in which my parents lay. It gave me one small ray of consolation to know that these two people, my mother and my father, who had loved each other so much, were not separated in death. It was a gift they couldn't thank me for and that made it all the more precious in my eyes.

There was so much I wished I could do over, but that was one act I would never want to undo. May they rest in peace: my wonderful parents.

MY PARENTS' APARTMENT

My father willed his Ramat Gan apartment to me and as he had asked I keep it in the family in Mama's memory. Each time I visit the apartment I am transported back to the first few days I spent there, visiting with my parents after their escape from Baghdad. It was bare of furnishings except for some creaky folding chairs borrowed from my sisters. But the sparse surroundings didn't dampen the pleasure we found in each other after so many years of separation. I especially remember the surge of love and joy I felt, seeing how Mama still worried about my pants being pressed and my shirt being mended. That apartment was where my father and I at long last made peace, and where he and my family grew to know and love each other. After Baba's death, it provided shelter for my Uncle Sion, who had depleted all his savings to raise a dowry for his sister Nazeema. And the apartment was the place my brother and sisters gathered for comfort when we said our last goodbyes to my sisters Jamila and Reyna, who died a few days apart in 2002.

My parents' apartment –
First Floor on the right hand side under the tree shade.

During my life, my family and I moved many times - from one town to another, from one state to another, and from one country to another. We had many "homes." But my parents' apartment in Ramat Gan was the one constant in our lives. It is the one place that my family and I have known the longest. It isn't big or fancy. But it is our refuge nonetheless, an island of caring and peace in the midst of a turbulent world. I cherish the memories of those who lived within its walls.

AZIZA LEAVES THE FOLD

Since Aziza's birth I had been saving money for her university education. I did the same with Loolwa from the day she was born.

Aziza was a top student at Lowell High, a first-rate public prep school in San Francisco, despite her continuous struggle with the remaining vestiges of hyperactivity. She spent long hours doing homework and consulting with her classmates over the phone about homework problems. I marveled at her perseverance. Sometimes when I went to her bedroom late at night to see that she was well covered, I was touched to find our little girl still up working or in the middle of reciting the Amidah, the silent evening prayer, before going to bed. Often it was past one in the morning.

Aziza – Senior at Lowell High, April 81

Aziza always wanted to help in carrying the family's burden. While in middle and high school, she offered several times to deliver morning papers and with the money earned help the family meet its financial obligations. I thanked Aziza for her offer but never took her up on it. I always felt that children should be allowed to concentrate on their schoolwork, that it was unfair to burden them with responsibilities that might adversely affect their ability to focus on their schooling. I also worried about Aziza's safety, if she were to deliver papers in the wee hours of the night or at dawn, and shared that concern with her. But I wish I had focused more on Aziza's feelings, on the fact that she must have felt uncomfortable being dependent and wanted to give back to the family, instead of focusing on the cold facts of safety and interference with schoolwork. I wish I had directed my attention to thinking of ways in which Aziza could help without putting her safety at risk or adversely affecting her ability to devote herself to her studies. What she needed was a sense she was doing something to help the family, that she was paying her dues so to speak. I know that now. I wish I had thought about it at the time.

COLLEGE

Aziza's wanting to help pay her way came into play again just before she began applying to college.

Aziza entered a competition, sponsored by a club in San Francisco, for the best presentation on a subject of social interest. The winner was awarded, I believe, $1000 toward college tuition. While I appreciated Aziza's decision to enter the competition, I purposely did not offer help with her essay for fear of dominating or unduly influencing what she was working on. It was her first venture outside the school framework, and I wanted it to be hers.

I attended Aziza's presentation on the evening the Club's judges sat to listen to what the competitors had to say. It touched my heart to see my little girl waging her first public battle. I felt a tremendous sense of love and appreciation for her. I was very impressed by the substance of what she had to say, but I saw also how she struggled with the delivery. The prize went to another contestant whose essay did not have anywhere the substance Aziza's essay had, but who must have rehearsed with a coach several times before coming that evening. She gave a smooth delivery. The judges loved her.

I looked at Aziza. She looked serene and she looked beautiful. It was hard for me to see her defeated. My heart went out to her. Why did I not help her? Why did I assume that every parent would stay away from their children and let the competition be strictly between the contestants? I had a lot of experience with public speaking. Why did I not share it with Aziza? I wanted to let her do her own thing without interference from me. But then where does one draw the line? Should I have refrained from helping my children with their homework too? I do not know what the right answer is. But to this day I hurt when I think of that evening.

Because Aziza took advanced placement courses and did very well in them, she was offered early admission at the University of California (UC) in Berkeley. I was delighted and so was she. UC Berkeley is a top institution. In addition, UC's tuition fee for residents of California was nominal by comparison with the fees at comparable institutions of higher learning. I felt the money I had saved would be enough to pay for Aziza's college and a good part of her graduate school. Making sure that my children could acquire all the university education they desired was on top of my list of priorities.

I felt it would be nice if I were to teach at UC Berkeley while my daughter attended college there. I applied for, and received, a visiting Faculty appointment at the Department of Economics at UC Berkeley, starting in 1981-82, the academic year Aziza was scheduled to start college.

Berkeley, however, was not the only college to which Aziza had applied. There were other colleges on the East Coast, and Aziza went to visit them. She went to look at Brandeis, Columbia and Wellesley. Aziza fell in love with Wellesley. When she called that evening from Waltham, Mass, she was all excited about her visit to Wellesley.

"Daddy, I just love it here. I want to go to Wellesley."

I was stunned. Wellesley's tuition fee was several multiples of UC Berkeley's.

"Aziza I don't have enough money to send you to Wellesley. If you go to Berkeley I will have enough for your college and for your graduate school, too. Even if we don't take graduate school into account, I don't have enough money to pay for four years at Wellesley."

I could hear my daughter crying over the phone.

"I would much rather go to Wellesley. I will pay for my graduate school. I love Wellesley. I don't want to go anywhere else."

" I will think about it," I said. "But are you sure you want to take a chance on not having enough money to pay for all four years at Wellesley and not having any left for graduate school"

"Yes, I am. I promise I won't ask for help for graduate work. I love Wellesley. Would you promise to think it over and try to send me to Wellesley," Aziza said while still crying.

"I will," I promised.

Last statement of balance of funds saved for Aziza's
education from her childhood

I took a close look at the matter. Before Aziza's call, I thought we had everything in place. If Aziza attended

Wellesley, I would probably be so much in debt by the time she had finished, I might not be able to help with her graduate school. That might very well mean she might not attend graduate school. But should that not be her choice? What was more important – a financial plan or my daughter's happiness? What use would it be for Aziza to have money to attend graduate school if that had to come at the expense of her happiness? What should count most?

I felt Aziza's happiness should take precedence, and decided I would go along with her preference to go to Wellesley. Aziza was happy.

I look back at that decision as one of the few decisions I made in my life that I never regretted. I feel I could not have done better.

Aziza kept her end of the bargain. When she attended graduate school she carried most of the financial burden herself. My financial contribution to her graduate education was marginal. She never asked for help.

Currently Aziza is on the Faculty at Hebrew University's Department of Sociology.

AN ABORTIVE MOVE TO NEW YORK

No sooner had we settled on Wellesley than my early conditioning came into play.

In Iraq, families stayed together. Children did not leave their parents' home until it was time to get married. It was true that I had left the nest at an early age and not for marriage, but that was not normal, and the circumstances under which I did it were extraordinary. I knew that in the United States children left home when they went to college, but somehow it never penetrated my consciousness that could happen in our little family. I could not see the family breaking up. I could not see us living three thousand miles away from Aziza. If we could not keep the family together, at least we should try to minimize the distance that separated us.

I was still not aware of Aziza's desire to get away from us when I put our house in San Francisco on the market. If Aziza were going to be on the East Coast, Joan and I thought we should be there, too. Loolwa, as it turned out, was in full agreement. She was terrified of earthquakes and told us it would be better to get away from San Francisco where we might one day end up "under the rubble." I accepted a position as Vice President of National Economic Research Associates, a large firm that did research work in energy and the environment. Their headquarters were located in New York's World Trade Center complex.

NATIONAL ECONOMIC RESEARCH ASSOCIATES, INC.
CONSULTING ECONOMISTS
FIVE WORLD TRADE CENTER, NEW YORK, N.Y. 10048
TELEPHONE: 212-524-7800

J. DANIEL KHAZZOOM
VICE PRESIDENT

Because Loolwa and Aziza were still in school, I went to New York by myself and stayed in a hotel. The family would follow as soon as the school year was over. We put a down payment on a house in Mamaroneck and accepted an offer on our house in San Francisco. Everything seemed to be falling into place.

Then the deal on our house in San Francisco fell through. It was a blow, but I was also finding it difficult to adjust to the crowdedness, tempo and atmosphere of life in New York City. One evening as I was walking on the street, I noticed a huge man accosting a woman. I was no match for him in physical size and strength so I ran across the street and hailed a police car. The officers chose not to interfere. A group of three men passed this woman by without as much as a glance in her direction. Nobody was paying attention to the harassed woman, except for an older woman who had seen what was happening and kept screaming, "Police, Police" to no avail.

I walked into my hotel, called Joan and said I was returning to San Francisco. I couldn't take life in New York.

My position at UC Berkeley was still open, and I could start teaching there in September of that year (1981). While my appointment was in the Economics Department, I was also associated with the Energy and Resources Group of which Bart McGuire was chairperson. Bart welcomed me enthusiastically. We had never met before, but Bart had read some of my publications. It felt good to be recognized and accepted. I looked forward to teaching at Berkeley where Bart was confident that funding would be forthcoming to offer me a permanent position in his group.

Years later when I was a Gilbert White Fellow at the Resources for the Future (RFF) in Washington D.C., I remembered my meeting with Bart and how good it felt to be recognized for the work I had done. At the RFF I was welcomed, too, and made to feel at home. One of the section heads there, on hearing my name, greeted me warmly and told me how much his section depended on a book I had written about estimating the demand for electricity in a utility service area and incorporating in the estimates the contribution of conservation measures.

"We couldn't have advanced as much as we have without your work," he told me.

It always feels good to be recognized, but even more than that, it feels good to have made a difference.

I am sure that Joan, too, felt good when she made a difference in our lives with the money she made from selling her work.

Around the time I began to teach in Berkeley, Joan arranged to get on the San Francisco street artists program. She made jewelry and Jewish ceremonial objects to sell from her stand in downtown San Francisco. It was very slow at first. But I remember the first Passover Aziza was in college and I did not have enough money to pay for the special food for the holiday. It was then that Joan handed me four hundred dollars she took in that week, to meet those expenses. I cannot begin to explain how good that felt.

We are divorced now, but every Passover I still send Joan $400 as a present, so that she can feel as good as I did on that unforgettable Passover.

BIDDING AZIZA FAREWELL

The last Sabbath we spent together before Aziza left for college was one that will always stay in my memory.

We were spending the weekend in Calistoga, something we all liked to do. Calistoga is famous for its mineral hot springs and geyser. Loolwa led the *kiddush* on Friday night. She looked beautiful wearing her headgear with her braces showing, but I could see the pain in her eyes. That was going to be the first crack in our family. Tears streamed down her cheeks as she recited the *kiddush*, but she pressed on. It was painful to see a child experiencing the pain of separation for the first time. That image of little Loolwa tearfully reciting the *kiddush* remains etched in my memory.

Joan and I looked sadly at each other. But when I looked at Aziza, I could see joy and elation lighting up her face. It was then that I really got the full message.

"Aziza really wants to get away. She will be happy to be away from the family," I thought.

Although I had left my own family at about Aziza's age, it was still a heartbreaking moment for me. I wondered if Aziza would have gone to Berkeley if I had not accepted a position there. It was futile to speculate on that. It was one of the hardest moments of my life.

Aziza's departure left a void. But I was consoled by the fact that Loolwa was with us. Loolwa was six years younger than Aziza. She wouldn't be attending college for another six years. We would still be a family for another six

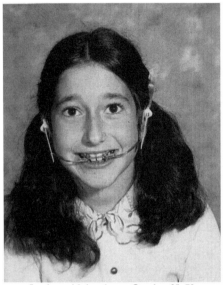

Loolwa with headgear, October 25, 79

The four of us, photographed before Aziza left for Wellesley

years, a long time I thought. But time flew. The six years passed very fast.

Aziza did her junior year at UC Berkeley in order to help stretch the money we had on hand, since UC Berkeley's tuition fee was a fraction of Wellesley's. During that year Aziza taught at Beth Israel's religious school and earned her own money. One day she surprised me with a big cup of frozen yogurt from Berkeley's famous Yogurt Park as I had just finished my lecture that day. We sat together in the campus' yard and ate our frozen yogurt together. I saw a lot of Aziza that year, and I remember that year fondly.

Aziza receiving the diploma from Wellesley's president.

That year introduced Aziza to Berkeley's Sociology faculty, who were very impressed with her intelligence and hard work. That was an asset that came in handy when Aziza graduated from Wellesley and applied for graduate work at UC Berkeley. Berkeley took her back with open arms.

When I Learned Aziza Is Lesbian

When Aziza graduated from Wellesley, she chose to stay in the Boston area, and work with children with learning difficulties. It was a stressful work because some of the children were violent, and some came from homes where the environment was not conducive to learning. But having had to struggle with hyperactivity herself during her younger years, Aziza felt a responsibility to these children. She wanted to help them. During this period, Aziza and I often talked over the phone.

One summer night, we were on the phone for a very long time. I was worried that it was past midnight on the east coast, and several times I felt it was time to end the conversation. Aziza, however, seemed to want to stay on the line, as if she wanted to hang in there, not wanting to let go. It was unusual for her to hold long phone conversations, but I seemed to be getting the message "Please, don't go away." I did not want to be intrusive and probe into her inner feelings, so I stayed on the line for as long as she wanted. When we said goodnight, I felt very disturbed. My daughter must be struggling with an awful burden, I felt - something that was weighing her down. What could it be? At the same time, I wondered if I were not making a big deal of something that was purely accidental. I thought I should talk it over with Joan.

Joan had a worried look on her face when I went to see her. She was aware I had been on the phone with Aziza. Aziza was not like her usual self, I said. Was she OK? Did Joan know of something that Aziza was having particular difficulty with or suffering from?

Joan looked sadly at me. Yes, she did know of something.

"Aziza thinks she is gay, and is afraid of telling you".

I was not shook up when Joan told me that my daughter was gay. I just wanted to know if I had heard correctly what Joan had said. Joan confirmed that I heard it right. How did Joan know? She had visited Aziza in Boston a couple of weeks before and Aziza had told her about it.

I think what hurt me most was that my daughter was afraid of me; afraid to share with me something that weighed so heavily on her soul for fear that I might reject her. Where was a child to seek love and warmth in time of duress if not from a parent? How did Aziza sleep nights when she had to live with fear of rejection by her father? I had feared incurring my father's wrath when I was growing up. I did not want my children to feel as I had.

I remember that day, when, as a ten year old and against my father's express command, I had rented a bicycle, hit an electric pole at high speed and injured my wrist badly. I was very far away from home. My right hand was no longer functional and I was too new in bike riding to ride with only one hand holding the handle bar. But in spite of all my misery at that point, the one thing I kept worrying about was my father's wrath. I could not look for understanding from him. I would hear him pouring his anger at my violation of the law he had laid down: no bike riding.

I did not want my children to react to me the way I reacted to my father. That was not how I wanted to bring up my children. I remember the time of the blackout that hit the eastern seaboard in the mid sixties. We lived in Yonkers then, and Aziza was three years old. She had just finished taking her nightly bath when the blackout hit the area. The apartment was pitch-black, and we had only a few candles in the house. I put two candles in the bathroom as I dressed Aziza, but Aziza kept asking that I turn on the light. I explained the lights were out not because I had turned them off, but because something had happened that I had no control over. But Aziza kept insisting that she did not like the two candles and wanted the electric light back on. I became impatient with her and I yelled when I told her that I could not give her the light she wanted. Aziza got upset with me for yelling. She started crying, lunged at me and attacked me with several punches. I doubled up in laughter. I picked up little Aziza, gave her a big hug and apologized to her for yelling. Most of all I was delighted to see that my child felt free to take me on for yelling at her. That was something I never had the courage to do with my father. I had to let my father get away with yelling and beating. Aziza would not let me get away with it. She was not afraid of me. I did something wrong and she was not going to stand for it. I felt that was exactly how I wanted my children to be. I did not want them to grow up being afraid of me.

I do not know what exactly went on in her mind that made her afraid to tell me she was a lesbian. It might be that she was mindful of the fact that we were observant Jews and that my reaction would probably be conditioned by the biblical injunction against homosexuality. Yet all I felt from the moment Joan told me that Aziza was lesbian was a sense of compassion for Aziza. My heart went out to her as I thought of the sense of fear and isolation she must have experienced when she wrestled with telling me about her homosexuality and the fear that I might turn my back on her. I wanted to call her right then and reassure her of my unconditional love for her. But Joan thought it was too late to call. It was past midnight, and Aziza shared the apartment with a roommate who might resent the telephone ringing so late at night.

I could not sleep that night. I had a lecture the following morning. When I got to my office, I had a few minutes on hand before the start of the lecture. I called Aziza. I got the answering machine.

"Aziza, mommy told me about what you told her in Boston. I am calling to tell you that I love you ..." and then I was overwhelmed by a gush of emotions, and I choked. I could not complete my sentence. The words would not come out. I started sobbing. While waiting until I could collect myself, I covered the mouthpiece. I did not want the answering machine to pick up my sobbing. But the answering machine, not detecting any sound, cut off the connection. It took me a while to gather myself together. By then it was time for me to head for my lecture.

In the evening Aziza called. She sounded very sad. She said when she heard how I choked in the middle of my message she wanted to kill herself for doing that to me. I told her she did not do anything terrible, that I stood by her as I did before, that I loved her as much as I did before. I wanted to hug her and to reassure her in person that I stood with her no matter what she was. But since I could not leave because of my classes, I asked her if she was free to come to San Francisco. She said she was. I believe that by that time she had left her position in the school of children with learning difficulties. I bought her a return ticket. Aziza was with us in San Francisco that week.

On her arrival home, Aziza indicated she wanted to share her story with Loolwa and get the burden off her chest. Both Joan and I felt there was no reason for her to live in hiding from anyone. Loolwa had taken a nap that afternoon. Aziza woke Loolwa up and told her that she was a lesbian. They hugged and kissed.

That evening all four of us said the evening prayers together. I put my arms around Aziza for most of the duration of the prayers. I felt very close to her, I felt very protective of my daughter. I wanted her to know I was with her, regardless. I was aware how the majority of the public reacted to homosexuality. I was aware also of the biblical injunction against homosexuality, but Judaism also mandated compassion in the administering and the interpretation of biblical laws. I felt no conflict between my being an observant Jew, on the one hand, and the love I felt for and the sense of identification I had with fellow human beings who happened to be homosexual.

At the end of the prayers, I put my two hands on Aziza in the traditional setting for reciting the blessing, and recited the biblical blessing for her: May God bless you and keep you; may God shine God's countenance upon you and be kind to you; may God lift up God's face to you and grant you peace.

I felt the divine presence was shining over all of us that night.

CONFERENCE OF THE DOUBLY BLESSED – JEWISH AND LESBIAN

Aziza left Boston and moved to Oakland, California. Not long after, the Jewish Bulletin of San Francisco announced that a conference of The Doubly Blessed – Jewish and Lesbian was scheduled to be held in the Bay Area. At the same time I learned of the publication of a book on Jewish gays. I decided to attend the conference to learn about the specific problems confronting Jewish lesbians and gain insights that might help me be a better father for Aziza.

I bought the book for Aziza and sent it to her with a note about the upcoming conference. I told her I was planning on attending the conference and asked her if she had any interest in attending too.

We went together to the conference.

I felt a keen sense of kinship with the conference participants. But that was not because my daughter happened to be a lesbian. I had identified with the struggle of gays for a place under the sun in the same way I identified with the struggle of the Jewish people for survival. Several years before I learned Aziza was a lesbian, I spoke to Sha'ar Zahav Synagogue, a congregation of gays and lesbians in the Castro district of San Francisco. That was shortly after the establishment of the congregation. I loved being in that synagogue that evening, and I told my audience how much I appreciated the fact that they chose to adhere to Judaism and establish that beautiful synagogue in spite of the fact that they had been shunned by mainstream Jews. I spoke to them about the history of Babylonian Jewry, and I marveled at the extent of their knowledge and interest in the history of that community. It was a memorable evening.

Attending the conference of the doubly blessed with Aziza opened my eyes to the many unique problems facing Jewish lesbians even within the gay community. I was one of a half dozen men attending the gathering and I noticed how my presence was greeted by many with a great deal of affection, noticing that I was accompanying my daughter, and by some with reservation. At one point I asked one of the speakers for a clarification and was blasted by the woman sitting next to me for "doing what men always do". Aziza came to my defense. I was not angered or disturbed by the hostility. I felt I understood the feeling of the woman who made that remark, and felt empathy with her.

I remember that conference with a great deal of affection. It brought Aziza and me even closer together. At the end of that conference Aziza sent me a tender letter. I want it to be part of my memoirs.

I walk through life with the knowledge that you are always behind me, supporting me, + that is very important to me. A lot of times I don't want to talk about things, like breaking up w/ Gini, because I am shy, or not sure I can explain things, or because talking will make me much too sad. Also when I talk about something that hurts me it makes you hurt too, sometimes it even hurts you more than me, (which hurts me), + that can be difficult for me. But regardless of whether I talk to you or not you are always behind me + I always know it - I just want you to know how (Back of card)

Dear Daddy,

I like this card because the kid has just gotten toilet paper all over the bathroom + thinks its very funny - I thought you would appreciate it too. I think you would call the kid a rascal. I don't think Mommy will like the card, though; I think it will make her anxious.

I wanted to let you know how much I appreciated your giving me the book about gay Jews. Even more than the words in the book, the fact that you would buy it is really important to me.

important that is to me.

Love,

Aziza

CONTEMPORARY AMERICAN PHOTOGRAPHERS

Photograph ©Lawrence Robins 1985
Baby in the Bathroom
©Palm Press 1986
1442 A Walnut Street
Berkeley, Ca 94709
APH262-125   CAN-195

Aziza's letter

BLOCKED VISION

I was sitting in my office at UC Berkeley in 1983 when it happened. A big cotton ball floated in front of my eyes and I couldn't see around it or beyond it. I got to my feet shakily. I felt disoriented. I decided to get home to San Francisco. Without thinking things through, and without any plan of action, I made my way to the stairs. At the top of the stairs I hesitated. I couldn't see the steps clearly and was afraid to move forward. Finally my hand found the railing and my feet moved slowly, carefully feeling for each step as I went down. I am not quite sure how I made it to the parking lot.

I slipped into the driver's seat and sat there, wondering what to do. This was a strange world in which I found myself. What was happening to me? I experimented by placing a hand over one eye and then the other. I found I could see out of my right eye. The huge cotton ball was squarely in front of my left eye. With one hand on the wheel and one hand over my left eye, I drove home to San Francisco.

At home I looked at the mirror. My left eye looked normal. But I could not see anything through it. The big white ball blocked everything. I was sure something was wrong, but I was afraid to call my ophthalmologist. A few years before he had told me that my left eye vision suffered from a mild cataract. But what I had experienced that day was something totally new. I hoped that the big while cotton ball would go away with rest and a good night's sleep.

The following day came before I could pick up enough courage to call my ophthalmologist and leave a message. The ball did not go away, and I was feeling as disoriented as I did the day before.

Within a few minutes the ophthalmologist called me back.

"Come right in. I will see you immediately."

That was unusual. My ophthalmologist never returned calls immediately.

At the clinic he determined I had hemorrhaged and blood had blocked my vision. I needed to be operated on, but the operation could not be scheduled for two weeks.

Those two weeks were a terrible period. I gave my lectures as scheduled, and I tried very hard to be my normal self. But frequently I lost my train of thought and felt as if I were floating in a different world with no idea where I was. Sometimes I began writing on the blackboard, but was unable to complete what I had started to write. At times, I was seized by a spell of dizziness and felt I was about to fall. Normally my teaching assistants (TA) sat in my lectures, and through this whole period they were particularly solicitous of me, protecting me as much as they could. Noticing that I sometimes turned to the lectern and held it tightly when I thought I was about to fall, my head TA moved his seat next to the lectern to be closer to me should I need help.

The day before the surgery, I went to the hospital for pre-surgery preparation. My ophthalmologist presented me with a choice. The surgery could be performed using a tried and true method, or I could become a guinea pig and volunteer for an experimental method of cataract surgery.

I knew the risks, and I knew how important my eyes were to me. I also knew how much the community in this country had given me. I wanted to give back to the society of which I was now a part. I also was committed to research and to pushing the frontiers of knowledge. That was after all what drove my own research work.

I elected to be a guinea pig. I signed the paper declaring my desire to be part of the experiment, with full knowledge of the risk the experimental operation entailed.

I was scheduled to be operated on early on the following day. Joan and Loolwa said they would come to see me half an hour before my operation, but the nurse came to wheel me to the operating room an hour before schedule. I felt bad that I would not be able to see Joan and Loolwa before my operation. But just as I was wheeled out of the door of my room, Joan and Loolwa showed up. My daughter, wearing a reassuring smile looked sleepy, as if she had just tumbled out of bed. She looked slim and tall and she was beautiful. I felt as if my guardian angel had come to reassure me, to give me her blessing. Loolwa was always special. Her arrival on earth soon after my mother's death made her always seem heaven sent. I knew I would be all right.

I was back at home on Friday of that week. I removed the eye bandage, and a wonderful thing happened. I turned my head to look at a map that hung on the wall. It was a present a friend had given us five years before. For five years I saw that map in monochrome yellow. But with my eye patch removed, I saw a new map in dazzling bright colors. I was amazed. Colors had reappeared in my world! I felt a surge of love for life run through my veins. I appreciated being alive and being able to see. Life presents its problems, but it also brings us blessings in Technicolor.

We moved to the dining room to recite the *kiddush*. We had the lights turned off, but the Sabbath seven-candle candelabra burnt brightly atop Loolwa's piano. We wanted to celebrate the Sabbath by candlelight. As I looked at the candles, I saw two sets. Both looked authentic. I realized I had a problem. For two years afterwards I saw double. During those two years it was difficult to read or do intensive visual work. Often I had to keep my left eye covered. I reported the double vision to my ophthalmologist. He tried to cure it, but nothing helped. In time my brain managed to make the adjustment, and the double vision finally vanished.

Eight years later my right eye was operated on for cataracts, using the same procedure used on my left eye. I did not experience any double vision his time. My ophthalmologist told me that the double-vision glitch I reported in what had been an experimental procedure was worked out.

It felt good to know my volunteering for the experimental surgery might have had a share in that little advancement to the frontiers of knowledge.

SUFFERING SAN FRANCISCO'S FOG

The weather in Berkeley was better than the weather in San Francisco. Winter and spring were beautiful in San Francisco, when we could sit in our large dining room and look down at our beautiful view of the ocean. But in summer and early fall, San Francisco was covered with thick fog for days on end. It was smothering. When I got up in the morning, thick fog that looked like gray cotton covered the windows in our house. I could not see beyond it. The opaque fog made me feel as if someone were holding his hand around my throat, choking me, cutting off my supply of air. I struggled for air. I could not breathe.

The newspaper was delivered to our home every morning. But when I went to pick it up, it was soggy and damp from the moisture-laden air.

It was also cold and windy during most of the summer and early fall. Having grown up in the Middle East where the sun shone brightly during the summer, summertime always conjured up images of outdoor living for me. Psychologically, it was hard for me to adjust to the idea that during summertime we should be sitting with electric heaters in front of us, turned on full blast, just to stay warm. I saw pictures on the television of people walking in shorts and short-sleeved shirts in towns just outside San Francisco, and felt sick sitting in the cold and miserable weather of San Francisco. I longed for the sun and the warm breezes. I wanted so much to be with those who were enjoying a good swim out in the open. I wanted to be sun bathing with the people I saw on television. I felt I was a prisoner in San Francisco. I hated living in that city. I hated its rotten weather.

There are people who need sunrays and I was one of them. No one in my family appreciated my plight. People seemed to understand that someone might not be able breathe because of allergies. All three other members of my family suffered from allergies. But no one seemed to appreciate how much I struggled to breathe because of that dreadful fog.

Most weekdays I traveled south of the Peninsula and did my work in libraries or coffee shops where I was away from the fog and where I could see sunshine. But I remember feeling like a fugitive, always on the run, to get away from the fog. I remember many times in mid afternoon when the fog in San Francisco was so enveloping, so gray, that it felt as if it were night. When I had finally driven far enough away to come from under the fog, I could scarcely believe my eyes when I saw the sunshine. It was hard to believe that what I saw was real, that there were parts of the state so close to San Francisco where the sun was still out. It had felt like nighttime just a few minutes before.

My constant escape to sunny places was disruptive to my work and peace of mind. Still, it was a relief to be able to get out from under the fog's yoke. There was, however, no escape, on the Sabbath when I could not get in the car and drive to where the sun shone.

Finally my family agreed that we should move to the East bay, to be away from the fog, but at the time Aziza was still attending Lowell High. So we decided to wait until she graduated a few years later. I thought it a sacrifice I should make. I did not want to have Aziza's schooling disrupted. Better I should deal with the fog, as best I could, than interfere with Aziza's schooling.

Following our abortive attempt to move to New York, I thought that now that Aziza had finished Lowell High, we should put our house on the market again and move to Berkeley where the weather conditions were better. But now Loolwa was in line to attend Lowell High in two years time. Loolwa wanted to have the same opportunity as Aziza and attend a top high school. The thought that now I should wait six more years under the misery of fog was depressing. But I thought it fair that Loolwa should get an equal chance as Aziza to attend a top prep school. I dropped the idea of moving away from the fog for the time being. I would wait for six more years until Loolwa graduated from Lowell High and then move out of San Francisco.

By now I was teaching at UC Berkeley. For years after that during my tenure at Berkeley, my escape from the fog was to leave for my office on Berkeley's campus early everyday during the summertime, and return to San Francisco at nightfall. The Sabbath remained a problem, because I did not drive on the Sabbath, and had no way of escaping San Francisco and its fog.

Eventually, we decided to rent an apartment every summer in Sacramento, where the sun shone brightly throughout the summer, and spend the Sabbaths there. Sacramento is located a hundred miles northeast of San Francisco. I drove there on Thursday afternoon or Friday morning and Joan came on Friday afternoon as soon as Loolwa was finished with school. It was a compromise that gave me relief while awaiting Loolwa's completion of Lowell.

LOOLWA, TOO, LEAVING

Throughout her years of growing up, Loolwa was out front with her emotions and very conscious of the four of us being a family unit. Loolwa's emotions were close to the surface, and she expressed herself openly about them. Loolwa, my mother's namesake, seemed to relate to the world as my mother did.

Loolwa was a very careful child, focused on her belongings and where she had put them. This, too, was her sense of herself. She was very put together. I remember one time when she questioned this facet of her being and it was very difficult for her.

She and I went to a restaurant on Pier 39 in San Francisco's Fisherman's Wharf and enjoyed a soft drink together. Loolwa was about ten years old. She had a gorgeous little purse that she loved and took good care of. She kept her money and her meticulously folded paper tissue in that purse. She had had that purse for close to three years.

As usual, Loolwa was nicely dressed and her purse sat squarely on her shoulder. She had the money and she wanted to pay for our treat. She counted out the correct amount and proudly paid the bill. Unfortunately, this time she forgot to bring her purse with her when we left the restaurant, and I didn't notice it was missing. When we discovered the loss we hurried back to the restaurant, but the purse was gone. Loolwa was devastated.

'How could I have been so careless? It's terrible that I left my purse in the restaurant. How could I have done that?"

It was clear that it wasn't the loss of the purse that was affecting her, but her sense of the fact that she hadn't taken care. I put my arm around her shoulder.

"Even the most careful people can forget things. You are extremely careful with your belongings, and I am very proud of you. This was just an aberration. Try to forgive yourself. In the eternal scheme of things it's no big deal."

She dried her eyes, but I could see that the loss of the purse still bothered her. She kept reaching her right hand to her left shoulder as if the purse could reappear all by itself. She wanted to step back in time and have a second chance. But we don't always get second chances.

I remember when Loolwa expressed an interest in having a fish tank. Joan was opposed to the idea, worried that Loolwa would not take care of the fish and Joan would be stuck with the work.

Eventually, however, Loolwa prevailed. She bought the fish, the aquarium and a book on caring for fish. She cleaned the tank, and fed the fish daily. She gave names to the fish, and talked tenderly about them. She loved to sit and watch her little fish swim under the bright purple light, in and around the colorful rocks in the aquarium. She proudly pointed to "Frisky" the fast swimmer and the most energetic in the crowd who could get in and out of the big rock crevices with amazing speed.

One day Loolwa returned from school to find that Frisky had died. Frisky got caught between two rocks and could not free himself. It was the first death Loolwa had seen up close. Loolwa stood silently in front of the aquarium, tears streaming down her cheeks as she watched Frisky's lifeless body in the tank. I stood by Loolwa's side and put my arm around her to comfort her. She dipped her hand into the tank and freed Frisky. She held him in her hand and petted him tenderly, as he lay motionless in her hand. With teary eyes, Loolwa told me how Frisky loved to swim fast in and out of the big rocks and how he managed to get to the food Loolwa sprinkled in the tank before any other fish.

"And now he will not be swimming any more. There will never be Frisky", Loolwa said sadly.

I suggested that we bury Frisky in a quiet corner in our backyard, and mark his place of burial.

And so it was. Loolwa and I gave Frisky a fitting funeral and burial in our backyard. The fish was part of Loolwa's family and deserved a fitting send off.

Loolwa cared so much about the safety of the household. At night she would say:

"Did you lock up, Daddy? You didn't forget."

When she felt we were all safe behind locked doors, she would say her prayers and go to sleep peacefully. I watched over her tenderly as she lay sleeping. She was such a beautiful little girl.

Family was the center of Loolwa's existence. When she played with her toy people in the bathtub, they became a family for her. She always picked up four of them and called them "Four people in the family. This is the Daddy; this is the Mommy; and here is 'my sister my Aziza', and here is me." She would send the little creatures sailing up and down the bathtub as she splashed around happily. She was safe. She was with her family.

When Aziza, Loolwa and I were walking one Sabbath on our way to Adath Israel Synagogue for afternoon services, we came across an injured bird. Aziza and Loolwa stopped to help the bird.

"It can't defend itself," they said. "An animal could come along and eat it. We need to save it."

We were almost as far as the synagogue, but saving a life was more important than praying. Aziza and Loolwa picked up the little bird and carried it home. Joan was surprised to see us back so early, but when she saw the bird, she understood.

Even though we called the SPCA to come to the rescue, the bird didn't make it, and there was another creature to bury in the backyard. Life is fragile and can be ended in a second. There is so much danger around us, too, though we are not always aware of it.

When Loolwa was in high school there was a rash of kidnappings in the Bay Area and KGO, a local TV station, offered to help with putting together an ID card with vital information for each child. The ID card could be produced at a moment's notice in the unfortunate event that it was needed. We took Loolwa to the station and had her ID card issued. That card resided on my desk. I still have it on my desk, and sometimes I look at it and say a prayer of gratitude that my beautiful daughter was never kidnapped, a parent's worst nightmare.

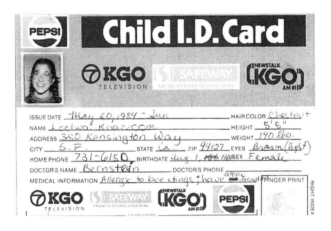

Loolwa's Child ID Card, in Loolwa's handwriting

Despite the lurking dangers Loolwa went on with her life. She was a top music student and delighted us with her playing on the flute, the piano and the guitar. She attended the San Francisco Conservatory of Music and she gave several recitals there. She wrote accompaniments for Babylonian Sh'bahoth, no mean accomplishment since they are composed in a different tonal scale from our western one.

Music was important to my daughter; family was important to her; and her Jewish heritage and the observance of Judaism held an important place in her life. She also had a deep concern for the welfare of others who might not be as fortunate as she.

A boy named Bobby wanted to visit his brother who lived far away, but did not have the money to pay for his trip. His story appeared on one of the local TV stations. I was very touched by the letter Loolwa wrote to Bobby and the money she and Aziza sent him. Loolwa, who had a keen sense of history, gave me her permission to duplicate the letter before mailing it to Bobby. Loolwa wrote: Dear Bobby, "My name is Loolwa

(Age 10) Khazzoom. I have sent you 50. This is for you to go to your brothers house and me to give this to you. I watched the news that told about you. The money that I'm giving you is most of my allowence, and will only give me 35c leftover but this is stacka that I want to give to you, out of my own will. I hope it will help you go to your brothers house. My sister (Age 16) is also giving you $1.00 out of her (one line missing – did not come out in the duplication)... you will get to your brothers house alright. By the way, stacka is a jewish charity that helps others. Love, Loolwa Khazzoom

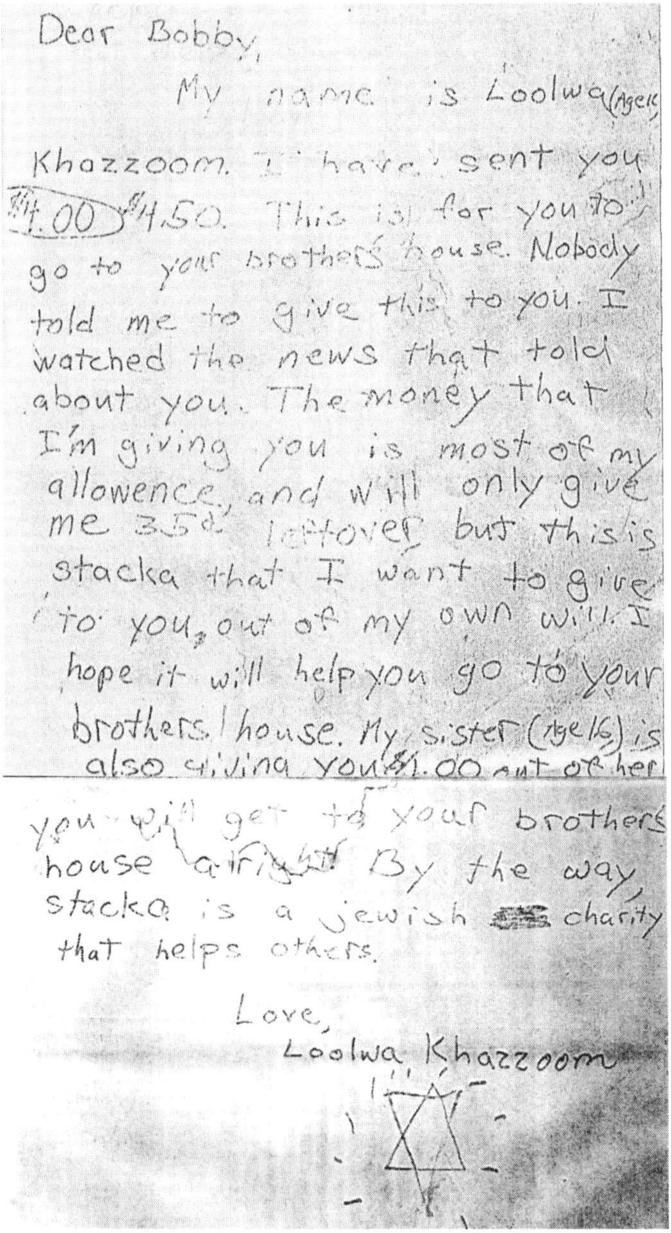

Dear Bobby,

My name is Loolwa (Age 10) Khazzoom. I have sent you $4.00 $4.50. This is for you to go to your brothers house. Nobody told me to give this to you. I watched the news that told about you. The money that I'm giving you is most of my allowence, and will only give me 35¢ leftover but this is stacka that I want to give to you, out of my own will. I hope it will help you go to your brothers house. My sister (Age 16) is also giving you $1.00 out of her

you will get to your brothers house airfare. By the way stacka is a Jewish charity that helps others.

Love,
Loolwa Khazzoom

(Damaged) copy of Loolwa's two-page letter to Bobby

Loolwa's care for others and her love of family never came in conflict with her religion, but her love of music did.

She was the first flutist in her high school, but she had to drop back to second flutist, since many of the concerts were performed on Friday nights and on Saturday, the Jewish Sabbath, a time when she could not perform. I never heard her complain about that. She took issue not with the religion, but with the school that did not take minorities, including the observant minorities, into account when events were scheduled.

Loolwa playing the flute on the day of her *Bath Miswah* celebration in our home in San Francisco, invited guests listening

She ran into problems with some of her teachers, too, because of religious observance. Many of them were accommodating when Loolwa asked for work in advance of holidays on which she could not attend school. She wanted to keep up with her class and do the work on her own. The High Holy Days often fell right at the beginning of the school year, a particularly difficult time to take time off from school. One time a math teacher of hers, a non- observant Jew, refused to tell her what material he would be covering during her absence, threw the math textbook at her, turned his back, and walked away.

The conflict between her school and her synagogue made a deep impression on Loolwa. In fact, when she wrote an essay as one of the requirements for admission to Harvard, she chose to write about this conflict. Later, she enlarged on it and it became her college thesis.

APPLYING FOR COLLEGE

Like her sister before her, Loolwa received early admission from the University of California, Berkeley, and was thus guaranteed a place in an outstanding university. Loolwa applied to five other colleges: Stanford, Harvard, Yale, Columbia and Barnard. The college Loolwa really wanted to attend was Harvard. It was my alma mater and maybe Loolwa wanted to follow in my footsteps. For me this was interesting since Aziza stayed as far away from my footsteps as she could. Aziza never took an economics class and, as far as I can remember, did not apply to Harvard. This didn't bother me in the slightest. I always felt my children should walk to the beat of their own drummers. Still it couldn't help but please me that Loolwa applied to Harvard.

Stanford invited Loolwa for an interview shortly after she had sent in her application. There, since she had applied to the music school, she was asked to audition. I drove her to Stanford for her interview.

Loolwa was well prepared and had played many times in public, often accompanied by her teacher from San Francisco's Conservatory of Music. At the audition in Stanford, Loolwa played Mozart's Flute Concerto No. 2, and a representative from Stanford's Music Department accompanied her flute on the piano. That accompanist was the only other person present in the auditorium and he was the worst, couldn't-care-less accompanist I have ever seen. . Loolwa had always played that flute concerto beautifully, and it was one of the concertos she had performed at San

Francisco's Conservatory of Music. But the accompanist kept changing pace and Loolwa kept trying to keep pace with him. I stood outside the auditorium where Loolwa was auditioning. It tore my heart to listen to what was happening.

When she left the audition Loolwa looked sad.

" Daddy, I did not do well." Loolwa told me, as she fought back tears.

It was not her fault. She knew her piece inside out.

"It is that sloppy accompanist," I said, as I held her close. "That man was awful."

Loolwa recovered fairly soon from that unfortunate experience. She was not particularly enthusiastic about attending Stanford and that might have played a part in her quick recovery.

The time for receiving answers from the colleges was approaching rapidly. Loolwa's hopes were high. Though somewhat anxious, Loolwa was confident as she waited to hear from the colleges to which she had applied. She had written an excellent paper for her Harvard entry. We all had high hopes of her getting admitted to Harvard.

The letters from the colleges all arrived on the same morning. Loolwa walked down the stairs in her furry blue bathrobe rubbing the sleep from her eyes. She looked just like a sleepy angel. I handed her the letters as she stood on the stairs and she opened them one by one.

She opened the one from Harvard first and I waited for her face to light up. Instead disappointment swept across her face and settled deep in her eyes. With trembling fingers she opened the next letter. It was from Yale. Another rejection. Next was Columbia's response. Another rejection. Loolwa did not lift her eyes to look around. Tears were streaming down her cheeks.

I watched her helplessly. There was nothing I could do to alleviate her pain. Harvard, Yale and Columbia had closed their doors to my daughter.

Barnard was her last choice. When she opened the letter from Barnard and found she was accepted she did not jump up and down with joy. I knew she felt as if she had been handed a consolation prize.

The day before, my daughter had been riding on the crest of a wave. Now she had been tossed brutally on the rocks near the shore. My heart bled for her. It was useless to point out that Barnard was an outstanding school with a fine reputation. In time, however, Loolwa came to appreciate the college that accepted her.

"It's much better being with other women in the lecture halls," she told me. "We can say anything we want when there are no men present."

I called Harvard's Admissions Office and inquired about the reason for rejecting Loolwa's application. The director of Admissions told me that the Admissions group who evaluated Loolwa's credentials was impressed with her achievement and felt that her paper was tops. However, there were so many top applicants that Harvard was forced to turn down many in order to keep the number of entrants within the limits of the college's capacity. I understood that, having sat myself on admissions committees to evaluate the credentials of applicants and had the unpleasant task of turning down some outstanding applicants for no reason other than space limitations.

I conveyed to Loolwa the outcome of my conversation with the Office of Admissions at Harvard. She understood, but I knew it was painful for her to realize that even though she had all the qualifications, she still could not make it.

A HILARIOUS ROOMMATE STORY

When Loolwa sent her letter of acceptance to Barnard she asked that she be assigned an observant Jewish roommate.

"It will be much easier to observe Jewish practices if my roommate does it, too," she told me.

When Barnard finished pairing roommates they sent a letter to Loolwa notifying her of the name of her roommate. The letter did not comment on her request for an observant

Jewish roommate but simply gave her her roommate's last name - Smith. A disappointed Loolwa fired off a letter to Barnard protesting the fact that her roommate was Christian. She didn't know that a young observant Jewish woman whose last name was Smith had also fired off a letter to Barnard protesting that she was assigned an Arab roommate.

Barnard chose not to respond to either letter, but the matter was cleared up when we met the Smiths in Loolwa's dorm, as Joan and I went with Loolwa to help her move in. The Smiths had accompanied their daughter to her dorm that day for the same reason.

When we entered the room we noticed Mr. Smith wore a skullcap. Loolwa turned to me in amazement. He looked like an observant Jew.

"Could Smith be a Jewish name?" Loolwa wondered.

She moved toward her roommate, looked at her closely.

"Are you Jewish?" Loolwa asked.

"Yes, I am," came the answer.

"And are you Jewish?" Loolwa's roommate asked.

"Yes, I am an observant Jew," Loolwa answered.

Relieved to discover that their worries about their roommates turned out to be unfounded, the two young women held hands and danced around their room chanting in tones of delight: "We are Jewish! We are Jewish!"

FOOD FOR THE HOMELESS

Barnard was a wonderful college for a young Jewish woman. It had a huge *kasher* kitchen and dining hall. This was in sharp contrast to Wellesley, which Aziza attended, and where we had to assemble ten Jewish students who kept *kasher* in order to have the minimum number required for having *kasher* meals delivered daily to Wellesley. Joan and I went on *rosh hashana* to New York to be with Loolwa, and we ate together in the college dining room. There was food in abundance and lots of leftovers.

"There are so many homeless around here," Loolwa told me, "but the college throws away the leftovers. The college does not give the leftover food to the homeless."

Loolwa and I looked at each other. The dining hall was deserted. Who was going to know? It was *rosh hashana*, a time for sharing, for being joyful and mindful of our fellow human beings. Nobody should be hungry. We seized trays of untouched food, which were left on the tables, and went into the street looking for homeless people.

"This is Jewish food and we want to share it with you," Loolwa told the half dazed people sitting outside in the cold.

People took the food and were happy. Everybody smiled at my daughter and blessed her, except for one man who turned away in disgust.

"I would rather starve than eat Jewish food," he told us.

COURSE OF STUDY, LEADERSHIP, SKILL AT ORGANIZING

Loolwa was nothing if not ambitious. She took courses at the Jewish Theological Seminary (JTS) as well as at Barnard and when I visited her, I sat in on her classes in Jewish Studies. It felt good to be sharing in my daughter's life, studying Judaism with her.

I took a deep interest in Loolwa's education and loved it when she included me in her new life. She took a course in economics and called me some nights to discuss the class material and questions in economics. I loved being of help to my daughter and remember being on the phone with her at times until five in the morning, California time. By that time Loolwa had to get ready to go to class. I was very proud of her and, despite the physical distance that separated us, I felt as if she were still with us in San Francisco.

She was Jewish, but she was a Jew whose father came from an Arab land and she identified very much with the traditions of Babylonian Jewry. While attending Barnard Loolwa started a new organization, Student Organization of

Jews from Arab Countries (SOJAC) and proudly told me what she was doing. She framed the organization's logo with a message on it for me and gave it to me on one of her visits to San Francisco. My heart was bursting and I couldn't find words to respond. Loolwa was so wonderful.

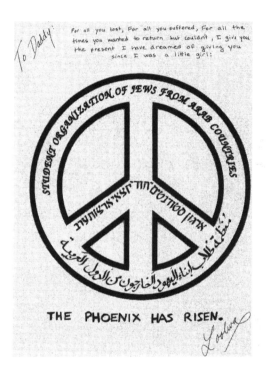

This was only one example of Loolwa's talent for organization. When Loolwa was attending Lowell High, the City of San Francisco announced a cutback in its budget for education, which would have adversely affected Lowell. Loolwa organized a big SOS – Save Our Schools – rally. She had top city and state officials come to speak at the rally in support of SOS. The huge turnout received wide coverage in newspapers, radio and television. Not long after, the city scrapped its plan to cut on its budget for education.

That was not Loolwa's first demonstration of leadership and skill in organizing. As a fourteen year old she organized the women at Kahal Joseph's Congregation in Los Angeles to join her en masse in defiance of the newly appointed Moroccan rabbi who discarded Babylonian songs, during the *Simhat Torah* celebration, in favor of Ashkenazi songs. Kahal Joseph was founded by Indian Jews of Babylonian descent, and its charter stipulated that the congregation be committed to Babylonian traditions, rituals and practices. Loolwa mobilized the women to join her in singing Babylonian songs at the top of their lungs, and they drowned out the rabbi and his followers. Soon men who stood on the sidelines joined Loolwa and the rest of the women in singing, clapping their hands and dancing to the tunes of the Babylonian songs. The rabbi and his few followers were stunned. They were furious with Loolwa for foiling their attempt at changing the character of the congregation. In a defiant mood and with tears in her eyes, Loolwa told the rabbi and his followers what she thought of them and their attempt at undermining the Babylonian traditions of the synagogue. Then to the cheers and delight of congregants she resumed leading the celebration and songs in the Babylonian traditions.

I watched my daughter in awe and admiration. The rabbi and his followers would not believe that a fourteen-year old child could have organized so effectively such a revolt, all on her own. They insisted I was behind it all, that Loolwa had acted at my behest. I told them they were nuts. I told them I supported what Loolwa had done, that I was proud of my daughter for standing up for her convictions.

Years later, while serving after her graduation from Barnard as program director at UC Berkeley's Hillel House, Loolwa organized a program in multiculturalism that attracted enormous crowds of students and encouraged dialog among students from many backgrounds. It was one of the most successful programs initiated at UC Berkeley's Hillel House, and in some ways paralleled the work she had done with SOJAC at Columbia. Within SOJAC's framework, Loolwa had initiated extensive dialog and group discussions with Arab students on Columbia's campus. I felt so proud of Loolwa's initiative. May it be that we live to see the day when dialog will replace violence and tolerance will replace man's inhumanity to man

THE DEVASTATING 1989 EARTHQUAKE

A few months after Loolwa had left for college, I talked with Joan about moving to Berkeley or another location in the Bay Area where I could escape San Francisco's fog. I felt that now that I had fulfilled my commitment of postponing the move first until Aziza, and then Loolwa, had finished Lowell, it was time for me to get the relief I had been waiting for. But Joan balked at the idea of moving out of San Francisco. Joan was making and selling jewelry in San Francisco and did not particularly welcome the idea of having to commute from Berkeley.

I was beginning to feel doomed to spend the rest of my life under San Francisco's rotten weather, when relief came from an unexpected quarter – the earthquake that hit the Bay Area in 1989.

On October 17th, 1989, I was in a plane on the runway in Los Angeles, waiting for the plane to take off for San Francisco. Suddenly an announcement came over the loudspeaker. The flight was canceled. A major earthquake had hit San Francisco. I deplaned with the other passengers and went to a hotel where I tried to call home. I couldn't reach anybody. I turned on the TV and learned that one part of the Bay Bridge, which connects San Francisco to Berkeley and the rest of the East Bay, had collapsed.

In the Jewish calendar, the earthquake occurred on *hol hamoed sukkoth*, the period of the four intervening days between the first and the last two days of the *sukkoth* holiday. We had built a beautiful *sukkah*, and invited Aziza to join us for dinner in the *sukkah* one evening. That evening, of all things, turned out to be the evening when the 1989 earthquake hit the area. Aziza was living in Berkeley, attending graduate school at UC Berkeley. I expected her to be crossing the bridge around the time the earthquake hit. Was she alive? Was she drowned in the waters of the Bay? I didn't know. I pictured her hurtling to her death when the bridge went down. I was terrified.

I could not get through to San Francisco, but Loolwa

was in New York where she was attending Barnard. Maybe she would know something. It was one o'clock in the morning in New York, but I called her anyway. If I had to wake her up, it was in a good cause. When Loolwa didn't answer her phone, I began to panic in earnest.

Columbia was not in a good neighborhood. Had Loolwa been mugged? Was she at that very moment lying on the street bleeding to death? The lack of information about the well being of my family was sapping my strength, but there was nothing I could do. I tried to sleep, but sleep evaded me. Picture after horrible picture kept going through my mind. Of what use was a telephone if I couldn't use it to connect with my family?

Next day, without having made contact with anyone in my family, I managed to get on a flight to San Francisco. I picked up my car at San Francisco's airport and drove to our home. But when I looked at our house my whole world went black. For several minutes after I first saw the house, I couldn't see anything at all. I saw black only. Though it was early in the afternoon, there was no light in my world. It was a dark black, moonless, starless night and my eyes couldn't pierce the blackness in which I was lost! Our house was built on a slope. Its front dropped, its back stayed put, and the house split in the middle. I couldn't take it in.

Joan had not been in the house when the earthquake hit, but her assistant Irit had. When the front of the house dropped, the door to the room in which Irit was working got stuck under the twisted lintel, and Irit was trapped inside. For months afterwards Irit would not stay in a room with the door closed.

Joan and I went through our house. Everything was in a shambles. My books in my office and in the library were scattered all over the floor. Furniture was overturned or lying at strange angles. Bits of broken crockery were all over the kitchen and the dining room. Pictures had fallen off the walls, their glass broken. Mirrors were lying in bits all over the place. I picked my way through the rubble and couldn't even feel glad we were alive. I could not face the devastation that had hurled its way into our lives. It was too much for me.

Bit by bit information made its way into corners of my brain. Aziza was safe in Berkeley. Loolwa was alive and well. Joan and I were both alive, too, but our house was deemed unsafe and was tagged in yellow, meaning that nobody, except for Joan and me were allowed into it.

INSURANCE – CAN YOU COUNT ON IT WHEN YOU NEED IT?

I called the insurance company. I was fortunate, I felt, to have earthquake insurance with a five per cent deductible, the lowest deductible possible. Surely most of the damage to our home would be covered, I thought.

The insurance assessors showed up and when they were done, we heard the news. According to them, the damage done was seven hundred dollars below the deductible. Repairing the house was our responsibility. I was sure the damage was much bigger than the insurance company's estimate. But where could I turn? I felt almost incapacitated.

It was then that Aziza came to the rescue.

Aziza sat with me and told me about FEMA and about the state agency that helped residents whose homes were damaged. She got their phone numbers and helped me file their forms.

FEMA sent their assessors out. When they looked at the basement, they said the damage there alone was about four times the insurance company's estimate for the whole (three-story) house.

I called the representative of the insurance company with the news, and they sent their people out a second time. This time the insurance company estimated the damage to substantially exceed the full value of the insurance on the house. They arranged to have the house shored up. That little episode had its own fallout.

Some time later the company that did the shoring up sued me in small claims court for their money since the insurance company had not paid the bill. I went to court and the shoring company did not show up.

"Do you know why you are here?" the judge asked me.

"I don't. I never authorized this company to do any work on my house. It was between them and my insurance company. I was not involved." I said.

The claim was dismissed, but I still felt as if I had walked through a looking glass, just as Alice had.

The people from the insurance company pulled another fast one. They told us the house was underinsured and that it was our responsibility to pay for the repair cost that exceeded the amount stipulated in our policy. I couldn't believe their claim the house was underinsured since Joan had called just a few months before to raise the insurance on the house by another one hundred thousand dollars. At that point, the agent told her we were insured to the maximum and would not sell us any more insurance. When we drew this little fact to the attention of the insurance company, it said the call had never happened.

Eventually, things got straightened out. We filed a suit against the insurance company for bad faith and had their records subpoenaed. I went through the records one by one and found the record of Joan's call and the agent's note that told her we had the maximum coverage and were denied the additional one hundred thousand dollar coverage. With that document in evidence, the insurance company chose to settle. By that time the front of our house in San Francisco had sunk further.

We bought a house we liked in Berkeley, and sold our house in San Francisco.

Our new home at 2901 Ashby Avenue, Berkeley

I breathed a sigh of relief. Finally I got out from under San Francisco's fog. But it took a devastating earthquake to do it.

VAGARIES OF RESEARCH WORK

In the late 1980's, I launched a major research effort sponsored by the US Environmental Protection Agency (EPA). The goal was to quantify the impact of enhanced automobile fuel efficiency on the emissions regulated by EPA.

Contrary to expectations, my preliminary results indicated that, because of the way EPA regulated automobile emissions, enhanced automobile fuel efficiency resulted in an increase, rather than a decrease, in the regulated emissions of new automobiles. This finding, which flew in the face of expectations, resulted from the EPA's choice of specifying the allowable amount of emissions in terms of grams per mile traveled instead of grams per gallon of fuel burned. For many, including the EPA, the distinction was too subtle to notice, but in practice, it had far reaching consequences, and was the reason for my unexpected preliminary results.

I alerted EPA to my findings and pointed out that, if my research sustained my preliminary results, the EPA would have to change its method of regulating automobile emissions.

My funding was cut off, and I no longer had access to EPA's data files to complete my research work.

It was a depressing period. I could have sued for the data I needed under the Freedom of Information Act. But that was a protracted and costly process. I was almost resigned to giving up on the work I had invested in the project, when I discovered that Congress had an interest in the subject I was investigating. Congress subpoenaed the documents and data I needed to continue my investigation. I was grateful to the Congress. It took me two years to complete my research work.

I submitted my results to the Journal of Environmental Economics and Management (JEEM). I remember one of the referees remarking, "Finally, someone called the spade a spade". My study appeared in the March 1995 issue of JEEM, "An Econometric Model of the Regulated Emission for Fuel Efficient New Vehicles".

663

In spite of the recognition the article received, EPA's method of regulating automobile emissions remained unchanged, as far as I know, to this day.

MY LAST PROFESSIONAL ACCOMPLISHMENT

PAY-AT-THE-PUMP AUTO INSURANCE

PAY-AT-THE-PUMP (PATP) auto insurance is a proposal to abolish the current system of lump-sum payments for automobile insurance and replace it by a surcharge on fuel price - say, 30c or 40c per gallon - to cover the cost of auto insurance.

PATP has several attributes. It reduces the average insurance cost, eliminates the problem of uninsured motorists, and reduces gasoline usage, which yields environmental benefits and reduces our vulnerability to a cut-off in oil imports. The insurance industry opposed changing the existing auto insurance system. The auto industry also opposed PATP – its argument being that, by raising gasoline price, PATP induces people to switch to more fuel-efficient vehicles, which according to the auto industry reduces vehicle safety and results in increased fatalities. In the face of this combined opposition, PATP failed to be adopted in any state where it was proposed.

I got interested in PATP initially through my research work on the safety implications of fuel-efficient vehicles. My findings were that, contrary to the auto industry's claims, enhanced fuel efficiency need not result in reduced automobile safety, and that, properly done, may in fact result in enhanced fleet safety. On April 11, 1991 I appeared before the U.S. Senate Subcommittee of the Committee on Consumer, Science, and Technology, and shared my findings with the subcommittee in a testimony titled "A Critique and Evaluation of Econometric Models of the Fuel Economy and Highway Fatalities". Three years later, I published my research results in a book titled "An Econometric Model of Fuel Economy and Single-Vehicle Highway Fatalities," Greenwich, CT: JAI Press, 1994.

Having addressed the PATP safety issues raised by the auto industry, I turned to turn to the concerns raised by the insurance industry. I felt that instead of piling up on the stock of basic research on PATP and its wonderful attributes, it might be more productive to start thinking in terms of what it takes to redesign PATP to make it more responsive to the concerns of the insurance industry, without impairing its ability to make the contributions it can make. My hope was that this would increase the chance of PATP's adoption.

In 1997 I received a large grant from EPA to undertake a study on the subject and to organize a conference on PATP at the end of my study. 1997 was also the year when I was privileged to be elected as the Gilbert F. White Fellow of Resources for the Future. I spent 1997-1998 in Washington, DC and directed my full attention to PATP.

To the conference I invited researchers from insurance companies, trade associations, insurance-agent organizations, community and neighborhood organizations, state legislatures, auto industry, oil companies, environment organizations, state regulatory agencies, US Departments of Energy, US Department of Transportation, the White House, the Brookings Institution and universities. I encountered a great deal of resistance from the insurance industry to the idea of attending the conference or contributing in any way to any discussion that might lead to the emergence of an "acceptable" version of PATP. Several major insurance companies boycotted the conference. Some who privately said they were interested in the idea of participating in the conference were afraid of retaliation or other form of repercussions if it became known that they supported the idea of a PAY-AT-THE-PUMP insurance. Some, after hesitation, agreed to attend, but only as observers and without taking part in any discussion. Interestingly, two executives from two insurance companies who initially were reluctant to accept the invitation to attend, but finally chose to participate, told me at the end of the conference that they had changed their mind about PATP and now supported the revised version of PATP that emerged from our deliberations during the conference.

We held the conference on January 11, 1999 at Resources for the Future, in Washington DC. To encourage the participants to speak candidly without concern for repercussions, no reporters were present in the workshop and no tape recording was allowed. The work during the conference itself was intensive. For several participants PATP was a highly charged topic. But none of that seemed to pose a problem. It seemed as if everyone was interested in learning and sharing what they knew with the rest. The discussion was focused.

A FIRST – SEPHARDI *KASHER* MEAL FOR CONFERENCE PARTICIPANTS

In planning for the conference, I had to plan also what to serve for breakfast and lunch. Being a vegetarian who keeps *kashruth*, I decided that we would serve *kasher* vegetarian meals all the way through. I had never attended any conference that served *kasher* meals. But why not, I thought? There is always a first. Why not make my conference the first to serve *kasher* vegetarian meals? In fact being a Sephardi Jew, why not go all the way and make all the meals Sephardi-*kasher*-vegetarian? That should be even more innovative.

I contacted David Dahan, an Israeli of Moroccan background, who was the chef at Washington's Jewish Community Center. David was excited about the idea and he put a lot steam behind it. He planned sumptuous Sephardi vegetarian breakfast and lunch. As it turned out the food cost came out to less than half of what I was told it would've cost had the meals been catered by a regular Washington catering house.

It was a riot when I announced we would be having *kasher* Sephardi vegetarian meals. Several attendants yelled out their pleasure about the novelty. A couple of participants who were Jewish and who identified themselves as non observant Jews told me how pleased they were that I chose to serve *kasher* meals of the Sephardi variety.

In the summer of 2000 I published the results of my study in an article titled "PAY-AT-THE-PUMP Auto Insurance", in the Journal of Insurance Regulation.

Of all the professional conferences I attended or organized during my lifetime, I remember the PATP conference as the best I ever attended. That conference was also my last professional endeavor. I feel fortunate that my career ended on such a high note.